S0-ARA-045

MAXIMUM LIFESPAN

ED PARK

◆

JOVE LEKSELL

PILEUS PRODUCTIONS

MAXIMUM LIFESPAN

© 2010 Pileus Productions

Creator, Writer : Edward Park

Cover Artist, Penciler, Inker, Colorist, Letterer: Jove Leksell

Published in the United States by Pileus Productions, LLC
Santa Ana, California

ISBN-13: 978-0-9840594-0-9
Hardcover, First English Edition)

Library of Congress: 2009932436

Printed in China By C&C Printing

10 9 8 7 6 5 4 3 2 1

CONTENTS: Bioethics / Cloning / Cognitive Science / Consciousness / Cybernetics / Drugs / Emerging technologies / Genetic Engineering / Graphic Novel / Human Rights / Immortality / Mitochondrial DNA / Mythology / Philosophy / Post-cyberpunk / Social Inequality / Speculative Fiction / Telomeres / Transgenic / Transhuman / Virtual Reality

Subject: Speculative Fiction — Science Fiction -- Transhumanism

This book is a work of fiction. With the exception of certain public figures, actual people are depicted only with their verbal consent. Any resemblance to other people, corporations or events is purely coincidental.

All rights reserved. Apart from "Fair Use" conventions, no part of this book may be reproduced or utilized in any form, by any means, electronic or mechanical, including photocopying, recording or any information storage and retrieval system, without permission, in writing, from the publisher.

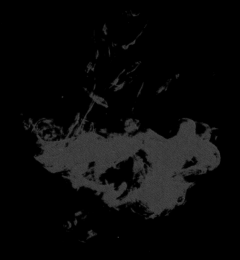

DEDICATED TO WON SUK PARK, FOR
SHARING HIS PASSION FOR LEARNING.

AND TO YOUNG JOO OH, FOR TEACHING
US TO FORGE DREAMS INTO REALITY

EDWARD PARK
CREATOR, WRITER

JAN-OVE [JOVE] LEKSELL
PENCILER, INKER, COLORIST, LETTERER

"I DON'T WANT TO ACHIEVE IMMORTALITY
THROUGH MY WORK...

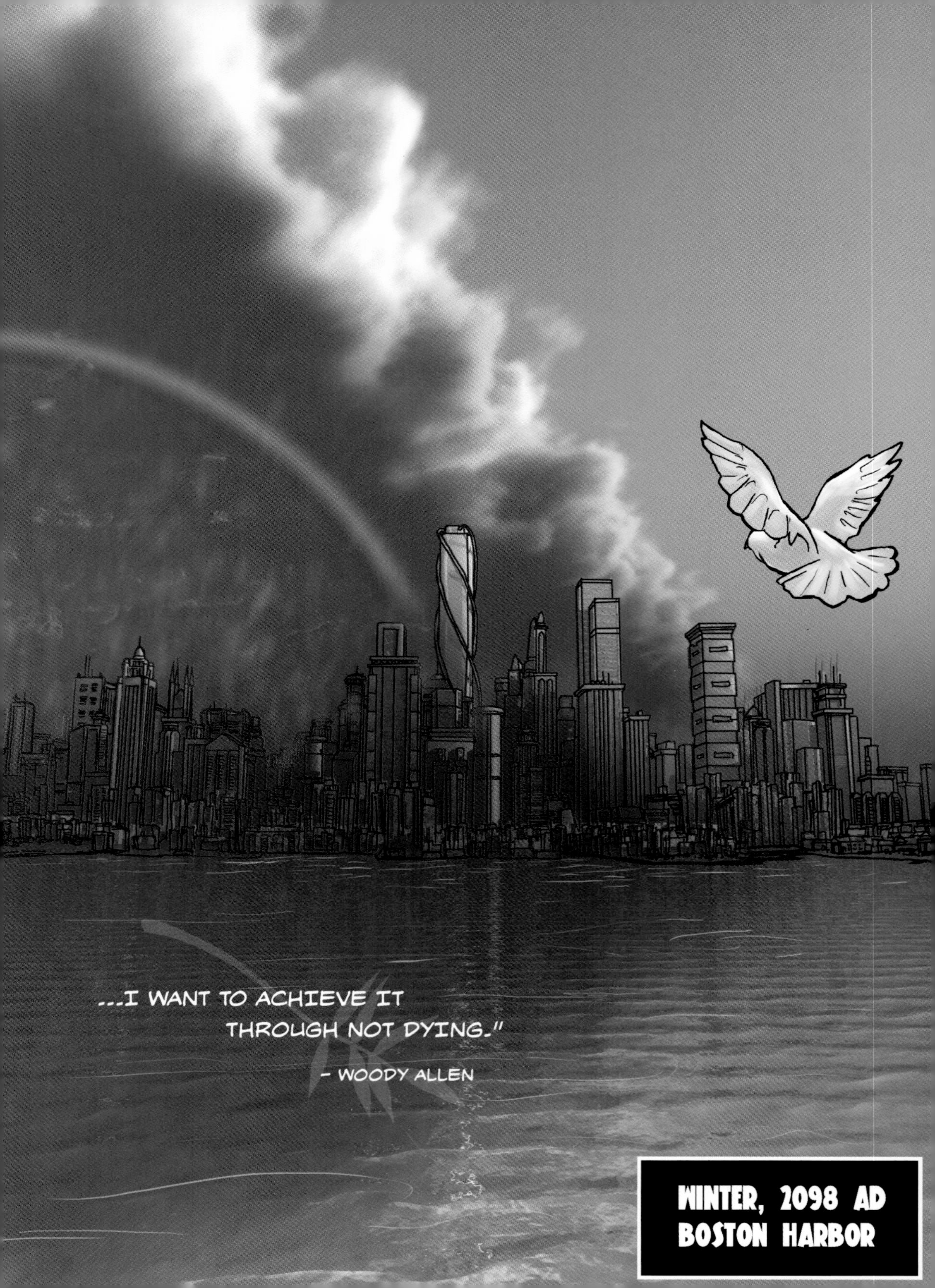
...I WANT TO ACHIEVE IT THROUGH NOT DYING."
- WOODY ALLEN
WINTER, 2098 AD
BOSTON HARBOR

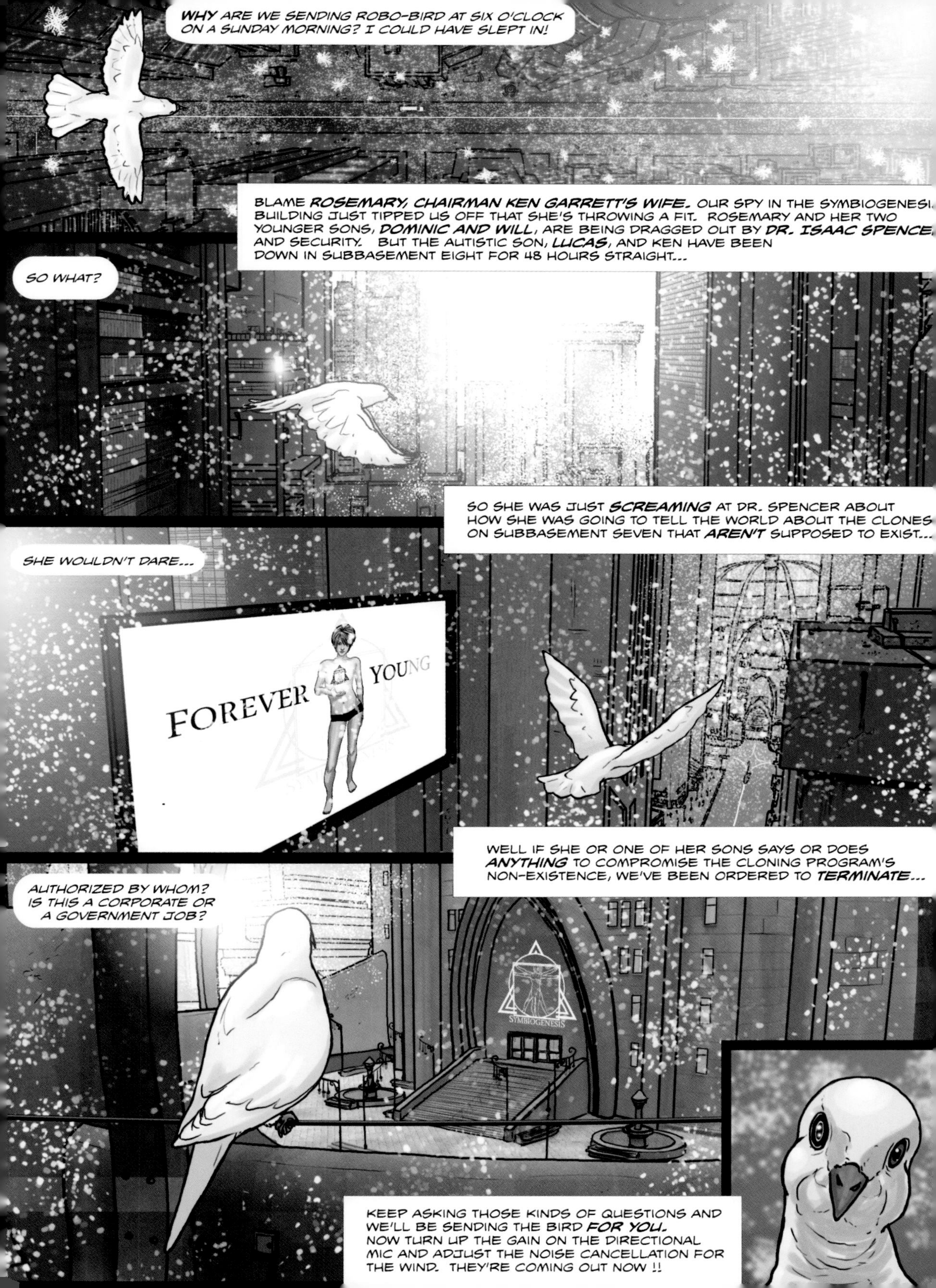

WHY ARE WE SENDING ROBO-BIRD AT SIX O'CLOCK ON A SUNDAY MORNING? I COULD HAVE SLEPT IN!
BLAME ROSEMARY, CHAIRMAN KEN GARRETT'S WIFE. OUR SPY IN THE SYMBIOGENESIS BUILDING JUST TIPPED US OFF THAT SHE'S THROWING A FIT. ROSEMARY AND HER TWO YOUNGER SONS, DOMINIC AND WILL, ARE BEING DRAGGED OUT BY DR. ISAAC SPENCER AND SECURITY. BUT THE AUTISTIC SON, LUCAS, AND KEN HAVE BEEN DOWN IN SUBBASEMENT EIGHT FOR 48 HOURS STRAIGHT...
SO WHAT?
SO SHE WAS JUST SCREAMING AT DR. SPENCER ABOUT HOW SHE WAS GOING TO TELL THE WORLD ABOUT THE CLONES ON SUBBASEMENT SEVEN THAT AREN'T SUPPOSED TO EXIST...
SHE WOULDN'T DARE...
FOREVER YOUNG
WELL IF SHE OR ONE OF HER SONS SAYS OR DOES ANYTHING TO COMPROMISE THE CLONING PROGRAM'S NON-EXISTENCE, WE'VE BEEN ORDERED TO TERMINATE...
AUTHORIZED BY WHOM? IS THIS A CORPORATE OR A GOVERNMENT JOB?
SYMBIOGENESIS
KEEP ASKING THOSE KINDS OF QUESTIONS AND WE'LL BE SENDING THE BIRD FOR YOU. NOW TURN UP THE GAIN ON THE DIRECTIONAL MIC AND ADJUST THE NOISE CANCELLATION FOR THE WIND. THEY'RE COMING OUT NOW !!

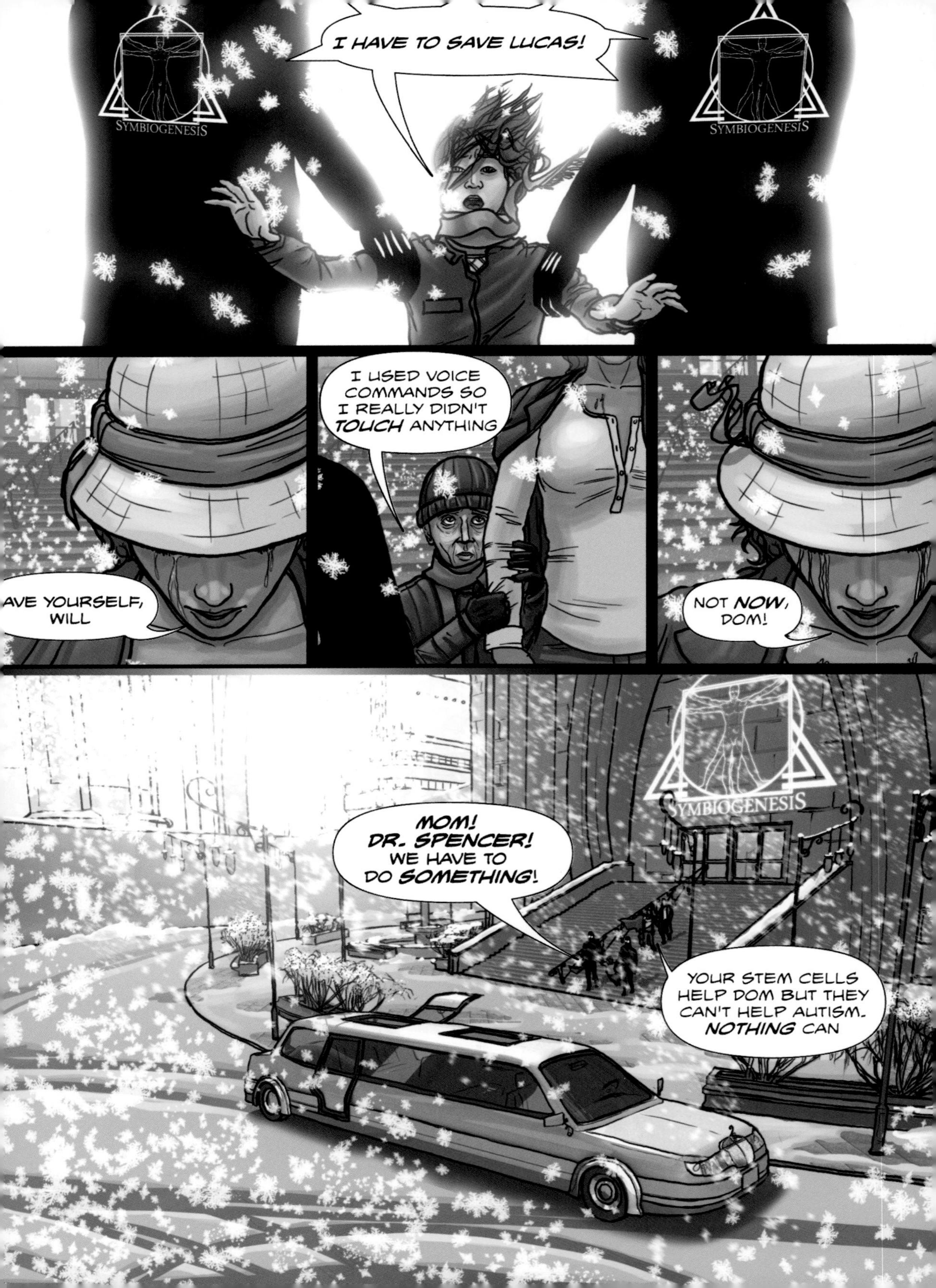
SYMBIOGENESIS
I HAVE TO SAVE LUCAS!
SYMBIOGENESIS
AVE YOURSELF, WILL
I USED VOICE COMMANDS SO I REALLY DIDN'T TOUCH ANYTHING
NOT NOW, DOM!
SYMBIOGENESIS
MOM! DR. SPENCER! WE HAVE TO DO SOMETHING!
YOUR STEM CELLS HELP DOM BUT THEY CAN'T HELP AUTISM. NOTHING CAN

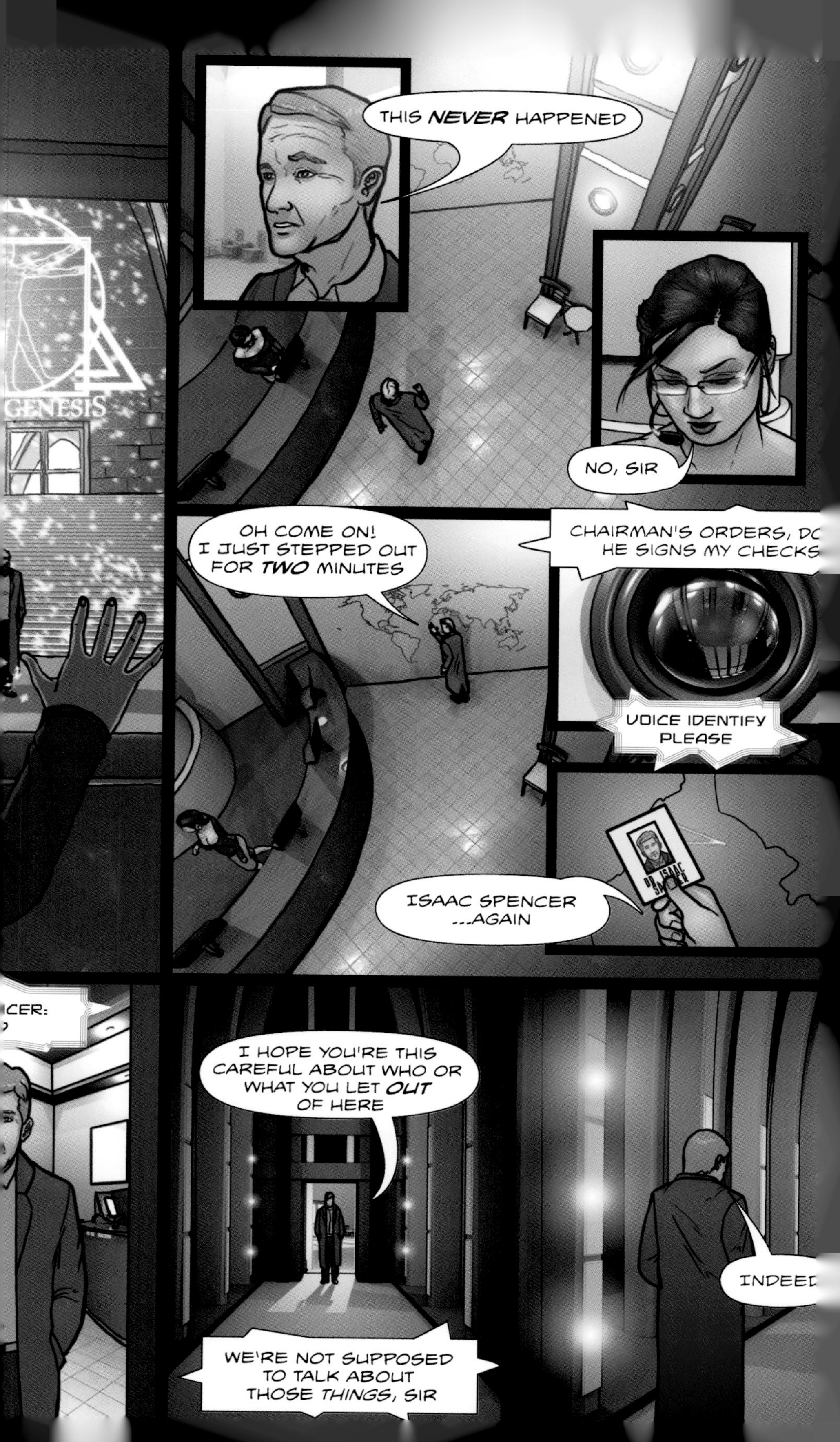
GENESIS
THIS *NEVER* HAPPENED
NO, SIR
OH COME ON! I JUST STEPPED OUT FOR *TWO* MINUTES
CHAIRMAN'S ORDERS, D
HE SIGNS MY CHECKS
VOICE IDENTIFY PLEASE
ISAAC SPENCER ...AGAIN
I HOPE YOU'RE THIS CAREFUL ABOUT WHO OR WHAT YOU LET *OUT* OF HERE
WE'RE NOT SUPPOSED TO TALK ABOUT THOSE *THINGS*, SIR
INDEED

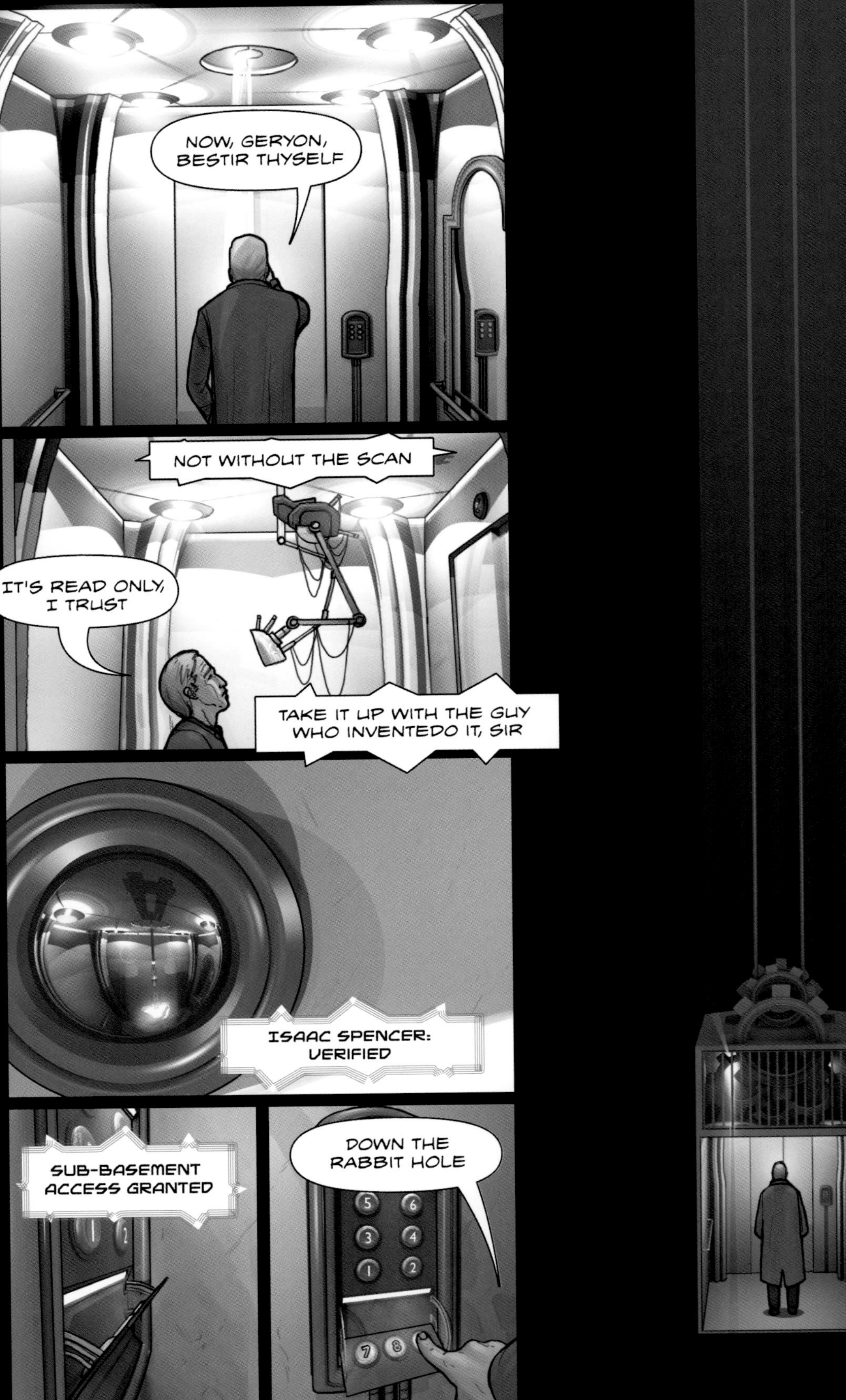
NOW, GERYON, BESTIR THYSELF
NOT WITHOUT THE SCAN
IT'S READ ONLY, I TRUST
TAKE IT UP WITH THE GUY WHO INVENTEDO IT, SIR
ISAAC SPENCER: VERIFIED
SUB-BASEMENT ACCESS GRANTED
DOWN THE RABBIT HOLE
5
6
3
4
1
2
7
8

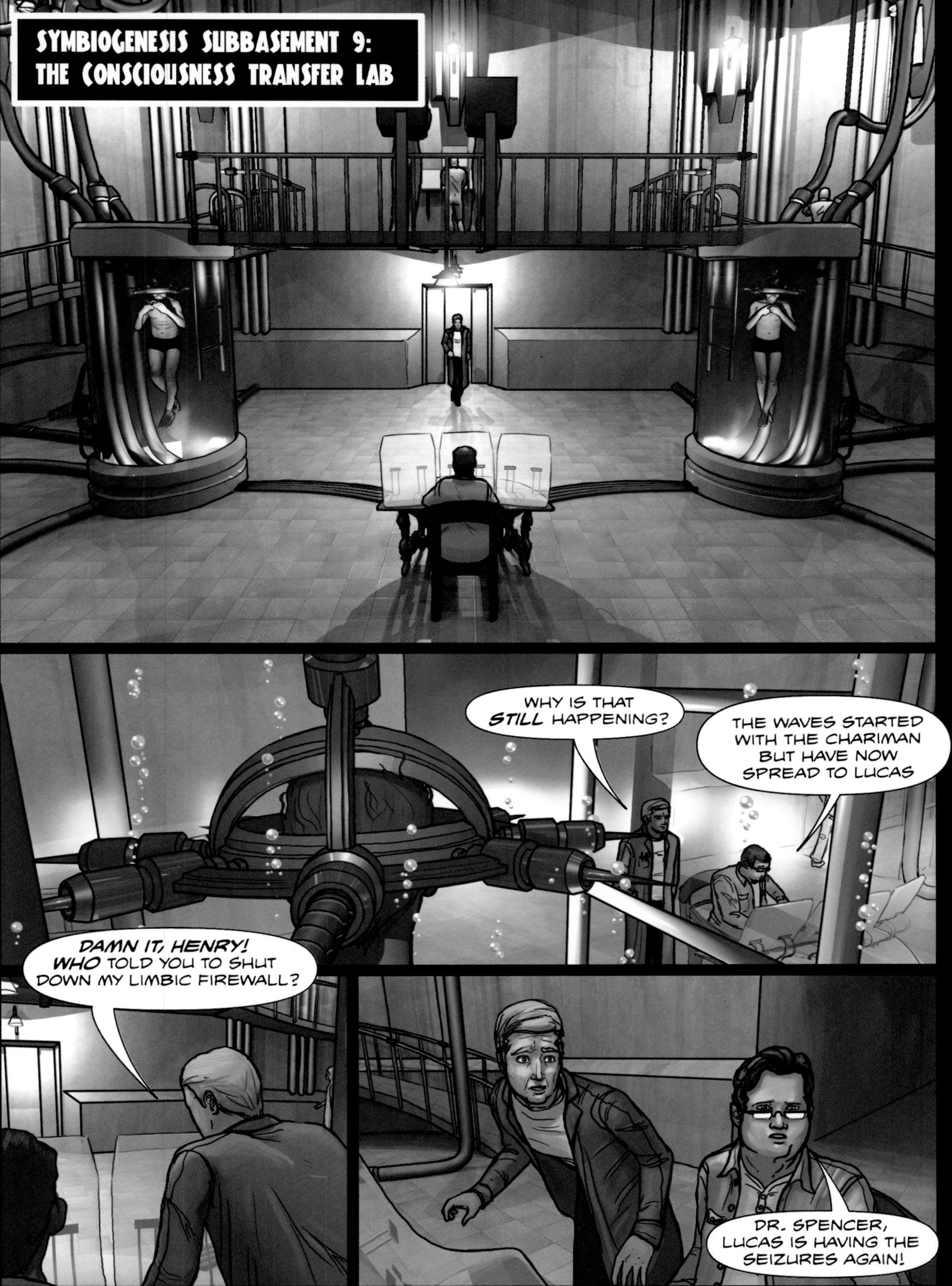
SYMBIOGENESIS SUBBASEMENT 9: THE CONSCIOUSNESS TRANSFER LAB
WHY IS THAT STILL HAPPENING?
THE WAVES STARTED WITH THE CHARIMAN BUT HAVE NOW SPREAD TO LUCAS
DAMN IT, HENRY! WHO TOLD YOU TO SHUT DOWN MY LIMBIC FIREWALL?
DR. SPENCER, LUCAS IS HAVING THE SEIZURES AGAIN!

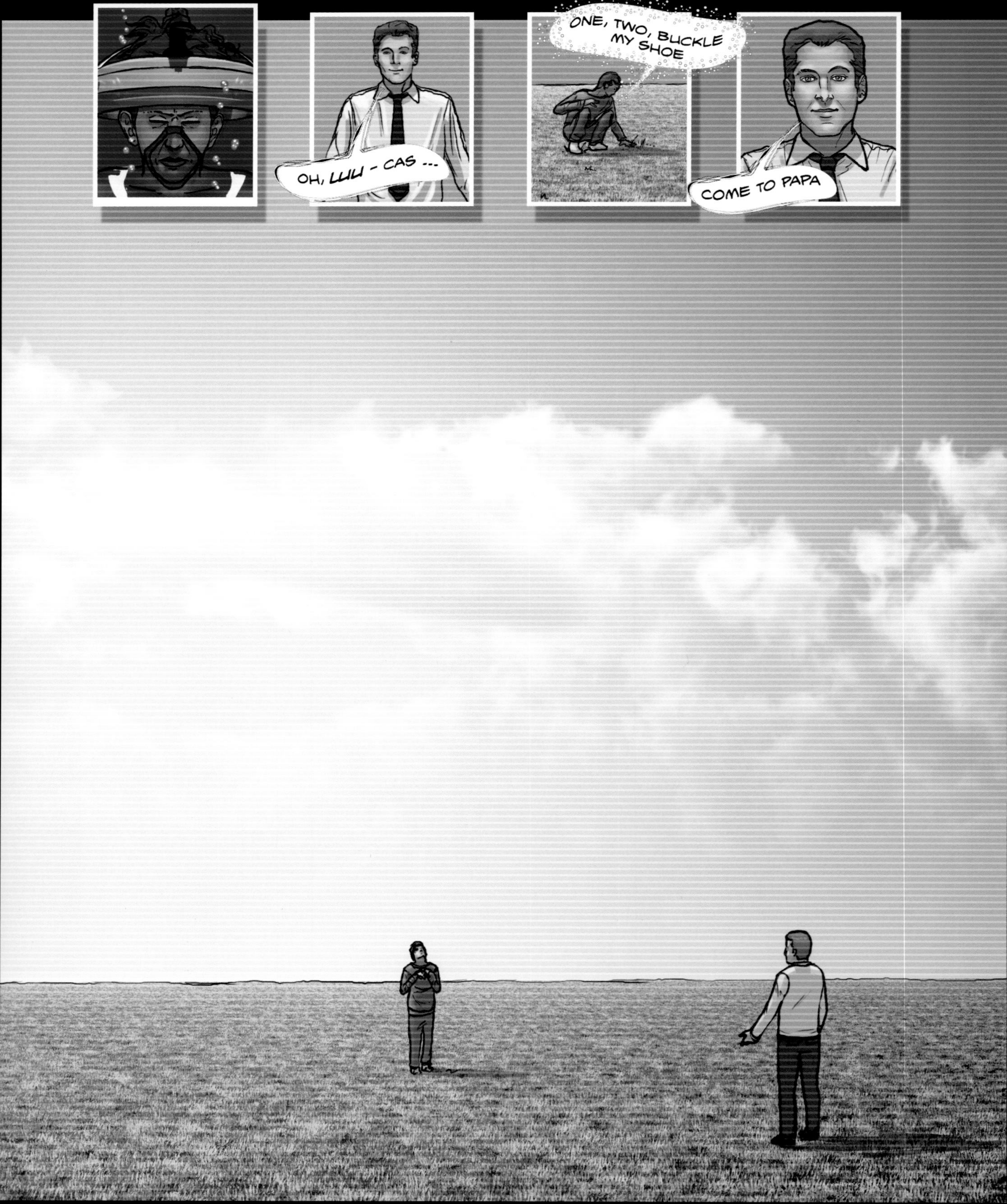
OH, LULU - CAS ...
ONE, TWO, BUCKLE MY SHOE
COME TO PAPA

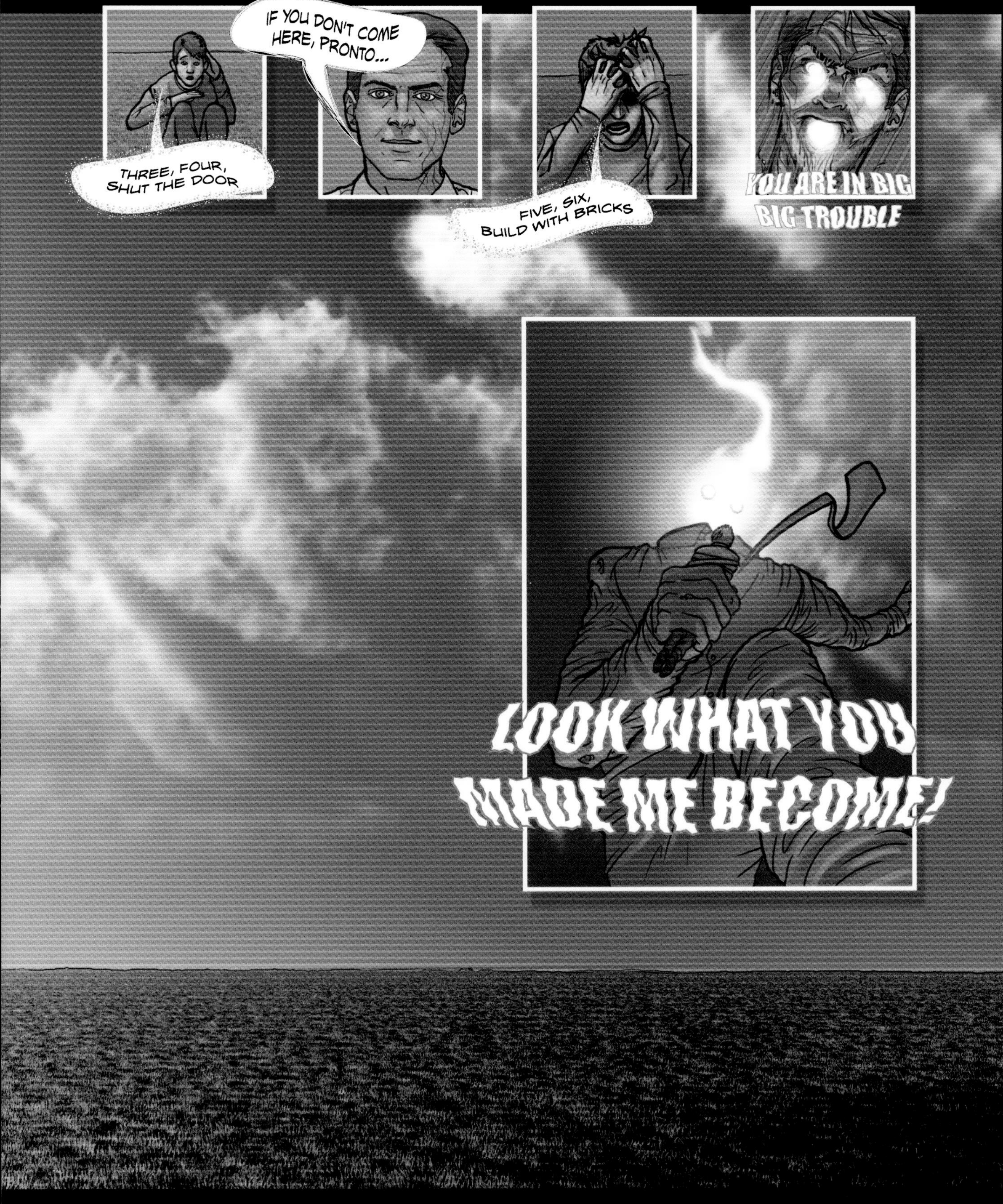
THREE, FOUR, SHUT THE DOOR
IF YOU DON'T COME HERE, PRONTO...
FIVE, SIX, BUILD WITH BRICKS
YOU ARE IN BIG BIG TROUBLE
LOOK WHAT YOU MADE ME BECOME!

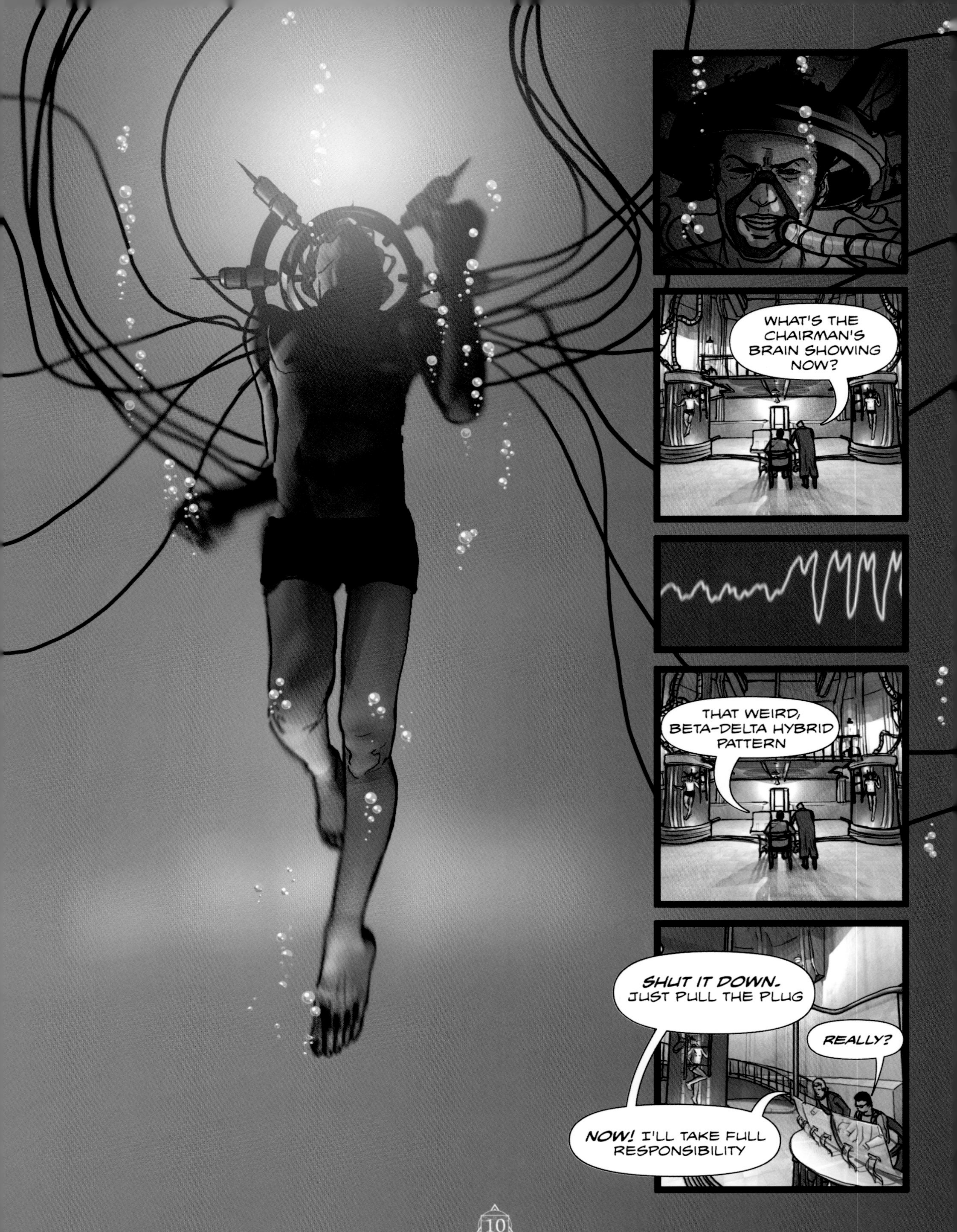
WHAT'S THE CHAIRMAN'S BRAIN SHOWING NOW?
THAT WEIRD, BETA-DELTA HYBRID PATTERN
SHUT IT DOWN. JUST PULL THE PLUG
REALLY?
NOW! I'LL TAKE FULL RESPONSIBILITY

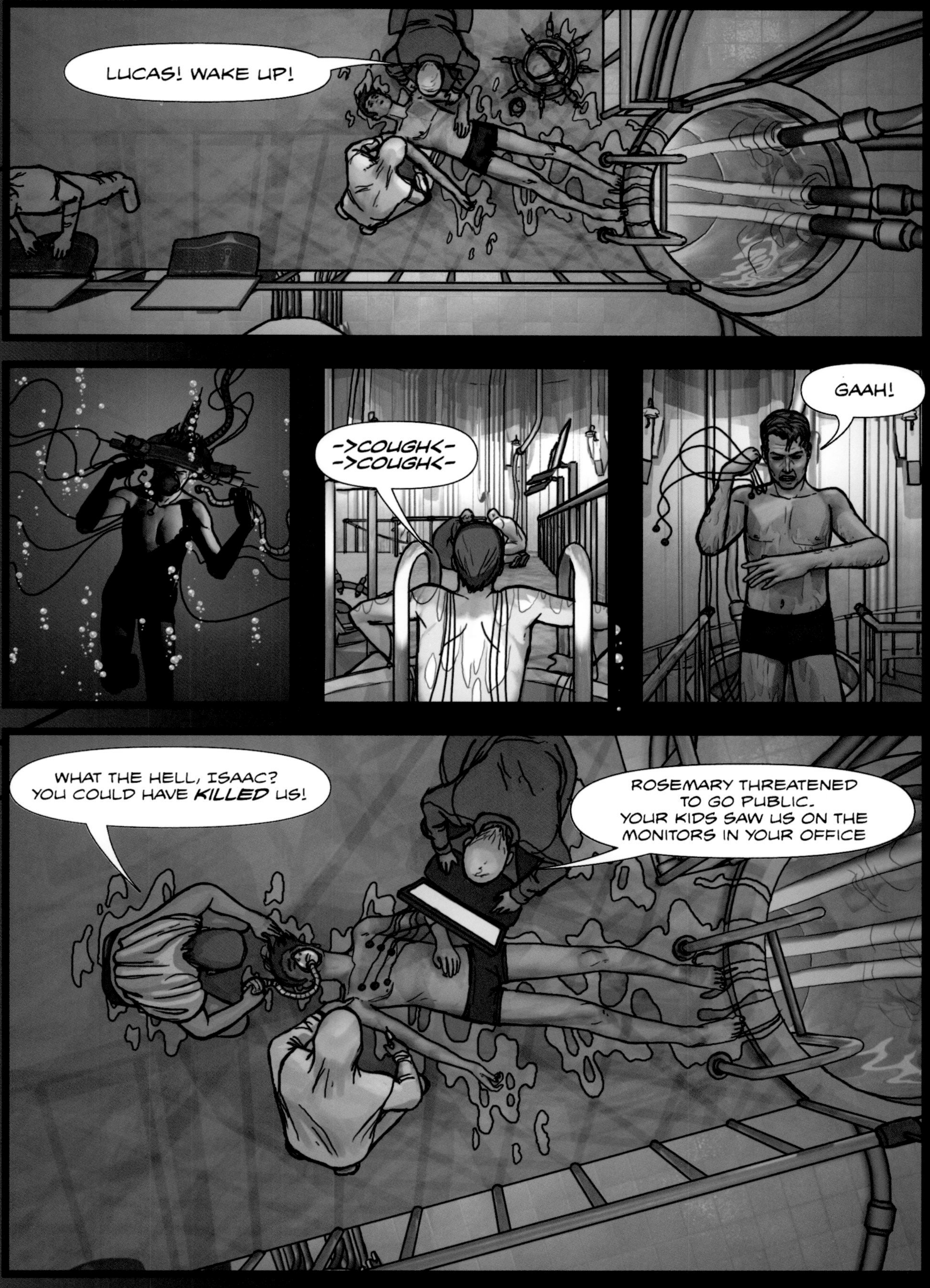
LUCAS! WAKE UP!
->COUGH<-
->COUGH<-
GAAH!
WHAT THE HELL, ISAAC? YOU COULD HAVE KILLED US!
ROSEMARY THREATENED TO GO PUBLIC. YOUR KIDS SAW US ON THE MONITORS IN YOUR OFFICE

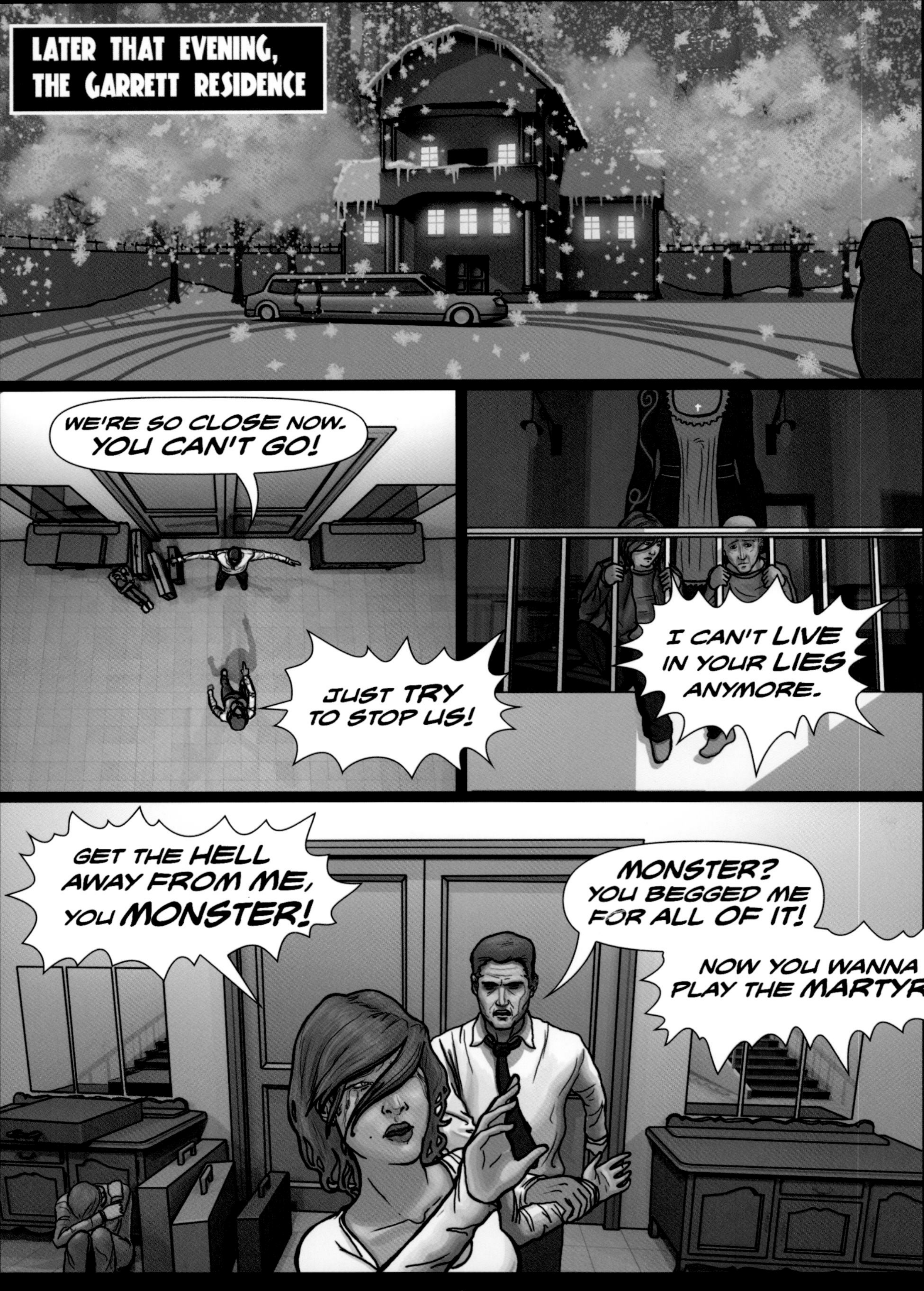
LATER THAT EVENING, THE GARRETT RESIDENCE
WE'RE SO CLOSE NOW. YOU CAN'T GO!
JUST TRY TO STOP US!
I CAN'T LIVE IN YOUR LIES ANYMORE.
GET THE HELL AWAY FROM ME, YOU MONSTER!
MONSTER? YOU BEGGED ME FOR ALL OF IT!
NOW YOU WANNA PLAY THE MARTYR?

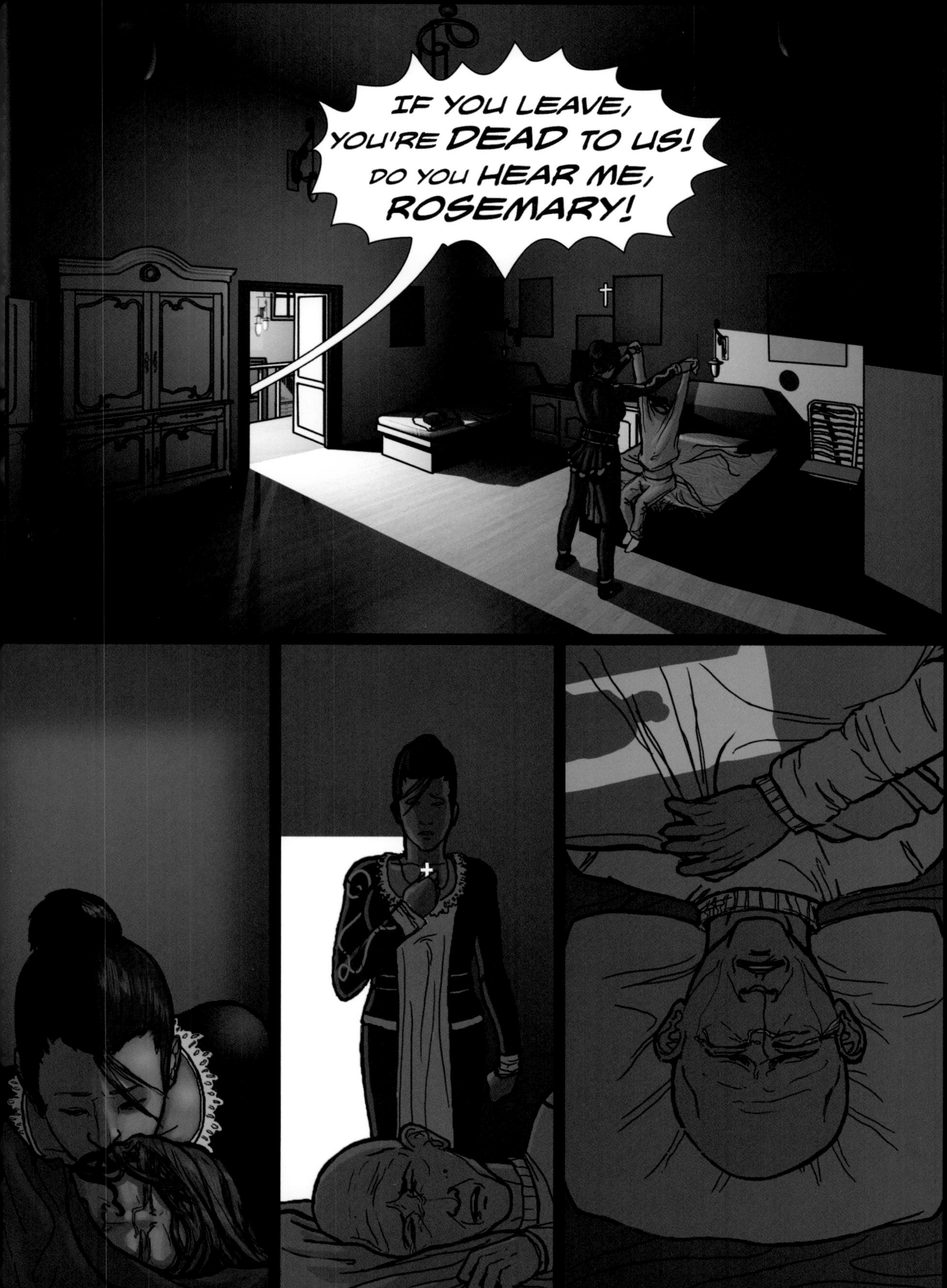
IF YOU LEAVE, YOU'RE DEAD TO US! DO YOU HEAR ME, ROSEMARY!

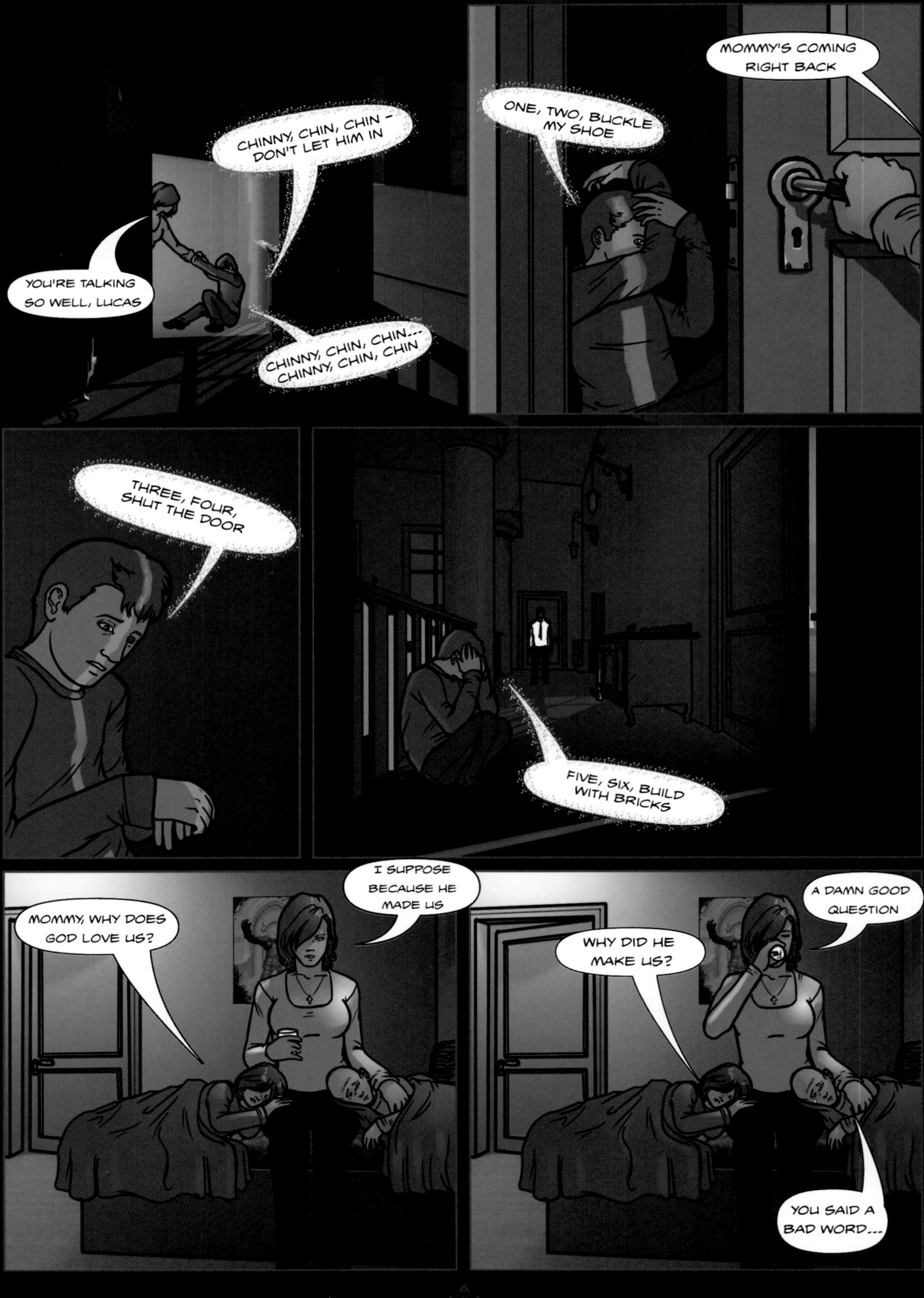
CHINNY, CHIN, CHIN - DON'T LET HIM IN
YOU'RE TALKING SO WELL, LUCAS
CHINNY, CHIN, CHIN... CHINNY, CHIN, CHIN
ONE, TWO, BUCKLE MY SHOE
MOMMY'S COMING RIGHT BACK
THREE, FOUR, SHUT THE DOOR
FIVE, SIX, BUILD WITH BRICKS
MOMMY, WHY DOES GOD LOVE US?
I SUPPOSE BECAUSE HE MADE US
WHY DID HE MAKE US?
A DAMN GOOD QUESTION
YOU SAID A BAD WORD...

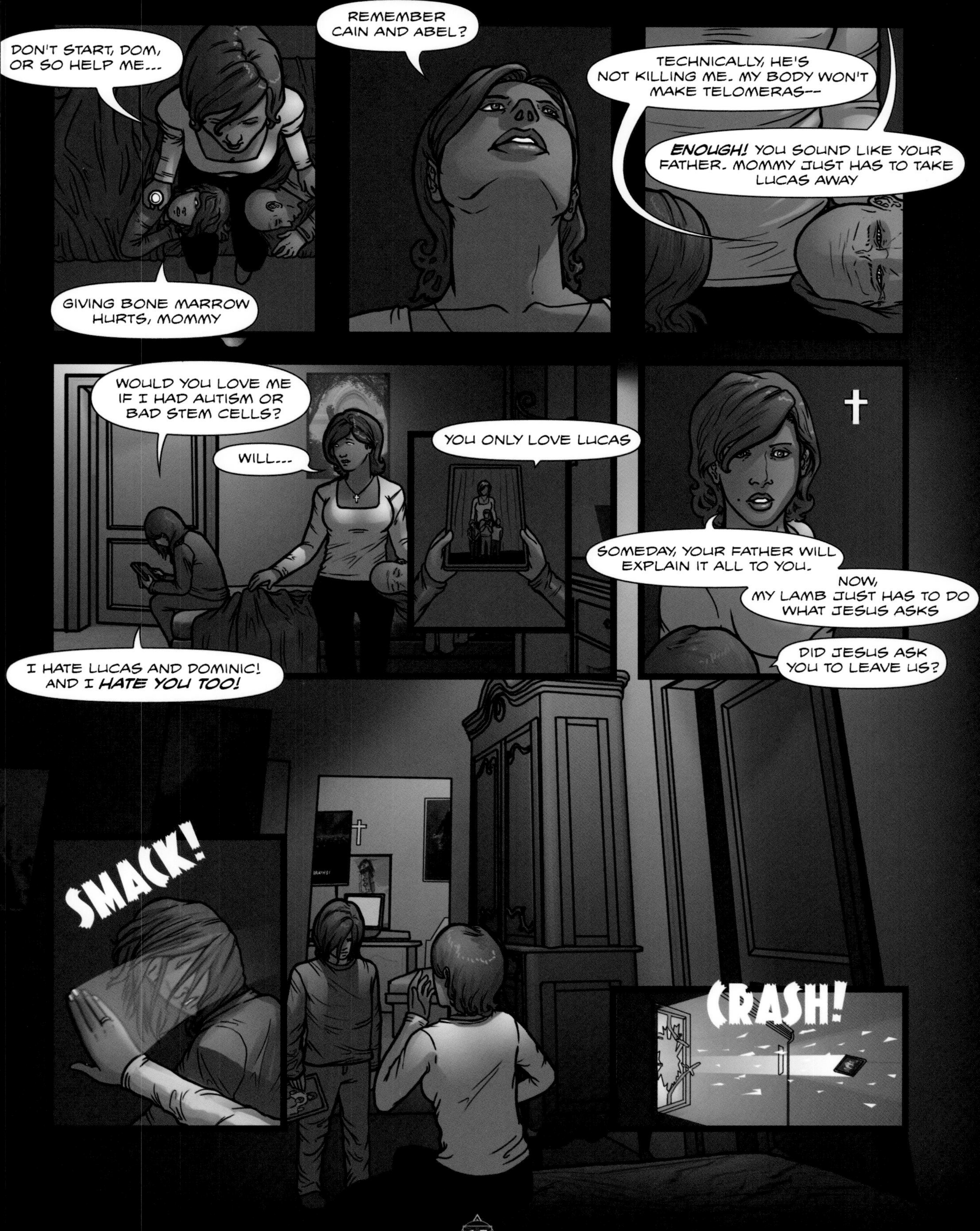
DON'T START, DOM, OR SO HELP ME...
GIVING BONE MARROW HURTS, MOMMY
REMEMBER CAIN AND ABEL?
TECHNICALLY, HE'S NOT KILLING ME. MY BODY WON'T MAKE TELOMERAS--
ENOUGH! YOU SOUND LIKE YOUR FATHER. MOMMY JUST HAS TO TAKE LUCAS AWAY
WOULD YOU LOVE ME IF I HAD AUTISM OR BAD STEM CELLS?
WILL...
YOU ONLY LOVE LUCAS
I HATE LUCAS AND DOMINIC! AND I HATE YOU TOO!
SOMEDAY, YOUR FATHER WILL EXPLAIN IT ALL TO YOU.
NOW, MY LAMB JUST HAS TO DO WHAT JESUS ASKS
DID JESUS ASK YOU TO LEAVE US?
SMACK!
CRASH!

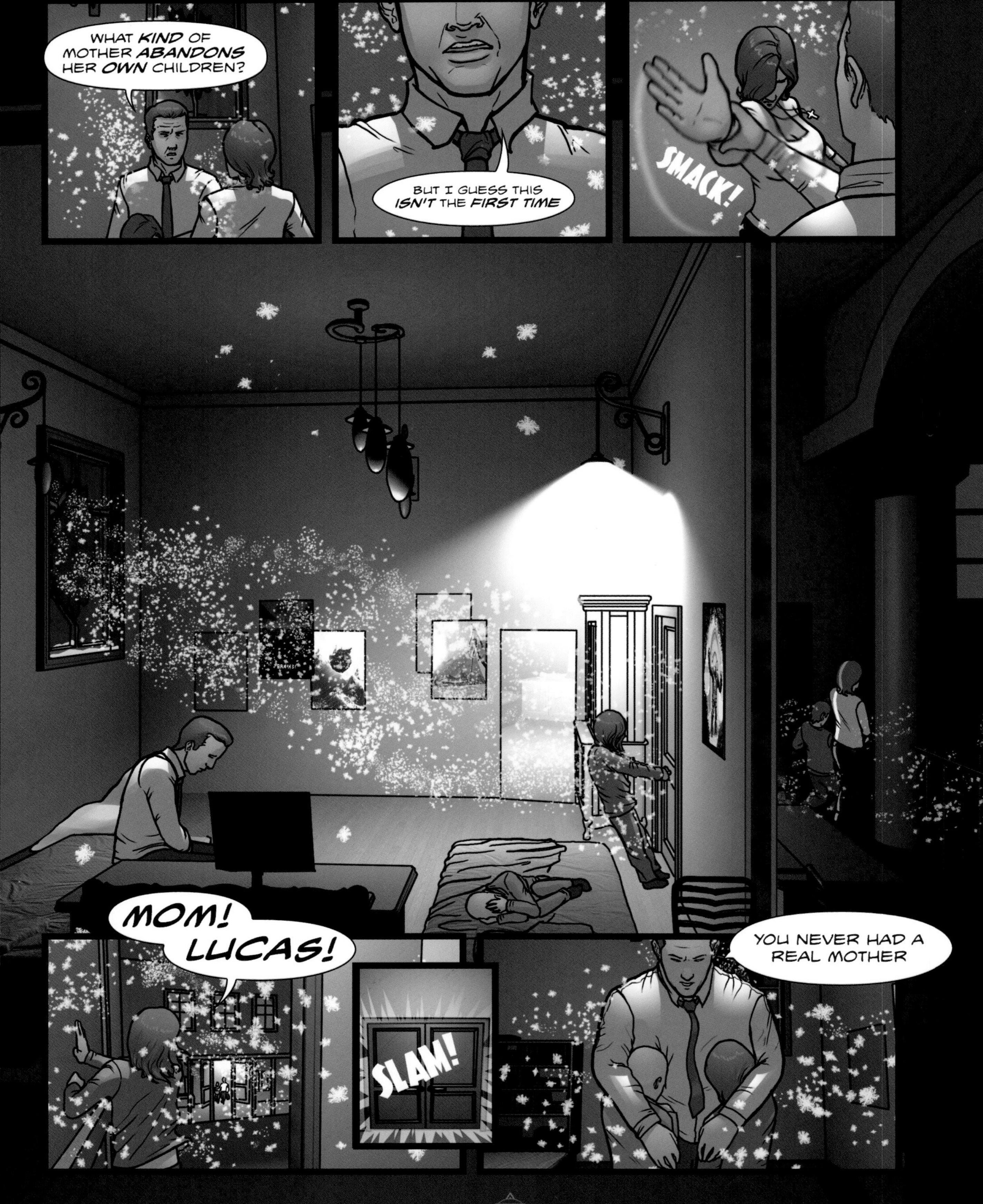
WHAT KIND OF MOTHER ABANDONS HER OWN CHILDREN?
BUT I GUESS THIS ISN'T THE FIRST TIME
SMACK!
MOM! LUCAS!
SLAM!
YOU NEVER HAD A REAL MOTHER

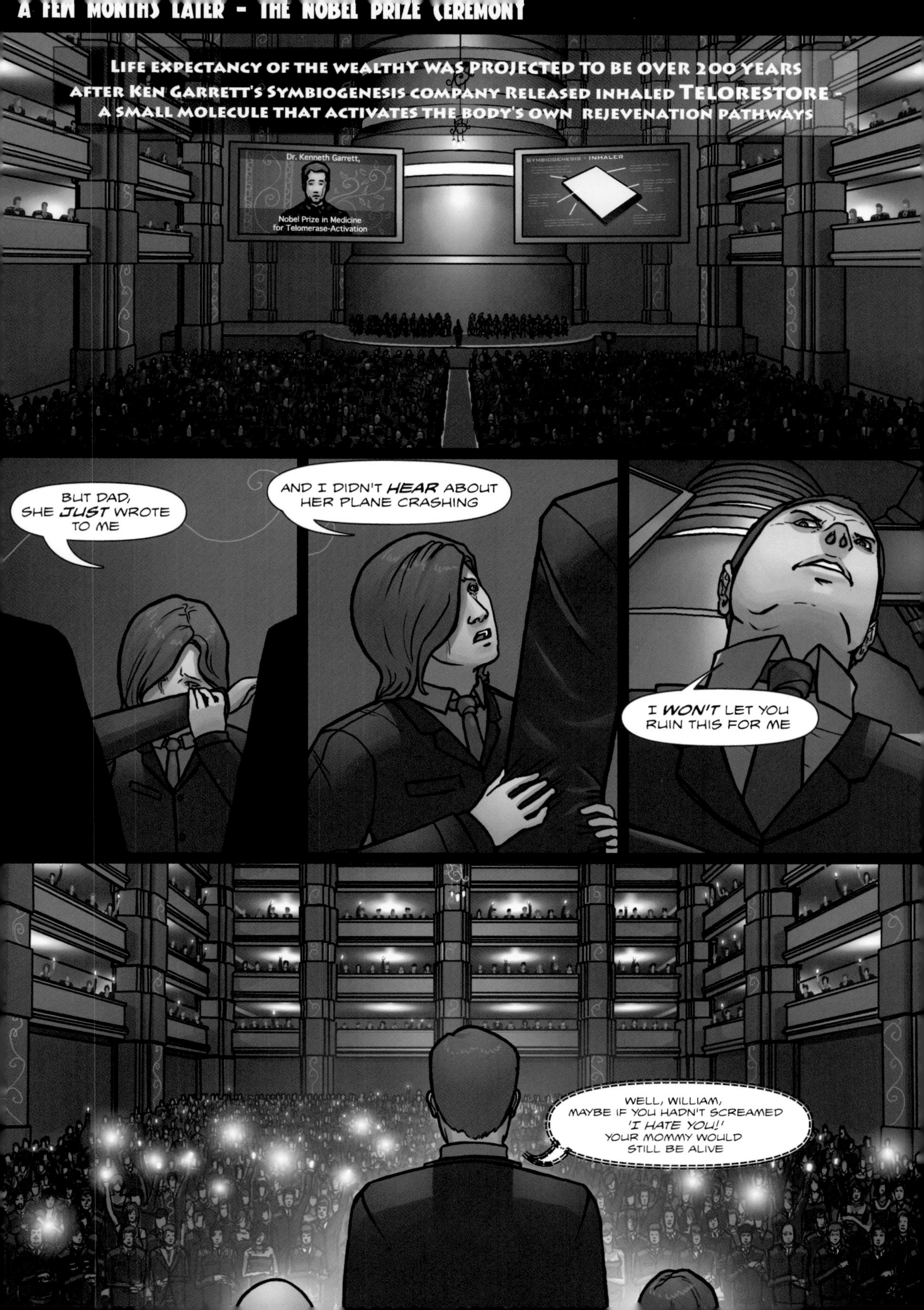
A FEW MONTHS LATER - THE NOBEL PRIZE CEREMONY
LIFE EXPECTANCY OF THE WEALTHY WAS PROJECTED TO BE OVER 200 YEARS AFTER KEN GARRETT'S SYMBIOGENESIS COMPANY RELEASED INHALED TELORESTORE - A SMALL MOLECULE THAT ACTIVATES THE BODY'S OWN REJEVENATION PATHWAYS
Dr. Kenneth Garrett,
Nobel Prize in Medicine for Telomerase-Activation
SYMBIOGENESIS - INHALER
BUT DAD, SHE *JUST* WROTE TO ME
AND I DIDN'T *HEAR* ABOUT HER PLANE CRASHING
I *WON'T* LET YOU RUIN THIS FOR ME
WELL, WILLIAM, MAYBE IF YOU HADN'T SCREAMED *'I HATE YOU!'* YOUR MOMMY WOULD STILL BE ALIVE

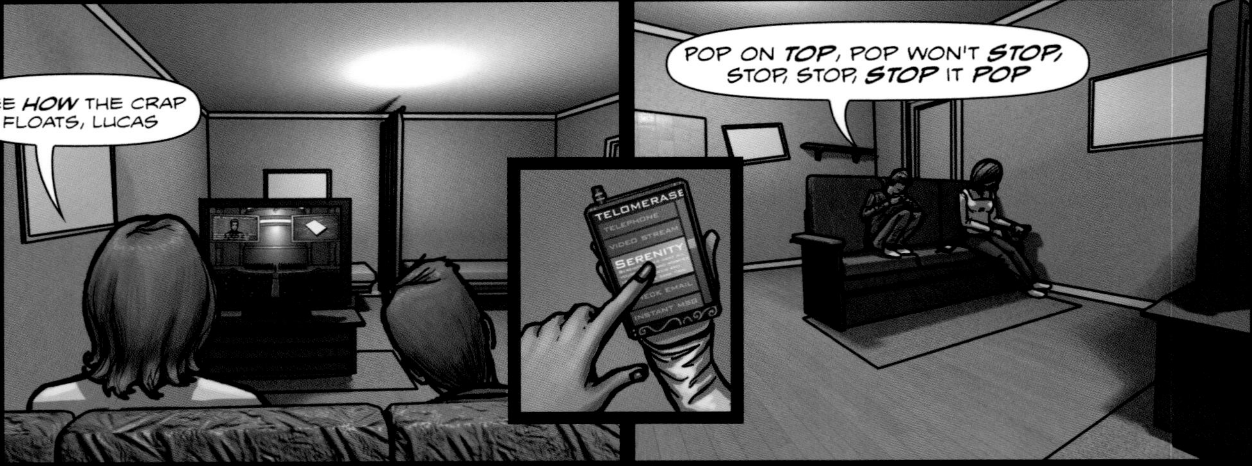
SEE *HOW* THE CRAP FLOATS, LUCAS
TELOMERASE
TELEPHONE
VIDEO STREAM
SERENITY
POP ON *TOP*, POP WON'T *STOP*, STOP, STOP, *STOP* IT *POP*

BUT LIKE TIRES OR BRAKES ON A VINTAGE CAR,
KIDNEYS AND OTHER ORGANS WORE OUT AFTER THE FIRST 100 YEARS.

SIMON VISSER'S PROMETHEUS CORPORATION CORNERED THE MARKET ON SYNTHETIC REPLACEMENT ORGANS THAT PROVED NOTORIOUSLY EXPENSIVE AND UNRELIABLE.

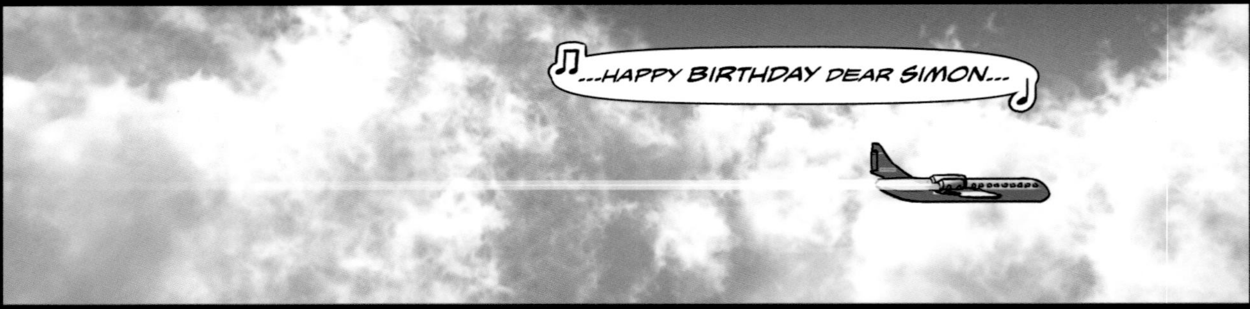
...HAPPY BIRTHDAY DEAR SIMON...

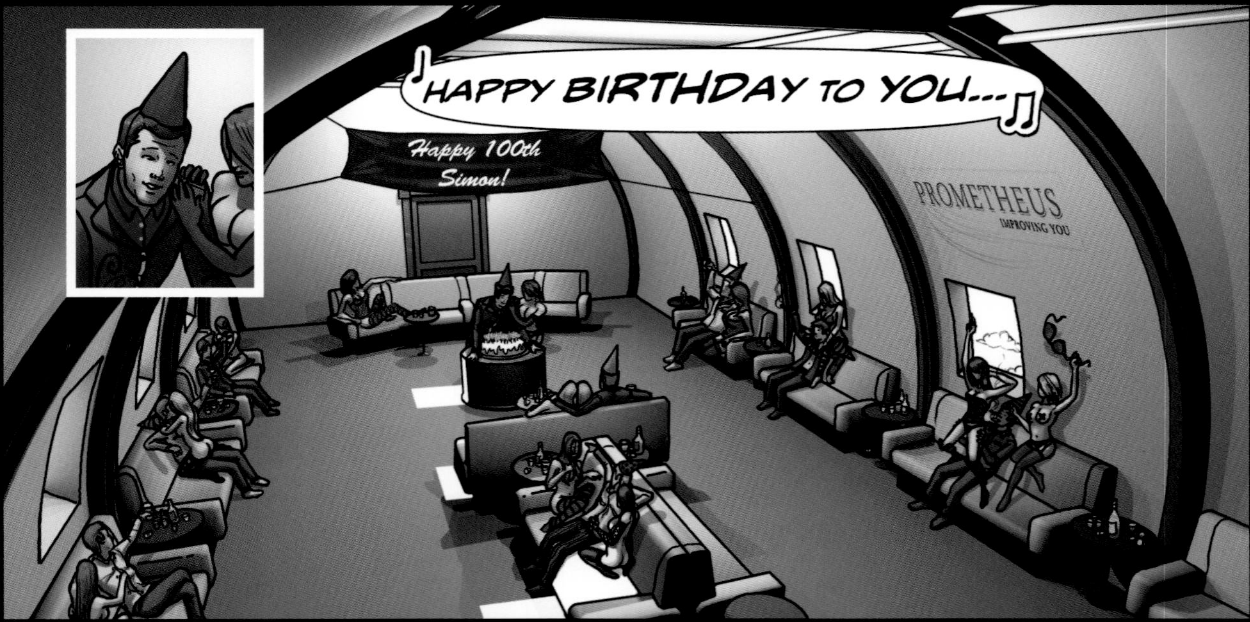
HAPPY BIRTHDAY TO YOU...
Happy 100th Simon!
PROMETHEUS
IMPROVING YOU

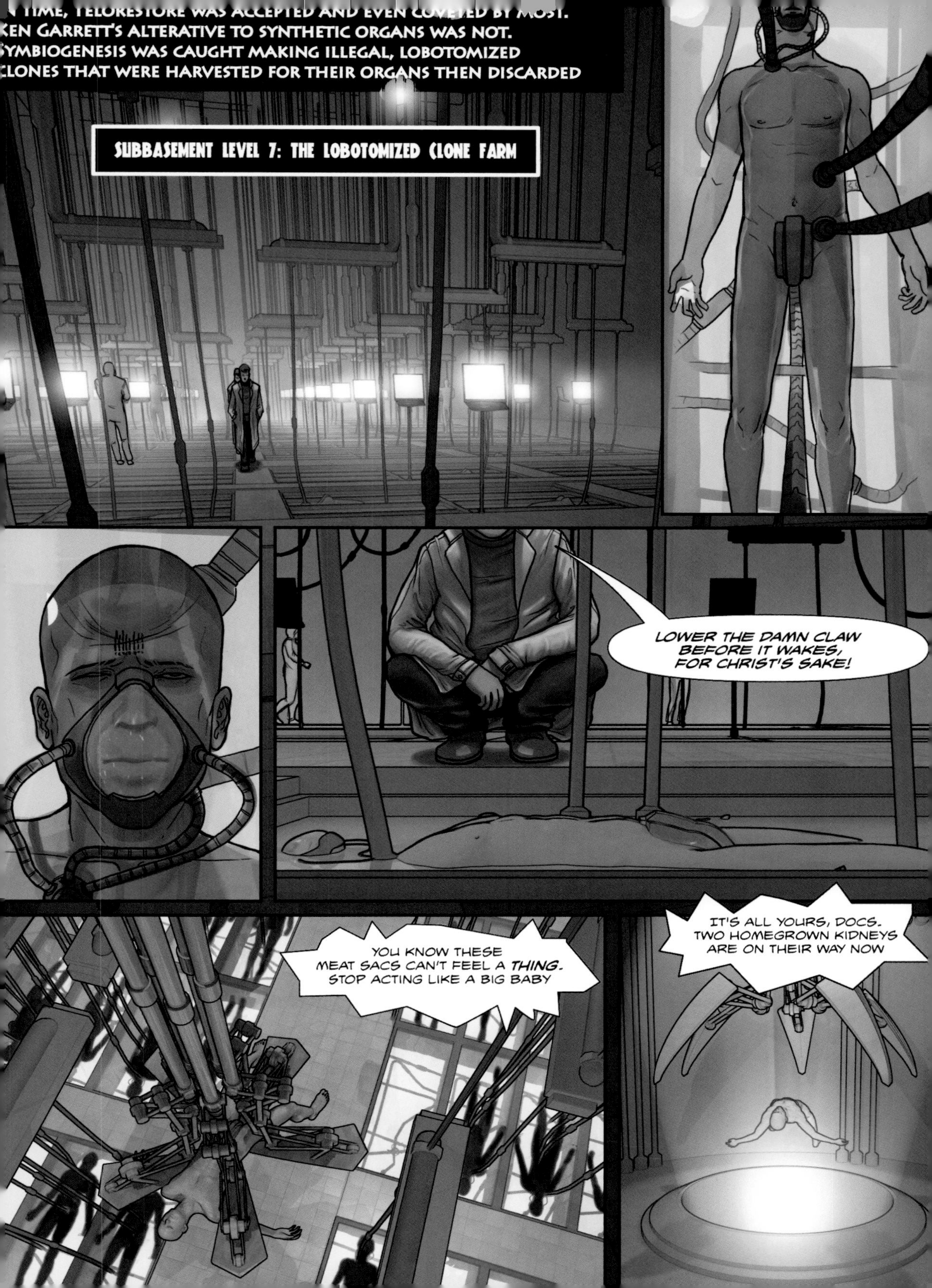
N TIME, TELORESTORE WAS ACCEPTED AND EVEN COVETED BY MOST.
KEN GARRETT'S ALTERATIVE TO SYNTHETIC ORGANS WAS NOT.
YMBIOGENESIS WAS CAUGHT MAKING ILLEGAL, LOBOTOMIZED
CLONES THAT WERE HARVESTED FOR THEIR ORGANS THEN DISCARDED
SUBBASEMENT LEVEL 7: THE LOBOTOMIZED CLONE FARM
LOWER THE DAMN CLAW BEFORE IT WAKES, FOR CHRIST'S SAKE!
YOU KNOW THESE MEAT SACS CAN'T FEEL A THING. STOP ACTING LIKE A BIG BABY
IT'S ALL YOURS, DOCS. TWO HOMEGROWN KIDNEYS ARE ON THEIR WAY NOW

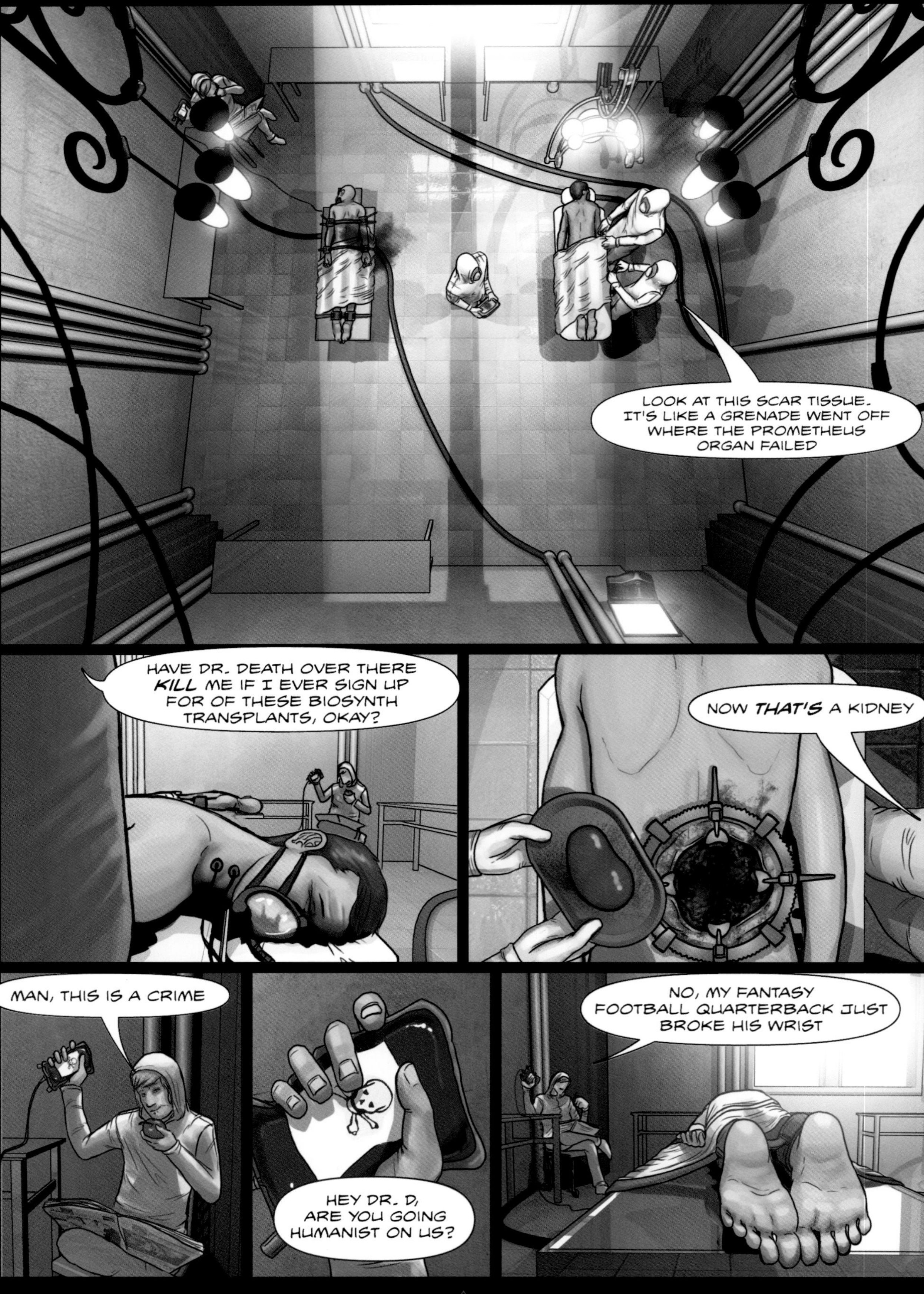
LOOK AT THIS SCAR TISSUE. IT'S LIKE A GRENADE WENT OFF WHERE THE PROMETHEUS ORGAN FAILED
HAVE DR. DEATH OVER THERE KILL ME IF I EVER SIGN UP FOR OF THESE BIOSYNTH TRANSPLANTS, OKAY?
NOW THAT'S A KIDNEY
MAN, THIS IS A CRIME
HEY DR. D, ARE YOU GOING HUMANIST ON US?
NO, MY FANTASY FOOTBALL QUARTERBACK JUST BROKE HIS WRIST

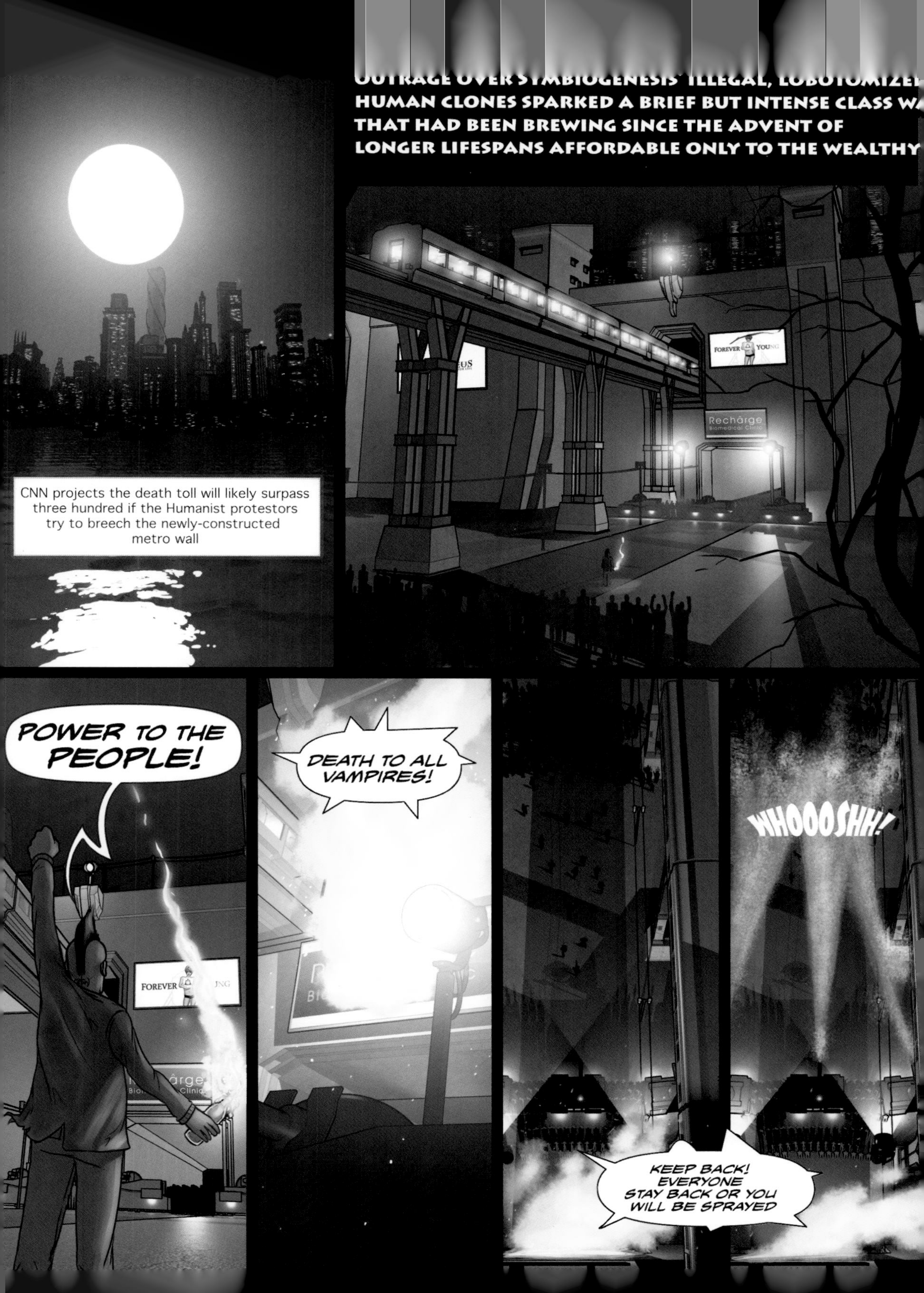
OUTRAGE OVER SYMBIOGENESIS' ILLEGAL, LOBOTOMIZE
HUMAN CLONES SPARKED A BRIEF BUT INTENSE CLASS W
THAT HAD BEEN BREWING SINCE THE ADVENT OF
LONGER LIFESPANS AFFORDABLE ONLY TO THE WEALTHY
CNN projects the death toll will likely surpass three hundred if the Humanist protestors try to breech the newly-constructed metro wall
FOREVER YOUNG
Rechârge
Biomedical Clinic
POWER TO THE PEOPLE!
DEATH TO ALL VAMPIRES!
WHOOOSHH!
KEEP BACK! EVERYONE STAY BACK OR YOU WILL BE SPRAYED

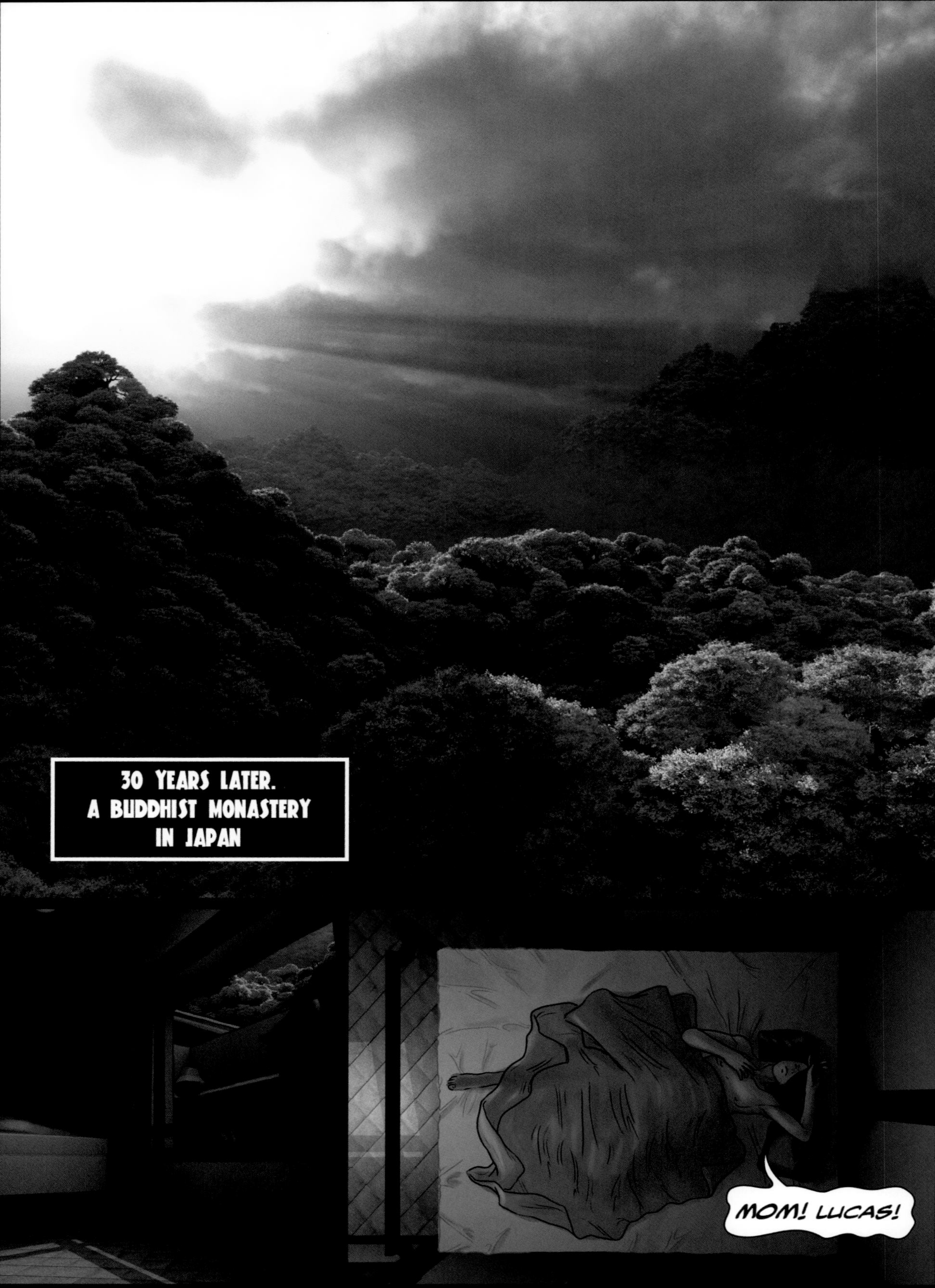
30 YEARS LATER.
A BUDDHIST MONASTERY
IN JAPAN
MOM! LUCAS!

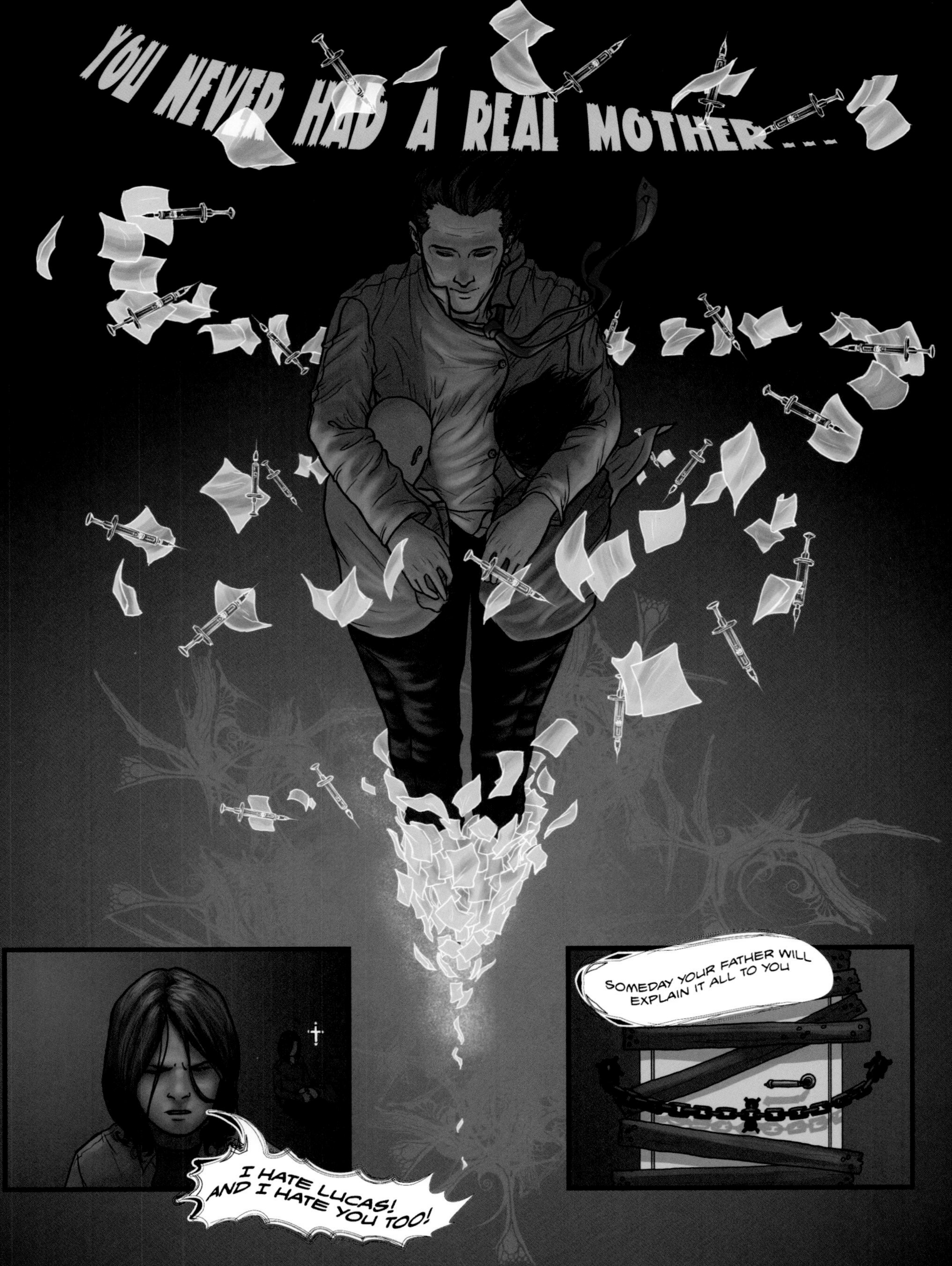
YOU NEVER HAD A REAL MOTHER...
I HATE LUCAS! AND I HATE YOU TOO!
SOMEDAY YOUR FATHER WILL EXPLAIN IT ALL TO YOU

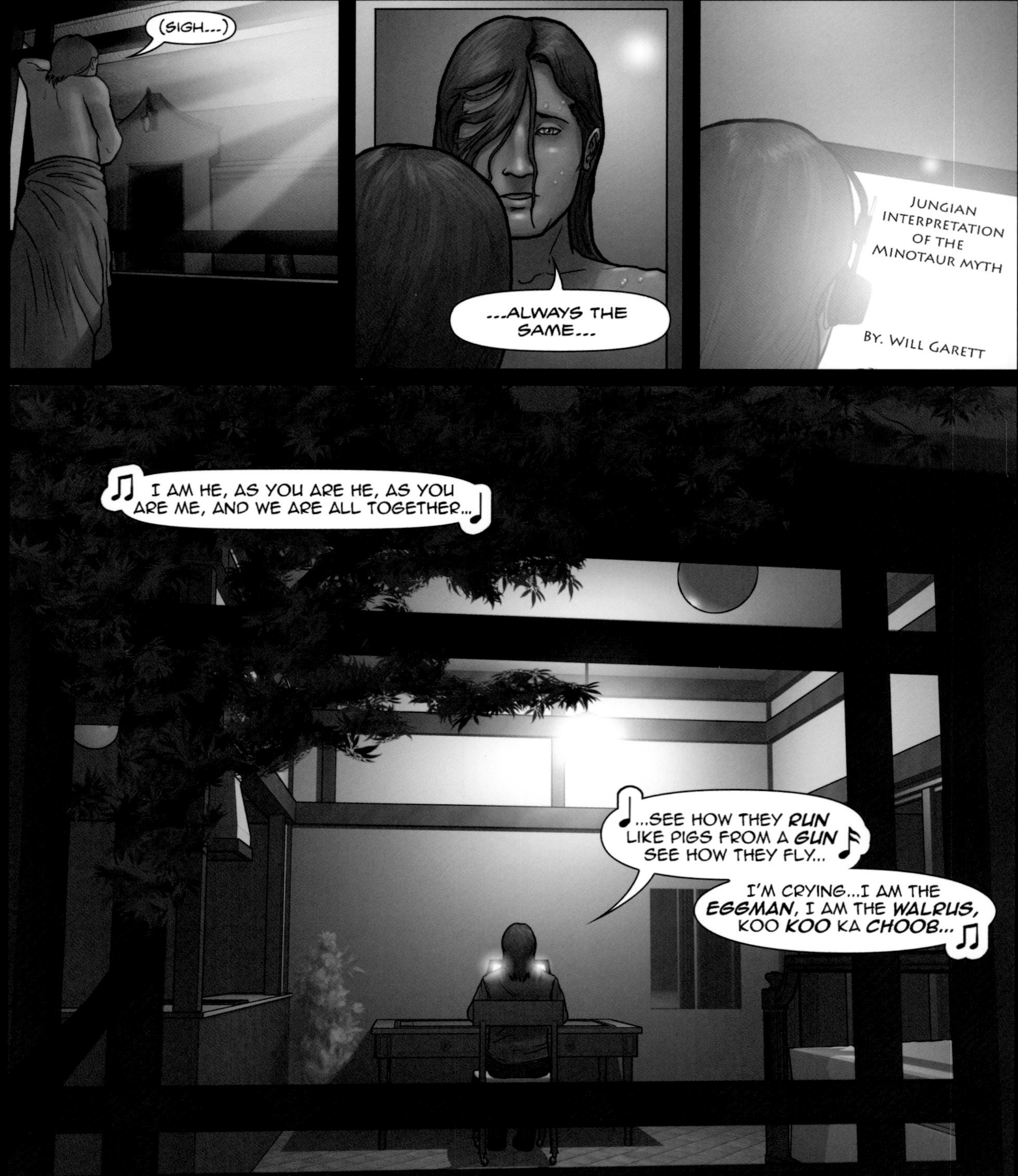
(SIGH...)
...ALWAYS THE SAME...
JUNGIAN INTERPRETATION OF THE MINOTAUR MYTH
BY. WILL GARETT
♫ I AM HE, AS YOU ARE HE, AS YOU ARE ME, AND WE ARE ALL TOGETHER...♩
♩...SEE HOW THEY RUN LIKE PIGS FROM A GUN SEE HOW THEY FLY...♪
I'M CRYING...I AM THE EGGMAN, I AM THE WALRUS, KOO KOO KA CHOOB...♫

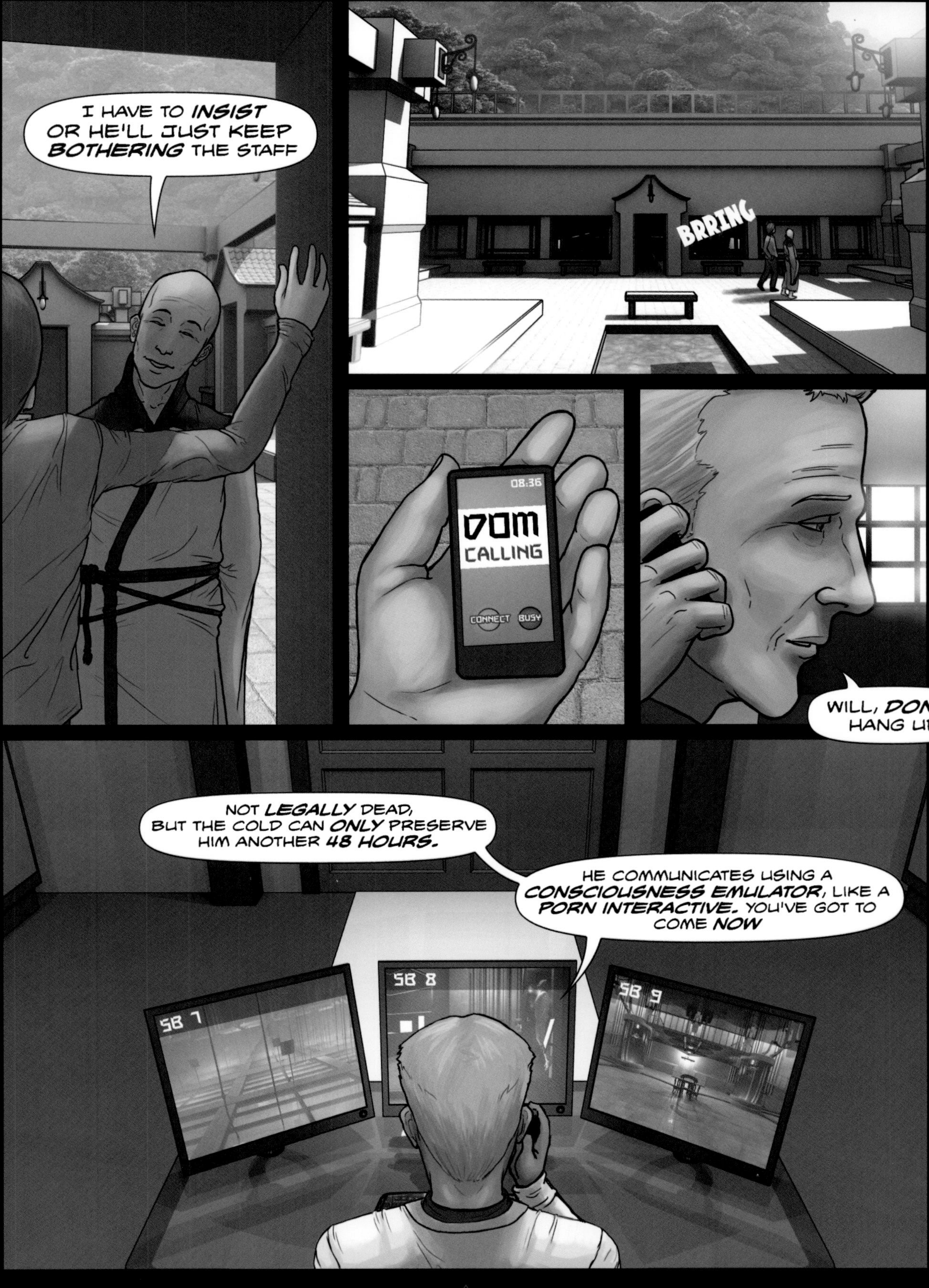
I HAVE TO INSIST OR HE'LL JUST KEEP BOTHERING THE STAFF
BRRING
08:36
DOM CALLING
CONNECT
BUSY
WILL, DON'T HANG UP
NOT LEGALLY DEAD, BUT THE COLD CAN ONLY PRESERVE HIM ANOTHER 48 HOURS.
HE COMMUNICATES USING A CONSCIOUSNESS EMULATOR, LIKE A PORN INTERACTIVE. YOU'VE GOT TO COME NOW
SB 7
SB 8
SB 9

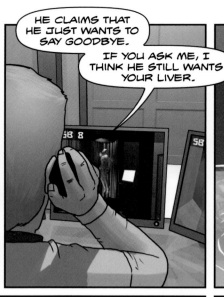

I THOUGHT YOU TOLD HIM I DON'T *WANT* YOUR JOB

HE CLAIMS THAT HE JUST WANTS TO SAY GOODBYE.

IF YOU ASK ME, I THINK HE STILL WANTS YOUR LIVER.

LET HIM BUY ONE FROM PROMETHEUS

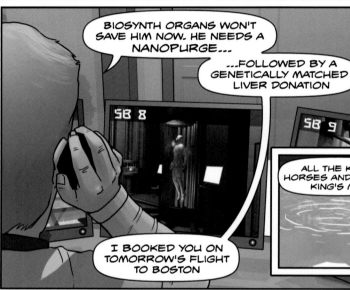

BIOSYNTH ORGANS WON'T SAVE HIM NOW. HE NEEDS A NANOPURGE...

...FOLLOWED BY A GENETICALLY MATCHED LIVER DONATION

I BOOKED YOU ON TOMORROW'S FLIGHT TO BOSTON

ALL THE KING'S HORSES AND ALL THE KING'S MEN

I WON'T GO THROUGH IT AGAIN. NOT FOR HIM. DON'T CALL BACK

CAN THAT PEBBLE DENY ITS RIPPLES?

I CAN'T BE CENTERED THERE.

BEING THERE IS LIKE BEING IN A HURRICANE

DANCE WITH THE WIND AND BETWEEN THE RAINDROPS

OUTSIDE SYMBIOGENESIS HEADQUARTERS

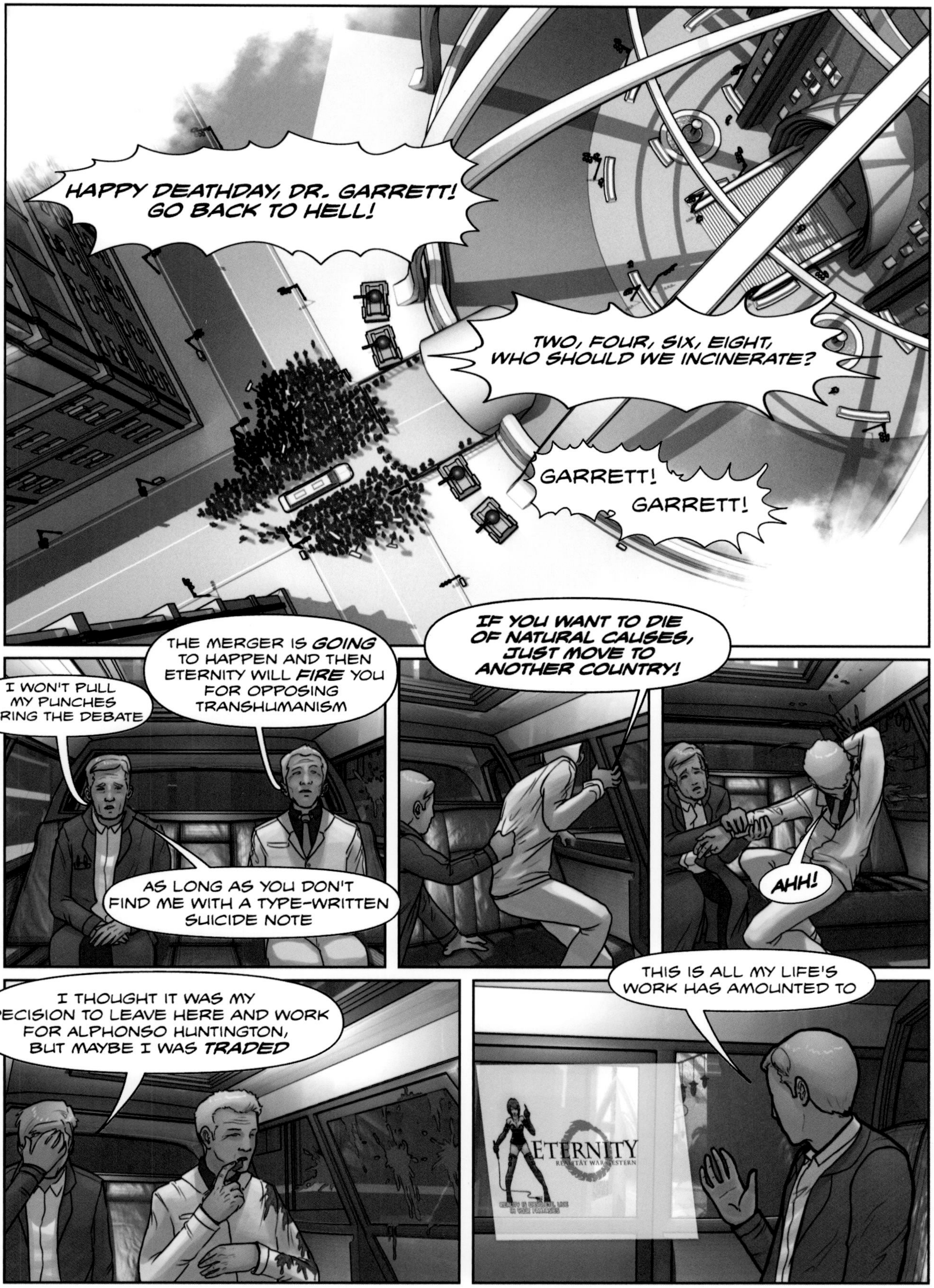

HAPPY DEATHDAY, DR. GARRETT! GO BACK TO HELL!
TWO, FOUR, SIX, EIGHT, WHO SHOULD WE INCINERATE?
GARRETT! GARRETT!
I WON'T PULL MY PUNCHES DURING THE DEBATE
THE MERGER IS *GOING* TO HAPPEN AND THEN ETERNITY WILL *FIRE* YOU FOR OPPOSING TRANSHUMANISM
AS LONG AS YOU DON'T FIND ME WITH A TYPE-WRITTEN SUICIDE NOTE
IF YOU WANT TO DIE OF NATURAL CAUSES, JUST MOVE TO ANOTHER COUNTRY!
AHH!
I THOUGHT IT WAS MY DECISION TO LEAVE HERE AND WORK FOR ALPHONSO HUNTINGTON, BUT MAYBE I WAS *TRADED*
THIS IS ALL MY LIFE'S WORK HAS AMOUNTED TO
ETERNITY

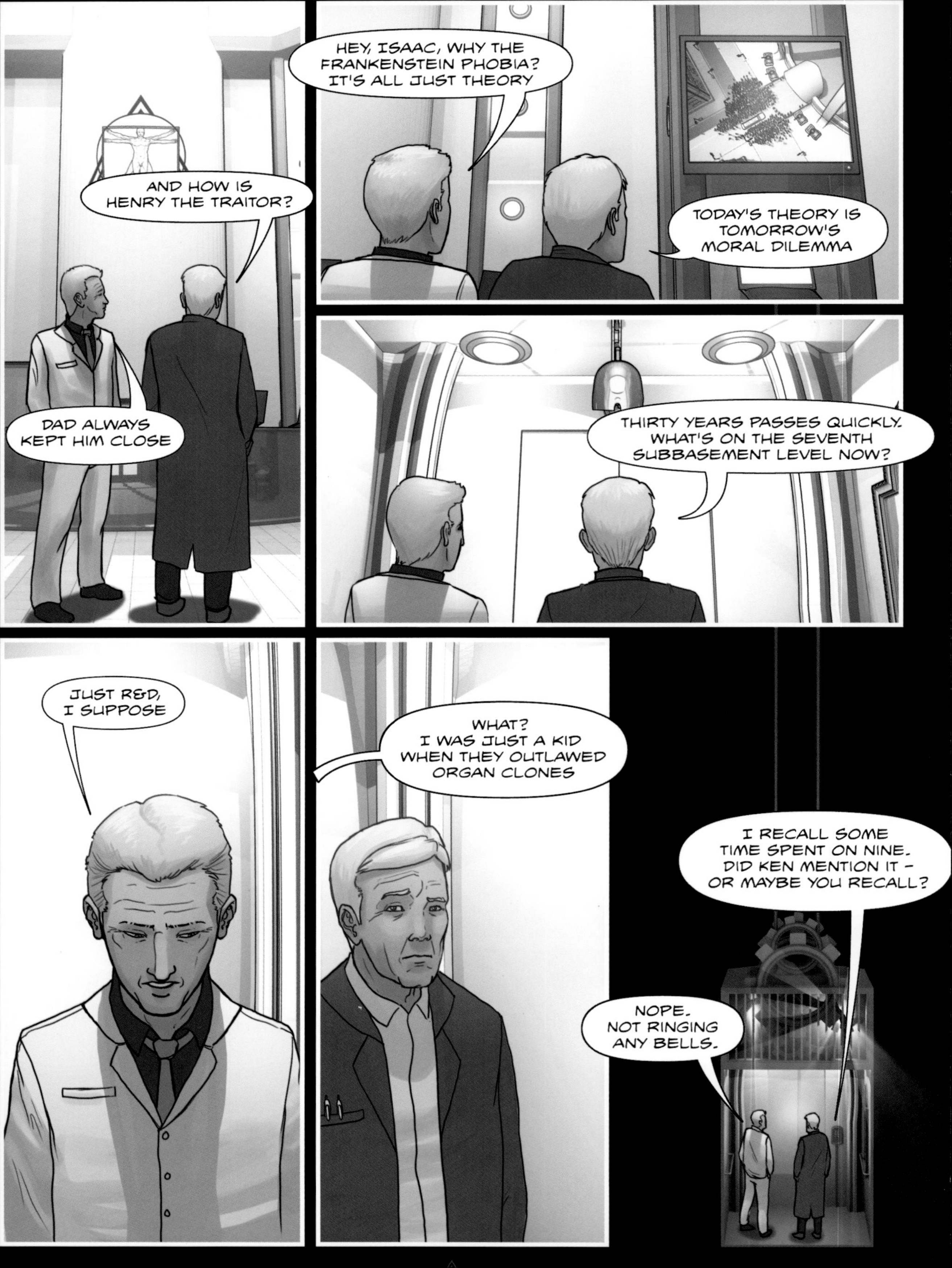
AND HOW IS HENRY THE TRAITOR?
DAD ALWAYS KEPT HIM CLOSE
HEY, ISAAC, WHY THE FRANKENSTEIN PHOBIA? IT'S ALL JUST THEORY
TODAY'S THEORY IS TOMORROW'S MORAL DILEMMA
THIRTY YEARS PASSES QUICKLY. WHAT'S ON THE SEVENTH SUBBASEMENT LEVEL NOW?
JUST R&D, I SUPPOSE
WHAT? I WAS JUST A KID WHEN THEY OUTLAWED ORGAN CLONES
I RECALL SOME TIME SPENT ON NINE. DID KEN MENTION IT - OR MAYBE YOU RECALL?
NOPE. NOT RINGING ANY BELLS.

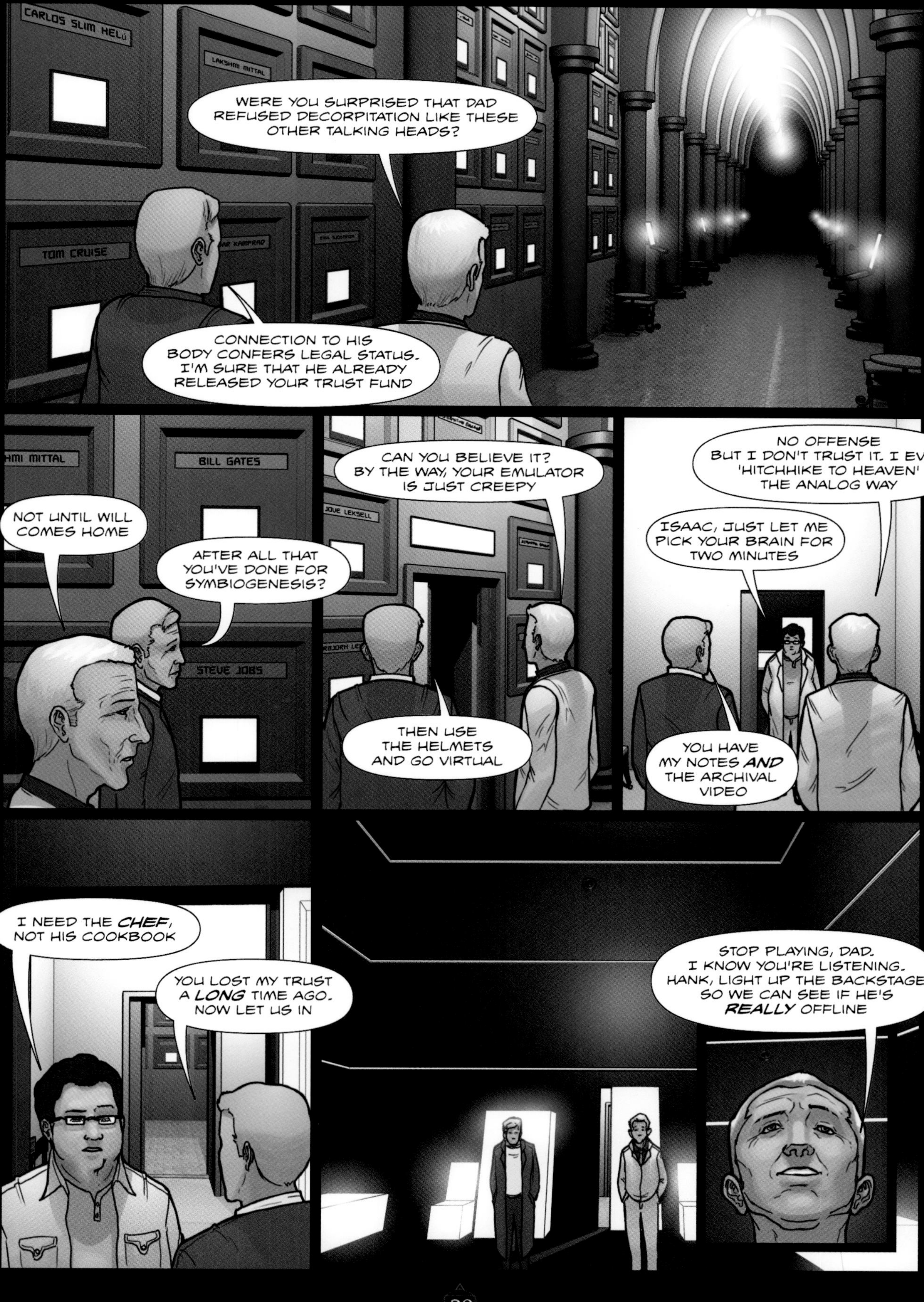
CARLOS SLIM HELÚ
LAKSHMI MITTAL
TOM CRUISE
WERE YOU SURPRISED THAT DAD REFUSED DECORPITATION LIKE THESE OTHER TALKING HEADS?
CONNECTION TO HIS BODY CONFERS LEGAL STATUS. I'M SURE THAT HE ALREADY RELEASED YOUR TRUST FUND
BILL GATES
STEVE JOBS
NOT UNTIL WILL COMES HOME
AFTER ALL THAT YOU'VE DONE FOR SYMBIOGENESIS?
CAN YOU BELIEVE IT? BY THE WAY, YOUR EMULATOR IS JUST CREEPY
THEN USE THE HELMETS AND GO VIRTUAL
NO OFFENSE BUT I DON'T TRUST IT. I EVEN 'HITCHHIKE TO HEAVEN' THE ANALOG WAY
ISAAC, JUST LET ME PICK YOUR BRAIN FOR TWO MINUTES
YOU HAVE MY NOTES AND THE ARCHIVAL VIDEO
I NEED THE CHEF, NOT HIS COOKBOOK
YOU LOST MY TRUST A LONG TIME AGO. NOW LET US IN
STOP PLAYING, DAD. I KNOW YOU'RE LISTENING. HANK, LIGHT UP THE BACKSTAGE SO WE CAN SEE IF HE'S REALLY OFFLINE

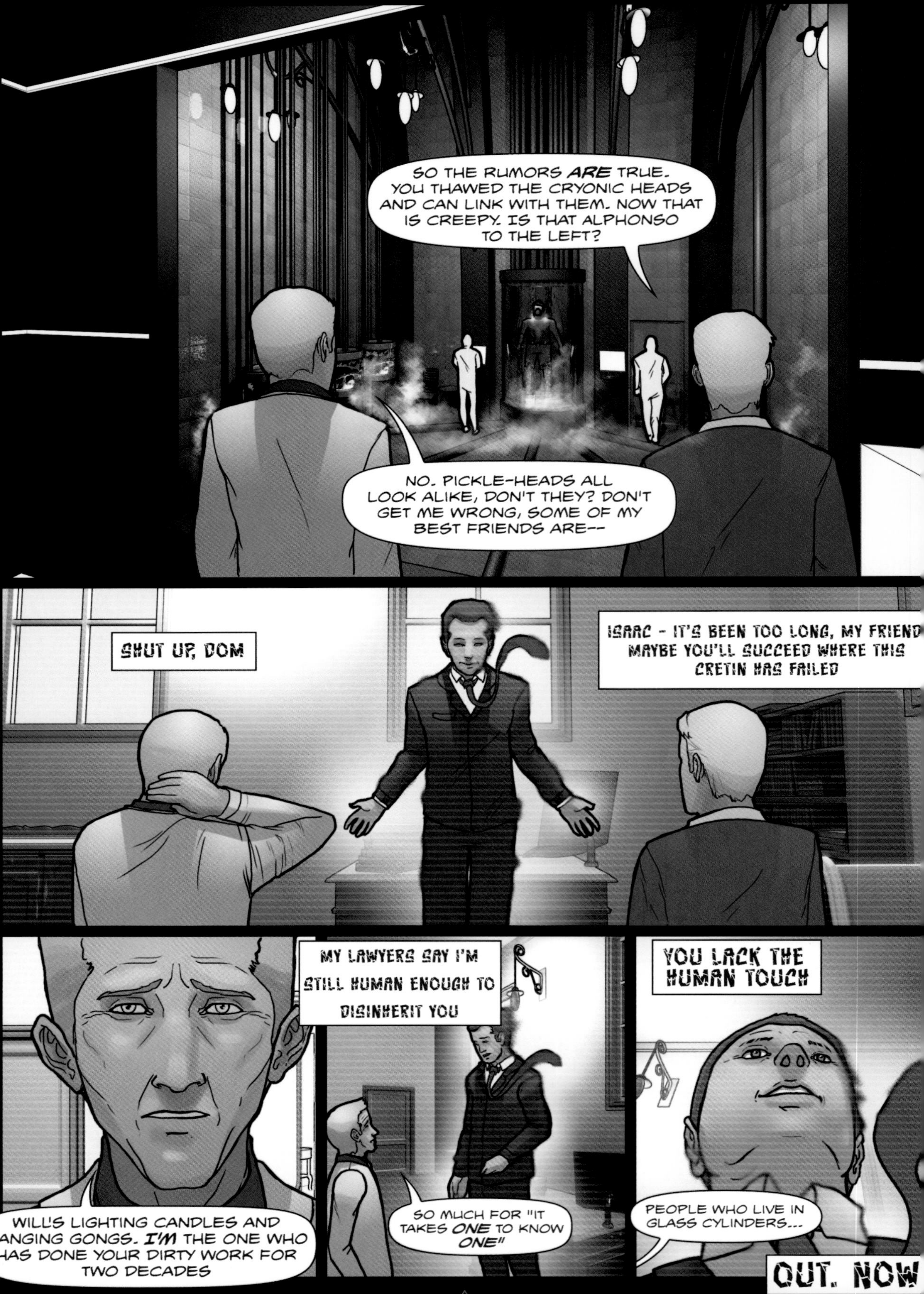
SO THE RUMORS ARE TRUE. YOU THAWED THE CRYONIC HEADS AND CAN LINK WITH THEM. NOW THAT IS CREEPY. IS THAT ALPHONSO TO THE LEFT?
NO. PICKLE-HEADS ALL LOOK ALIKE, DON'T THEY? DON'T GET ME WRONG, SOME OF MY BEST FRIENDS ARE--
SHUT UP, DOM
ISAAC - IT'S BEEN TOO LONG, MY FRIEND MAYBE YOU'LL SUCCEED WHERE THIS CRETIN HAS FAILED
WILL'S LIGHTING CANDLES AND BANGING GONGS. I'M THE ONE WHO HAS DONE YOUR DIRTY WORK FOR TWO DECADES
MY LAWYERS SAY I'M STILL HUMAN ENOUGH TO DISINHERIT YOU
SO MUCH FOR "IT TAKES ONE TO KNOW ONE"
YOU LACK THE HUMAN TOUCH
PEOPLE WHO LIVE IN GLASS CYLINDERS...
OUT. NOW

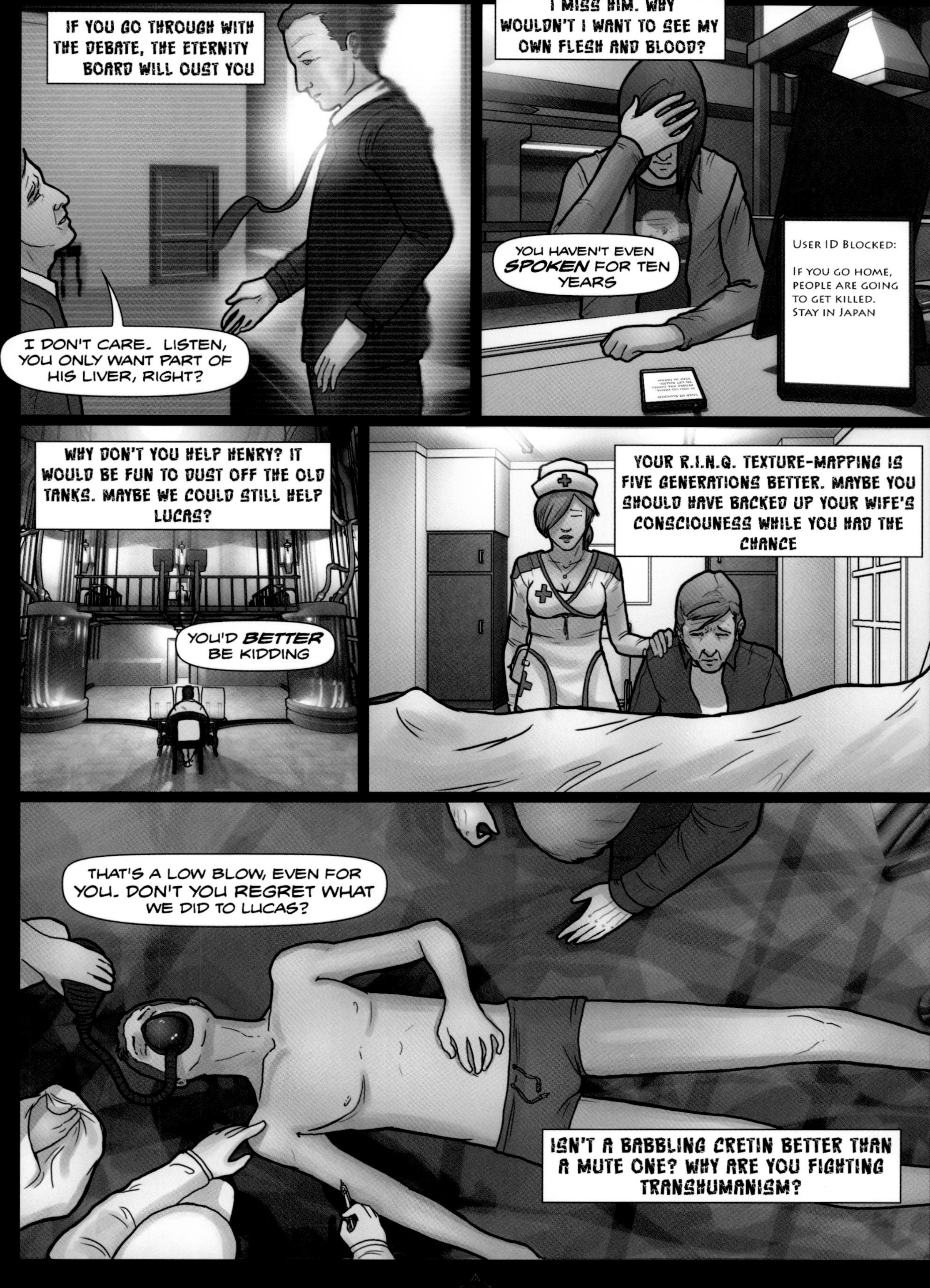

IF YOU GO THROUGH WITH THE DEBATE, THE ETERNITY BOARD WILL OUST YOU
I DON'T CARE. LISTEN, YOU ONLY WANT PART OF HIS LIVER, RIGHT?
I MISS HIM. WHY WOULDN'T I WANT TO SEE MY OWN FLESH AND BLOOD?
YOU HAVEN'T EVEN SPOKEN FOR TEN YEARS
USER ID BLOCKED:
IF YOU GO HOME, PEOPLE ARE GOING TO GET KILLED. STAY IN JAPAN
WHY DON'T YOU HELP HENRY? IT WOULD BE FUN TO DUST OFF THE OLD TANKS. MAYBE WE COULD STILL HELP LUCAS?
YOU'D BETTER BE KIDDING
YOUR R.I.N.Q. TEXTURE-MAPPING IS FIVE GENERATIONS BETTER. MAYBE YOU SHOULD HAVE BACKED UP YOUR WIFE'S CONSCIOUNESS WHILE YOU HAD THE CHANCE
THAT'S A LOW BLOW, EVEN FOR YOU. DON'T YOU REGRET WHAT WE DID TO LUCAS?
ISN'T A BABBLING CRETIN BETTER THAN A MUTE ONE? WHY ARE YOU FIGHTING TRANSHUMANISM?

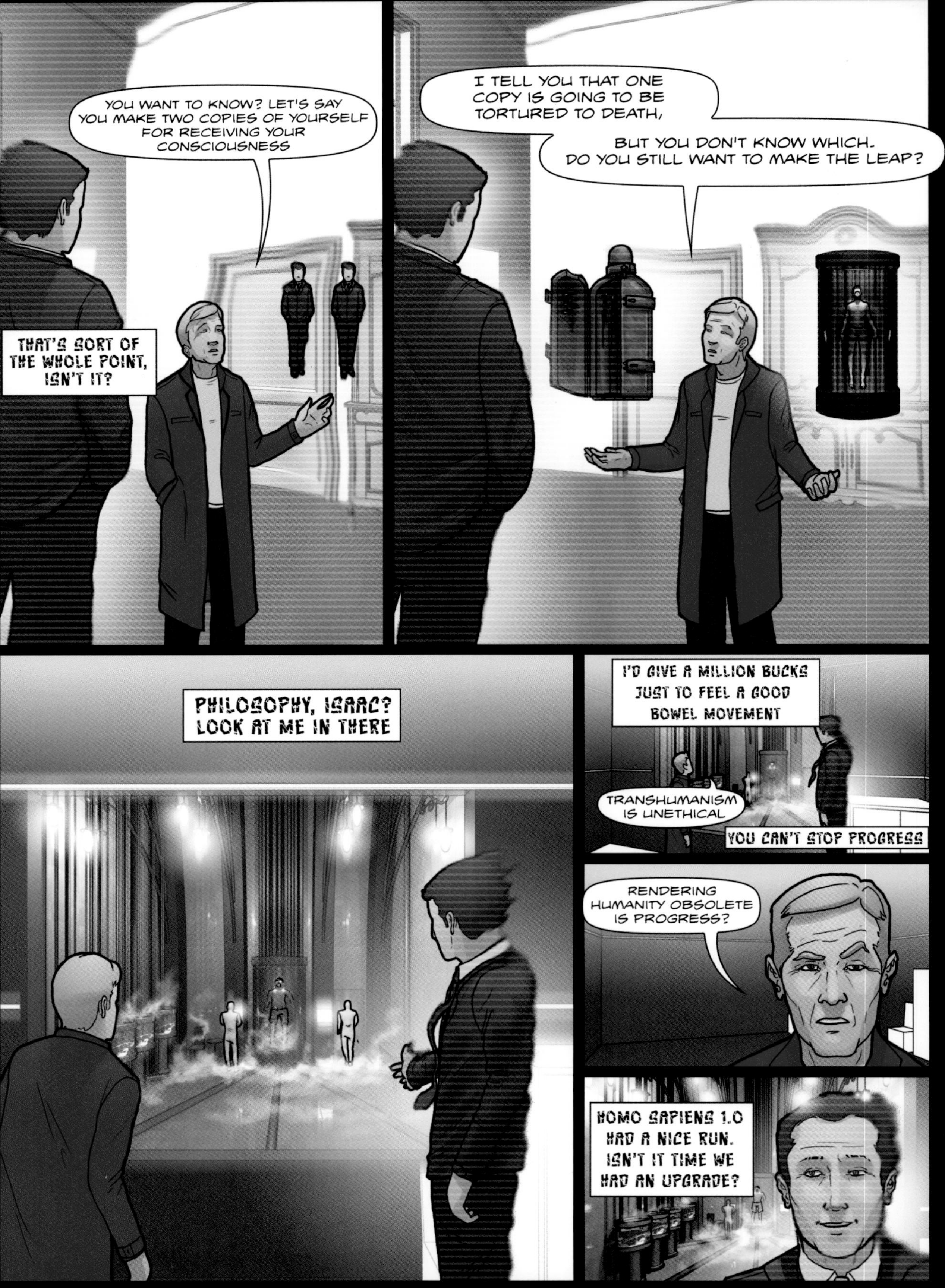

YOU WANT TO KNOW? LET'S SAY YOU MAKE TWO COPIES OF YOURSELF FOR RECEIVING YOUR CONSCIOUSNESS
THAT'S SORT OF THE WHOLE POINT, ISN'T IT?
I TELL YOU THAT ONE COPY IS GOING TO BE TORTURED TO DEATH,
BUT YOU DON'T KNOW WHICH. DO YOU STILL WANT TO MAKE THE LEAP?
PHILOSOPHY, ISAAC? LOOK AT ME IN THERE
I'D GIVE A MILLION BUCKS JUST TO FEEL A GOOD BOWEL MOVEMENT
TRANSHUMANISM IS UNETHICAL
YOU CAN'T STOP PROGRESS
RENDERING HUMANITY OBSOLETE IS PROGRESS?
HOMO SAPIENS 1.0 HAD A NICE RUN. ISN'T IT TIME WE HAD AN UPGRADE?

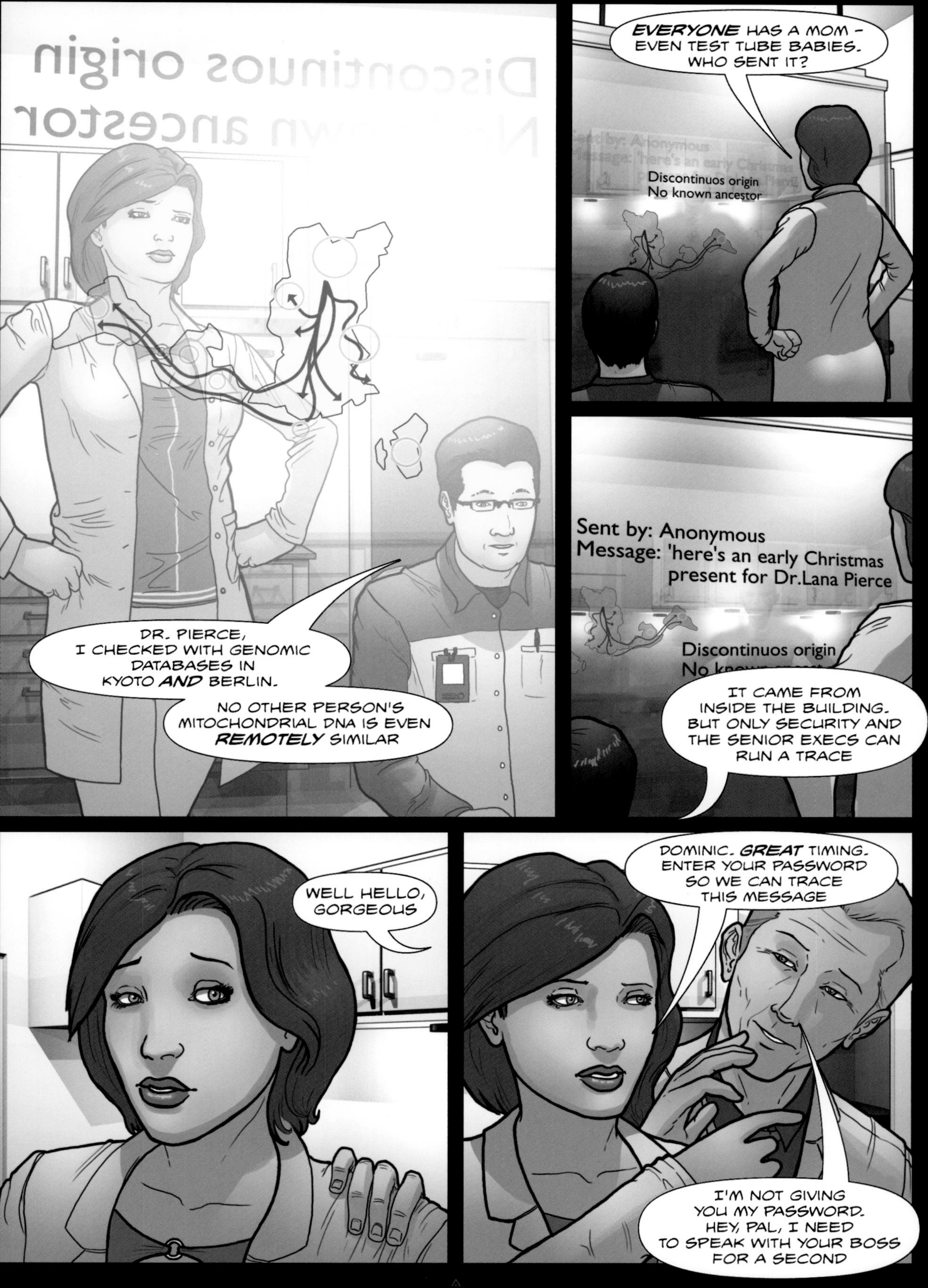
DR. PIERCE, I CHECKED WITH GENOMIC DATABASES IN KYOTO *AND* BERLIN.
NO OTHER PERSON'S MITOCHONDRIAL DNA IS EVEN *REMOTELY* SIMILAR
EVERYONE HAS A MOM - EVEN TEST TUBE BABIES. WHO SENT IT?
Discontinuos origin
No known ancestor
Sent by: Anonymous
Message: 'here's an early Christmas present for Dr.Lana Pierce
Discontinuos origin
IT CAME FROM INSIDE THE BUILDING. BUT ONLY SECURITY AND THE SENIOR EXECS CAN RUN A TRACE
WELL HELLO, GORGEOUS
DOMINIC. *GREAT* TIMING. ENTER YOUR PASSWORD SO WE CAN TRACE THIS MESSAGE
I'M NOT GIVING YOU MY PASSWORD. HEY, PAL, I NEED TO SPEAK WITH YOUR BOSS FOR A SECOND

HAVE YOU RECONSIDERED MY OFFER?

DIDN'T YOU HAVE A CRUSH ON HIM IN COLLEGE?

SO MANY OFFICE HOURS, BUT I NEVER HAD THE GUTS TO GO

JUST ENTER IT

USER ID: DOMINIC GARRETT
PASSWORD: *****
HINT: PET NAME

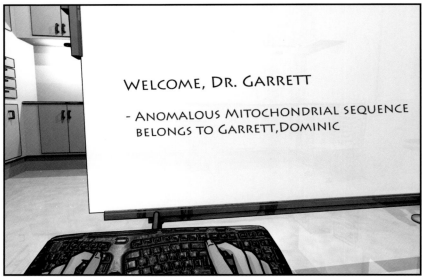

WELCOME, DR. GARRETT

- ANOMALOUS MITOCHONDRIAL SEQUENCE BELONGS TO GARRETT, DOMINIC

WHAT THE @#% !

WHY'D YOU CLOSE IT? *WHO* WAS IT?

CLEAR IT WITH LEGAL FIRST

THIS MERGER WILL CHANGE YOUR MOTHER'S MIND. RUTHIE CAN DOWNLOAD INTO HER OWN FRESH CLONE; I'LL PUT HER AT THE *TOP* OF THE LIST

WHY THE SUDDEN CONCERN OVER *MY* MOTHER?

NOW THAT HURTS. FACT IS, I'M SUDDENLY OVERCOME WITH AN URGE TO CALL MY *OWN* MOM

A SUBURBAN HOSPITAL

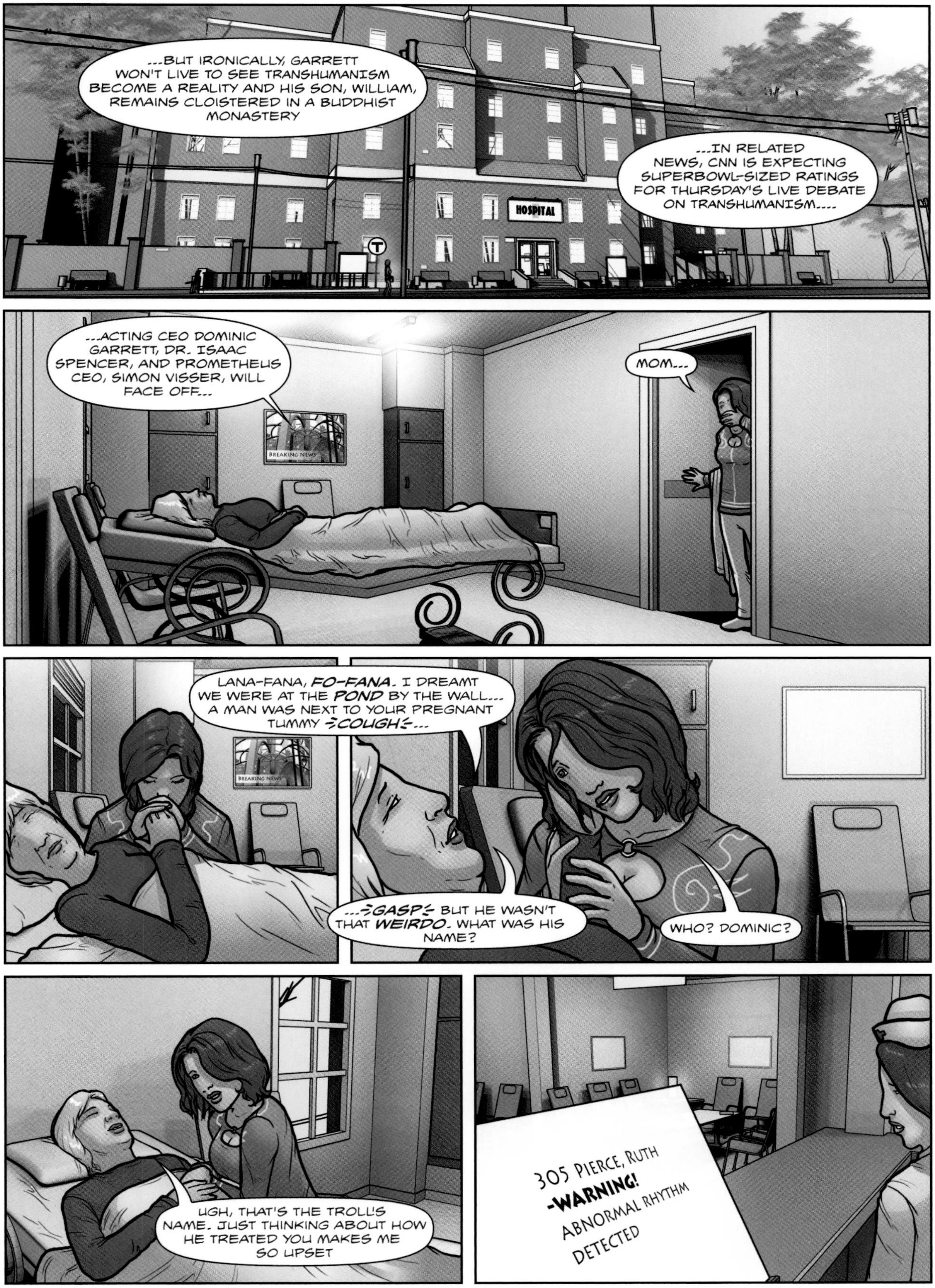

...BUT IRONICALLY, GARRETT WON'T LIVE TO SEE TRANSHUMANISM BECOME A REALITY AND HIS SON, WILLIAM, REMAINS CLOISTERED IN A BUDDHIST MONASTERY
HOSPITAL
...IN RELATED NEWS, CNN IS EXPECTING SUPERBOWL-SIZED RATINGS FOR THURSDAY'S LIVE DEBATE ON TRANSHUMANISM....
...ACTING CEO DOMINIC GARRETT, DR. ISAAC SPENCER, AND PROMETHEUS CEO, SIMON VISSER, WILL FACE OFF...
BREAKING NEWS
MOM...
LANA-FANA, FO-FANA. I DREAMT WE WERE AT THE POND BY THE WALL... A MAN WAS NEXT TO YOUR PREGNANT TUMMY *COUGH*...
BREAKING NEWS
...*GASP* BUT HE WASN'T THAT WEIRDO. WHAT WAS HIS NAME?
WHO? DOMINIC?
UGH, THAT'S THE TROLL'S NAME. JUST THINKING ABOUT HOW HE TREATED YOU MAKES ME SO UPSET
305 PIERCE, RUTH
-WARNING!
ABNORMAL RHYTHM
DETECTED

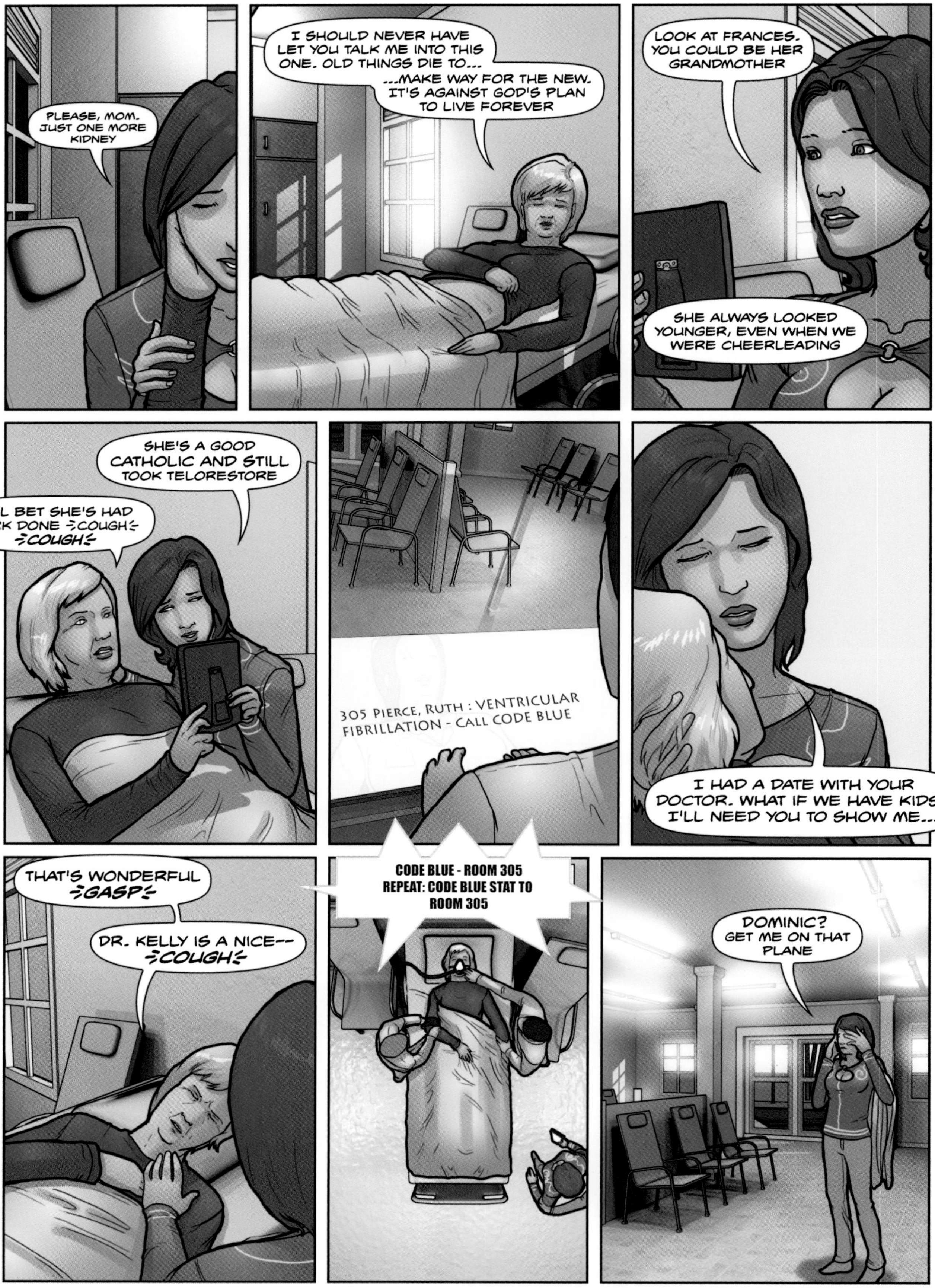
PLEASE, MOM. JUST ONE MORE KIDNEY
I SHOULD NEVER HAVE LET YOU TALK ME INTO THIS ONE. OLD THINGS DIE TO...
...MAKE WAY FOR THE NEW. IT'S AGAINST GOD'S PLAN TO LIVE FOREVER
LOOK AT FRANCES. YOU COULD BE HER GRANDMOTHER
SHE ALWAYS LOOKED YOUNGER, EVEN WHEN WE WERE CHEERLEADING
SHE'S A GOOD CATHOLIC AND STILL TOOK TELORESTORE
I'LL BET SHE'S HAD WORK DONE ≈COUGH≈ ≈COUGH≈
305 PIERCE, RUTH : VENTRICULAR FIBRILLATION - CALL CODE BLUE
I HAD A DATE WITH YOUR DOCTOR. WHAT IF WE HAVE KIDS? I'LL NEED YOU TO SHOW ME...
THAT'S WONDERFUL ≈GASP≈
DR. KELLY IS A NICE-- ≈COUGH≈
CODE BLUE - ROOM 305
REPEAT: CODE BLUE STAT TO ROOM 305
DOMINIC? GET ME ON THAT PLANE

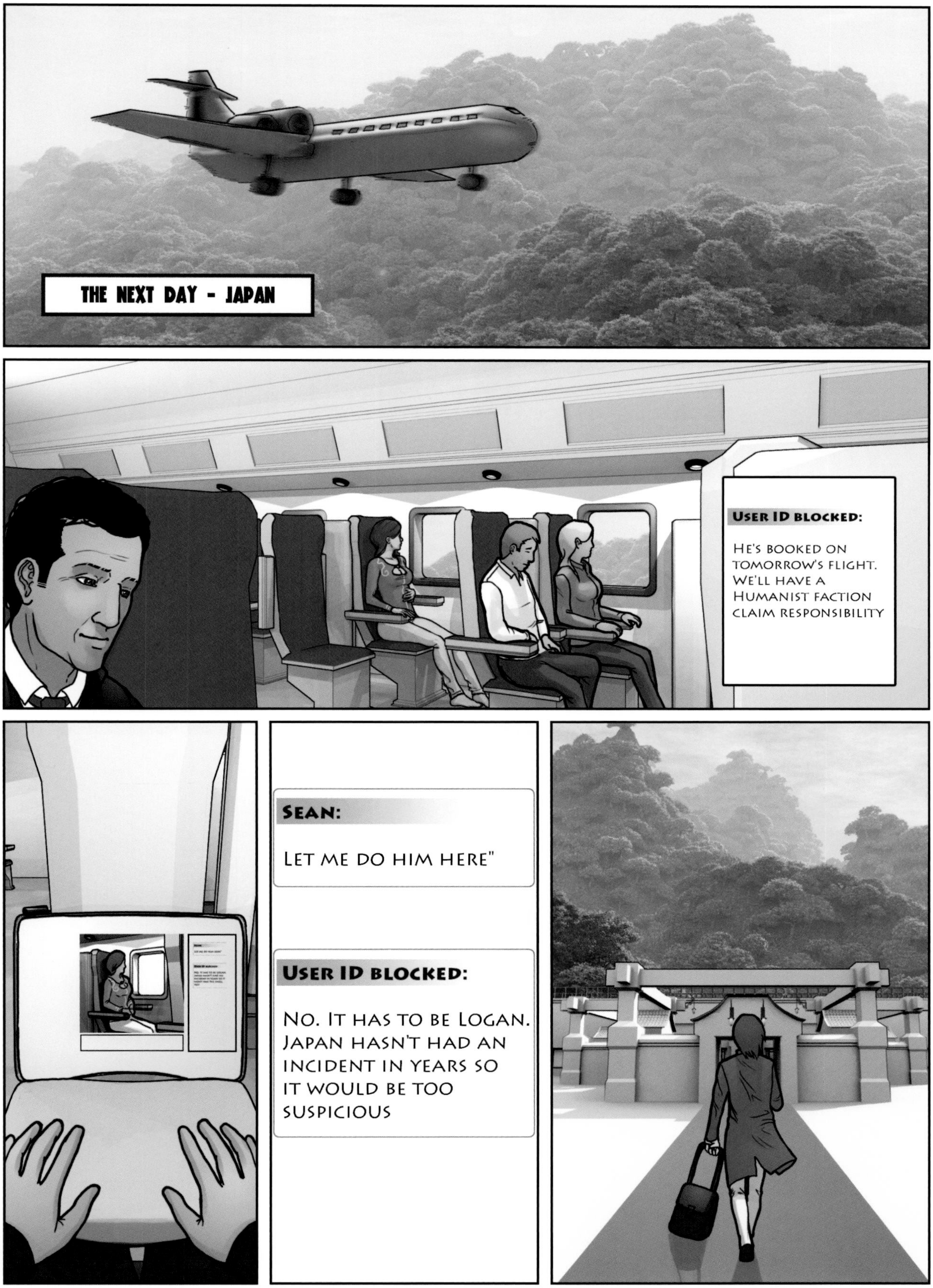
THE NEXT DAY - JAPAN
USER ID BLOCKED:
HE'S BOOKED ON TOMORROW'S FLIGHT. WE'LL HAVE A HUMANIST FACTION CLAIM RESPONSIBILITY
SEAN:
LET ME DO HIM HERE"
USER ID BLOCKED:
NO. IT HAS TO BE LOGAN. JAPAN HASN'T HAD AN INCIDENT IN YEARS SO IT WOULD BE TOO SUSPICIOUS

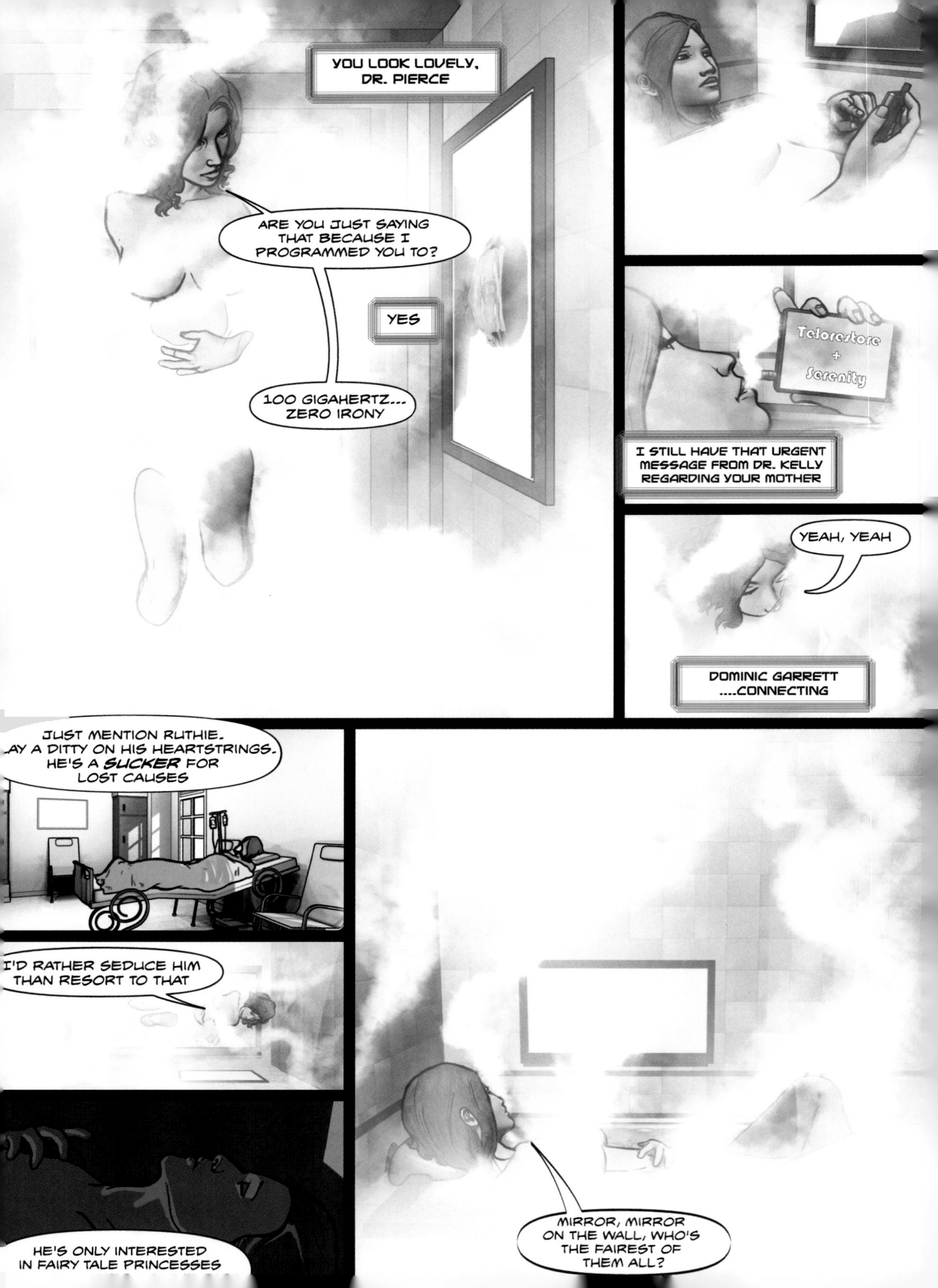
YOU LOOK LOVELY, DR. PIERCE
ARE YOU JUST SAYING THAT BECAUSE I PROGRAMMED YOU TO?
YES
100 GIGAHERTZ... ZERO IRONY
Teloréstore + Serenity
I STILL HAVE THAT URGENT MESSAGE FROM DR. KELLY REGARDING YOUR MOTHER
YEAH, YEAH
DOMINIC GARRETT ....CONNECTING
JUST MENTION RUTHIE. PLAY A DITTY ON HIS HEARTSTRINGS. HE'S A SUCKER FOR LOST CAUSES
I'D RATHER SEDUCE HIM THAN RESORT TO THAT
HE'S ONLY INTERESTED IN FAIRY TALE PRINCESSES
MIRROR, MIRROR ON THE WALL, WHO'S THE FAIREST OF THEM ALL?

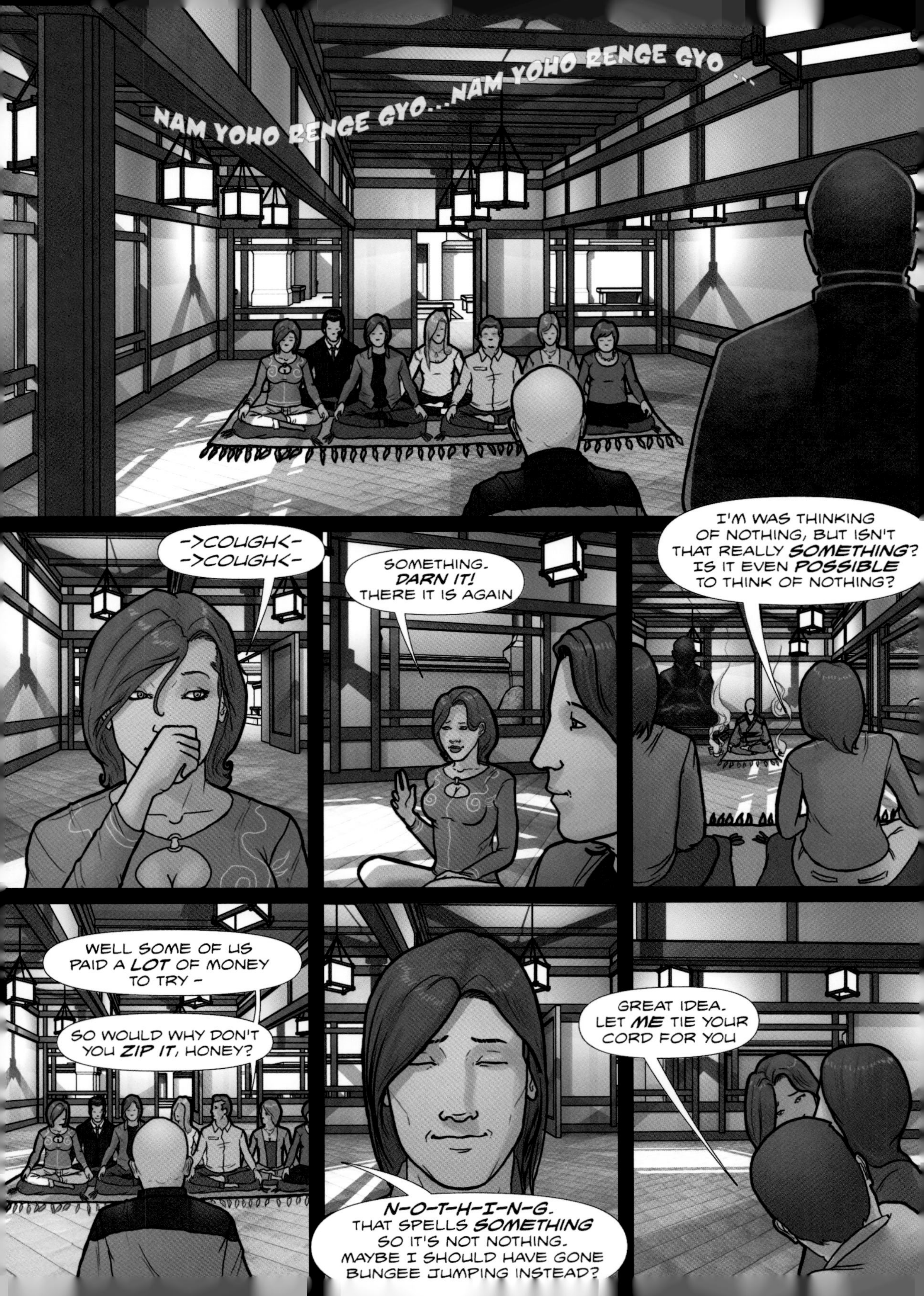
NAM YOHO RENGE GYO...NAM YOHO RENGE GYO
->COUGH<-
->COUGH<-
SOMETHING. DARN IT! THERE IT IS AGAIN
I'M WAS THINKING OF NOTHING, BUT ISN'T THAT REALLY SOMETHING? IS IT EVEN POSSIBLE TO THINK OF NOTHING?
WELL SOME OF US PAID A LOT OF MONEY TO TRY -
SO WOULD WHY DON'T YOU ZIP IT, HONEY?
N-O-T-H-I-N-G. THAT SPELLS SOMETHING SO IT'S NOT NOTHING. MAYBE I SHOULD HAVE GONE BUNGEE JUMPING INSTEAD?
GREAT IDEA. LET ME TIE YOUR CORD FOR YOU

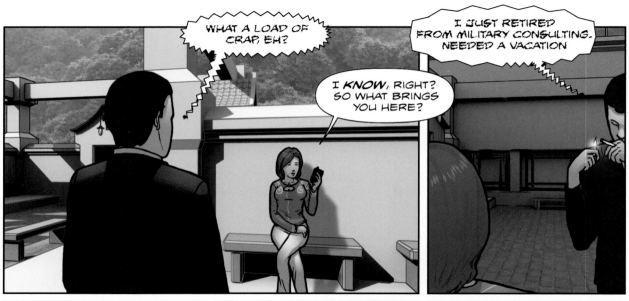

WHAT A LOAD OF CRAP, EH?

I KNOW, RIGHT? SO WHAT BRINGS YOU HERE?

I JUST RETIRED FROM MILITARY CONSULTING. NEEDED A VACATION

PRICEY LITTLE VACATION

WICKED PRICEY. BUT I CAME INTO SOME MONEY AFTER SELLING MY HOUSE. TOO MANY GHOSTS

GHOSTS?

DON'T ASK

A SMOKER WHO BELIEVES IN GHOSTS? WHAT CENTURY ARE YOU FROM?

OKAY, SMART-GIRL SO HAPPENS MY FAMILY WAS KILLED IN THAT HOUSE

I'M SO SORRY

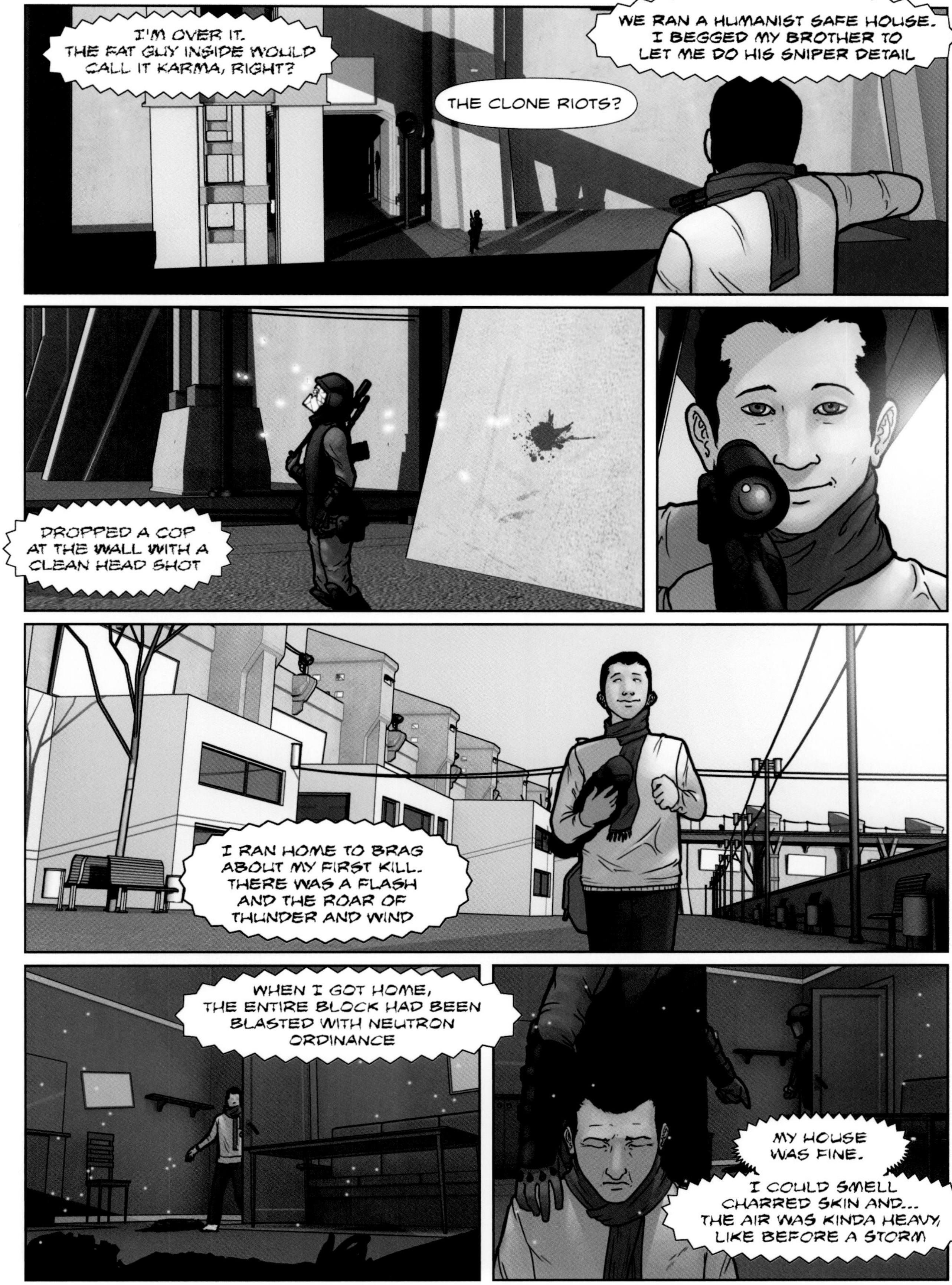
I'M OVER IT. THE FAT GUY INSIDE WOULD CALL IT KARMA, RIGHT?
THE CLONE RIOTS?
WE RAN A HUMANIST SAFE HOUSE. I BEGGED MY BROTHER TO LET ME DO HIS SNIPER DETAIL
DROPPED A COP AT THE WALL WITH A CLEAN HEAD SHOT
I RAN HOME TO BRAG ABOUT MY FIRST KILL. THERE WAS A FLASH AND THE ROAR OF THUNDER AND WIND
WHEN I GOT HOME, THE ENTIRE BLOCK HAD BEEN BLASTED WITH NEUTRON ORDINANCE
MY HOUSE WAS FINE.
I COULD SMELL CHARRED SKIN AND... THE AIR WAS KINDA HEAVY, LIKE BEFORE A STORM

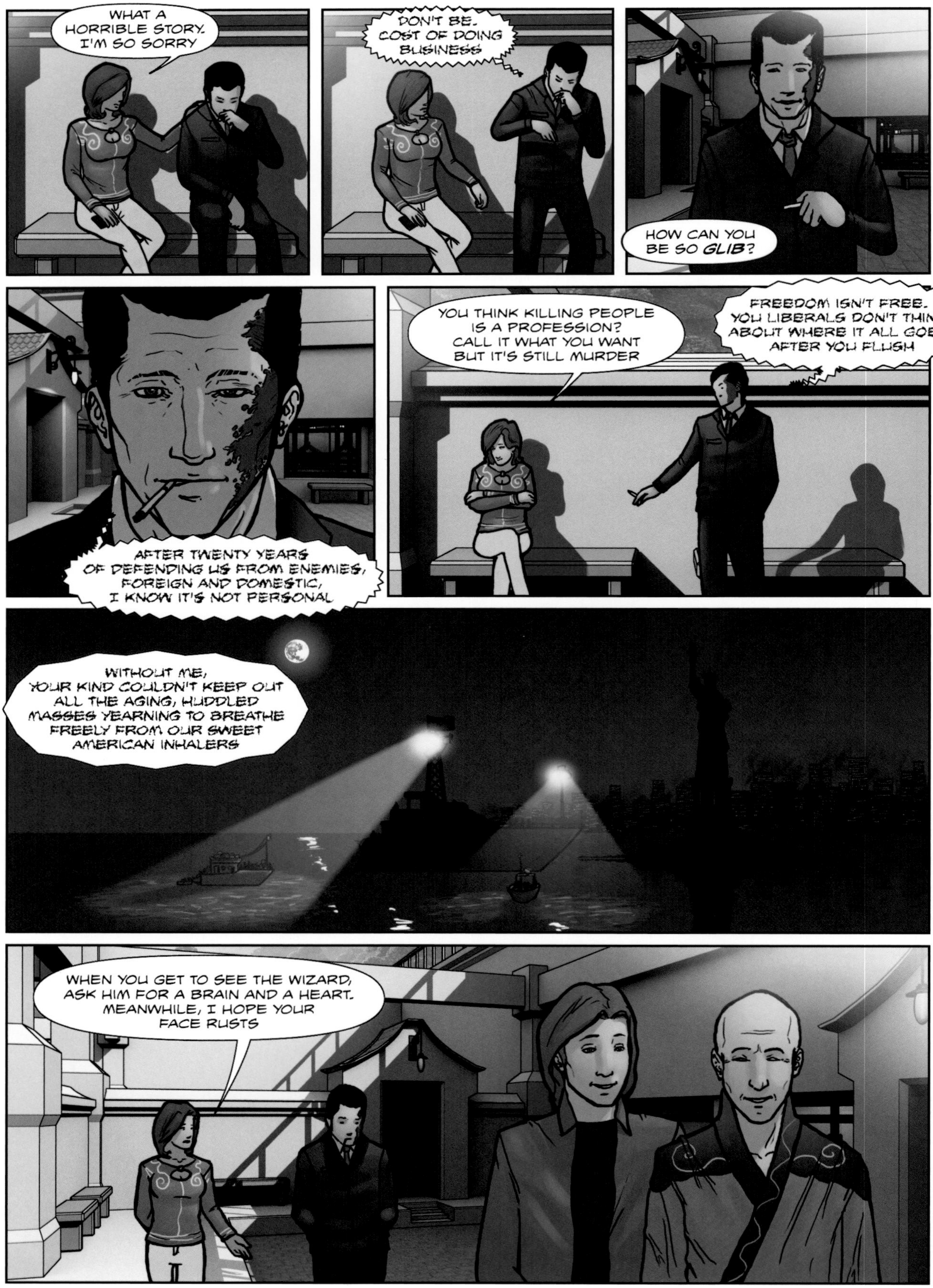
WHAT A HORRIBLE STORY. I'M SO SORRY
DON'T BE. COST OF DOING BUSINESS
HOW CAN YOU BE SO GLIB?
AFTER TWENTY YEARS OF DEFENDING US FROM ENEMIES, FOREIGN AND DOMESTIC, I KNOW IT'S NOT PERSONAL
YOU THINK KILLING PEOPLE IS A PROFESSION? CALL IT WHAT YOU WANT BUT IT'S STILL MURDER
FREEDOM ISN'T FREE. YOU LIBERALS DON'T THINK ABOUT WHERE IT ALL GOES AFTER YOU FLUSH
WITHOUT ME, YOUR KIND COULDN'T KEEP OUT ALL THE AGING, HUDDLED MASSES YEARNING TO BREATHE FREELY FROM OUR SWEET AMERICAN INHALERS
WHEN YOU GET TO SEE THE WIZARD, ASK HIM FOR A BRAIN AND A HEART. MEANWHILE, I HOPE YOUR FACE RUSTS

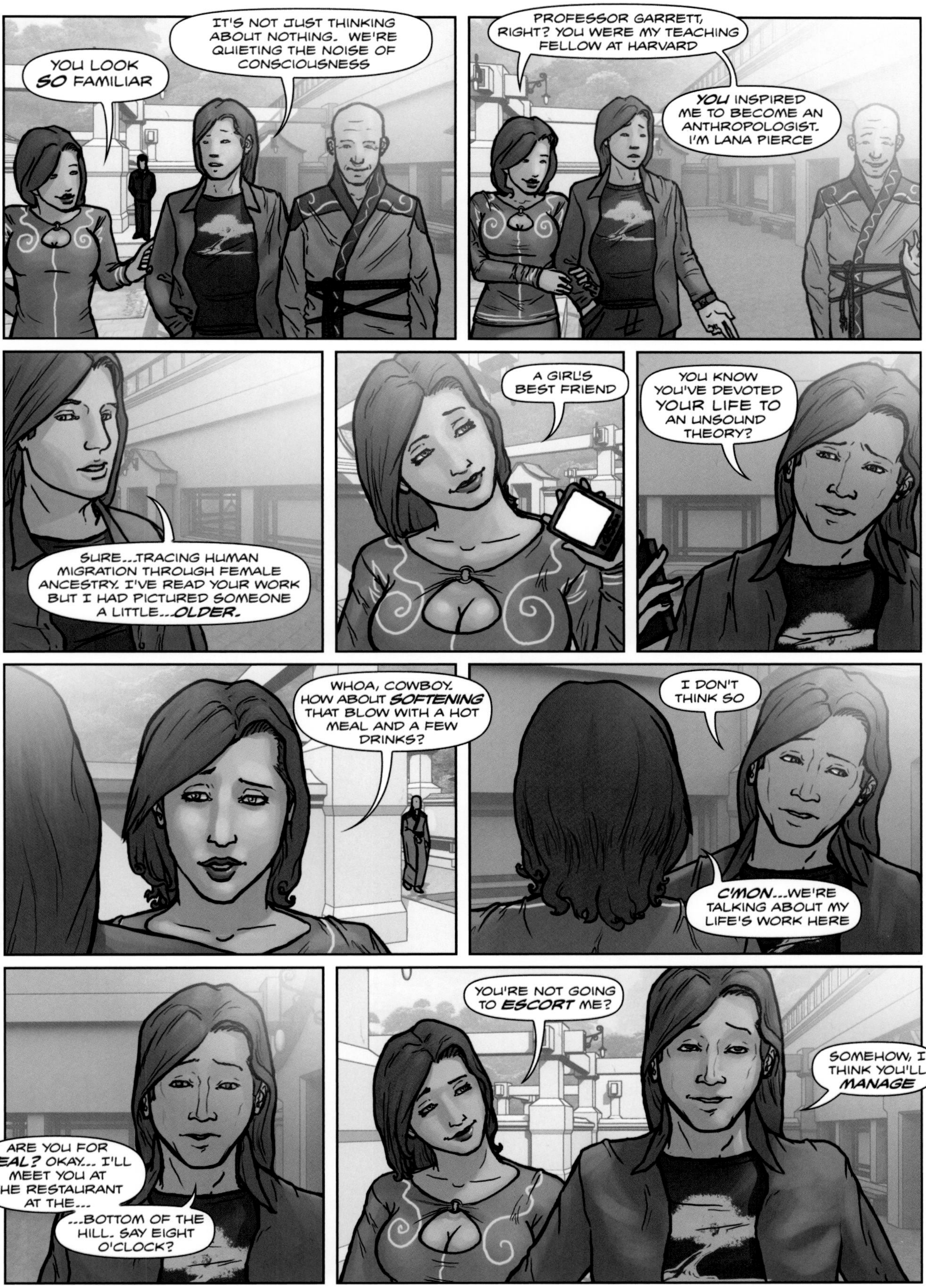
YOU LOOK SO FAMILIAR
IT'S NOT JUST THINKING ABOUT NOTHING. WE'RE QUIETING THE NOISE OF CONSCIOUSNESS
PROFESSOR GARRETT, RIGHT? YOU WERE MY TEACHING FELLOW AT HARVARD
YOU INSPIRED ME TO BECOME AN ANTHROPOLOGIST. I'M LANA PIERCE
SURE...TRACING HUMAN MIGRATION THROUGH FEMALE ANCESTRY. I'VE READ YOUR WORK BUT I HAD PICTURED SOMEONE A LITTLE...OLDER.
A GIRL'S BEST FRIEND
YOU KNOW YOU'VE DEVOTED YOUR LIFE TO AN UNSOUND THEORY?
WHOA, COWBOY. HOW ABOUT SOFTENING THAT BLOW WITH A HOT MEAL AND A FEW DRINKS?
I DON'T THINK SO
C'MON...WE'RE TALKING ABOUT MY LIFE'S WORK HERE
ARE YOU FOR REAL? OKAY... I'LL MEET YOU AT THE RESTAURANT AT THE...
...BOTTOM OF THE HILL. SAY EIGHT O'CLOCK?
YOU'RE NOT GOING TO ESCORT ME?
SOMEHOW, I THINK YOU'LL MANAGE

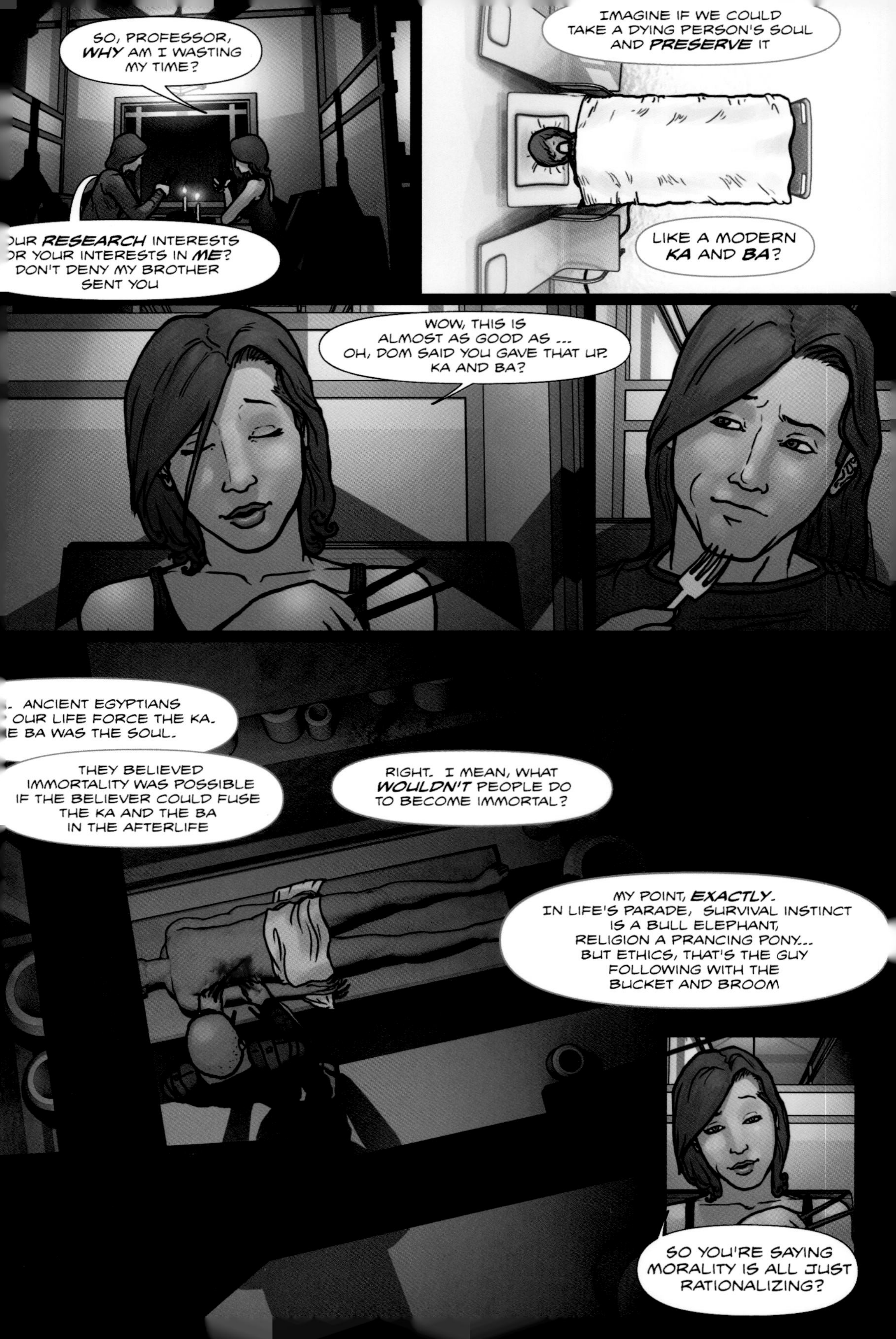
SO, PROFESSOR, WHY AM I WASTING MY TIME?
OUR RESEARCH INTERESTS OR YOUR INTERESTS IN ME? DON'T DENY MY BROTHER SENT YOU
IMAGINE IF WE COULD TAKE A DYING PERSON'S SOUL AND PRESERVE IT
LIKE A MODERN KA AND BA?
WOW, THIS IS ALMOST AS GOOD AS ... OH, DOM SAID YOU GAVE THAT UP. KA AND BA?
ANCIENT EGYPTIANS OUR LIFE FORCE THE KA. E BA WAS THE SOUL.
THEY BELIEVED IMMORTALITY WAS POSSIBLE IF THE BELIEVER COULD FUSE THE KA AND THE BA IN THE AFTERLIFE
RIGHT. I MEAN, WHAT WOULDN'T PEOPLE DO TO BECOME IMMORTAL?
MY POINT, EXACTLY. IN LIFE'S PARADE, SURVIVAL INSTINCT IS A BULL ELEPHANT, RELIGION A PRANCING PONY... BUT ETHICS, THAT'S THE GUY FOLLOWING WITH THE BUCKET AND BROOM
SO YOU'RE SAYING MORALITY IS ALL JUST RATIONALIZING?

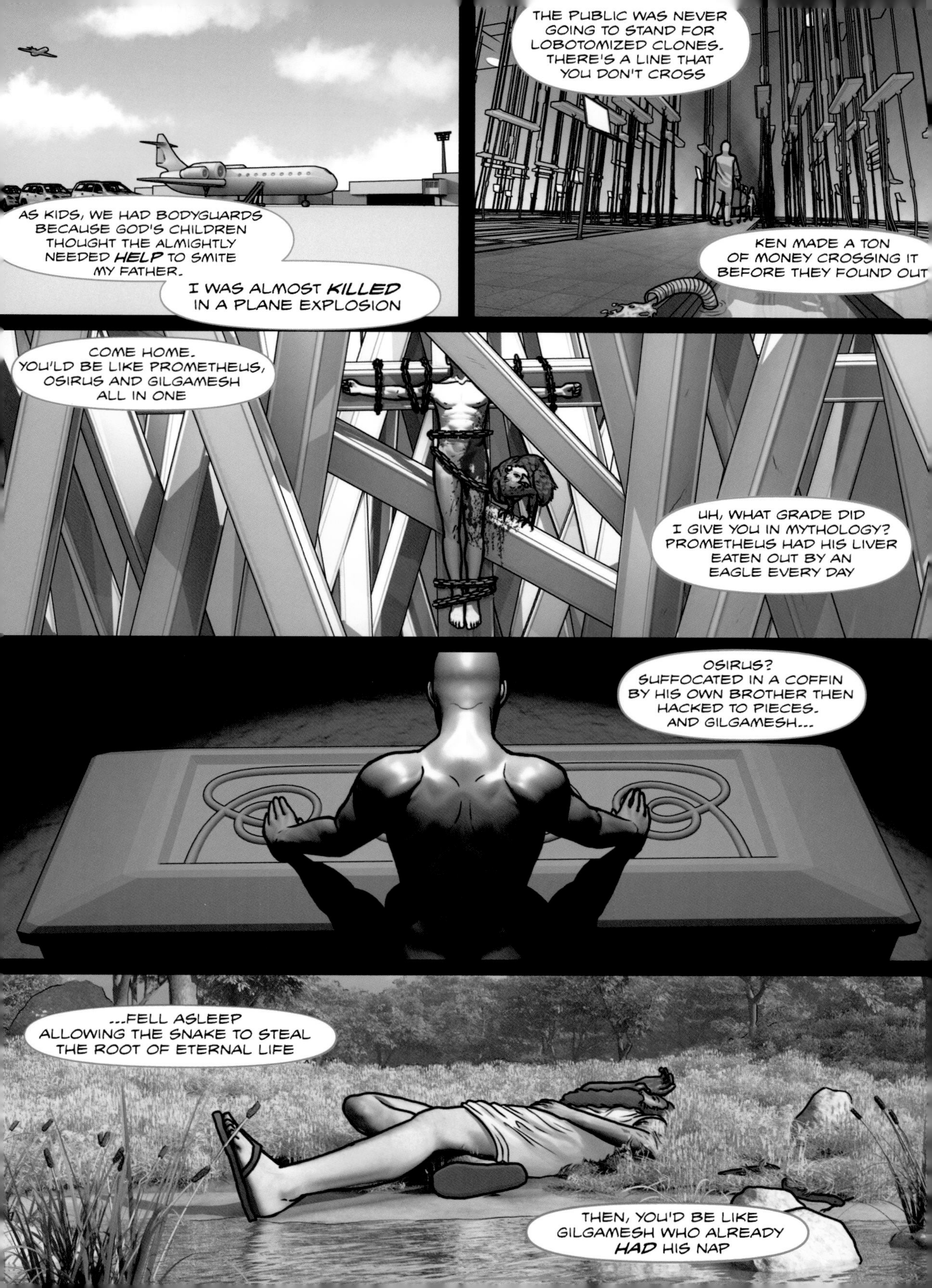
AS KIDS, WE HAD BODYGUARDS BECAUSE GOD'S CHILDREN THOUGHT THE ALMIGHTLY NEEDED *HELP* TO SMITE MY FATHER.
I WAS ALMOST *KILLED* IN A PLANE EXPLOSION
THE PUBLIC WAS NEVER GOING TO STAND FOR LOBOTOMIZED CLONES. THERE'S A LINE THAT YOU DON'T CROSS
KEN MADE A TON OF MONEY CROSSING IT BEFORE THEY FOUND OUT
COME HOME. YOU'LD BE LIKE PROMETHEUS, OSIRUS AND GILGAMESH ALL IN ONE
UH, WHAT GRADE DID I GIVE YOU IN MYTHOLOGY? PROMETHEUS HAD HIS LIVER EATEN OUT BY AN EAGLE EVERY DAY
OSIRUS? SUFFOCATED IN A COFFIN BY HIS OWN BROTHER THEN HACKED TO PIECES. AND GILGAMESH...
...FELL ASLEEP ALLOWING THE SNAKE TO STEAL THE ROOT OF ETERNAL LIFE
THEN, YOU'D BE LIKE GILGAMESH WHO ALREADY *HAD* HIS NAP

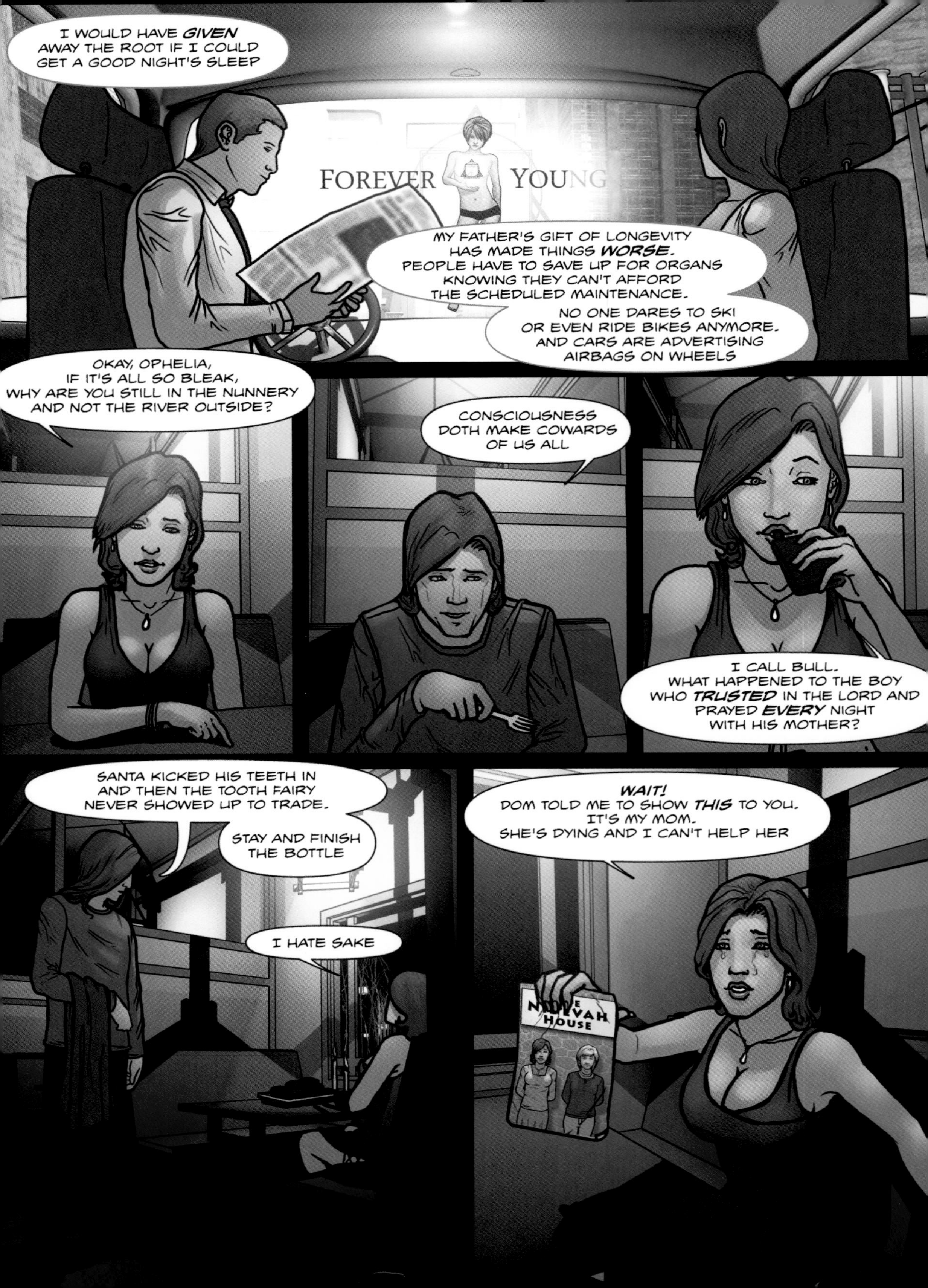

I WOULD HAVE *GIVEN* AWAY THE ROOT IF I COULD GET A GOOD NIGHT'S SLEEP
FOREVER YOUNG
MY FATHER'S GIFT OF LONGEVITY HAS MADE THINGS *WORSE.* PEOPLE HAVE TO SAVE UP FOR ORGANS KNOWING THEY CAN'T AFFORD THE SCHEDULED MAINTENANCE.
NO ONE DARES TO SKI OR EVEN RIDE BIKES ANYMORE. AND CARS ARE ADVERTISING AIRBAGS ON WHEELS
OKAY, OPHELIA, IF IT'S ALL SO BLEAK, WHY ARE YOU STILL IN THE NUNNERY AND NOT THE RIVER OUTSIDE?
CONSCIOUSNESS DOTH MAKE COWARDS OF US ALL
I CALL BULL. WHAT HAPPENED TO THE BOY WHO *TRUSTED* IN THE LORD AND PRAYED *EVERY* NIGHT WITH HIS MOTHER?
SANTA KICKED HIS TEETH IN AND THEN THE TOOTH FAIRY NEVER SHOWED UP TO TRADE.
STAY AND FINISH THE BOTTLE
I HATE SAKE
WAIT! DOM TOLD ME TO SHOW *THIS* TO YOU. IT'S MY MOM. SHE'S DYING AND I CAN'T HELP HER
HOUSE

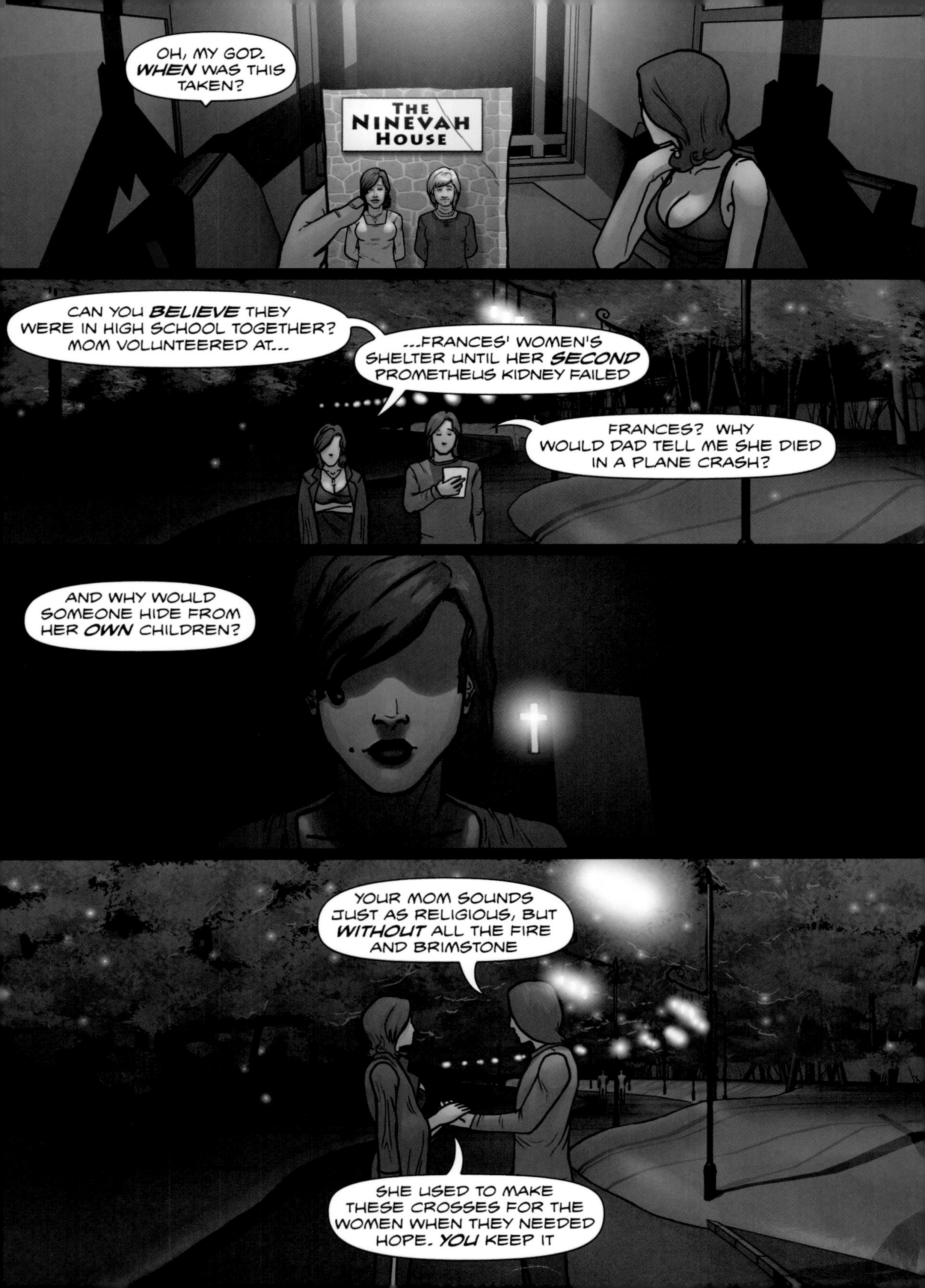

OH, MY GOD. WHEN WAS THIS TAKEN?
THE NINEVAH HOUSE
CAN YOU BELIEVE THEY WERE IN HIGH SCHOOL TOGETHER? MOM VOLUNTEERED AT...
...FRANCES' WOMEN'S SHELTER UNTIL HER SECOND PROMETHEUS KIDNEY FAILED
FRANCES? WHY WOULD DAD TELL ME SHE DIED IN A PLANE CRASH?
AND WHY WOULD SOMEONE HIDE FROM HER OWN CHILDREN?
YOUR MOM SOUNDS JUST AS RELIGIOUS, BUT WITHOUT ALL THE FIRE AND BRIMSTONE
SHE USED TO MAKE THESE CROSSES FOR THE WOMEN WHEN THEY NEEDED HOPE. YOU KEEP IT

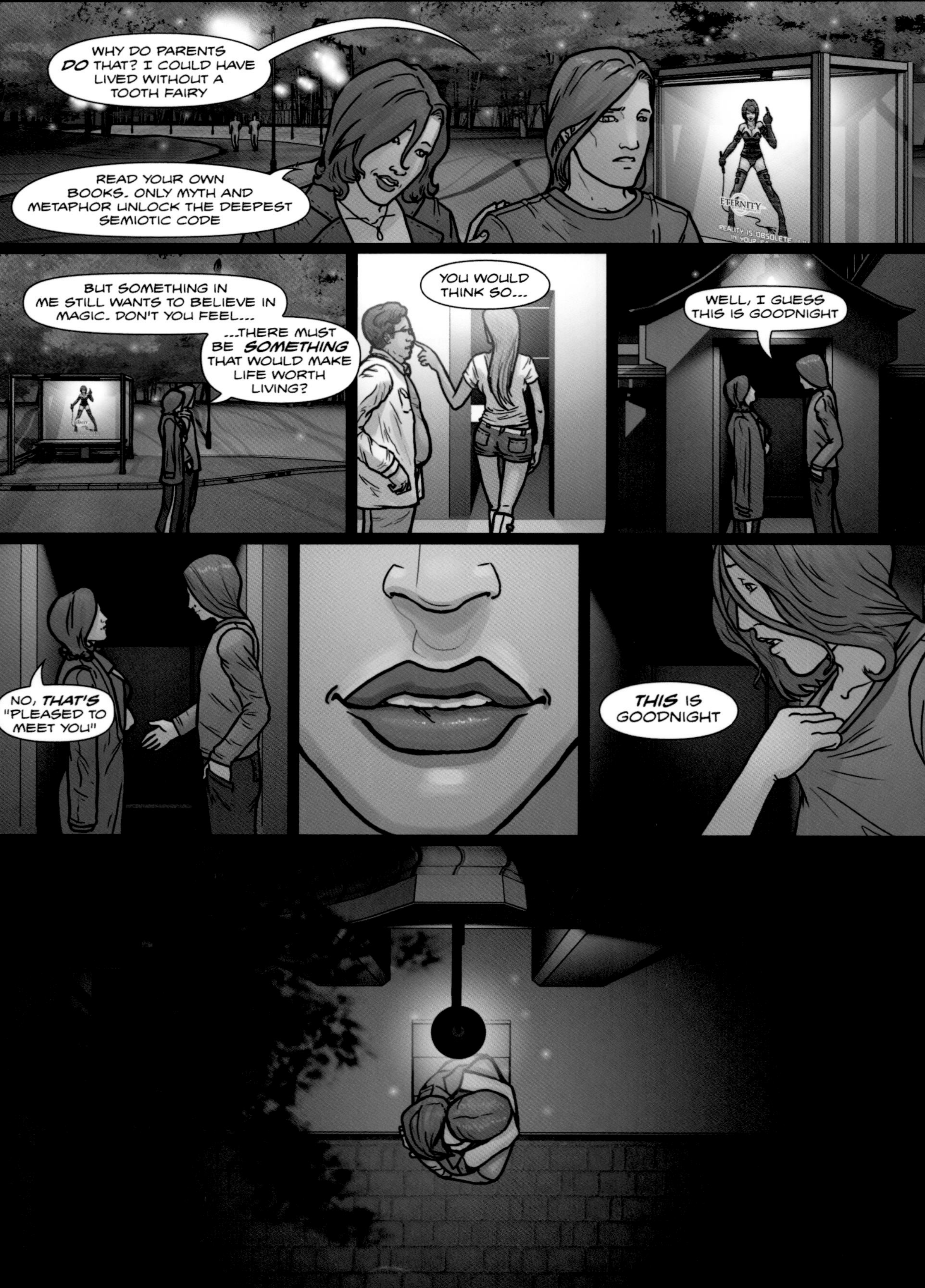
WHY DO PARENTS DO THAT? I COULD HAVE LIVED WITHOUT A TOOTH FAIRY
READ YOUR OWN BOOKS. ONLY MYTH AND METAPHOR UNLOCK THE DEEPEST SEMIOTIC CODE
ETERNITY
BUT SOMETHING IN ME STILL WANTS TO BELIEVE IN MAGIC. DON'T YOU FEEL...
...THERE MUST BE SOMETHING THAT WOULD MAKE LIFE WORTH LIVING?
YOU WOULD THINK SO...
WELL, I GUESS THIS IS GOODNIGHT
NO, THAT'S "PLEASED TO MEET YOU!"
THIS IS GOODNIGHT

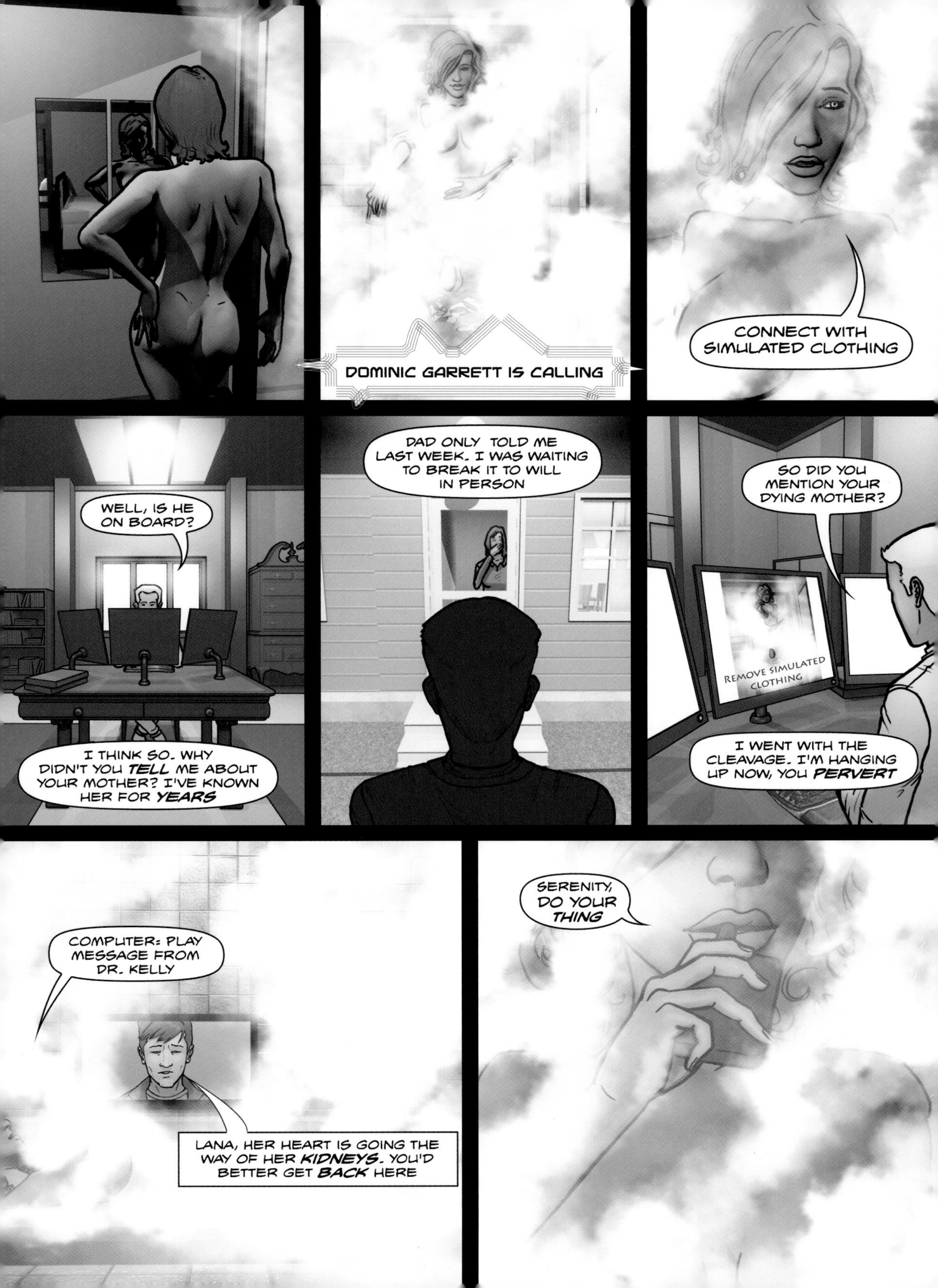
DOMINIC GARRETT IS CALLING
CONNECT WITH SIMULATED CLOTHING
WELL, IS HE ON BOARD?
I THINK SO. WHY DIDN'T YOU TELL ME ABOUT YOUR MOTHER? I'VE KNOWN HER FOR YEARS
DAD ONLY TOLD ME LAST WEEK. I WAS WAITING TO BREAK IT TO WILL IN PERSON
SO DID YOU MENTION YOUR DYING MOTHER?
REMOVE SIMULATED CLOTHING
I WENT WITH THE CLEAVAGE. I'M HANGING UP NOW, YOU PERVERT
COMPUTER: PLAY MESSAGE FROM DR. KELLY
LANA, HER HEART IS GOING THE WAY OF HER KIDNEYS. YOU'D BETTER GET BACK HERE
SERENITY, DO YOUR THING

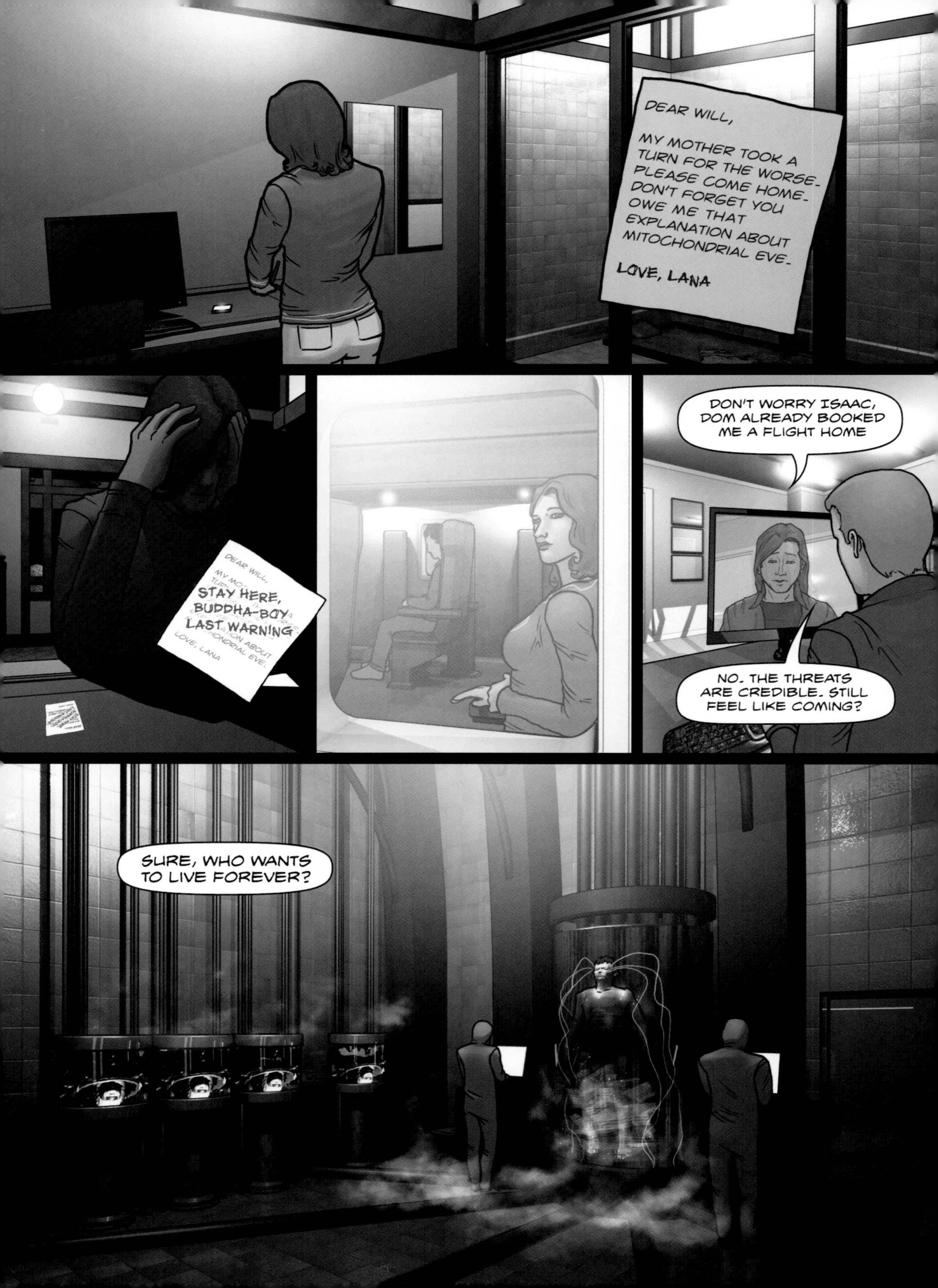
DEAR WILL,
MY MOTHER TOOK A TURN FOR THE WORSE. PLEASE COME HOME. DON'T FORGET YOU OWE ME THAT EXPLANATION ABOUT MITOCHONDRIAL EVE.
LOVE, LANA
STAY HERE, BUDDHA-BOY LAST WARNING
DON'T WORRY ISAAC, DOM ALREADY BOOKED ME A FLIGHT HOME
NO. THE THREATS ARE CREDIBLE. STILL FEEL LIKE COMING?
SURE, WHO WANTS TO LIVE FOREVER?

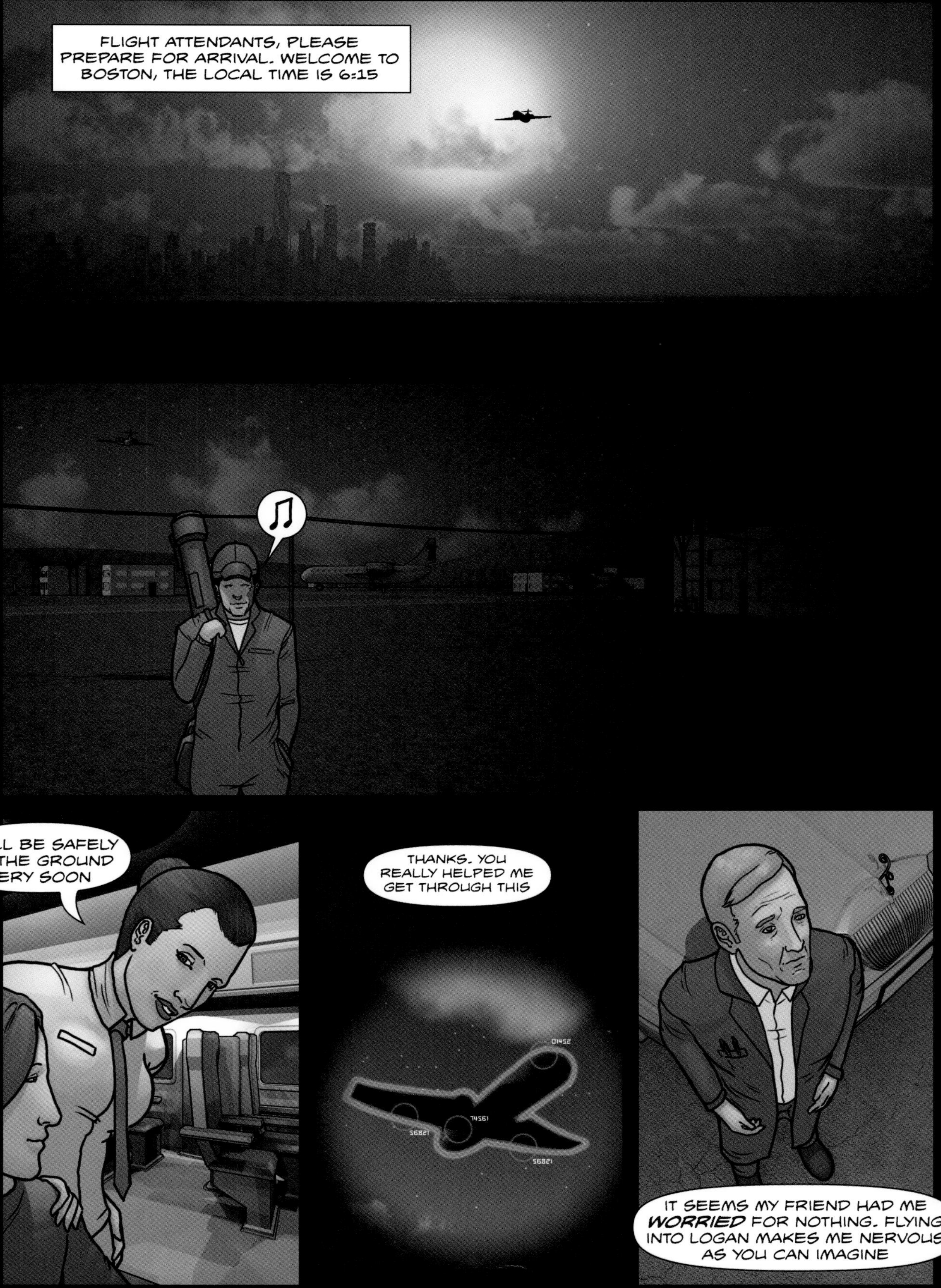
FLIGHT ATTENDANTS, PLEASE PREPARE FOR ARRIVAL. WELCOME TO BOSTON, THE LOCAL TIME IS 6:15
WE'LL BE SAFELY ON THE GROUND VERY SOON
THANKS. YOU REALLY HELPED ME GET THROUGH THIS
IT SEEMS MY FRIEND HAD ME *WORRIED* FOR NOTHING. FLYING INTO LOGAN MAKES ME NERVOUS AS YOU CAN IMAGINE

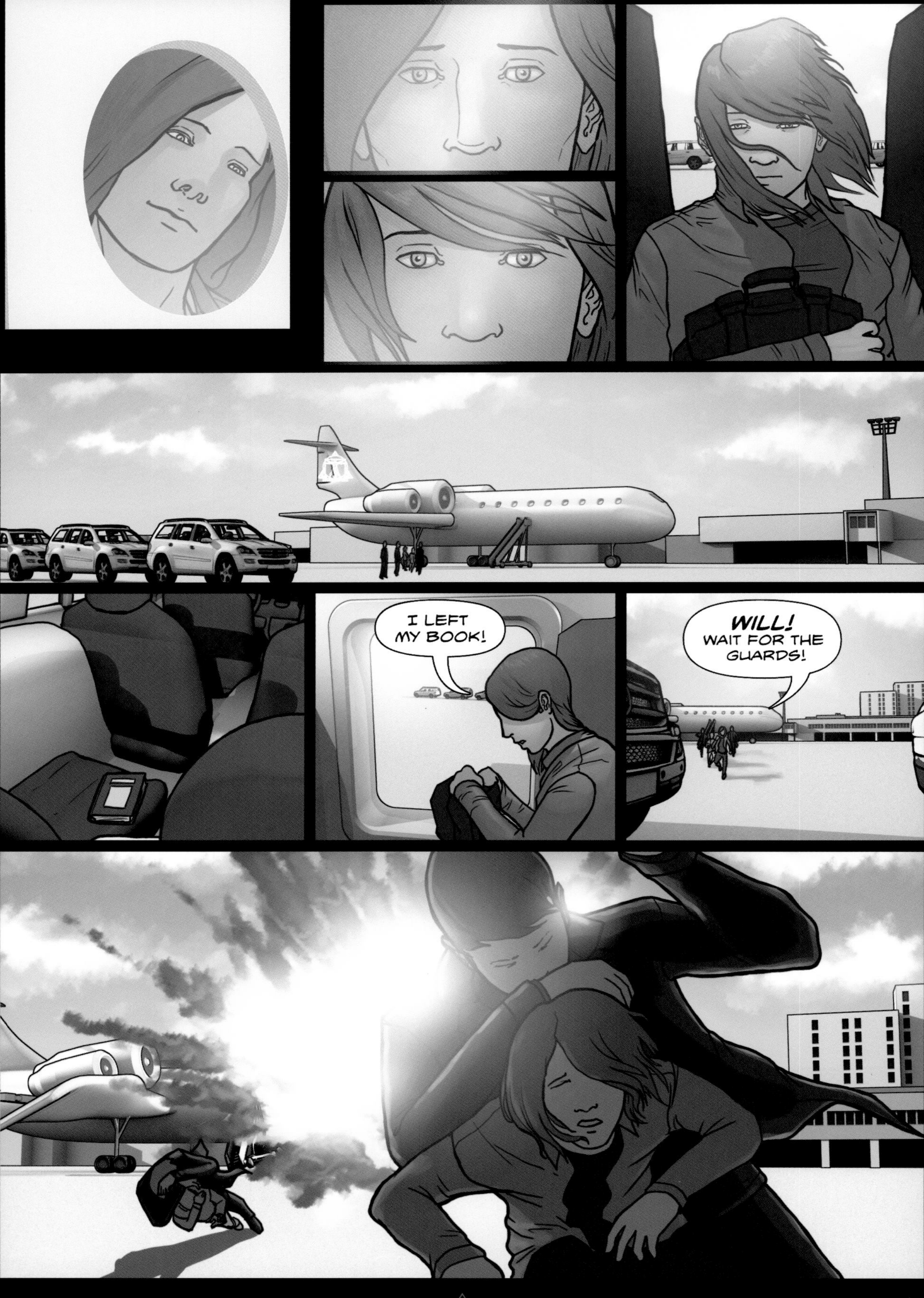
I LEFT MY BOOK!
WILL! WAIT FOR THE GUARDS!

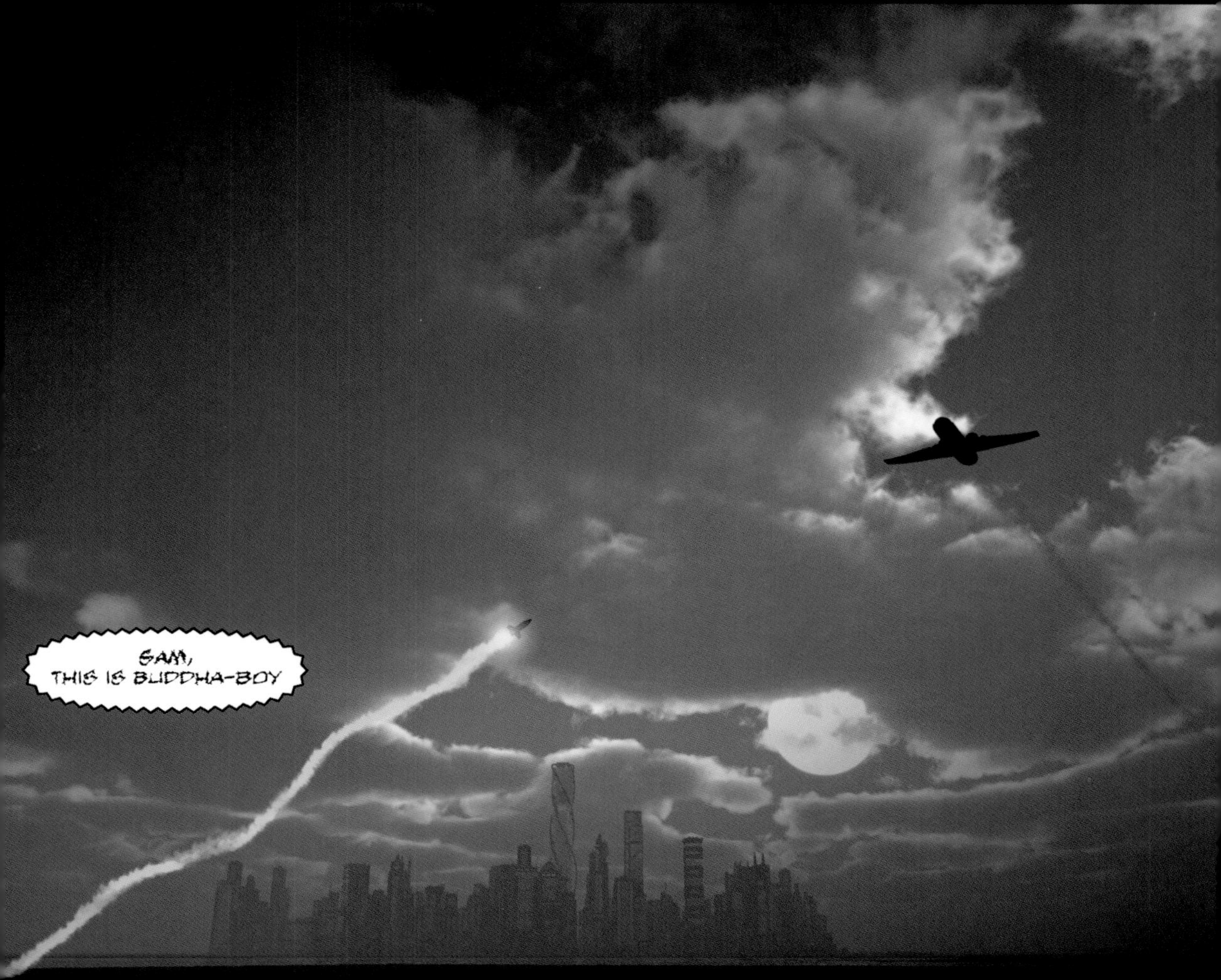
SAM,
THIS IS BUDDHA-BOY

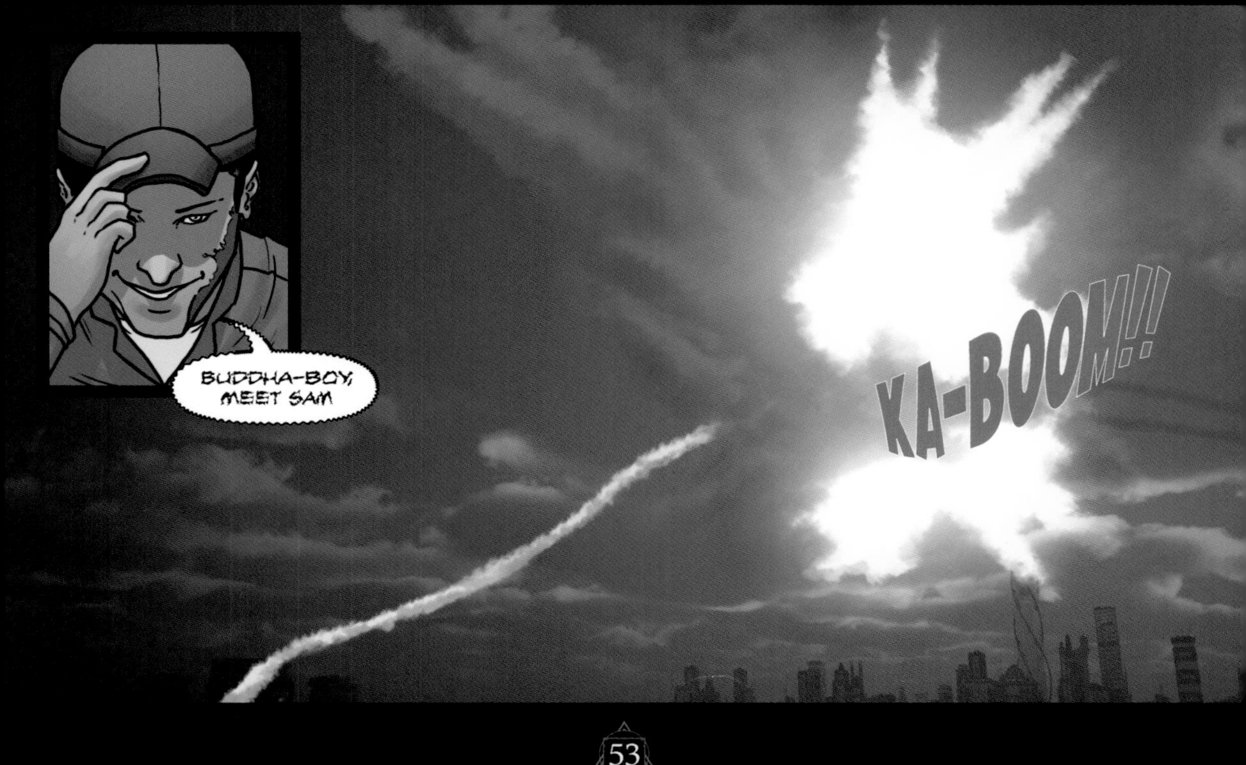
BUDDHA-BOY,
MEET SAM
KA-BOOM!!!

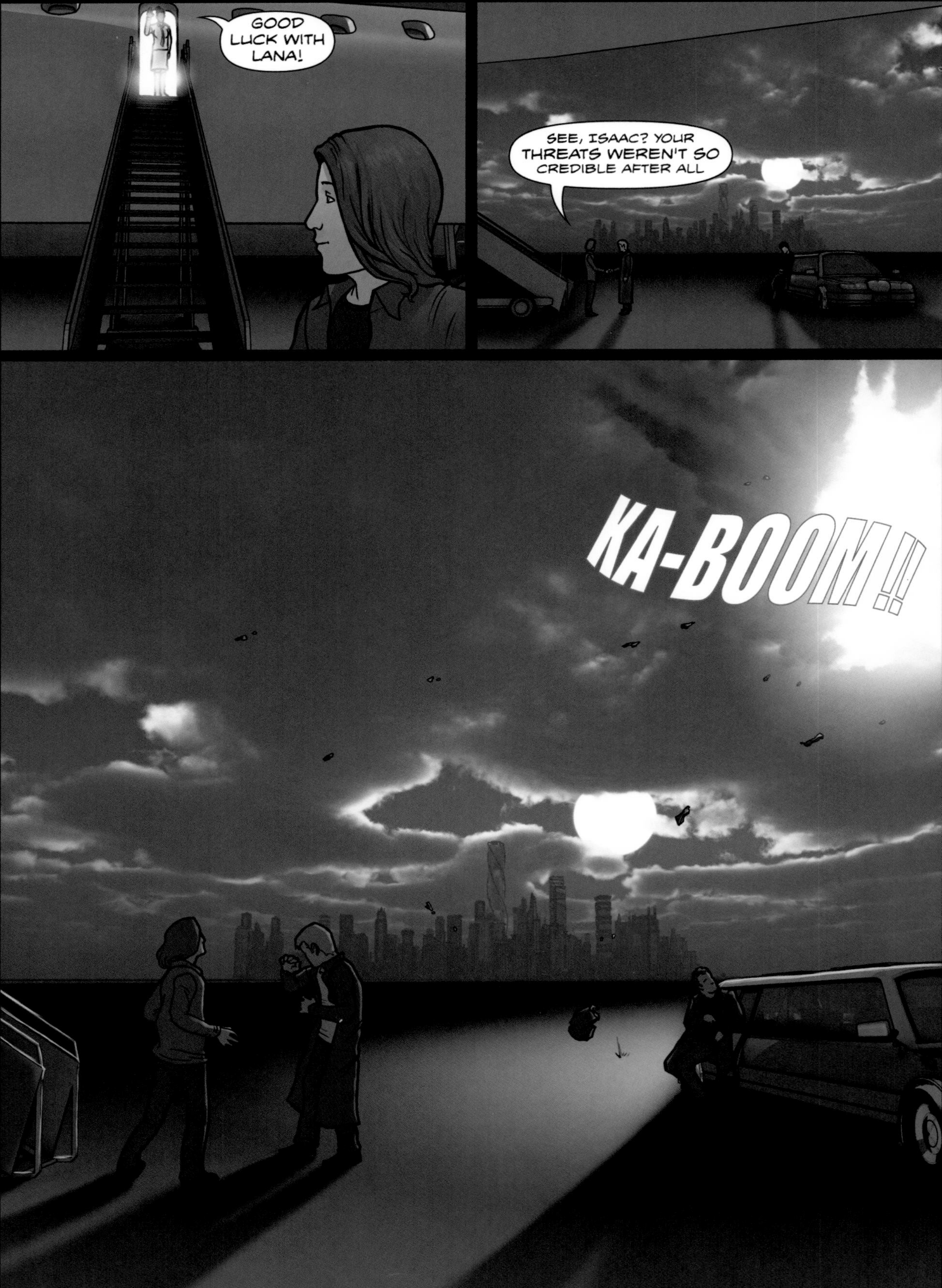
GOOD LUCK WITH LANA!
SEE, ISAAC? YOUR THREATS WEREN'T SO CREDIBLE AFTER ALL
KA-BOOM!!

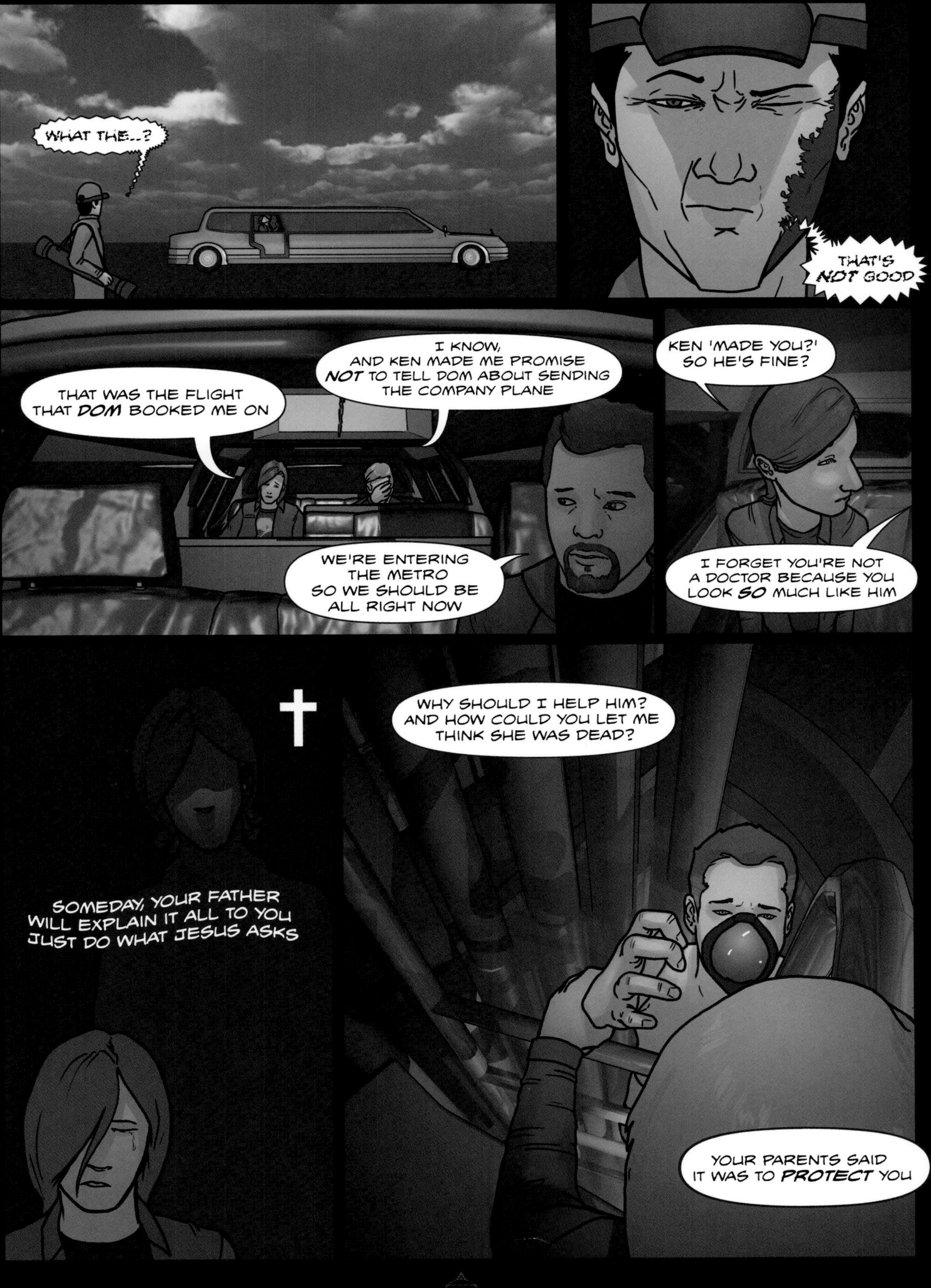

WHAT THE...?
THAT'S NOT GOOD
THAT WAS THE FLIGHT THAT DOM BOOKED ME ON
I KNOW, AND KEN MADE ME PROMISE NOT TO TELL DOM ABOUT SENDING THE COMPANY PLANE
WE'RE ENTERING THE METRO SO WE SHOULD BE ALL RIGHT NOW
KEN 'MADE YOU?' SO HE'S FINE?
I FORGET YOU'RE NOT A DOCTOR BECAUSE YOU LOOK SO MUCH LIKE HIM
SOMEDAY, YOUR FATHER WILL EXPLAIN IT ALL TO YOU JUST DO WHAT JESUS ASKS
WHY SHOULD I HELP HIM? AND HOW COULD YOU LET ME THINK SHE WAS DEAD?
YOUR PARENTS SAID IT WAS TO PROTECT YOU

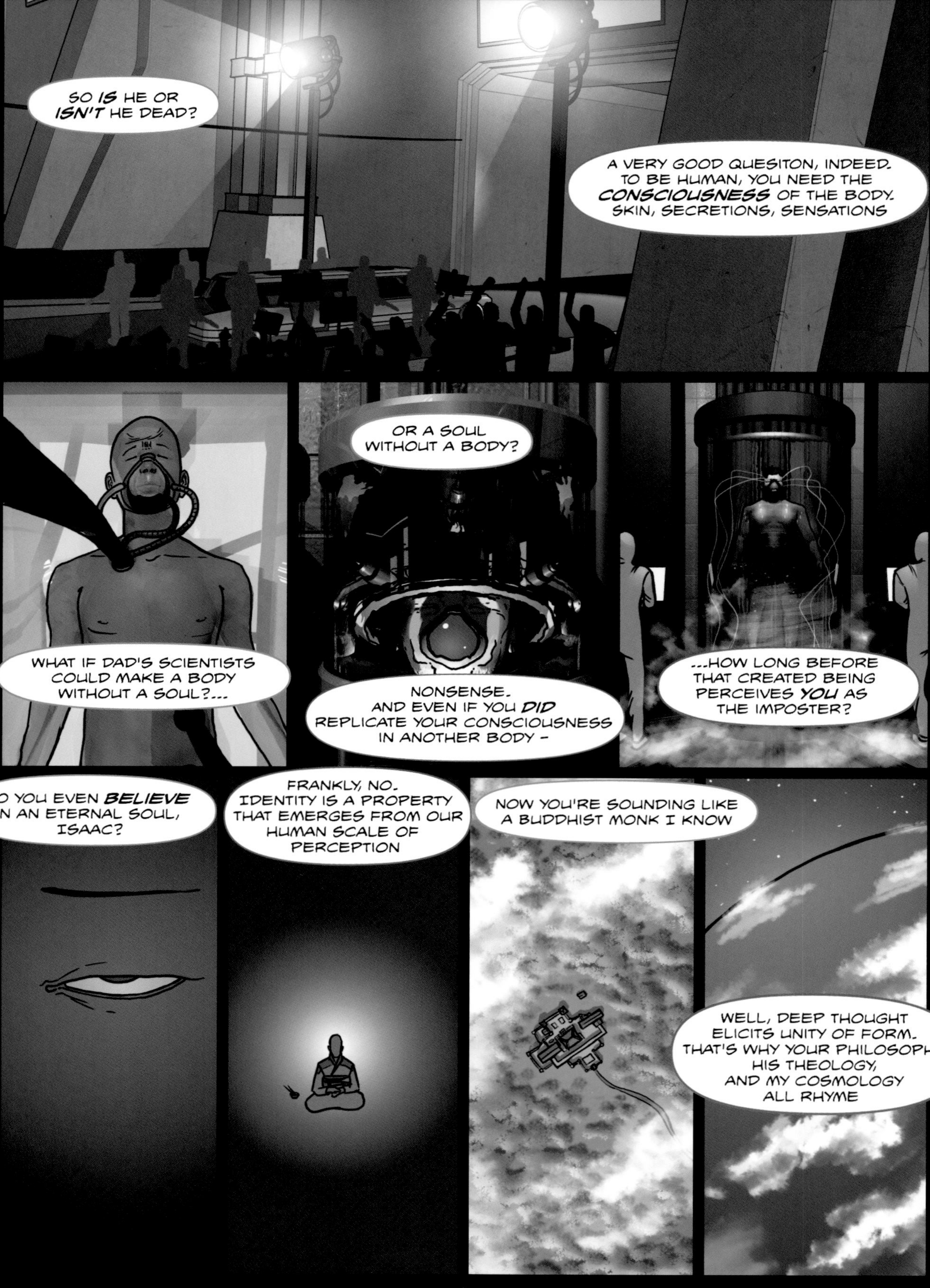
SO IS HE OR ISN'T HE DEAD?
A VERY GOOD QUESITON, INDEED. TO BE HUMAN, YOU NEED THE CONSCIOUSNESS OF THE BODY. SKIN, SECRETIONS, SENSATIONS
WHAT IF DAD'S SCIENTISTS COULD MAKE A BODY WITHOUT A SOUL?...
OR A SOUL WITHOUT A BODY?
NONSENSE. AND EVEN IF YOU DID REPLICATE YOUR CONSCIOUSNESS IN ANOTHER BODY -
...HOW LONG BEFORE THAT CREATED BEING PERCEIVES YOU AS THE IMPOSTER?
DO YOU EVEN BELIEVE IN AN ETERNAL SOUL, ISAAC?
FRANKLY, NO. IDENTITY IS A PROPERTY THAT EMERGES FROM OUR HUMAN SCALE OF PERCEPTION
NOW YOU'RE SOUNDING LIKE A BUDDHIST MONK I KNOW
WELL, DEEP THOUGHT ELICITS UNITY OF FORM. THAT'S WHY YOUR PHILOSOPHY, HIS THEOLOGY, AND MY COSMOLOGY ALL RHYME

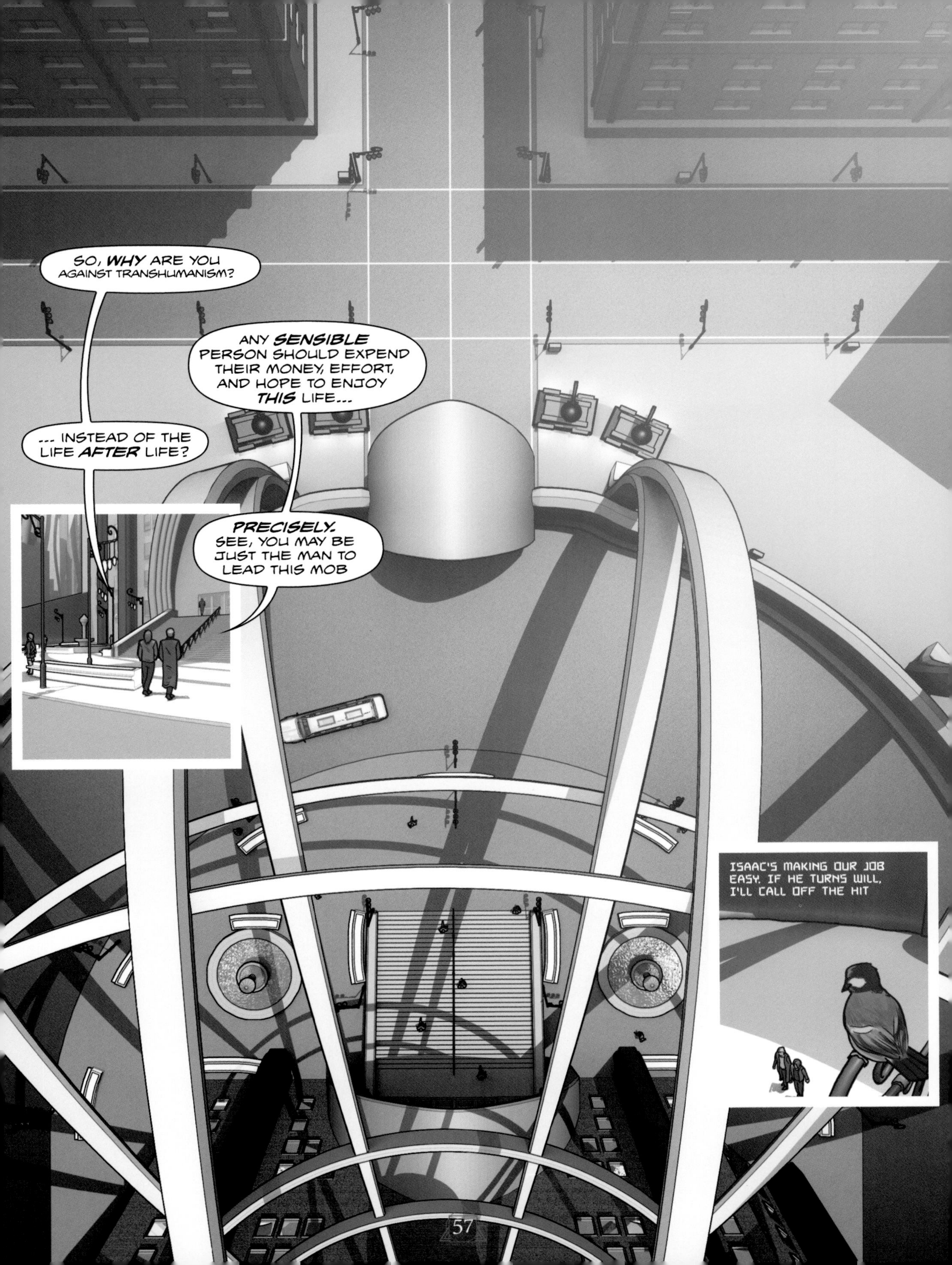
SO, WHY ARE YOU AGAINST TRANSHUMANISM?
ANY SENSIBLE PERSON SHOULD EXPEND THEIR MONEY, EFFORT, AND HOPE TO ENJOY THIS LIFE...
... INSTEAD OF THE LIFE AFTER LIFE?
PRECISELY. SEE, YOU MAY BE JUST THE MAN TO LEAD THIS MOB
ISAAC'S MAKING OUR JOB EASY. IF HE TURNS WILL, I'LL CALL OFF THE HIT

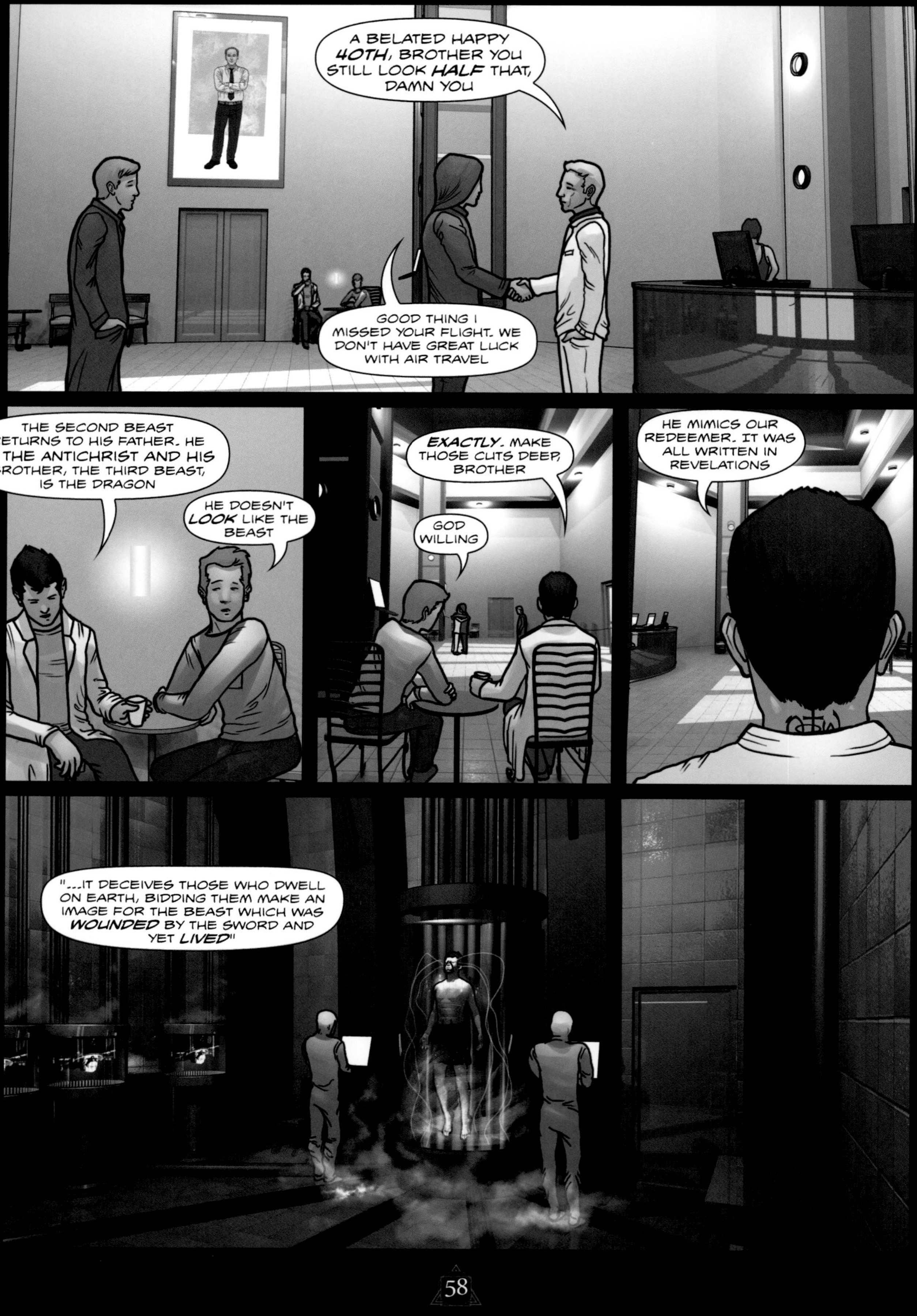
A BELATED HAPPY 40TH, BROTHER YOU STILL LOOK HALF THAT, DAMN YOU
GOOD THING I MISSED YOUR FLIGHT. WE DON'T HAVE GREAT LUCK WITH AIR TRAVEL
THE SECOND BEAST RETURNS TO HIS FATHER. HE IS THE ANTICHRIST AND HIS BROTHER, THE THIRD BEAST, IS THE DRAGON
HE DOESN'T LOOK LIKE THE BEAST
EXACTLY. MAKE THOSE CUTS DEEP, BROTHER
GOD WILLING
HE MIMICS OUR REDEEMER. IT WAS ALL WRITTEN IN REVELATIONS
"...IT DECEIVES THOSE WHO DWELL ON EARTH, BIDDING THEM MAKE AN IMAGE FOR THE BEAST WHICH WAS WOUNDED BY THE SWORD AND YET LIVED"

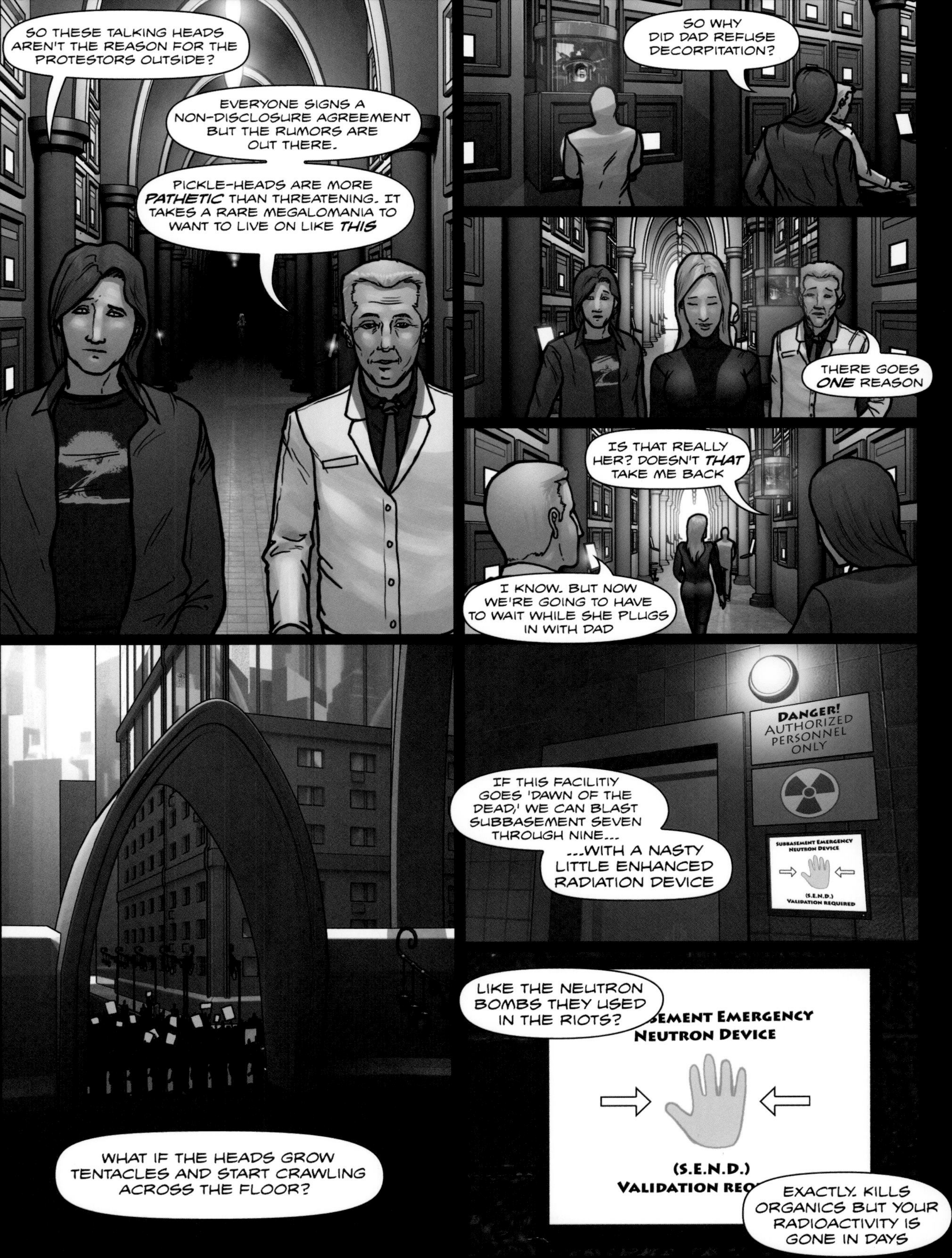
SO THESE TALKING HEADS AREN'T THE REASON FOR THE PROTESTORS OUTSIDE?
EVERYONE SIGNS A NON-DISCLOSURE AGREEMENT BUT THE RUMORS ARE OUT THERE.
PICKLE-HEADS ARE MORE *PATHETIC* THAN THREATENING. IT TAKES A RARE MEGALOMANIA TO WANT TO LIVE ON LIKE *THIS*
SO WHY DID DAD REFUSE DECORPITATION?
THERE GOES *ONE* REASON
IS THAT REALLY HER? DOESN'T *THAT* TAKE ME BACK
I KNOW. BUT NOW WE'RE GOING TO HAVE TO WAIT WHILE SHE PLUGS IN WITH DAD
WHAT IF THE HEADS GROW TENTACLES AND START CRAWLING ACROSS THE FLOOR?
DANGER! AUTHORIZED PERSONNEL ONLY
IF THIS FACILITIY GOES 'DAWN OF THE DEAD,' WE CAN BLAST SUBBASEMENT SEVEN THROUGH NINE...
...WITH A NASTY LITTLE ENHANCED RADIATION DEVICE
SUBBASEMENT EMERGENCY NEUTRON DEVICE
(S.E.N.D.) VALIDATION REQUIRED
LIKE THE NEUTRON BOMBS THEY USED IN THE RIOTS?
EMENT EMERGENCY NEUTRON DEVICE
(S.E.N.D.) VALIDATION REQ
EXACTLY. KILLS ORGANICS BUT YOUR RADIOACTIVITY IS GONE IN DAYS

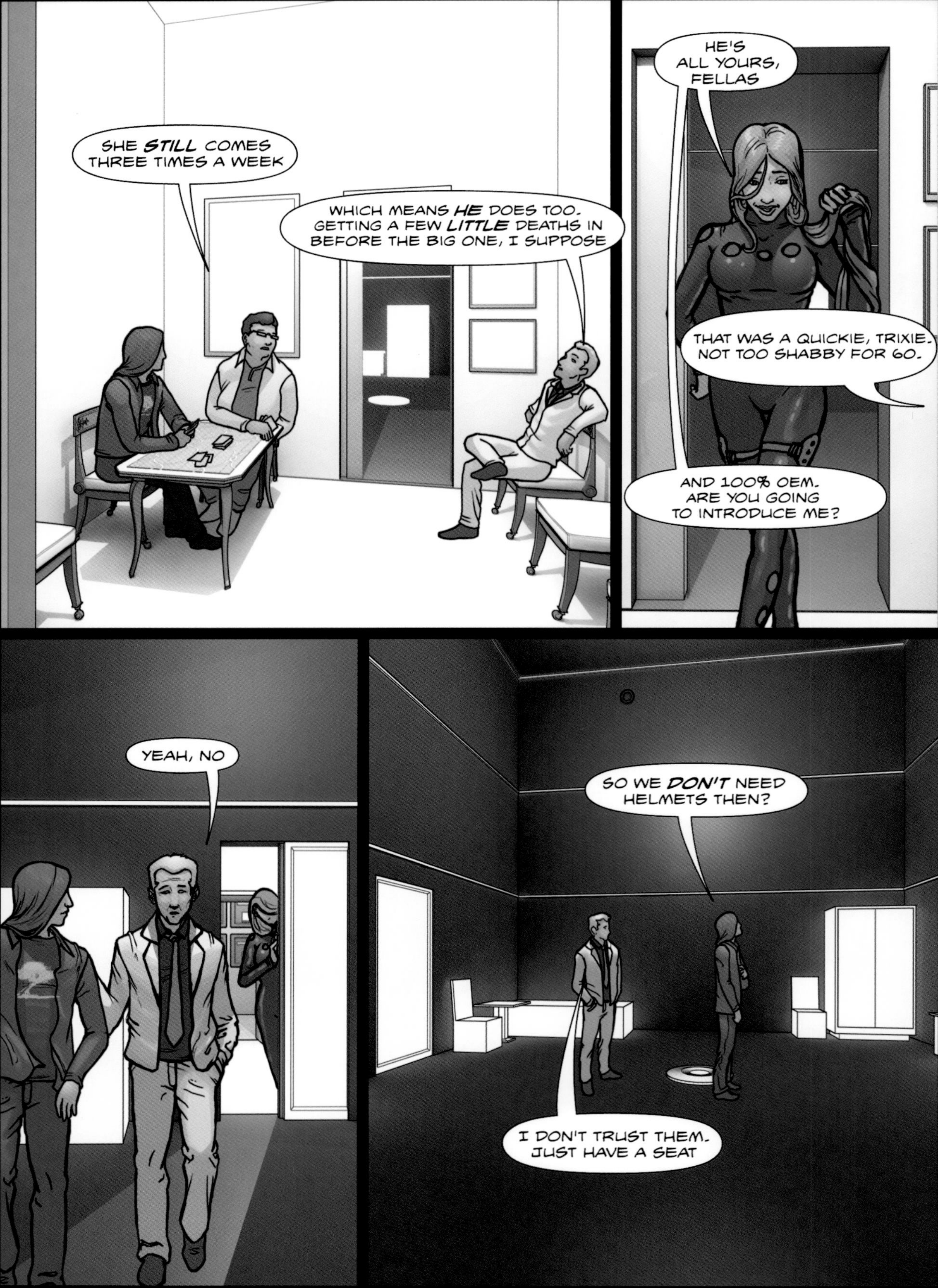

SHE *STILL* COMES THREE TIMES A WEEK
WHICH MEANS *HE* DOES TOO. GETTING A FEW *LITTLE* DEATHS IN BEFORE THE BIG ONE, I SUPPOSE
HE'S ALL YOURS, FELLAS
THAT WAS A QUICKIE, TRIXIE. NOT TOO SHABBY FOR 60.
AND 100% OEM. ARE YOU GOING TO INTRODUCE ME?
YEAH, NO
SO WE *DON'T* NEED HELMETS THEN?
I DON'T TRUST THEM. JUST HAVE A SEAT

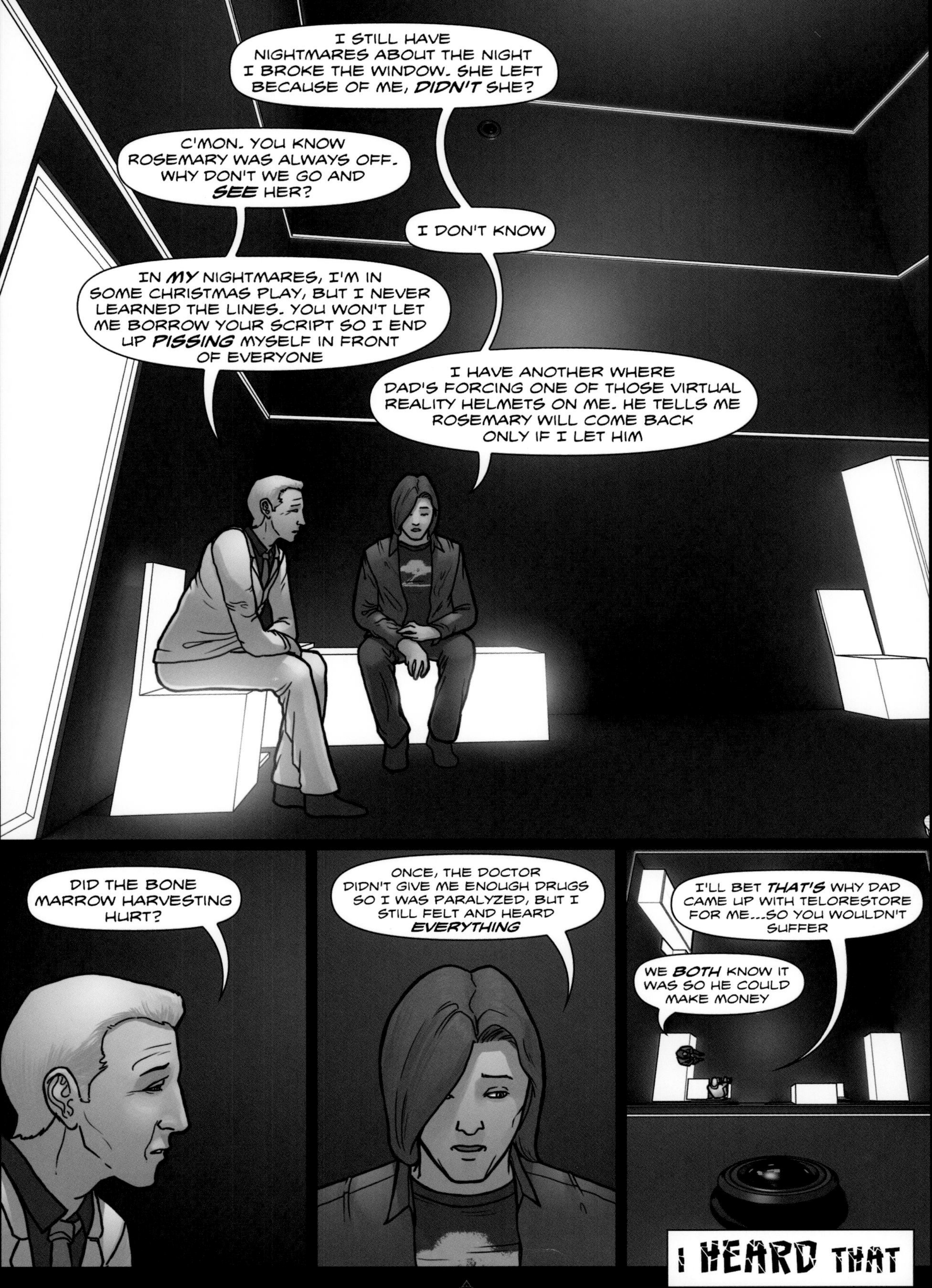
I STILL HAVE NIGHTMARES ABOUT THE NIGHT I BROKE THE WINDOW. SHE LEFT BECAUSE OF ME, *DIDN'T* SHE?
C'MON. YOU KNOW ROSEMARY WAS ALWAYS OFF. WHY DON'T WE GO AND *SEE* HER?
I DON'T KNOW
IN *MY* NIGHTMARES, I'M IN SOME CHRISTMAS PLAY, BUT I NEVER LEARNED THE LINES. YOU WON'T LET ME BORROW YOUR SCRIPT SO I END UP *PISSING* MYSELF IN FRONT OF EVERYONE
I HAVE ANOTHER WHERE DAD'S FORCING ONE OF THOSE VIRTUAL REALITY HELMETS ON ME. HE TELLS ME ROSEMARY WILL COME BACK ONLY IF I LET HIM
DID THE BONE MARROW HARVESTING HURT?
ONCE, THE DOCTOR DIDN'T GIVE ME ENOUGH DRUGS SO I WAS PARALYZED, BUT I STILL FELT AND HEARD *EVERYTHING*
I'LL BET *THAT'S* WHY DAD CAME UP WITH TELORESTORE FOR ME...SO YOU WOULDN'T SUFFER
WE *BOTH* KNOW IT WAS SO HE COULD MAKE MONEY
I HEARD THAT

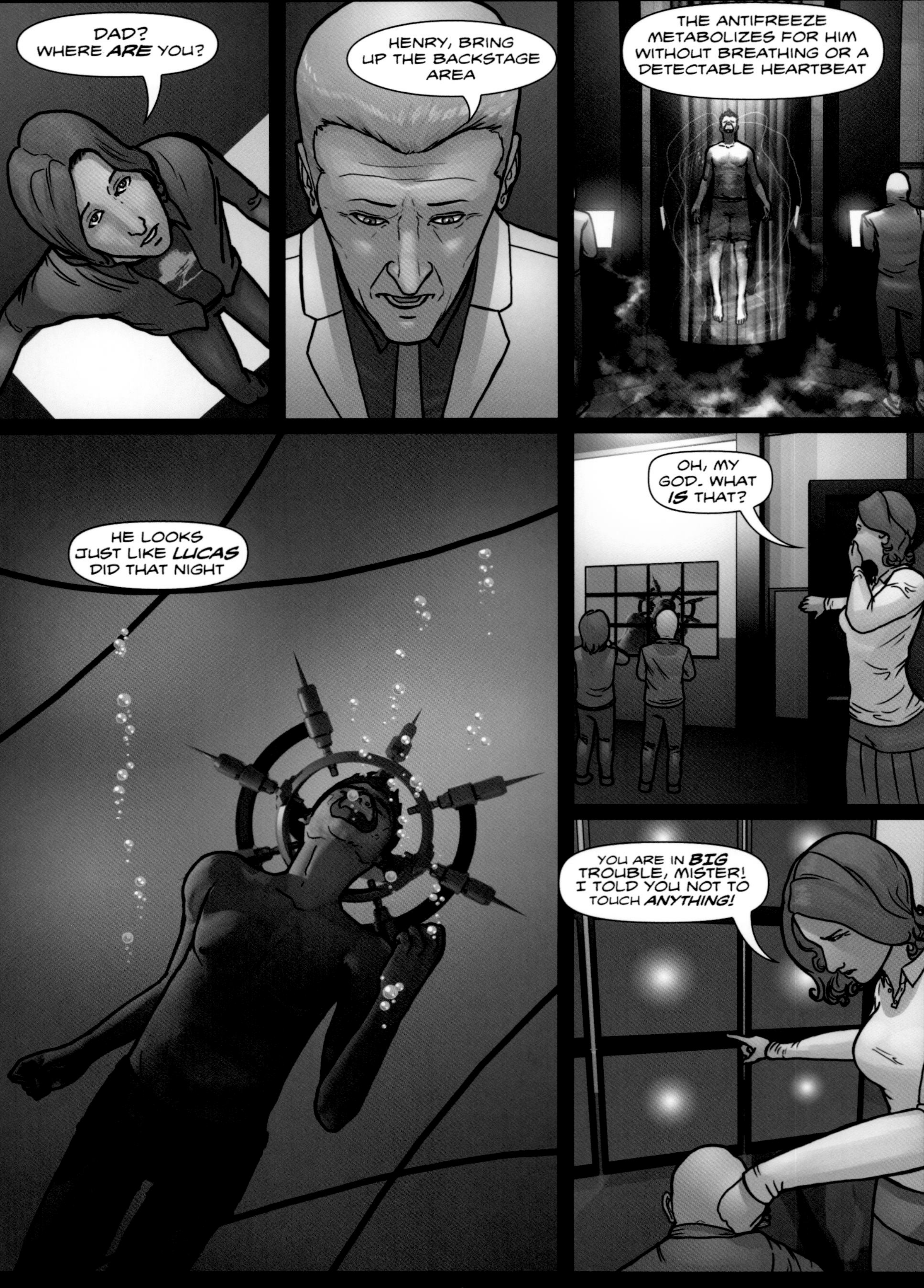
DAD? WHERE ARE YOU?
HENRY, BRING UP THE BACKSTAGE AREA
THE ANTIFREEZE METABOLIZES FOR HIM WITHOUT BREATHING OR A DETECTABLE HEARTBEAT
HE LOOKS JUST LIKE LUCAS DID THAT NIGHT
OH, MY GOD. WHAT IS THAT?
YOU ARE IN BIG TROUBLE, MISTER! I TOLD YOU NOT TO TOUCH ANYTHING!

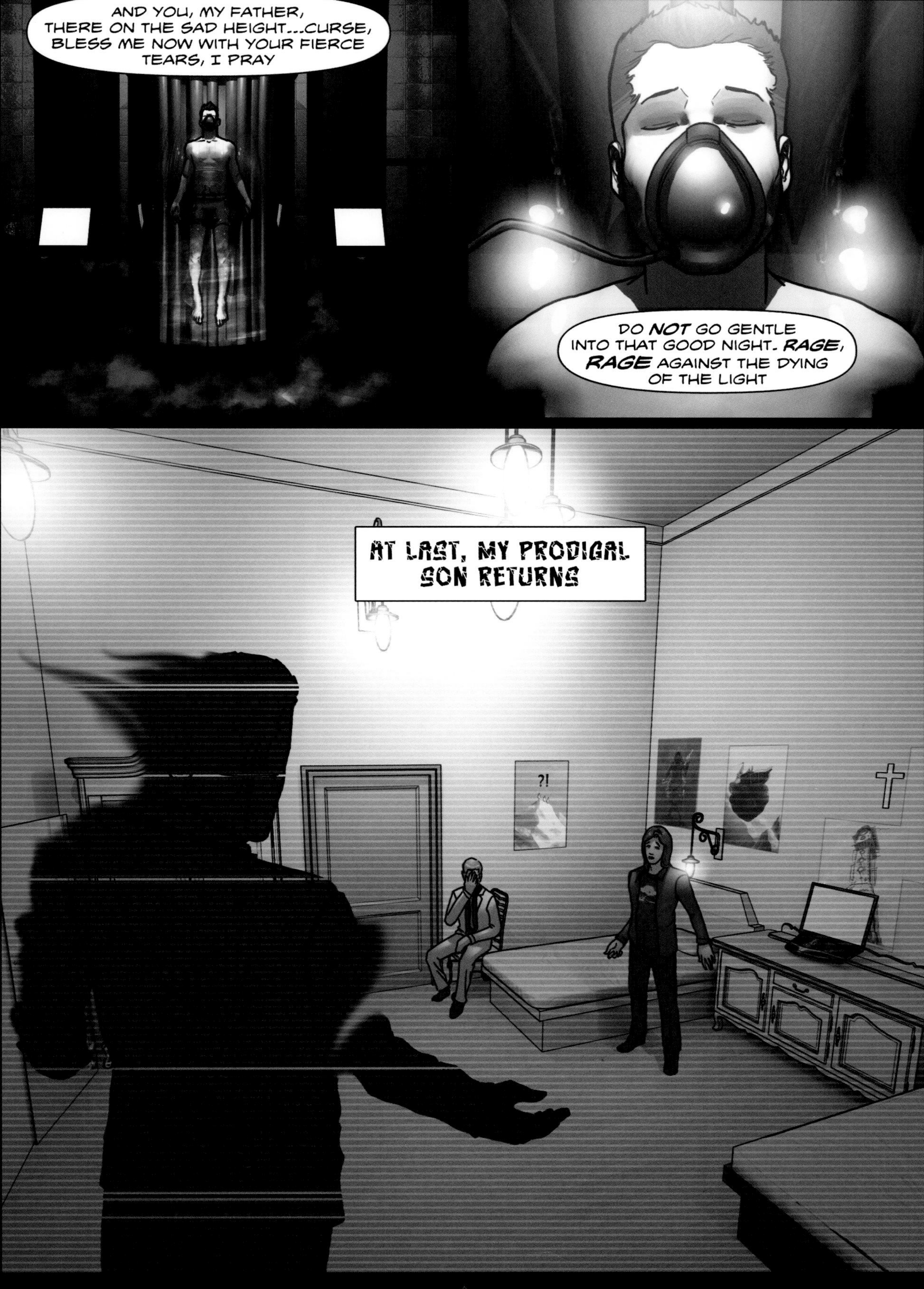
AND YOU, MY FATHER, THERE ON THE SAD HEIGHT...CURSE, BLESS ME NOW WITH YOUR FIERCE TEARS, I PRAY
DO NOT GO GENTLE INTO THAT GOOD NIGHT. RAGE, RAGE AGAINST THE DYING OF THE LIGHT
?!
AT LAST, MY PRODIGAL SON RETURNS

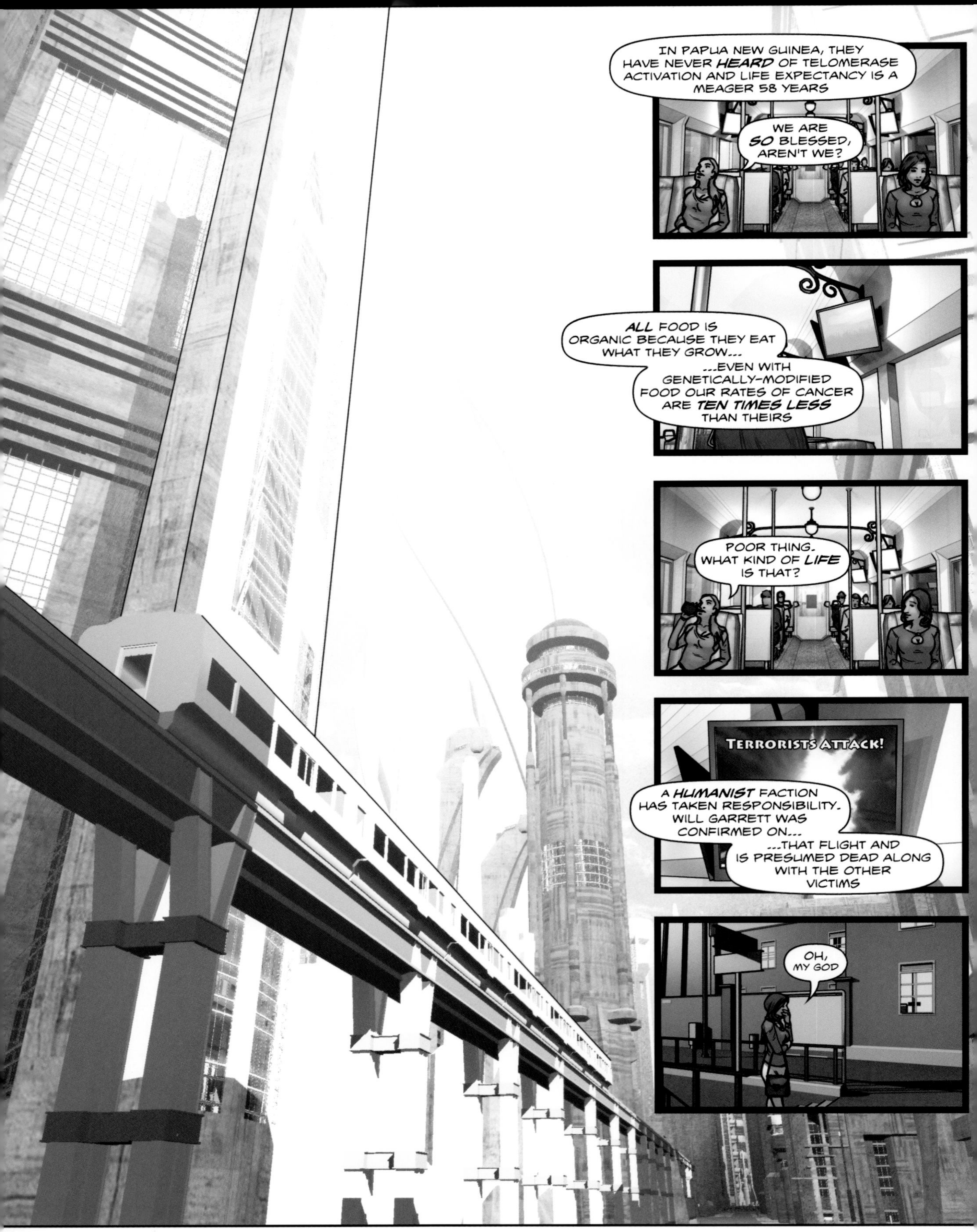
IN PAPUA NEW GUINEA, THEY HAVE NEVER HEARD OF TELOMERASE ACTIVATION AND LIFE EXPECTANCY IS A MEAGER 58 YEARS
WE ARE SO BLESSED, AREN'T WE?
ALL FOOD IS ORGANIC BECAUSE THEY EAT WHAT THEY GROW...
...EVEN WITH GENETICALLY-MODIFIED FOOD OUR RATES OF CANCER ARE TEN TIMES LESS THAN THEIRS
POOR THING. WHAT KIND OF LIFE IS THAT?
TERRORISTS ATTACK!
A HUMANIST FACTION HAS TAKEN RESPONSIBILITY. WILL GARRETT WAS CONFIRMED ON...
...THAT FLIGHT AND IS PRESUMED DEAD ALONG WITH THE OTHER VICTIMS
OH, MY GOD

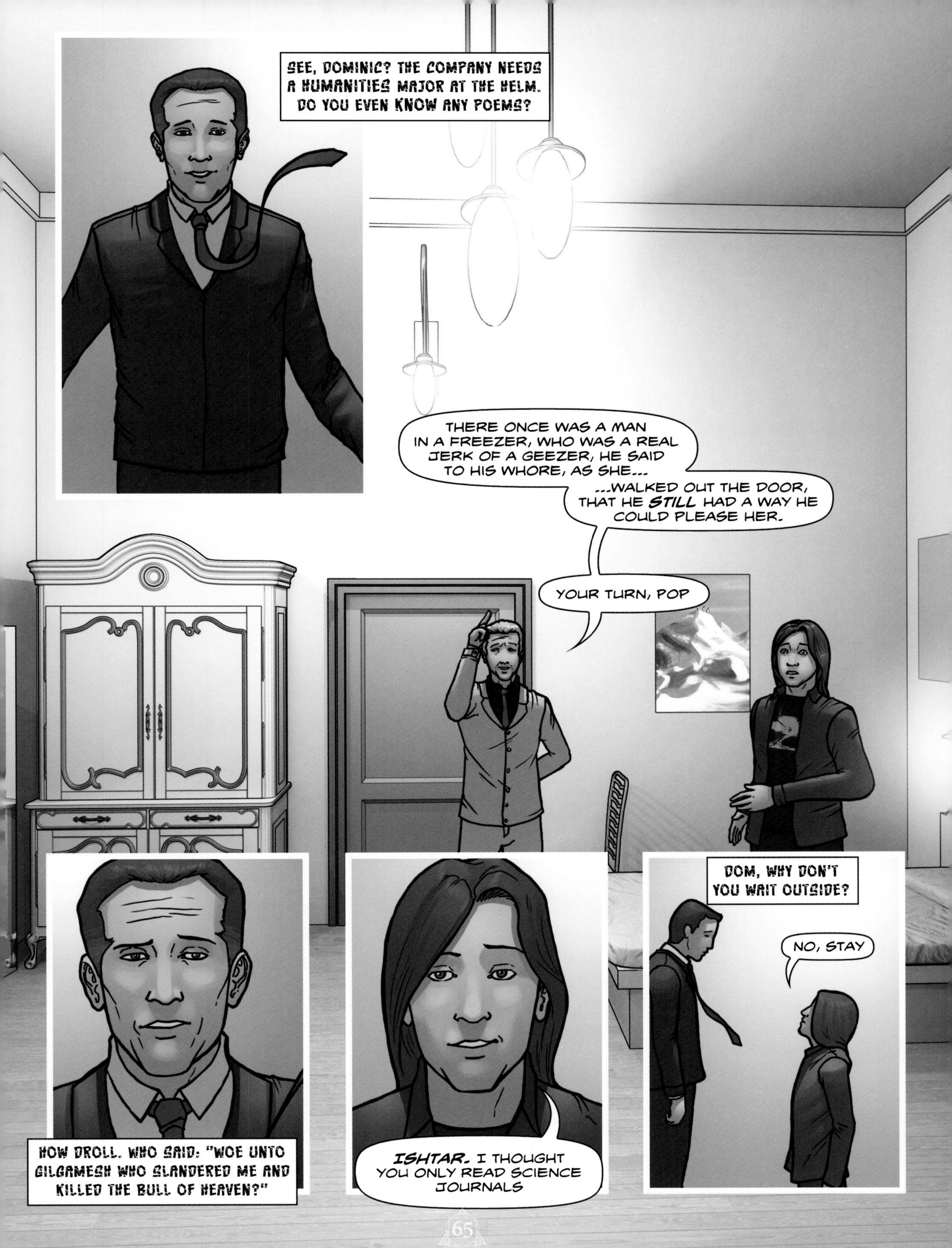

SEE, DOMINIC? THE COMPANY NEEDS A HUMANITIES MAJOR AT THE HELM. DO YOU EVEN KNOW ANY POEMS?
THERE ONCE WAS A MAN IN A FREEZER, WHO WAS A REAL JERK OF A GEEZER, HE SAID TO HIS WHORE, AS SHE...
...WALKED OUT THE DOOR, THAT HE STILL HAD A WAY HE COULD PLEASE HER.
YOUR TURN, POP
HOW DROLL. WHO SAID: "WOE UNTO GILGAMESH WHO SLANDERED ME AND KILLED THE BULL OF HEAVEN?"
ISHTAR. I THOUGHT YOU ONLY READ SCIENCE JOURNALS
DOM, WHY DON'T YOU WAIT OUTSIDE?
NO, STAY

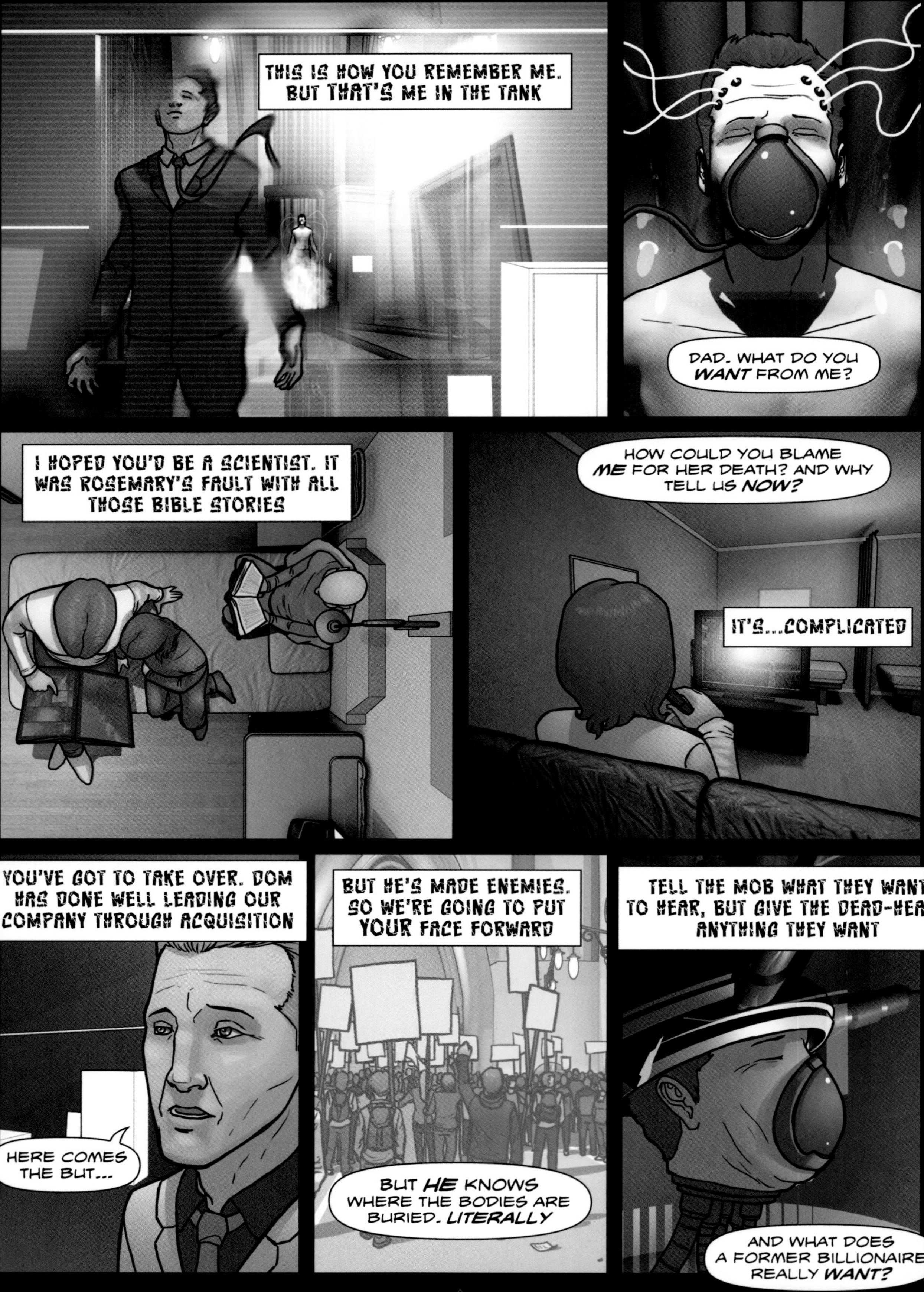
THIS IS HOW YOU REMEMBER ME. BUT THAT'S ME IN THE TANK
DAD. WHAT DO YOU *WANT* FROM ME?
I HOPED YOU'D BE A SCIENTIST. IT WAS ROSEMARY'S FAULT WITH ALL THOSE BIBLE STORIES
HOW COULD YOU BLAME *ME* FOR HER DEATH? AND WHY TELL US *NOW?*
IT'S...COMPLICATED
YOU'VE GOT TO TAKE OVER. DOM HAS DONE WELL LEADING OUR COMPANY THROUGH ACQUISITION
HERE COMES THE BUT...
BUT HE'S MADE ENEMIES. SO WE'RE GOING TO PUT YOUR FACE FORWARD
BUT *HE* KNOWS WHERE THE BODIES ARE BURIED. *LITERALLY*
TELL THE MOB WHAT THEY WANT TO HEAR, BUT GIVE THE DEAD-HEADS ANYTHING THEY WANT
AND WHAT DOES A FORMER BILLIONAIRE REALLY *WANT?*

A NECKTIE SHAPED LIKE A *FISH?*

FRESH NEW BODIES TO DOWNLOAD INTO

COME AGAIN?

LET IT GO, DOM

CLONES? NOT AGAIN

THAT DIDN'T GO OVER SO WELL LAST TIME

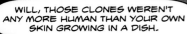

WE JUST DIDN'T SPIN IT RIGHT

SPIN? PEOPLE ARE GETTING *KILLED* AGAIN. I THINK WE'RE WELL PAST SPIN

IT IS THEIR DNA USED TO MAKE THEIR OWN CLONES. DOES A TOENAIL HAVE THE RIGHT TO LIFE...

...LIBERTY AND A HUNDRED DOLLAR PEDICURE?

BUT AT WHAT *COST?*

WILL, THOSE CLONES WEREN'T ANY MORE HUMAN THAN YOUR OWN SKIN GROWING IN A DISH.
FOR TRANSHUMANISM, YOU'LL WANT A *HEALTHY* CLONE

THIS IS ALL SO THAT THOSE HEADS OUTSIDE CAN TRANSFER TO NEW BODIES?

IF RELIGIONS TITHE 10%, WE COULD GET 20 EASILY...

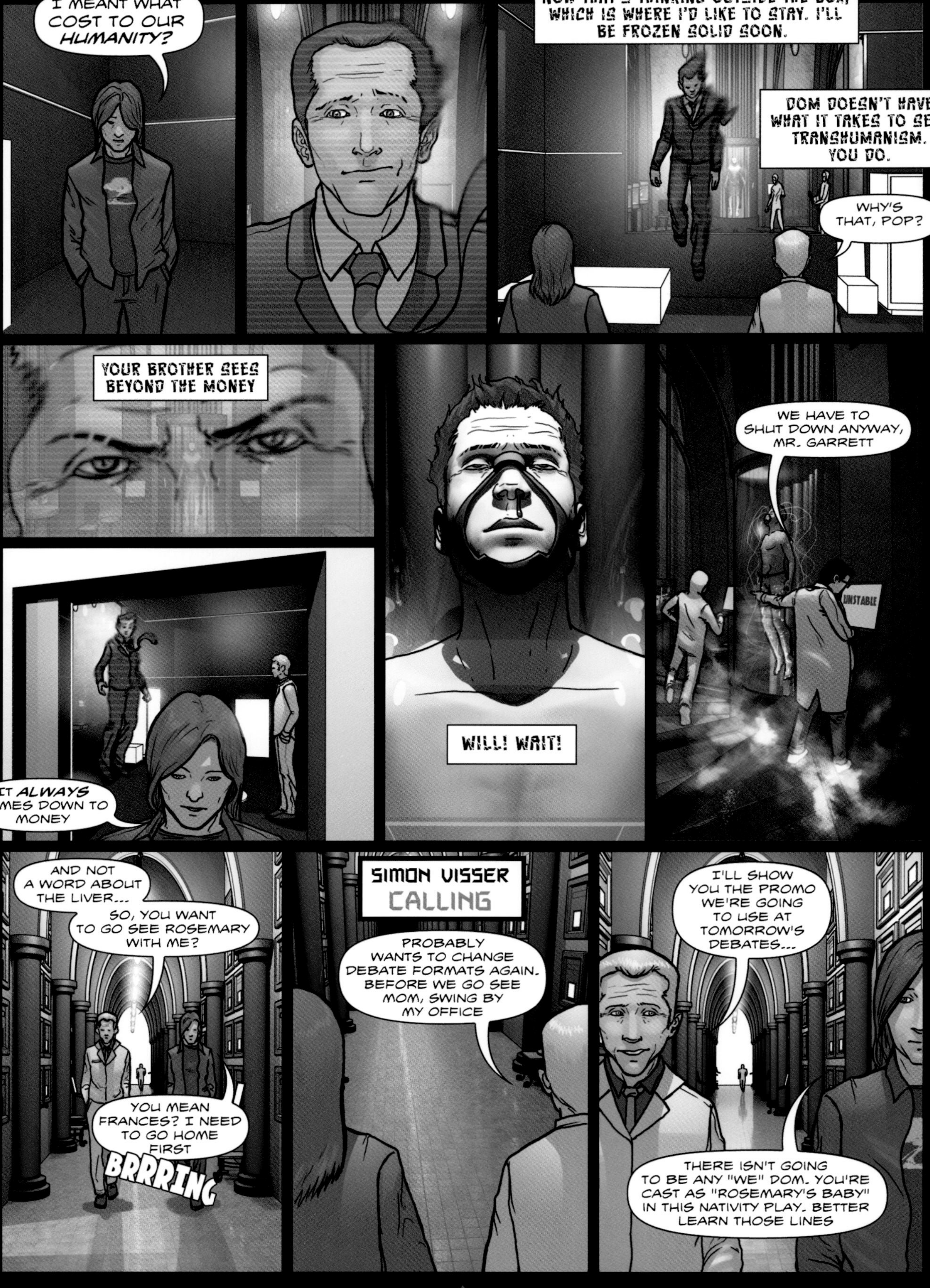

I MEANT WHAT COST TO OUR *HUMANITY?*
NOW THAT'S THINKING OUTSIDE THE BOX, WHICH IS WHERE I'D LIKE TO STAY. I'LL BE FROZEN SOLID SOON.
DOM DOESN'T HAVE WHAT IT TAKES TO SELL TRANSHUMANISM. YOU DO.
WHY'S THAT, POP?
YOUR BROTHER SEES BEYOND THE MONEY
IT *ALWAYS* COMES DOWN TO MONEY
WILL! WAIT!
WE HAVE TO SHUT DOWN ANYWAY, MR. GARRETT
UNSTABLE
AND NOT A WORD ABOUT THE LIVER...
SO, YOU WANT TO GO SEE ROSEMARY WITH ME?
YOU MEAN FRANCES? I NEED TO GO HOME FIRST
BRRRING
SIMON VISSER CALLING
PROBABLY WANTS TO CHANGE DEBATE FORMATS AGAIN. BEFORE WE GO SEE MOM, SWING BY MY OFFICE
I'LL SHOW YOU THE PROMO WE'RE GOING TO USE AT TOMORROW'S DEBATES...
THERE ISN'T GOING TO BE ANY "WE" DOM. YOU'RE CAST AS "ROSEMARY'S BABY" IN THIS NATIVITY PLAY. BETTER LEARN THOSE LINES

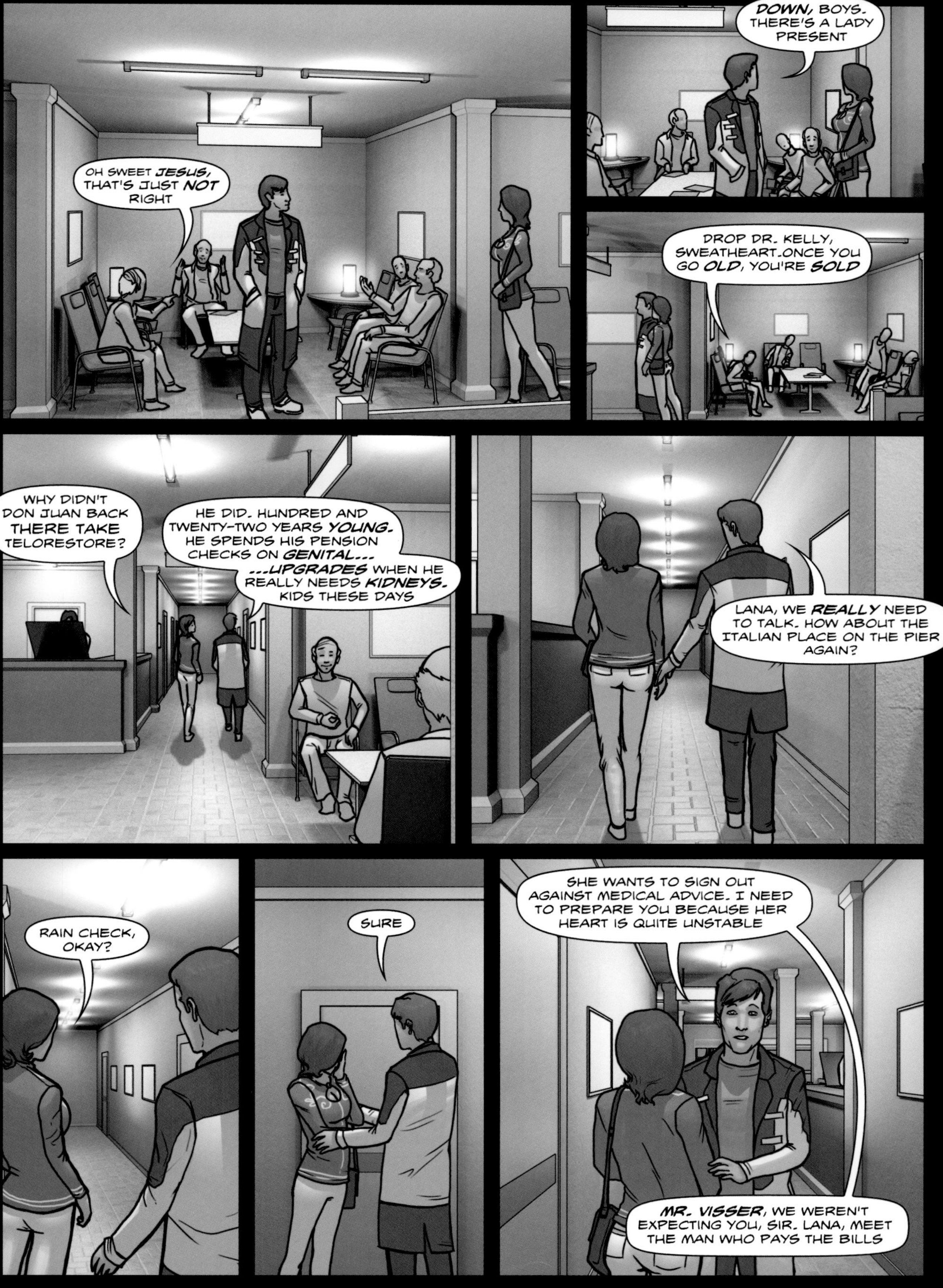
OH SWEET JESUS, THAT'S JUST NOT RIGHT
DOWN, BOYS. THERE'S A LADY PRESENT
DROP DR. KELLY, SWEATHEART. ONCE YOU GO OLD, YOU'RE SOLD
WHY DIDN'T DON JUAN BACK THERE TAKE TELORESTORE?
HE DID. HUNDRED AND TWENTY-TWO YEARS YOUNG. HE SPENDS HIS PENSION CHECKS ON GENITAL...
...UPGRADES WHEN HE REALLY NEEDS KIDNEYS. KIDS THESE DAYS
LANA, WE REALLY NEED TO TALK. HOW ABOUT THE ITALIAN PLACE ON THE PIER AGAIN?
RAIN CHECK, OKAY?
SURE
SHE WANTS TO SIGN OUT AGAINST MEDICAL ADVICE. I NEED TO PREPARE YOU BECAUSE HER HEART IS QUITE UNSTABLE
MR. VISSER, WE WEREN'T EXPECTING YOU, SIR. LANA, MEET THE MAN WHO PAYS THE BILLS

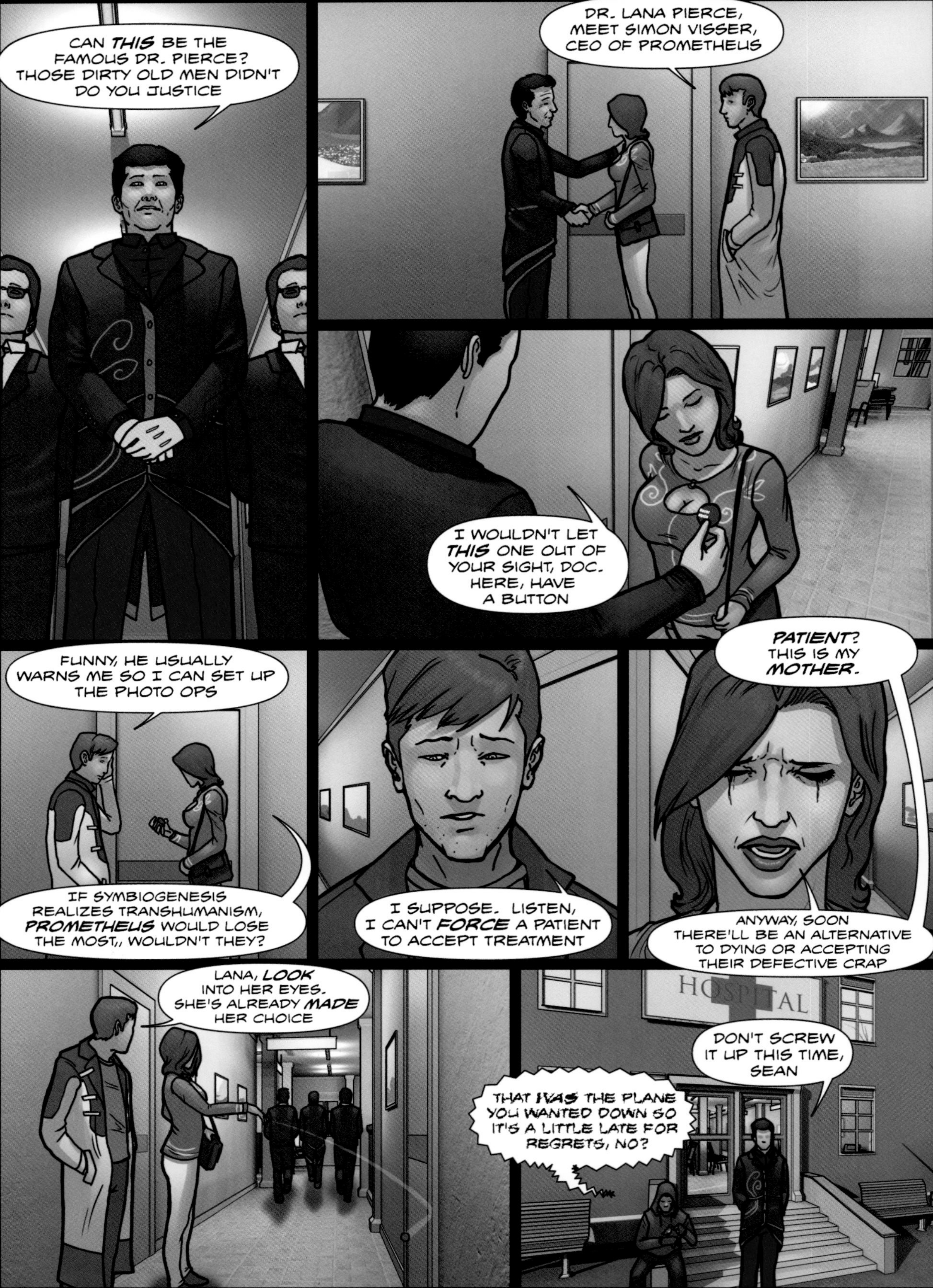
CAN THIS BE THE FAMOUS DR. PIERCE? THOSE DIRTY OLD MEN DIDN'T DO YOU JUSTICE
DR. LANA PIERCE, MEET SIMON VISSER, CEO OF PROMETHEUS
I WOULDN'T LET THIS ONE OUT OF YOUR SIGHT, DOC. HERE, HAVE A BUTTON
FUNNY, HE USUALLY WARNS ME SO I CAN SET UP THE PHOTO OPS
IF SYMBIOGENESIS REALIZES TRANSHUMANISM, PROMETHEUS WOULD LOSE THE MOST,, WOULDN'T THEY?
I SUPPOSE. LISTEN, I CAN'T FORCE A PATIENT TO ACCEPT TREATMENT
PATIENT? THIS IS MY MOTHER.
ANYWAY, SOON THERE'LL BE AN ALTERNATIVE TO DYING OR ACCEPTING THEIR DEFECTIVE CRAP
LANA, LOOK INTO HER EYES. SHE'S ALREADY MADE HER CHOICE
HOSPITAL
DON'T SCREW IT UP THIS TIME, SEAN
THAT WAS THE PLANE YOU WANTED DOWN SO IT'S A LITTLE LATE FOR REGRETS, NO?

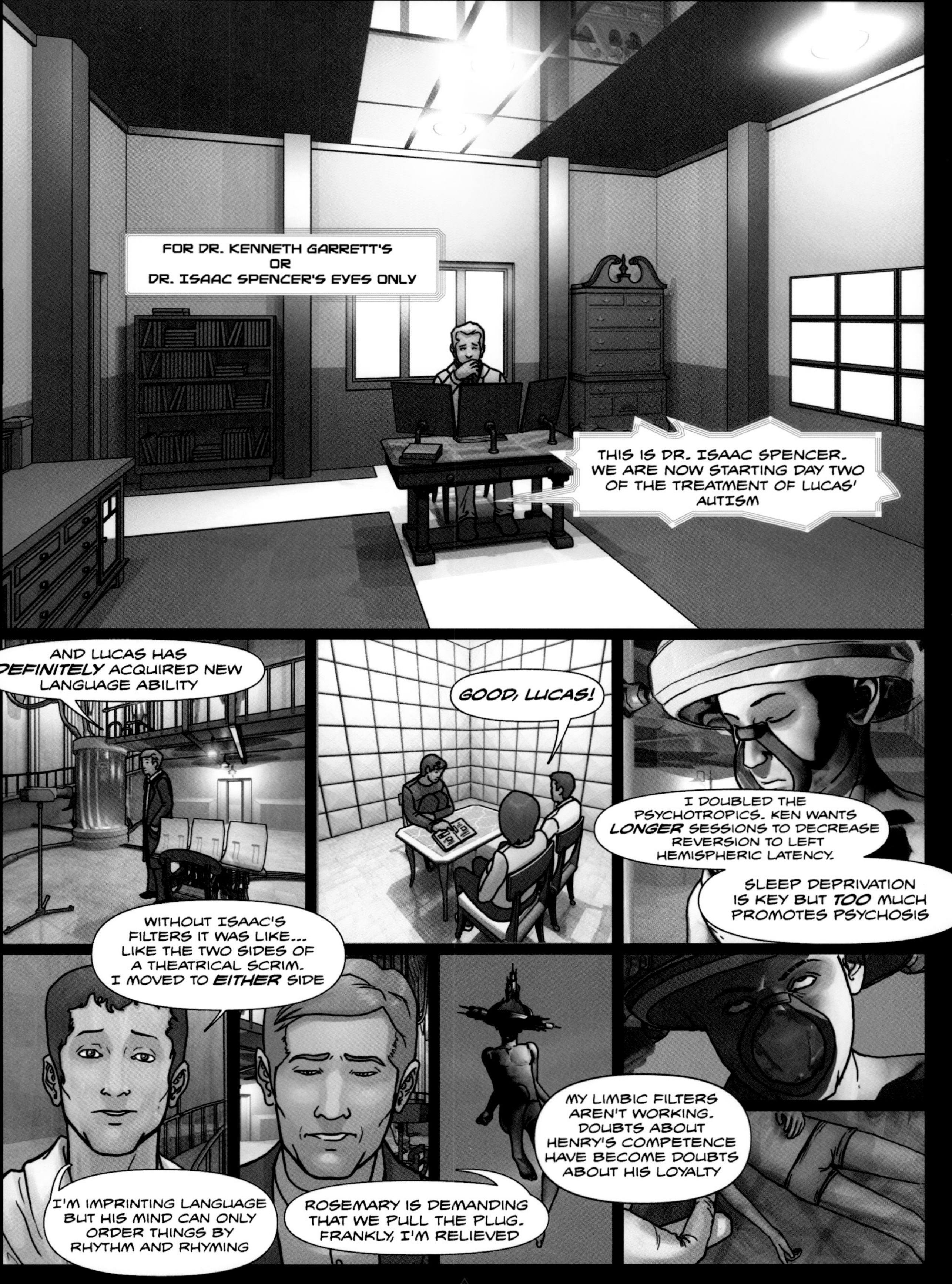

FOR DR. KENNETH GARRETT'S OR DR. ISAAC SPENCER'S EYES ONLY
THIS IS DR. ISAAC SPENCER. WE ARE NOW STARTING DAY TWO OF THE TREATMENT OF LUCAS' AUTISM
AND LUCAS HAS DEFINITELY ACQUIRED NEW LANGUAGE ABILITY
GOOD, LUCAS!
I DOUBLED THE PSYCHOTROPICS. KEN WANTS LONGER SESSIONS TO DECREASE REVERSION TO LEFT HEMISPHERIC LATENCY.
SLEEP DEPRIVATION IS KEY BUT TOO MUCH PROMOTES PSYCHOSIS
WITHOUT ISAAC'S FILTERS IT WAS LIKE... LIKE THE TWO SIDES OF A THEATRICAL SCRIM. I MOVED TO EITHER SIDE
I'M IMPRINTING LANGUAGE BUT HIS MIND CAN ONLY ORDER THINGS BY RHYTHM AND RHYMING
ROSEMARY IS DEMANDING THAT WE PULL THE PLUG. FRANKLY, I'M RELIEVED
MY LIMBIC FILTERS AREN'T WORKING. DOUBTS ABOUT HENRY'S COMPETENCE HAVE BECOME DOUBTS ABOUT HIS LOYALTY

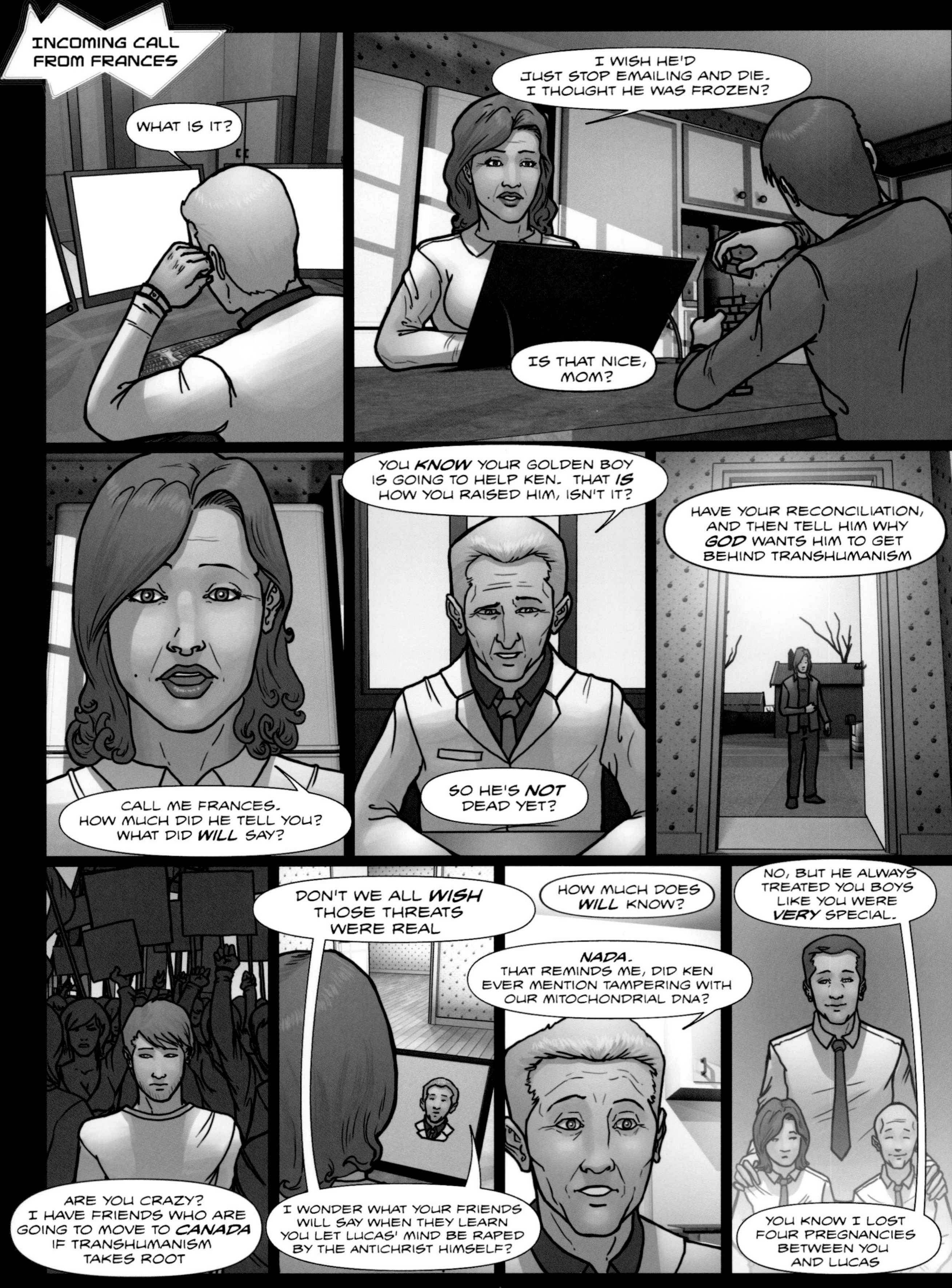
INCOMING CALL FROM FRANCES
WHAT IS IT?
I WISH HE'D JUST STOP EMAILING AND DIE. I THOUGHT HE WAS FROZEN?
IS THAT NICE, MOM?
CALL ME FRANCES. HOW MUCH DID HE TELL YOU? WHAT DID WILL SAY?
YOU KNOW YOUR GOLDEN BOY IS GOING TO HELP KEN. THAT IS HOW YOU RAISED HIM, ISN'T IT?
SO HE'S NOT DEAD YET?
HAVE YOUR RECONCILIATION, AND THEN TELL HIM WHY GOD WANTS HIM TO GET BEHIND TRANSHUMANISM
ARE YOU CRAZY? I HAVE FRIENDS WHO ARE GOING TO MOVE TO CANADA IF TRANSHUMANISM TAKES ROOT
DON'T WE ALL WISH THOSE THREATS WERE REAL
I WONDER WHAT YOUR FRIENDS WILL SAY WHEN THEY LEARN YOU LET LUCAS' MIND BE RAPED BY THE ANTICHRIST HIMSELF?
HOW MUCH DOES WILL KNOW?
NADA. THAT REMINDS ME, DID KEN EVER MENTION TAMPERING WITH OUR MITOCHONDRIAL DNA?
NO, BUT HE ALWAYS TREATED YOU BOYS LIKE YOU WERE VERY SPECIAL.
YOU KNOW I LOST FOUR PREGNANCIES BETWEEN YOU AND LUCAS

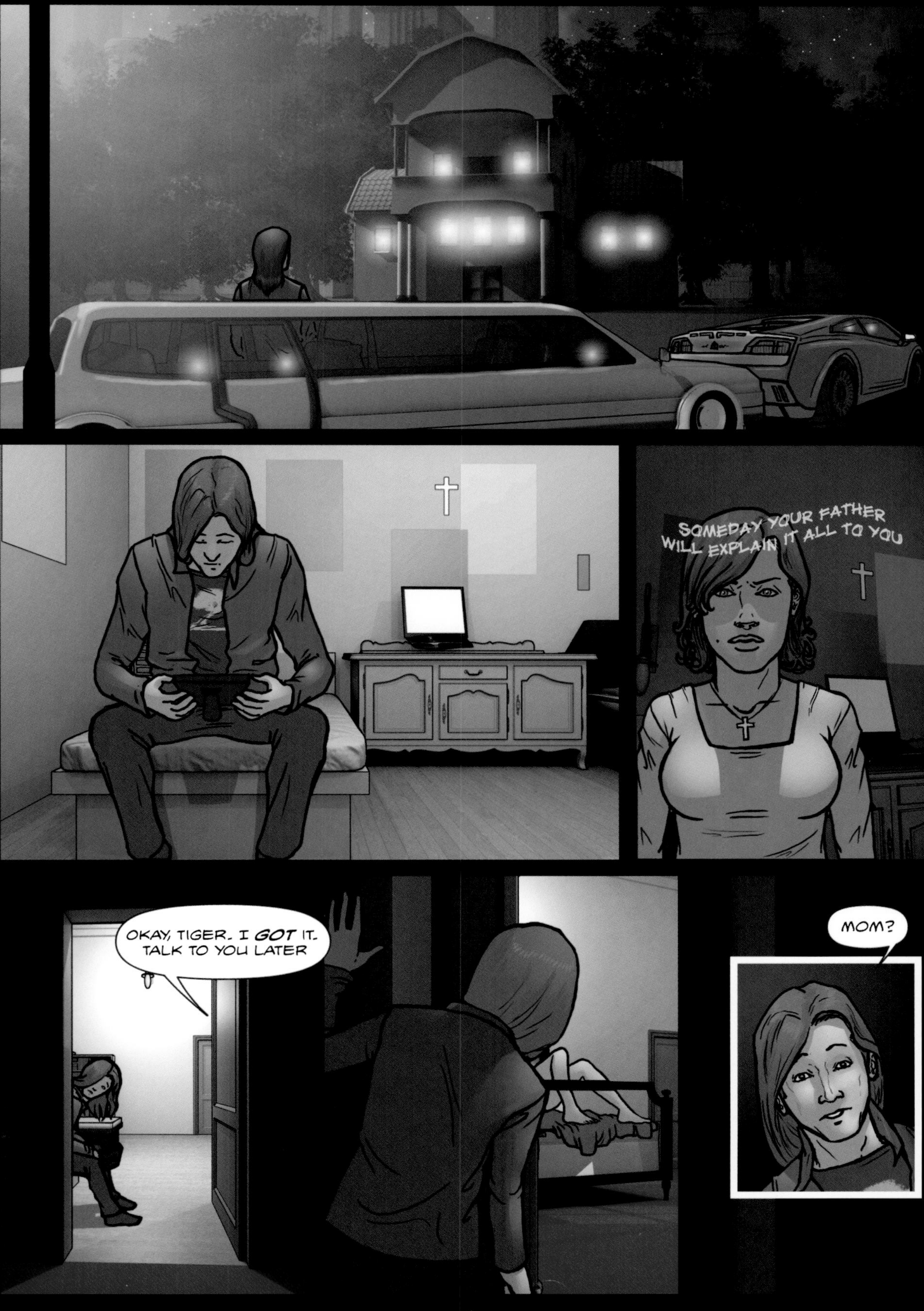
SOMEDAY YOUR FATHER WILL EXPLAIN IT ALL TO YOU
OKAY, TIGER. I *GOT* IT. TALK TO YOU LATER
MOM?

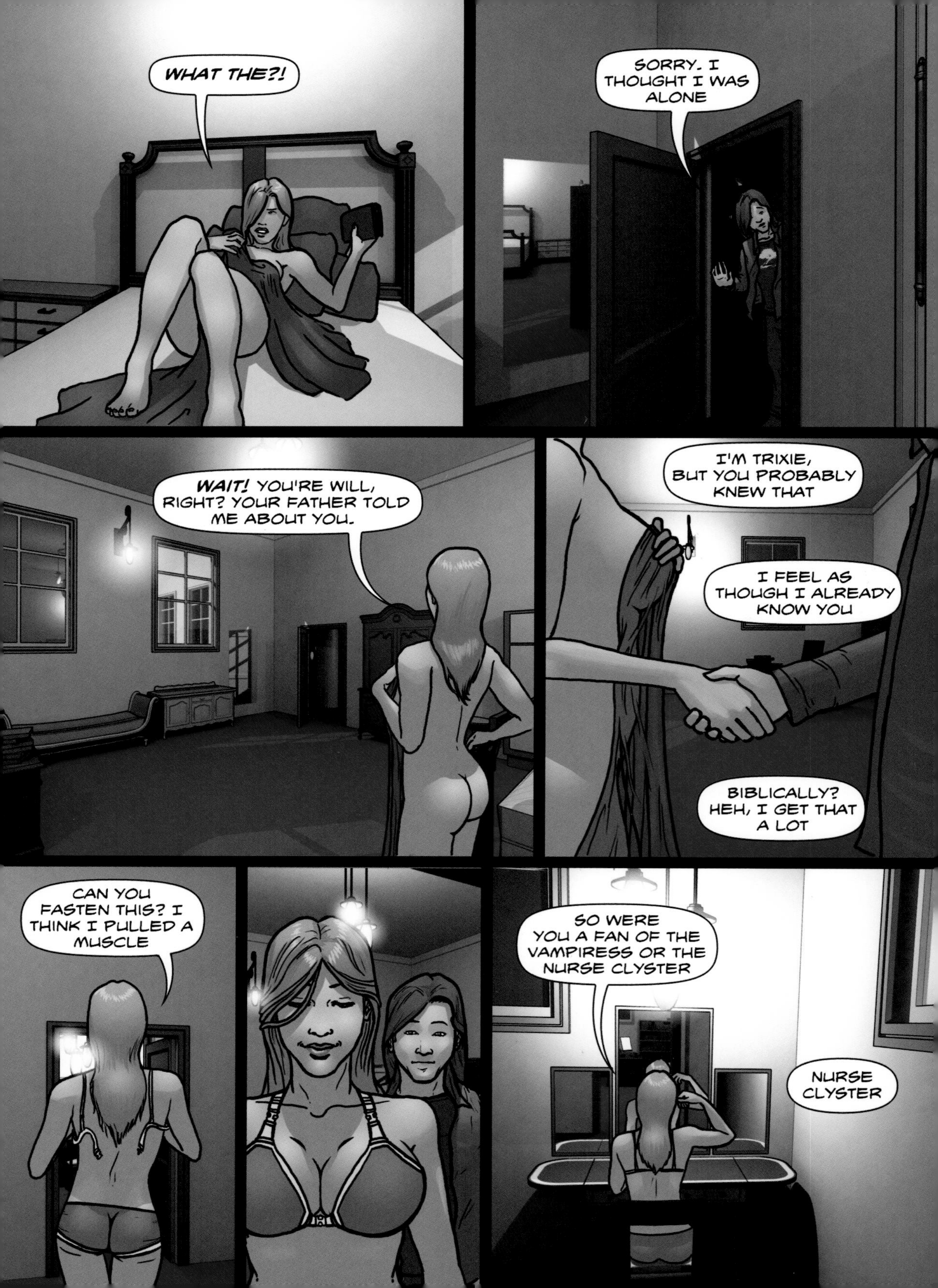
WHAT THE?!
SORRY. I THOUGHT I WAS ALONE
WAIT! YOU'RE WILL, RIGHT? YOUR FATHER TOLD ME ABOUT YOU.
I'M TRIXIE, BUT YOU PROBABLY KNEW THAT
I FEEL AS THOUGH I ALREADY KNOW YOU
BIBLICALLY? HEH, I GET THAT A LOT
CAN YOU FASTEN THIS? I THINK I PULLED A MUSCLE
SO WERE YOU A FAN OF THE VAMPIRESS OR THE NURSE CLYSTER
NURSE CLYSTER

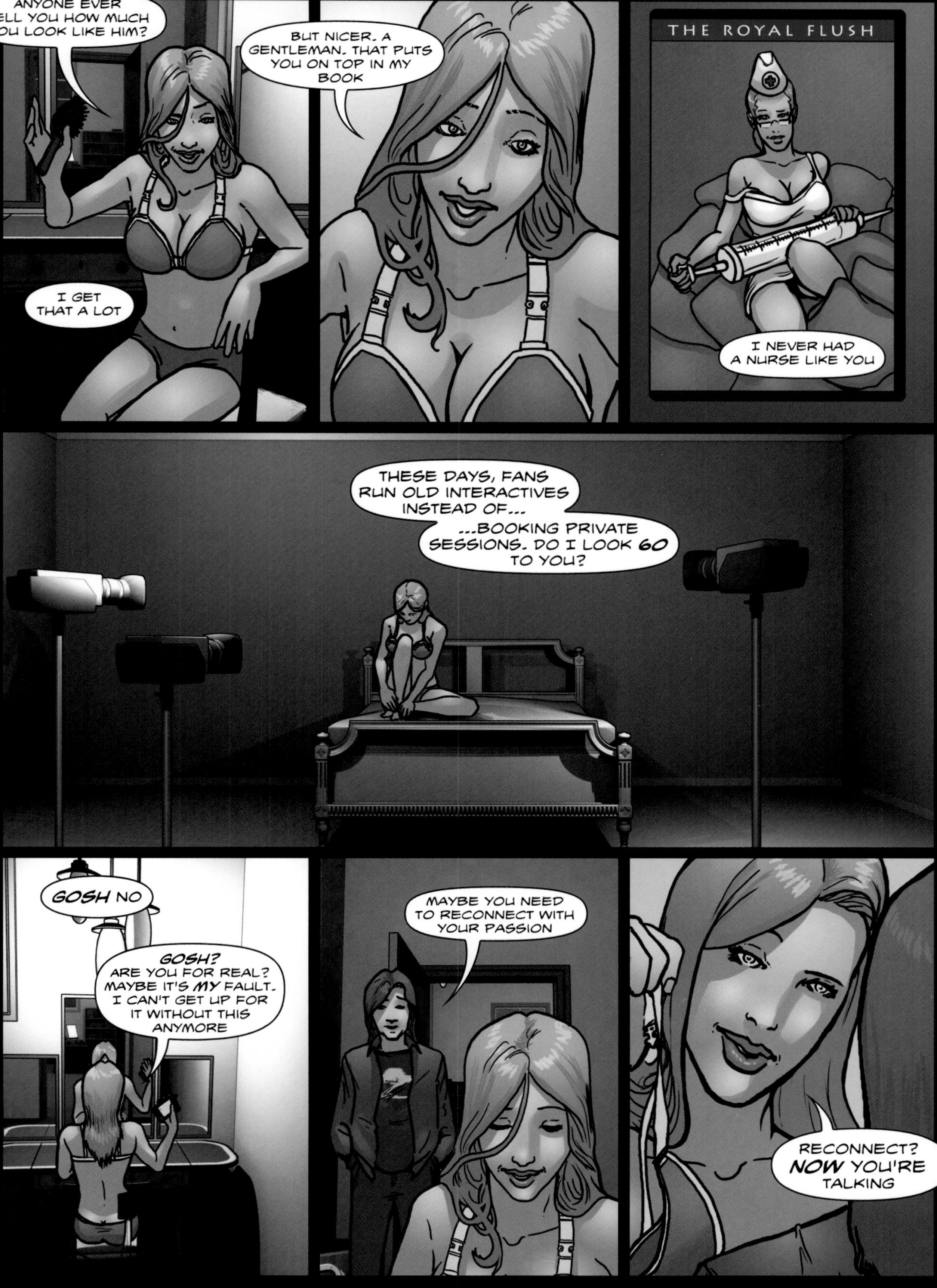
ANYONE EVER TELL YOU HOW MUCH YOU LOOK LIKE HIM?
I GET THAT A LOT
BUT NICER. A GENTLEMAN. THAT PUTS YOU ON TOP IN MY BOOK
THE ROYAL FLUSH
I NEVER HAD A NURSE LIKE YOU
THESE DAYS, FANS RUN OLD INTERACTIVES INSTEAD OF...
...BOOKING PRIVATE SESSIONS. DO I LOOK 60 TO YOU?
GOSH NO
GOSH? ARE YOU FOR REAL? MAYBE IT'S MY FAULT. I CAN'T GET UP FOR IT WITHOUT THIS ANYMORE
MAYBE YOU NEED TO RECONNECT WITH YOUR PASSION
RECONNECT? NOW YOU'RE TALKING

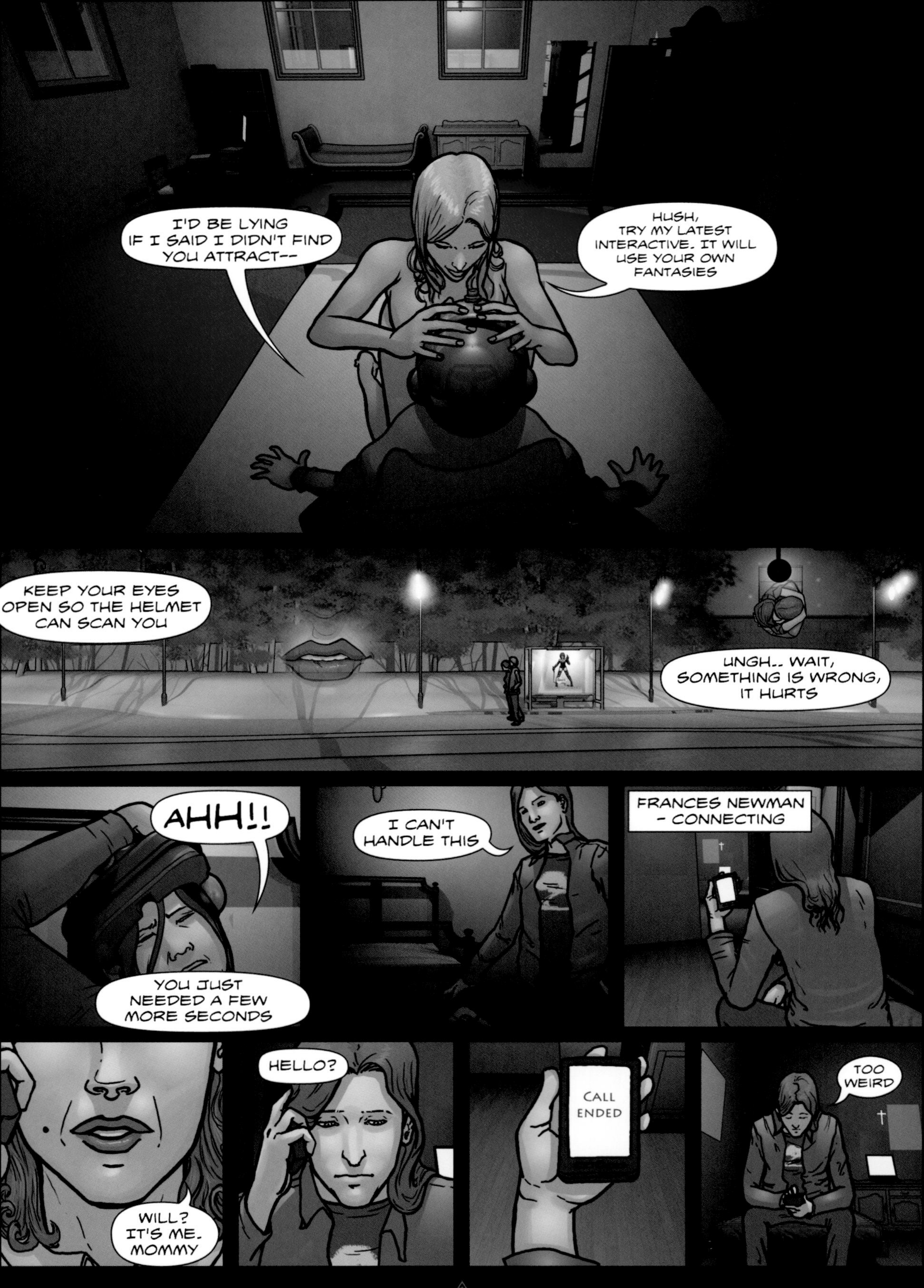
I'D BE LYING IF I SAID I DIDN'T FIND YOU ATTRACT--
HUSH, TRY MY LATEST INTERACTIVE. IT WILL USE YOUR OWN FANTASIES
KEEP YOUR EYES OPEN SO THE HELMET CAN SCAN YOU
UNGH.. WAIT, SOMETHING IS WRONG, IT HURTS
AHH!!
YOU JUST NEEDED A FEW MORE SECONDS
I CAN'T HANDLE THIS
FRANCES NEWMAN - CONNECTING
WILL? IT'S ME. MOMMY
HELLO?
CALL ENDED
TOO WEIRD

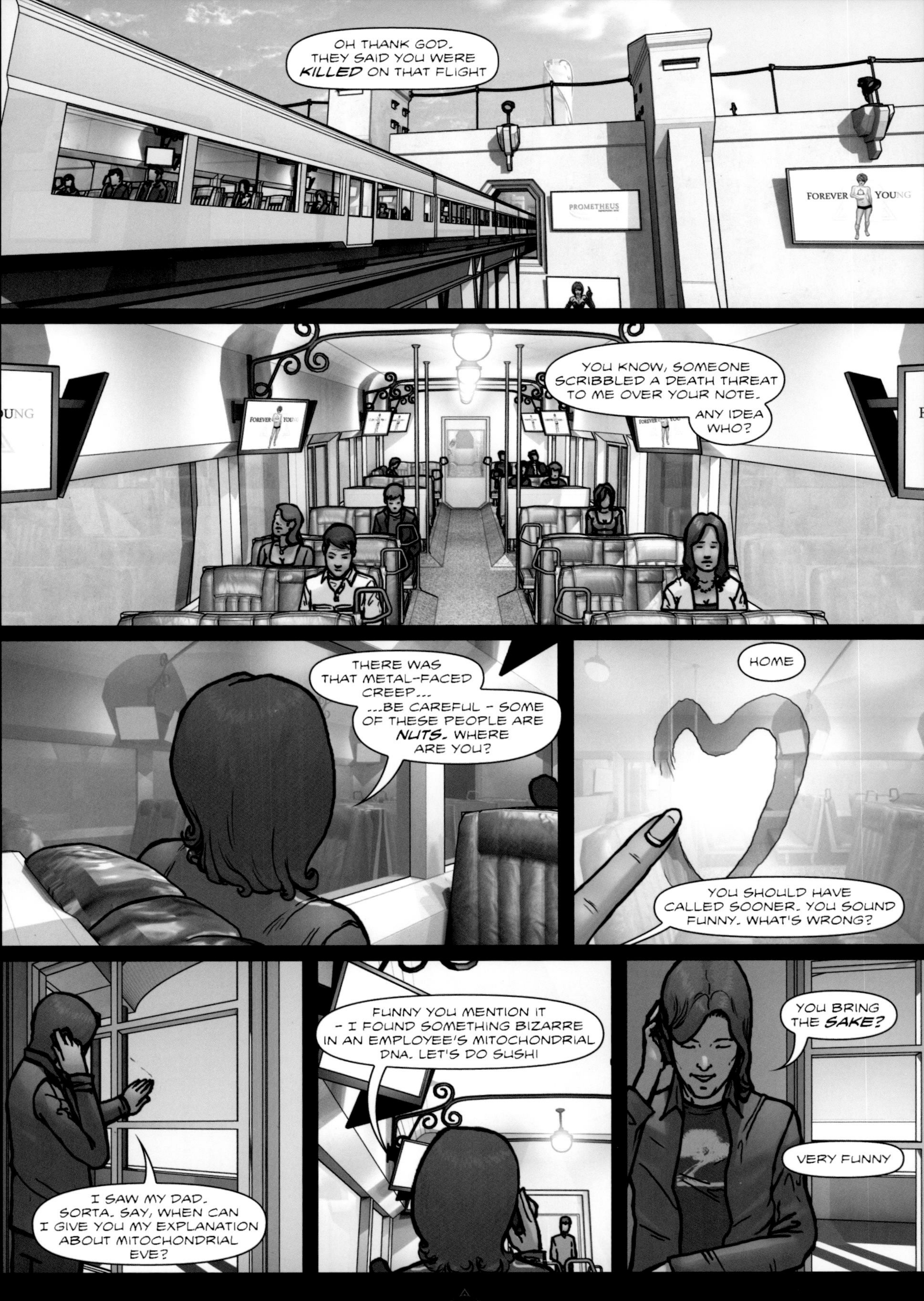
OH THANK GOD. THEY SAID YOU WERE *KILLED* ON THAT FLIGHT
PROMETHEUS
FOREVER YOUNG
YOU KNOW, SOMEONE SCRIBBLED A DEATH THREAT TO ME OVER YOUR NOTE.
ANY IDEA WHO?
THERE WAS THAT METAL-FACED CREEP...
...BE CAREFUL - SOME OF THESE PEOPLE ARE *NUTS.* WHERE ARE YOU?
HOME
YOU SHOULD HAVE CALLED SOONER. YOU SOUND FUNNY. WHAT'S WRONG?
I SAW MY DAD. SORTA. SAY, WHEN CAN I GIVE YOU MY EXPLANATION ABOUT MITOCHONDRIAL EVE?
FUNNY YOU MENTION IT - I FOUND SOMETHING BIZARRE IN AN EMPLOYEE'S MITOCHONDRIAL DNA. LET'S DO SUSHI
YOU BRING THE *SAKE?*
VERY FUNNY

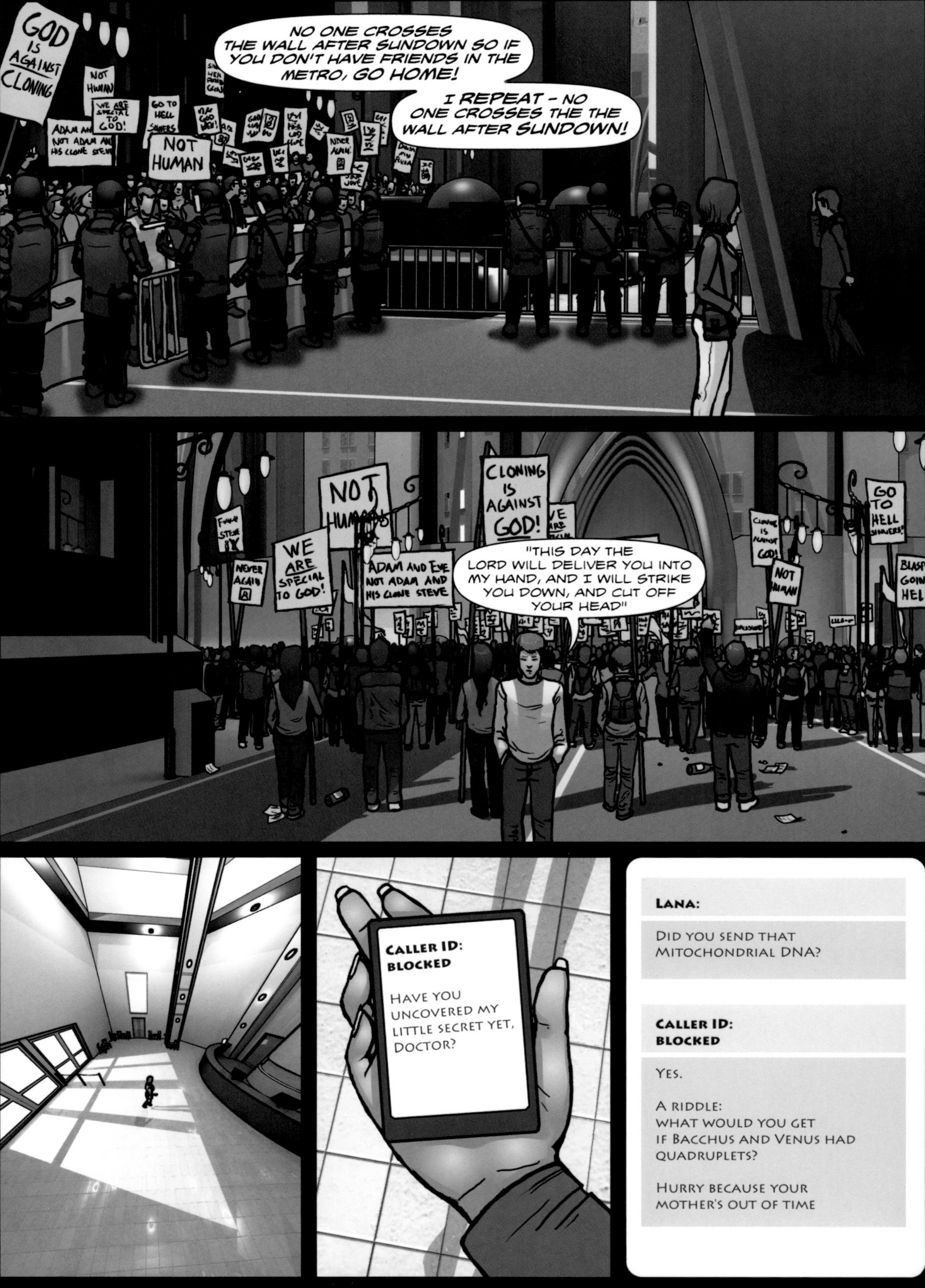
GOD IS AGAINST CLONING
NOT HUMAN
WE ARE SPECIAL TO GOD!
GO TO HELL SINNERS
ADAM AND EVE NOT ADAM AND HIS CLONE STEVE
NOT HUMAN
NO ONE CROSSES THE WALL AFTER SUNDOWN SO IF YOU DON'T HAVE FRIENDS IN THE METRO, GO HOME!
I REPEAT - NO ONE CROSSES THE THE WALL AFTER SUNDOWN!
NOT HUMAN
CLONING IS AGAINST GOD!
WE ARE SPECIAL TO GOD!
NEVER AGAIN
ADAM AND EVE NOT ADAM AND HIS CLONE STEVE
GO TO HELL SINNERS!
NOT HUMAN
"THIS DAY THE LORD WILL DELIVER YOU INTO MY HAND, AND I WILL STRIKE YOU DOWN, AND CUT OFF YOUR HEAD"
CALLER ID: BLOCKED
HAVE YOU UNCOVERED MY LITTLE SECRET YET, DOCTOR?
LANA:
DID YOU SEND THAT MITOCHONDRIAL DNA?
CALLER ID: BLOCKED
YES.
A RIDDLE:
WHAT WOULD YOU GET IF BACCHUS AND VENUS HAD QUADRUPLETS?
HURRY BECAUSE YOUR MOTHER'S OUT OF TIME

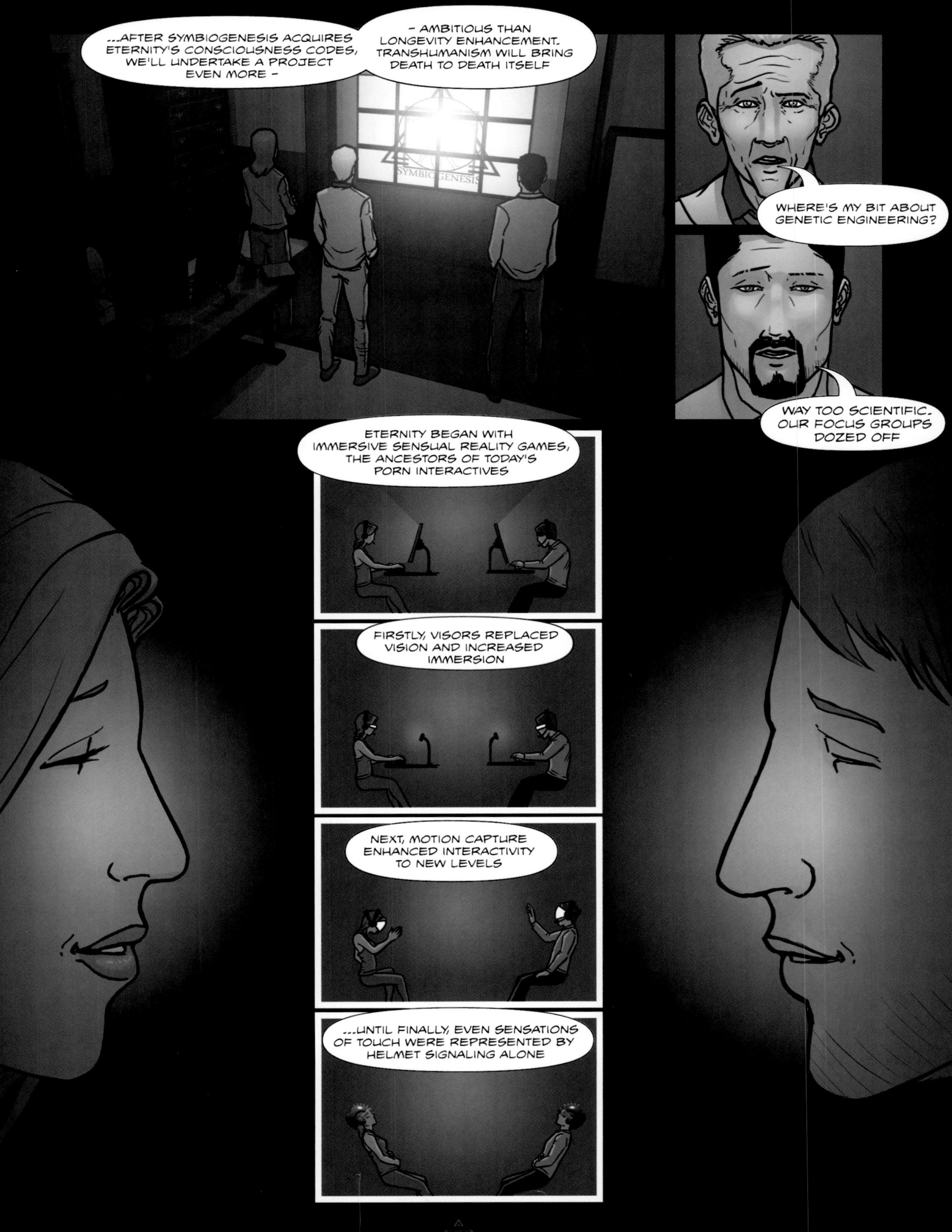
...AFTER SYMBIOGENESIS ACQUIRES ETERNITY'S CONSCIOUSNESS CODES, WE'LL UNDERTAKE A PROJECT EVEN MORE –
– AMBITIOUS THAN LONGEVITY ENHANCEMENT. TRANSHUMANISM WILL BRING DEATH TO DEATH ITSELF
SYMBIOGENESIS
WHERE'S MY BIT ABOUT GENETIC ENGINEERING?
WAY TOO SCIENTIFIC. OUR FOCUS GROUPS DOZED OFF
ETERNITY BEGAN WITH IMMERSIVE SENSUAL REALITY GAMES, THE ANCESTORS OF TODAY'S PORN INTERACTIVES
FIRSTLY, VISORS REPLACED VISION AND INCREASED IMMERSION
NEXT, MOTION CAPTURE ENHANCED INTERACTIVITY TO NEW LEVELS
...UNTIL FINALLY, EVEN SENSATIONS OF TOUCH WERE REPRESENTED BY HELMET SIGNALING ALONE

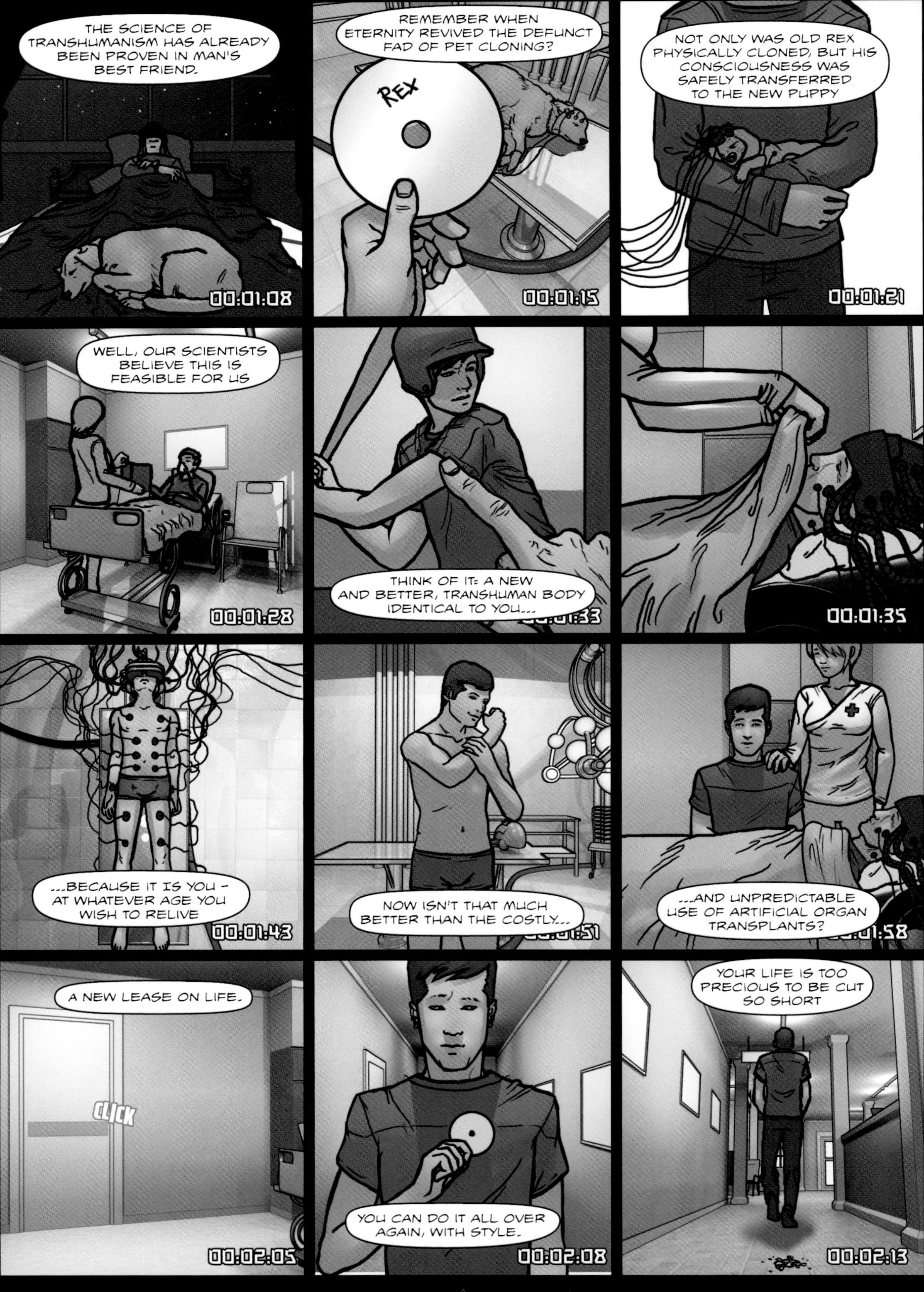
THE SCIENCE OF TRANSHUMANISM HAS ALREADY BEEN PROVEN IN MAN'S BEST FRIEND.
00:01:08
REMEMBER WHEN ETERNITY REVIVED THE DEFUNCT FAD OF PET CLONING?
REX
00:01:15
NOT ONLY WAS OLD REX PHYSICALLY CLONED, BUT HIS CONSCIOUSNESS WAS SAFELY TRANSFERRED TO THE NEW PUPPY
00:01:21
WELL, OUR SCIENTISTS BELIEVE THIS IS FEASIBLE FOR US
00:01:28
THINK OF IT: A NEW AND BETTER, TRANSHUMAN BODY IDENTICAL TO YOU...
00:01:35
...BECAUSE IT IS YOU - AT WHATEVER AGE YOU WISH TO RELIVE
00:01:43
NOW ISN'T THAT MUCH BETTER THAN THE COSTLY...
...AND UNPREDICTABLE USE OF ARTIFICIAL ORGAN TRANSPLANTS?
A NEW LEASE ON LIFE.
CLICK
00:02:05
YOU CAN DO IT ALL OVER AGAIN, WITH STYLE.
00:02:08
YOUR LIFE IS TOO PRECIOUS TO BE CUT SO SHORT
00:02:13

SURE, WE'RE ALL CONCERNED ABOUT SETTING LIMITS...

00:02:13

...ESPECIALLY AFTER LAST YEAR'S EXPOSÉS ABOUT PLANNED OBSOLESCENCE BY THE PROMETHEUS CORPORATION

THAT'S WHY WE'RE COMMITTED TO THESE THREE FUNDAMENTAL PRINCIPLES:

I CAN'T WAIT TO SEE THE LOOK ON SIMON'S FACE

00:02:21

1. NO ONE MAY BE COERCED INTO ACCEPTING LIFE-PROLONGING THERAPIES

00:02:29

2. CLONING WILL BE RESERVED FOR AUTOLOGOUS CONSCIOUSNESS TRANSFER, NOT FOR ORGAN HARVESTING

00:02:37

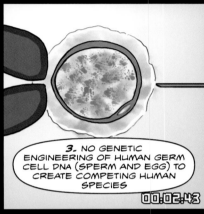

3. NO GENETIC ENGINEERING OF HUMAN GERM CELL DNA (SPERM AND EGG) TO CREATE COMPETING HUMAN SPECIES

00:02:43

BUT IF YOU DREAM OF IMMORTALITY, THIS MERGER WILL CREATE A SAFE AND ETHICAL MEANS TO PRESERVE ALL THE THINGS YOU ARE, FOR ALL OF ETERNITY...

00:02:50

TRANSHUMANISM... IT'S REINCARNATION FOR THE REST OF US

00:02:58

00:02:59

00:03:00

TELL ME THIS IS A JOKE

JOKE? THIS IS DELIVERANCE FOR THE PICKLE-HEADS...

...AND YOU'RE THE MAN BEHIND THE PLAN. WE'D BETTER GO SEE ROSEMARY BEFORE CURFEW

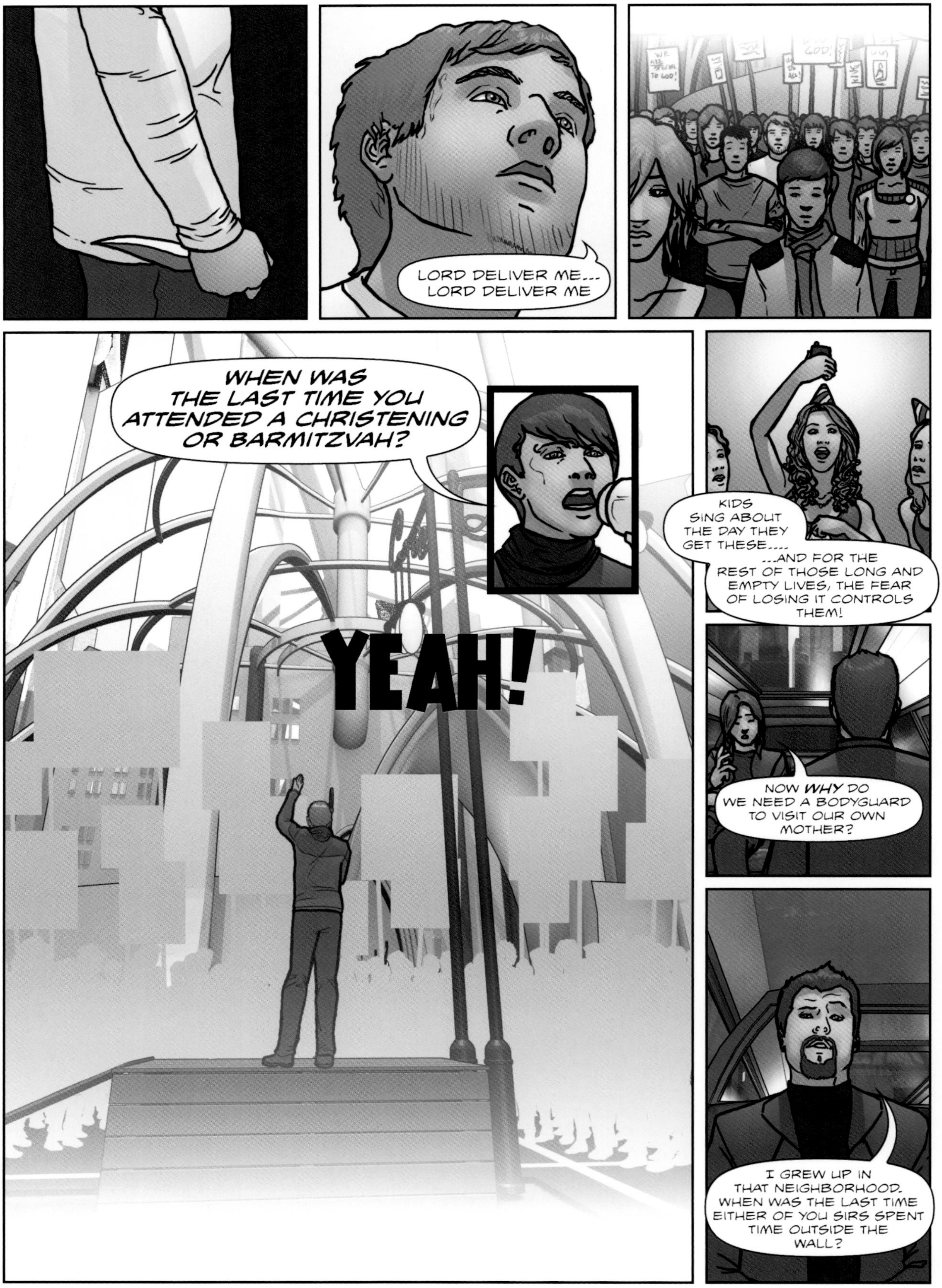
LORD DELIVER ME... LORD DELIVER ME
WHEN WAS THE LAST TIME YOU ATTENDED A CHRISTENING OR BARMITZVAH?
YEAH!
KIDS SING ABOUT THE DAY THEY GET THESE....
...AND FOR THE REST OF THOSE LONG AND EMPTY LIVES, THE FEAR OF LOSING IT CONTROLS THEM!
NOW *WHY* DO WE NEED A BODYGUARD TO VISIT OUR OWN MOTHER?
I GREW UP IN THAT NEIGHBORHOOD. WHEN WAS THE LAST TIME EITHER OF YOU SIRS SPENT TIME OUTSIDE THE WALL?

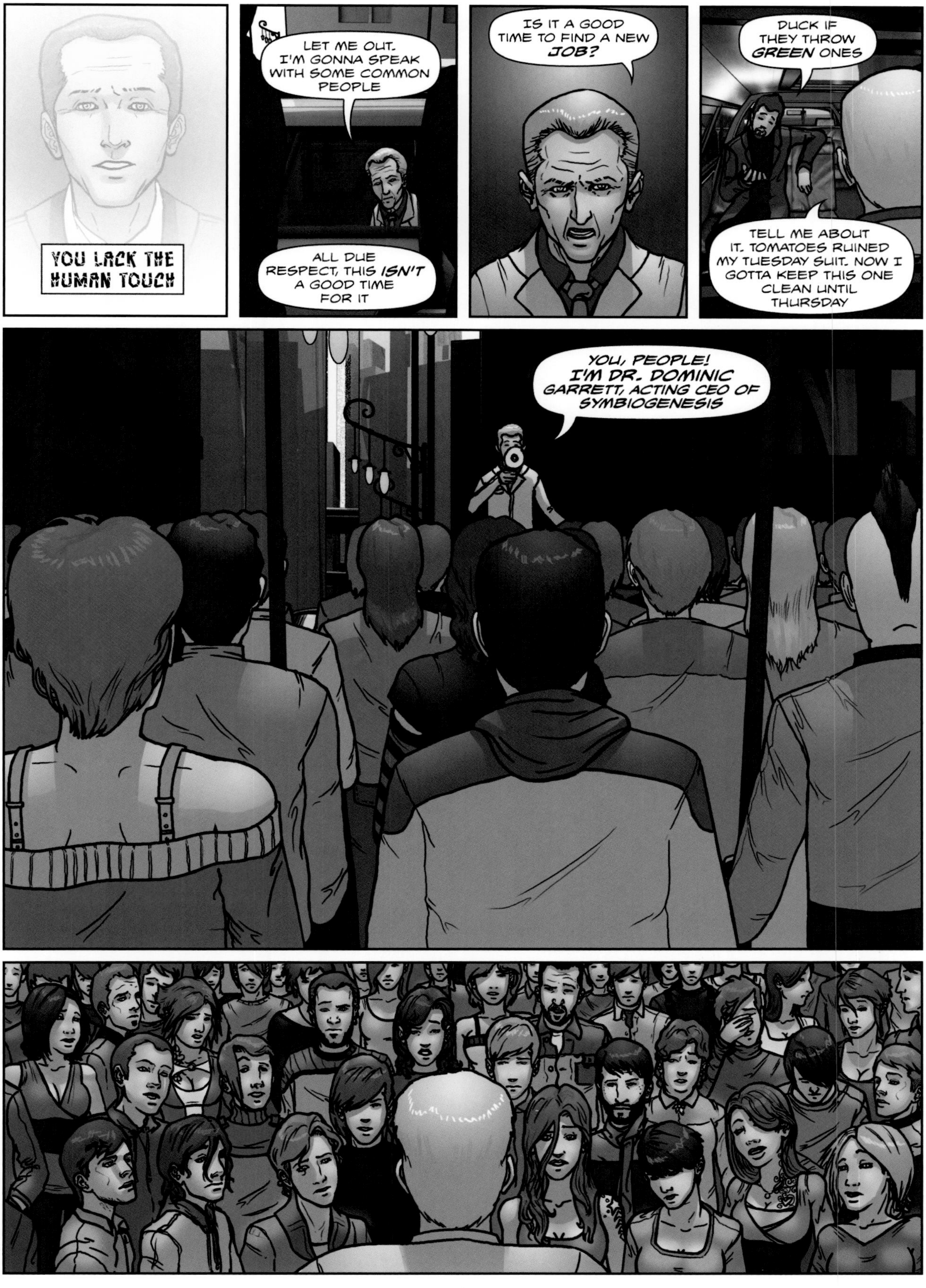
YOU LACK THE HUMAN TOUCH
LET ME OUT. I'M GONNA SPEAK WITH SOME COMMON PEOPLE
ALL DUE RESPECT, THIS ISN'T A GOOD TIME FOR IT
IS IT A GOOD TIME TO FIND A NEW JOB?
DUCK IF THEY THROW GREEN ONES
TELL ME ABOUT IT. TOMATOES RUINED MY TUESDAY SUIT. NOW I GOTTA KEEP THIS ONE CLEAN UNTIL THURSDAY
YOU, PEOPLE! I'M DR. DOMINIC GARRETT, ACTING CEO OF SYMBIOGENESIS

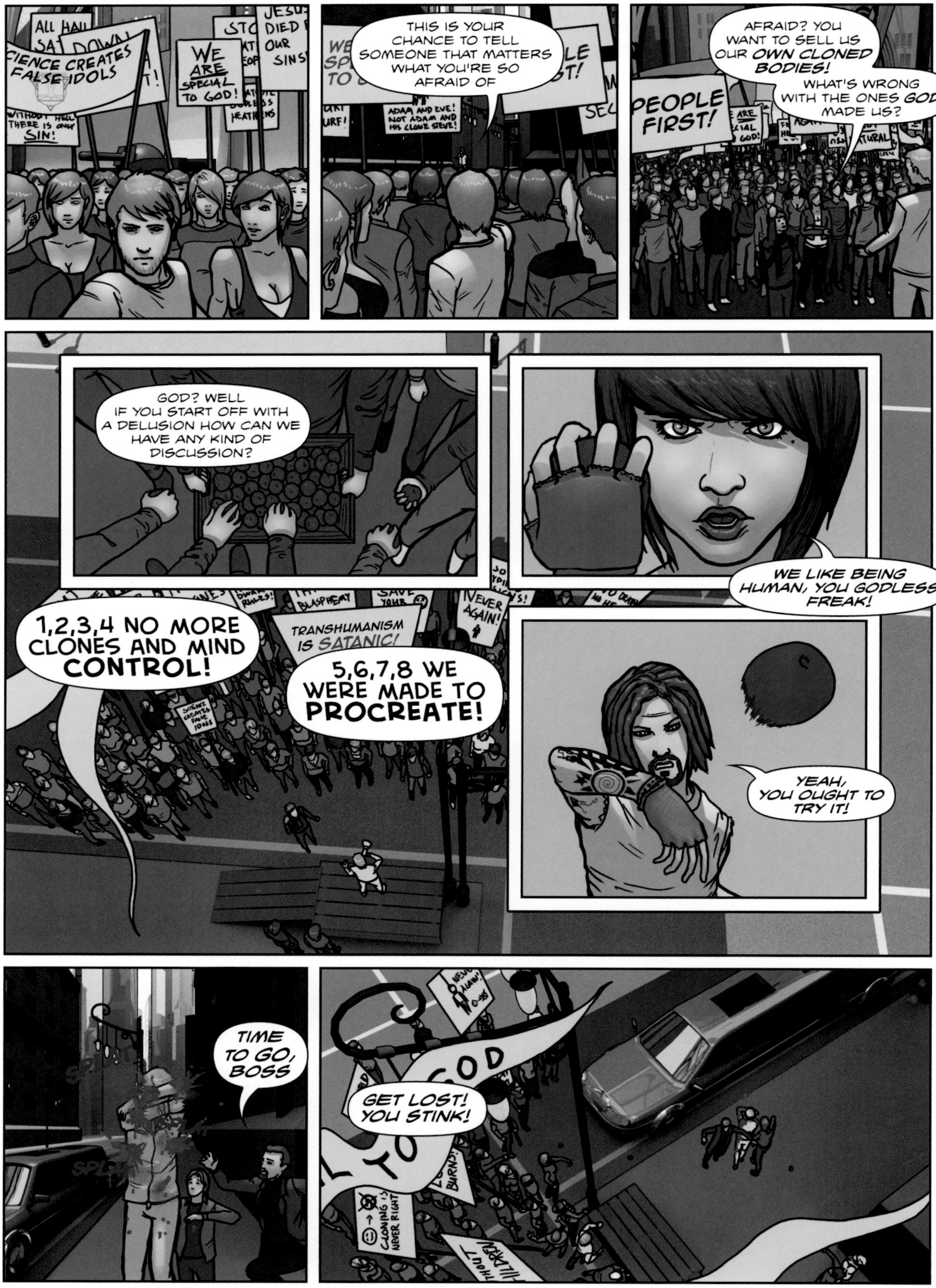
THIS IS YOUR CHANCE TO TELL SOMEONE THAT MATTERS WHAT YOU'RE SO AFRAID OF
AFRAID? YOU WANT TO SELL US OUR OWN CLONED BODIES!
WHAT'S WRONG WITH THE ONES GOD MADE US?
GOD? WELL IF YOU START OFF WITH A DELUSION HOW CAN WE HAVE ANY KIND OF DISCUSSION?
WE LIKE BEING HUMAN, YOU GODLESS FREAK!
1,2,3,4 NO MORE CLONES AND MIND CONTROL!
5,6,7,8 WE WERE MADE TO PROCREATE!
YEAH, YOU OUGHT TO TRY IT!
TIME TO GO, BOSS
GET LOST! YOU STINK!

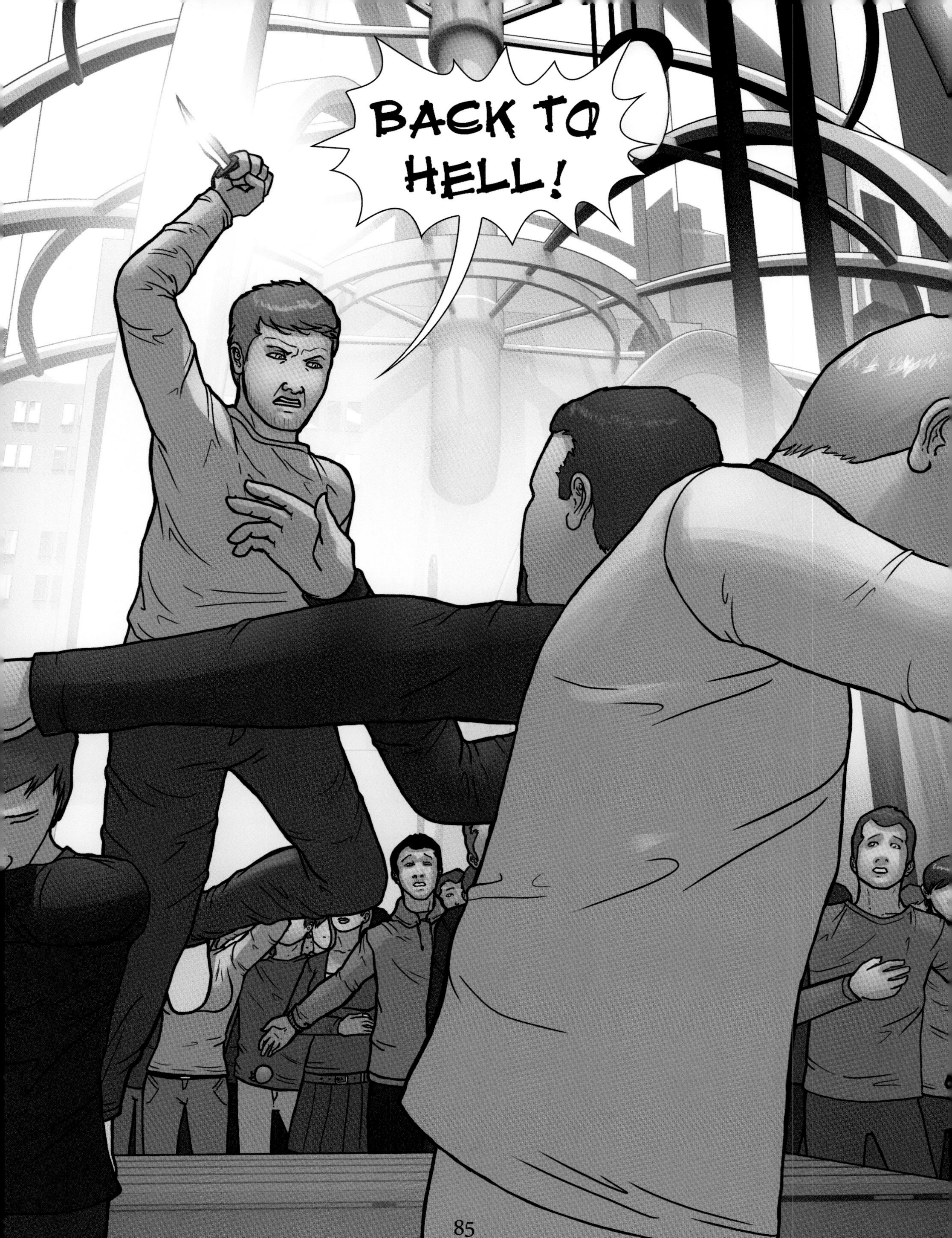
BACK TO HELL!

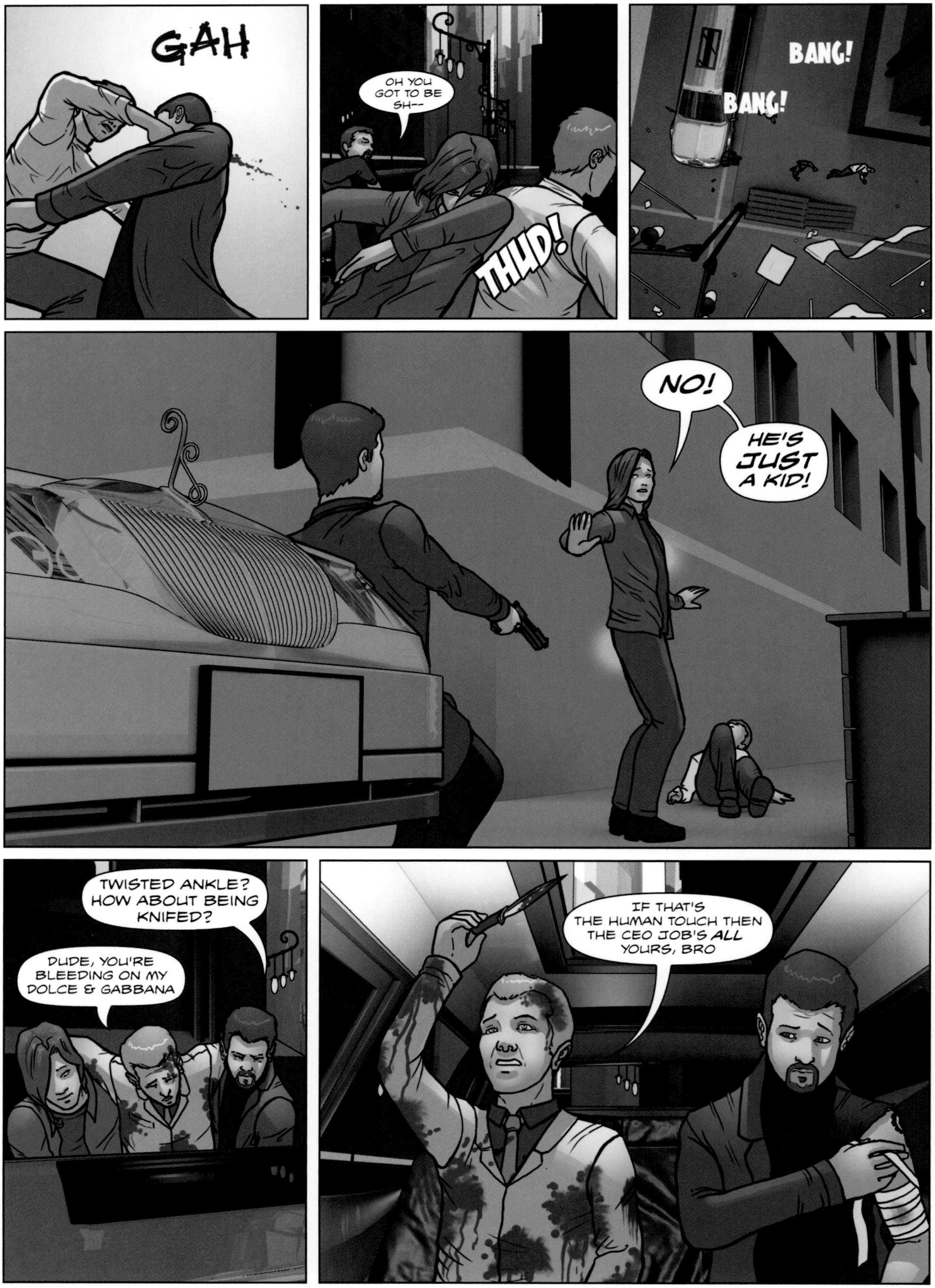
GAH
OH YOU GOT TO BE SH--
THUD!
BANG!
BANG!
NO!
HE'S JUST A KID!
TWISTED ANKLE? HOW ABOUT BEING KNIFED?
DUDE, YOU'RE BLEEDING ON MY DOLCE & GABBANA
IF THAT'S THE HUMAN TOUCH THEN THE CEO JOB'S *ALL* YOURS, BRO

NEAR ROSEMARY'S HOUSE

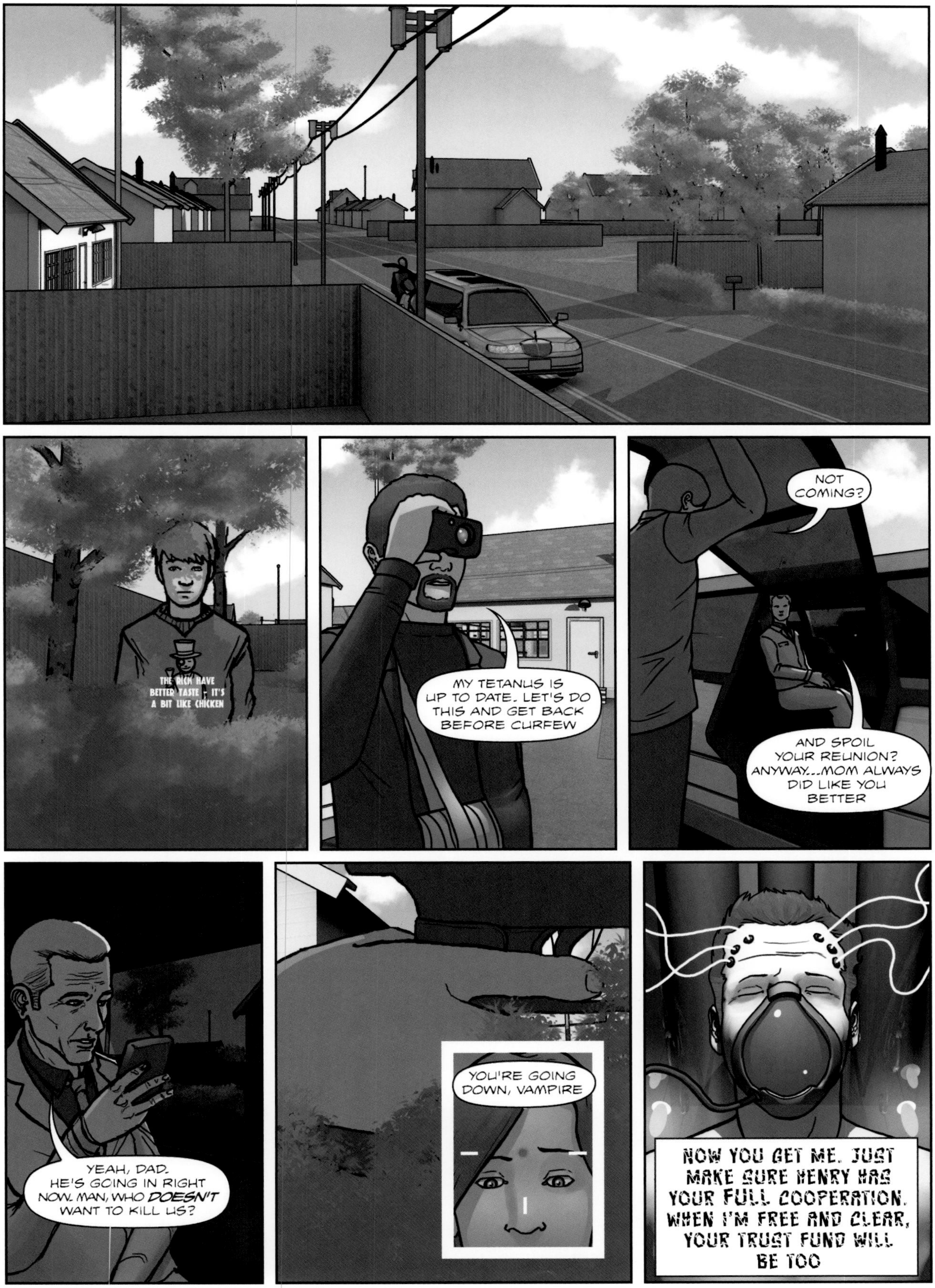
THE RICH HAVE BETTER TASTE - IT'S A BIT LIKE CHICKEN
MY TETANUS IS UP TO DATE. LET'S DO THIS AND GET BACK BEFORE CURFEW
NOT COMING?
AND SPOIL YOUR REUNION? ANYWAY...MOM ALWAYS DID LIKE YOU BETTER
YEAH, DAD. HE'S GOING IN RIGHT NOW. MAN, WHO *DOESN'T* WANT TO KILL US?
YOU'RE GOING DOWN, VAMPIRE
NOW YOU GET ME. JUST MAKE SURE HENRY HAS YOUR FULL COOPERATION. WHEN I'M FREE AND CLEAR, YOUR TRUST FUND WILL BE TOO

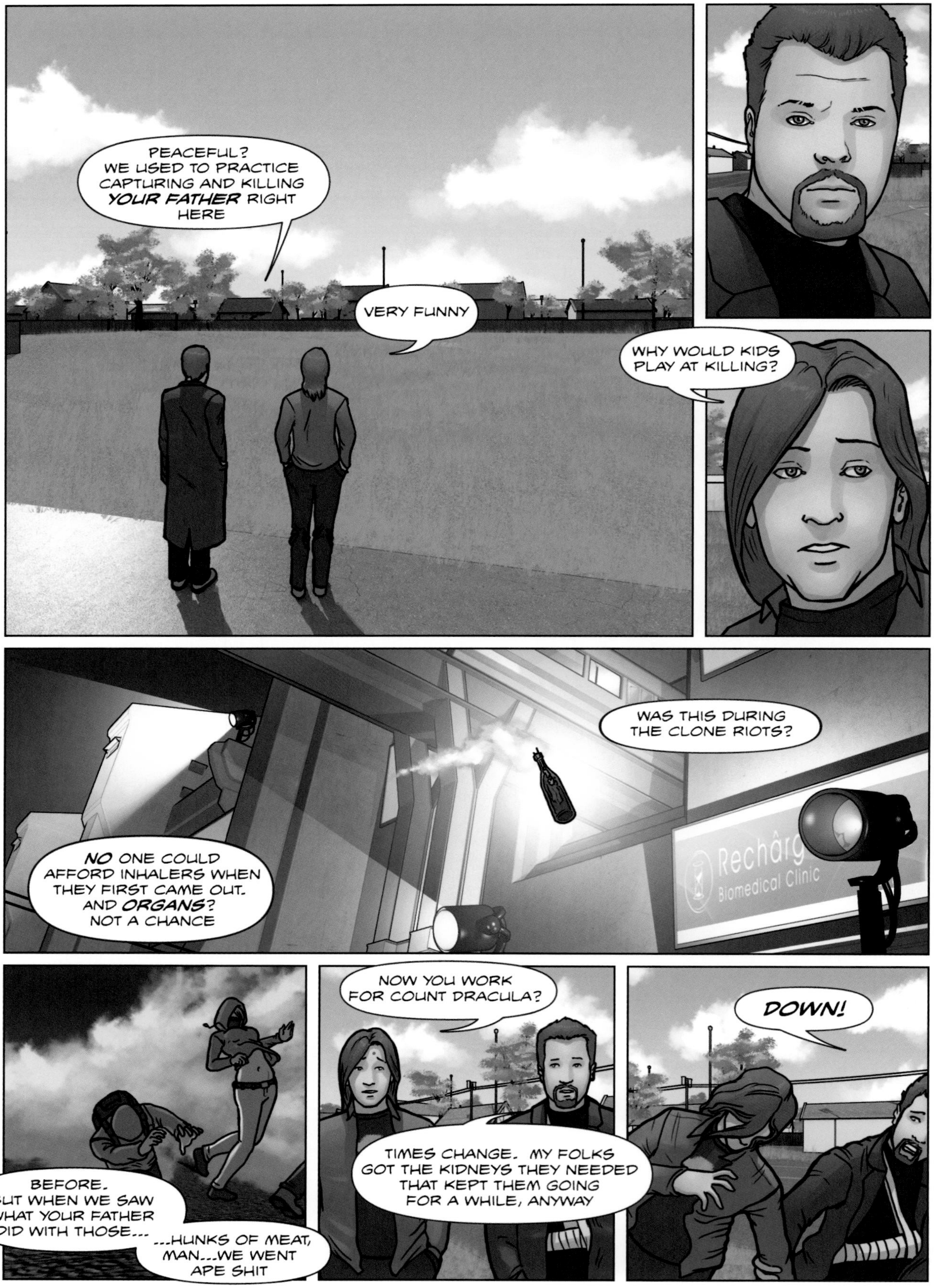
PEACEFUL? WE USED TO PRACTICE CAPTURING AND KILLING YOUR FATHER RIGHT HERE
VERY FUNNY
WHY WOULD KIDS PLAY AT KILLING?
WAS THIS DURING THE CLONE RIOTS?
NO ONE COULD AFFORD INHALERS WHEN THEY FIRST CAME OUT. AND ORGANS? NOT A CHANCE
Biomedical Clinic
BEFORE. BUT WHEN WE SAW WHAT YOUR FATHER DID WITH THOSE...
...HUNKS OF MEAT, MAN...WE WENT APE SHIT
NOW YOU WORK FOR COUNT DRACULA?
TIMES CHANGE. MY FOLKS GOT THE KIDNEYS THEY NEEDED THAT KEPT THEM GOING FOR A WHILE, ANYWAY
DOWN!

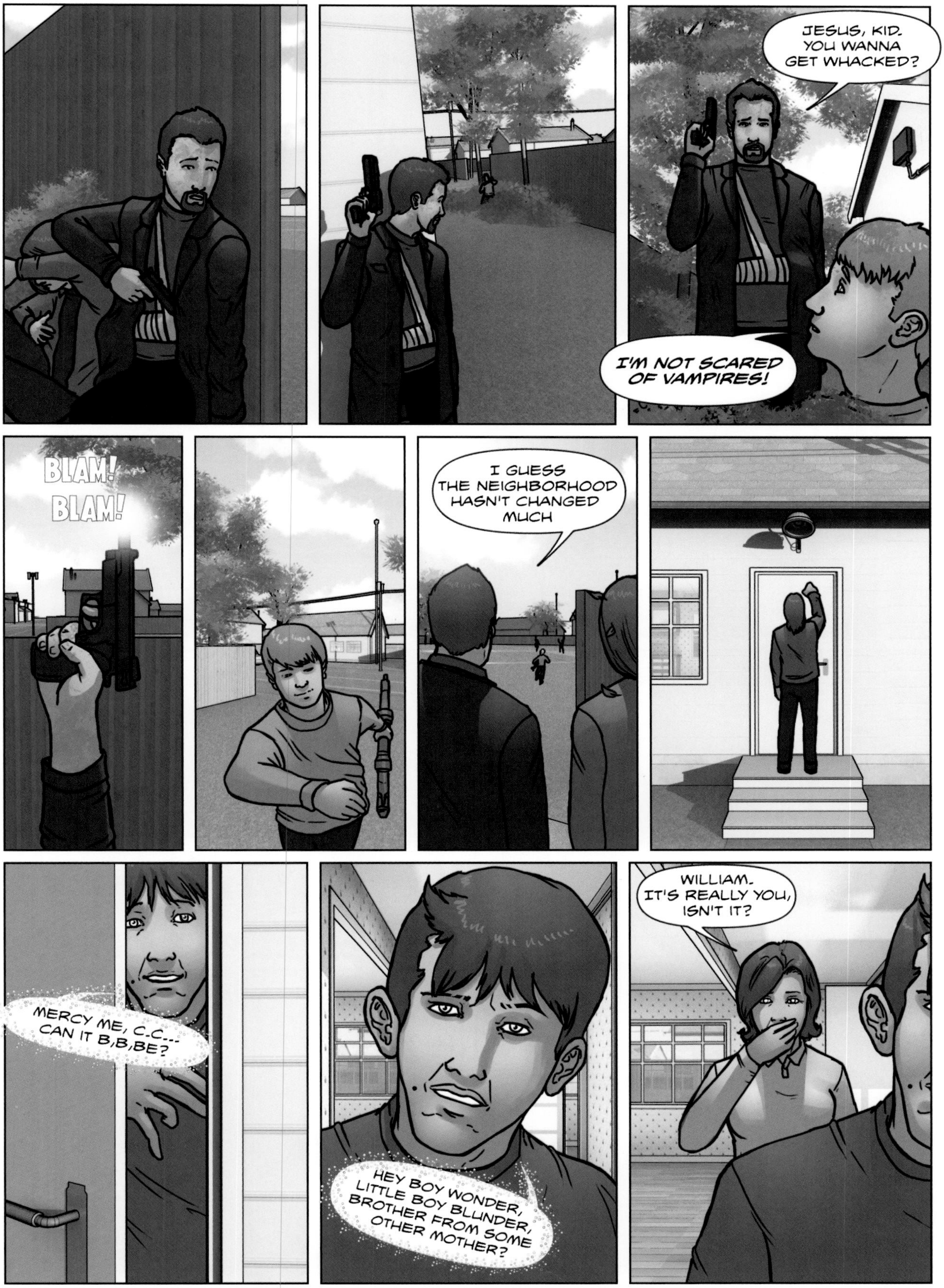
JESUS, KID. YOU WANNA GET WHACKED?
I'M NOT SCARED OF VAMPIRES!
BLAM!
BLAM!
I GUESS THE NEIGHBORHOOD HASN'T CHANGED MUCH
MERCY ME, C.C... CAN IT B,B,BE?
HEY BOY WONDER, LITTLE BOY BLUNDER, BROTHER FROM SOME OTHER MOTHER?
WILLIAM. IT'S REALLY YOU, ISN'T IT?

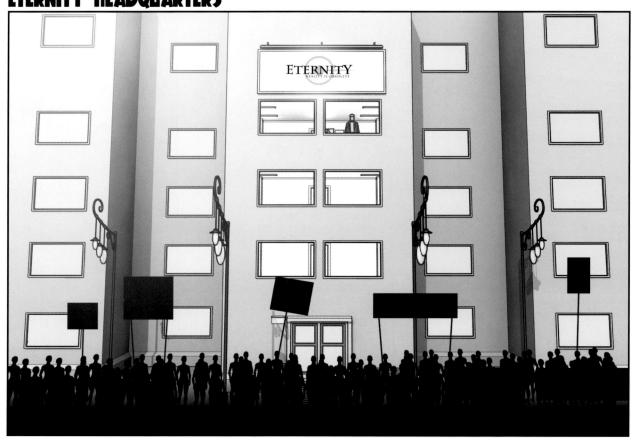

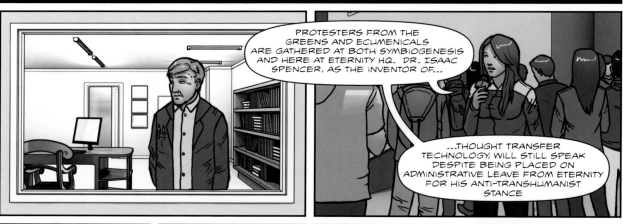

ETERNITY HEADQUARTERS

ETERNITY
REALITY IS OBSOLETE
PROTESTERS FROM THE GREENS AND ECUMENICALS ARE GATHERED AT BOTH SYMBIOGENESIS AND HERE AT ETERNITY HQ. DR. ISAAC SPENCER, AS THE INVENTOR OF...
...THOUGHT TRANSFER TECHNOLOGY, WILL STILL SPEAK DESPITE BEING PLACED ON ADMINISTRATIVE LEAVE FROM ETERNITY FOR HIS ANTI-TRANSHUMANIST STANCE
HOMELAND SECURITY MAY EXTEND THE CURFEWS GIVEN...
...THE BLOGOSPHERE CHATTER AND THE FIRST SURFACE-TO-AIR...
...STRIKE WE'VE SEEN SINCE THE CLONE RIOTS OVER TWO DECADES AGO
NO CLONES!
EVEN CITIES WITHOUT METROPOLIS FORTIFICATION ARE LIMITING ACCESS TO HIGH-VALUE TARGETS

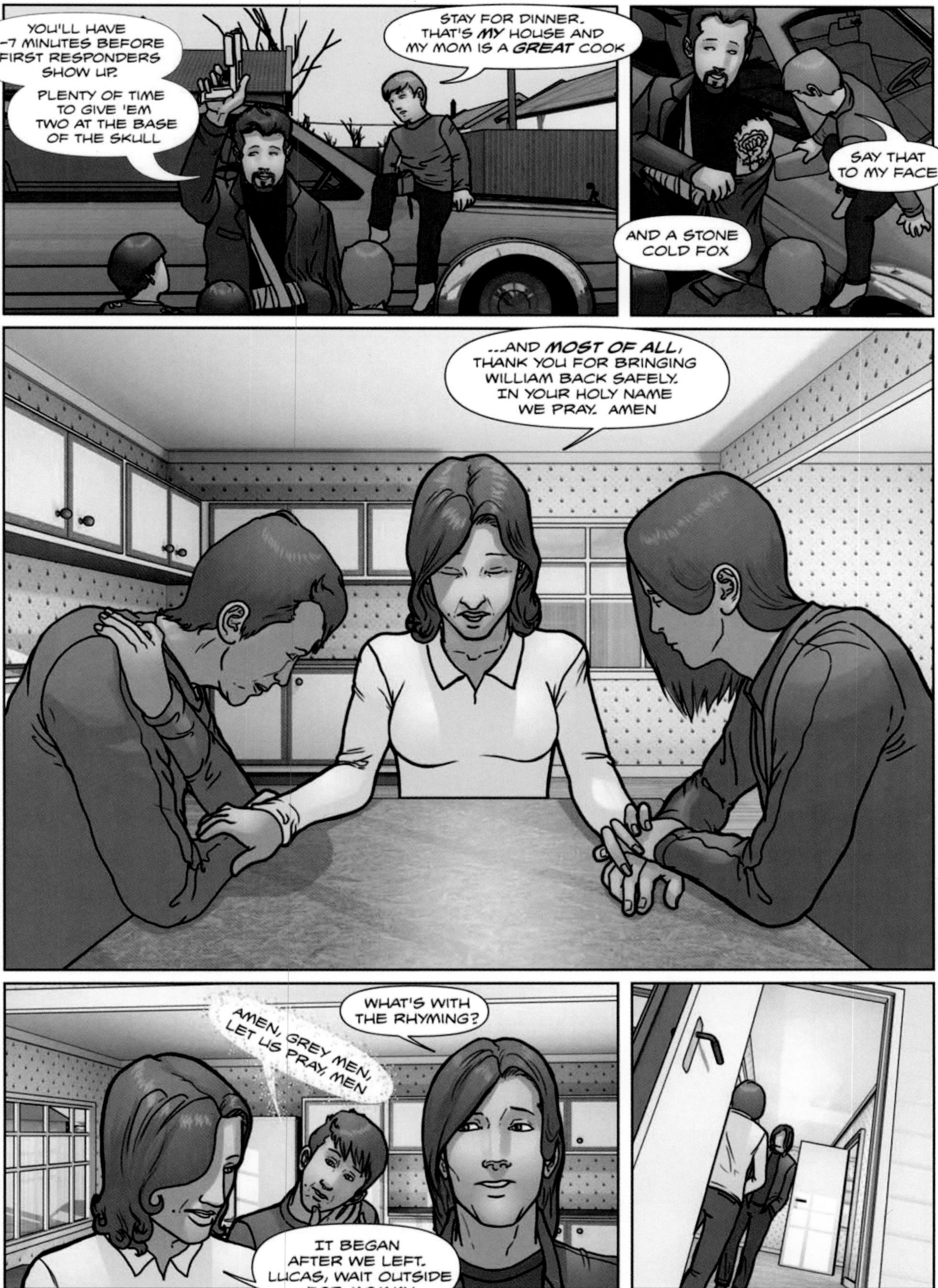

YOU'LL HAVE 5-7 MINUTES BEFORE FIRST RESPONDERS SHOW UP.
PLENTY OF TIME TO GIVE 'EM TWO AT THE BASE OF THE SKULL
STAY FOR DINNER. THAT'S MY HOUSE AND MY MOM IS A GREAT COOK
SAY THAT TO MY FACE
AND A STONE COLD FOX
...AND MOST OF ALL, THANK YOU FOR BRINGING WILLIAM BACK SAFELY. IN YOUR HOLY NAME WE PRAY. AMEN
AMEN, GREY MEN, LET US PRAY, MEN
WHAT'S WITH THE RHYMING?
IT BEGAN AFTER WE LEFT. LUCAS, WAIT OUTSIDE FOR MOMMY

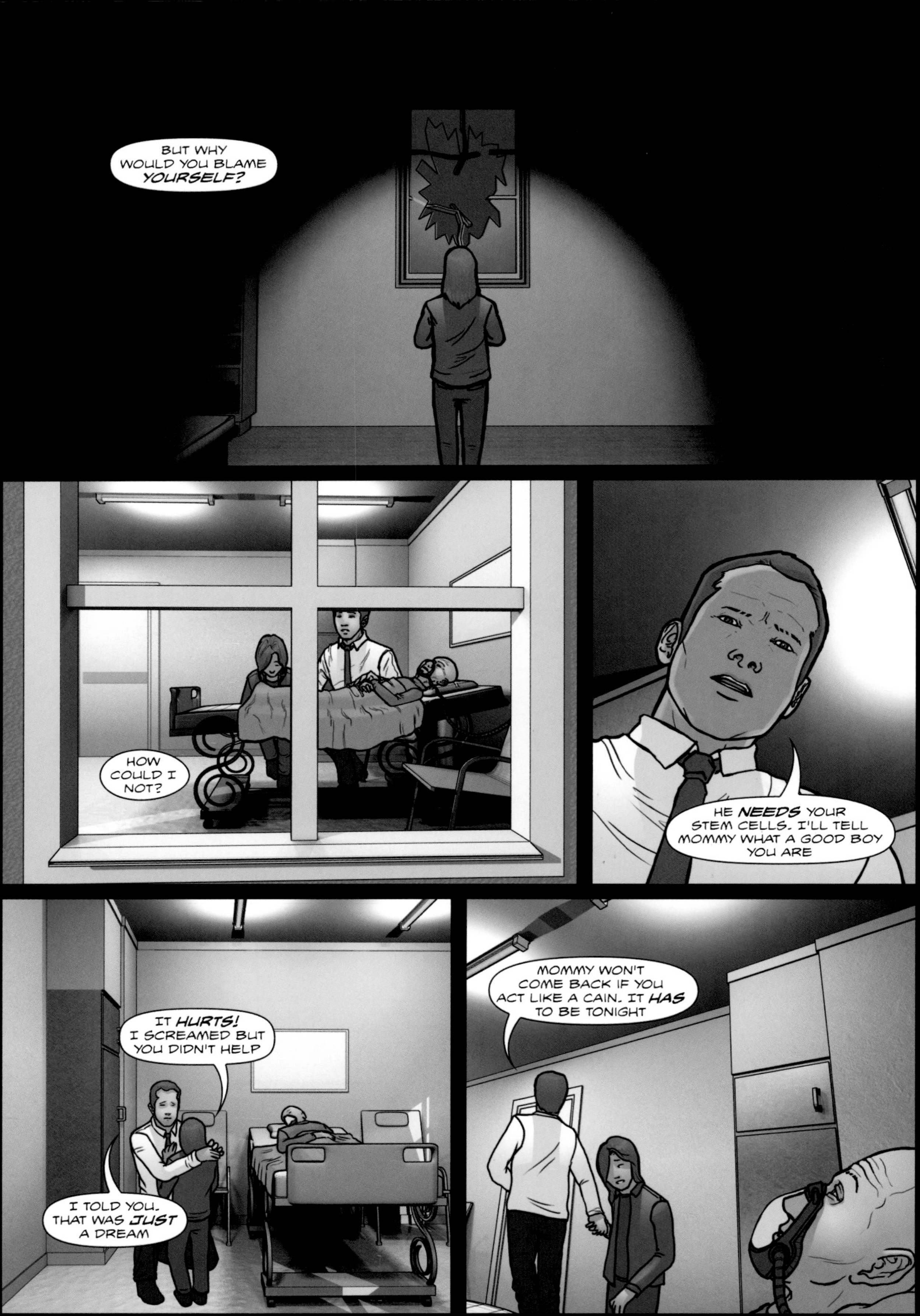
BUT WHY WOULD YOU BLAME *YOURSELF?*
HOW COULD I NOT?
HE *NEEDS* YOUR STEM CELLS. I'LL TELL MOMMY WHAT A GOOD BOY YOU ARE
IT *HURTS!* I SCREAMED BUT YOU DIDN'T HELP
I TOLD YOU. THAT WAS *JUST* A DREAM
MOMMY WON'T COME BACK IF YOU ACT LIKE A CAIN. IT *HAS* TO BE TONIGHT

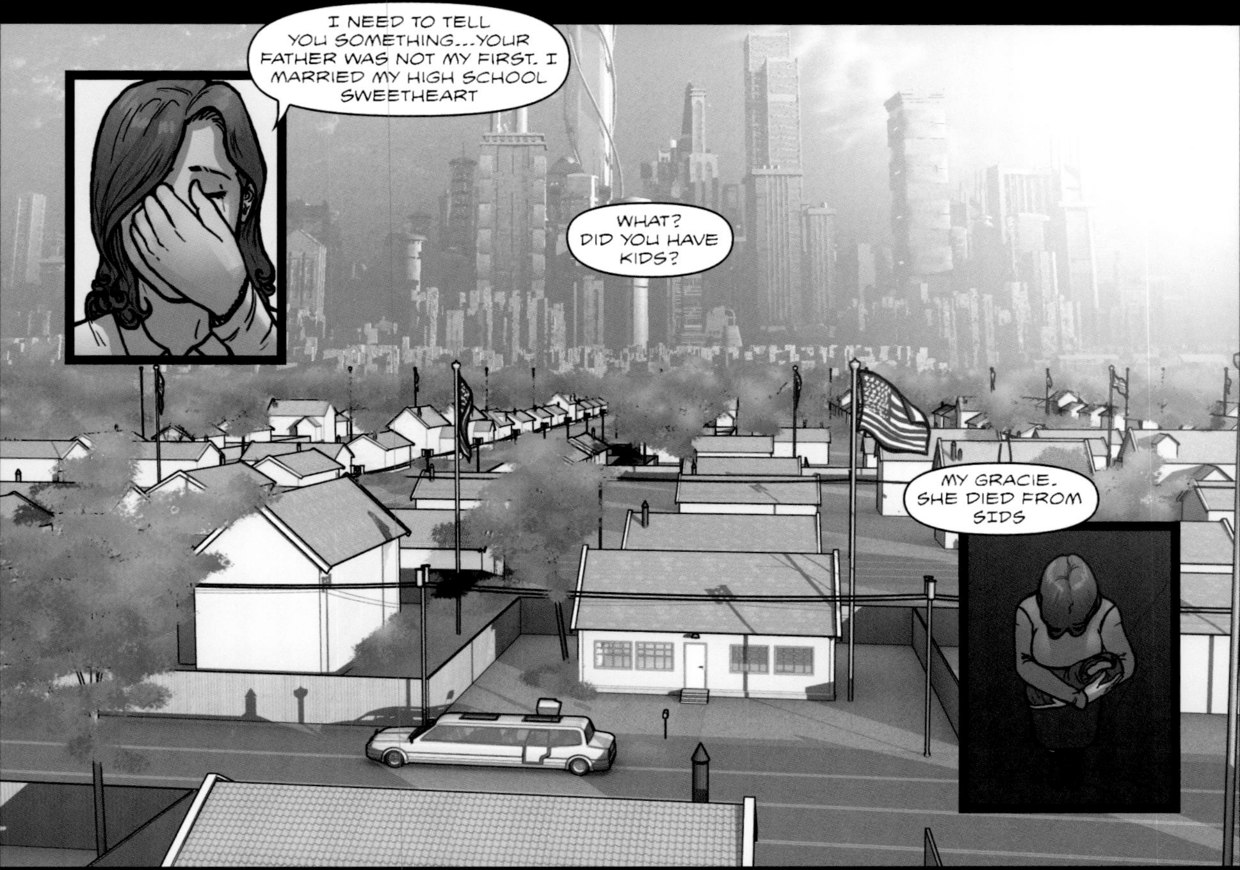
I NEED TO TELL YOU SOMETHING...YOUR FATHER WAS NOT MY FIRST. I MARRIED MY HIGH SCHOOL SWEETHEART
WHAT? DID YOU HAVE KIDS?
MY GRACIE. SHE DIED FROM SIDS

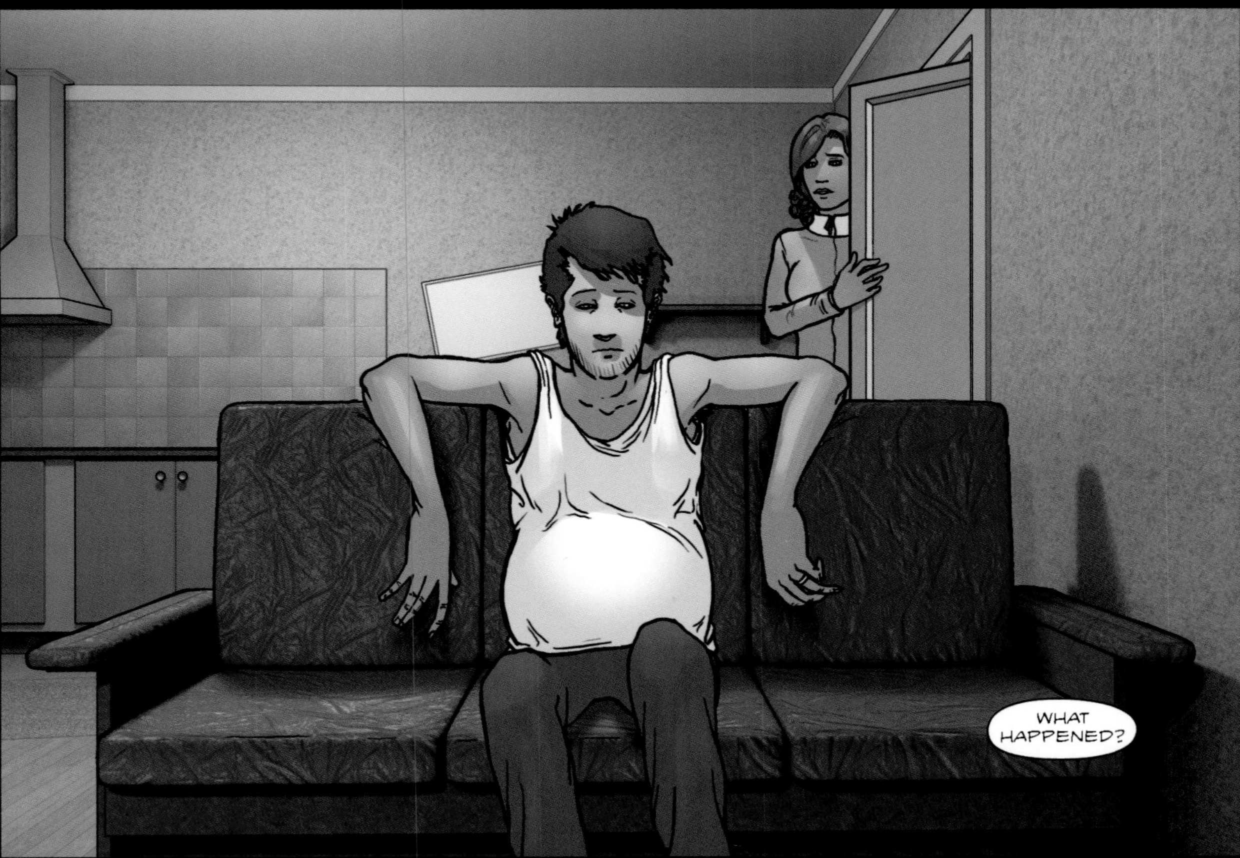
WHAT HAPPENED?

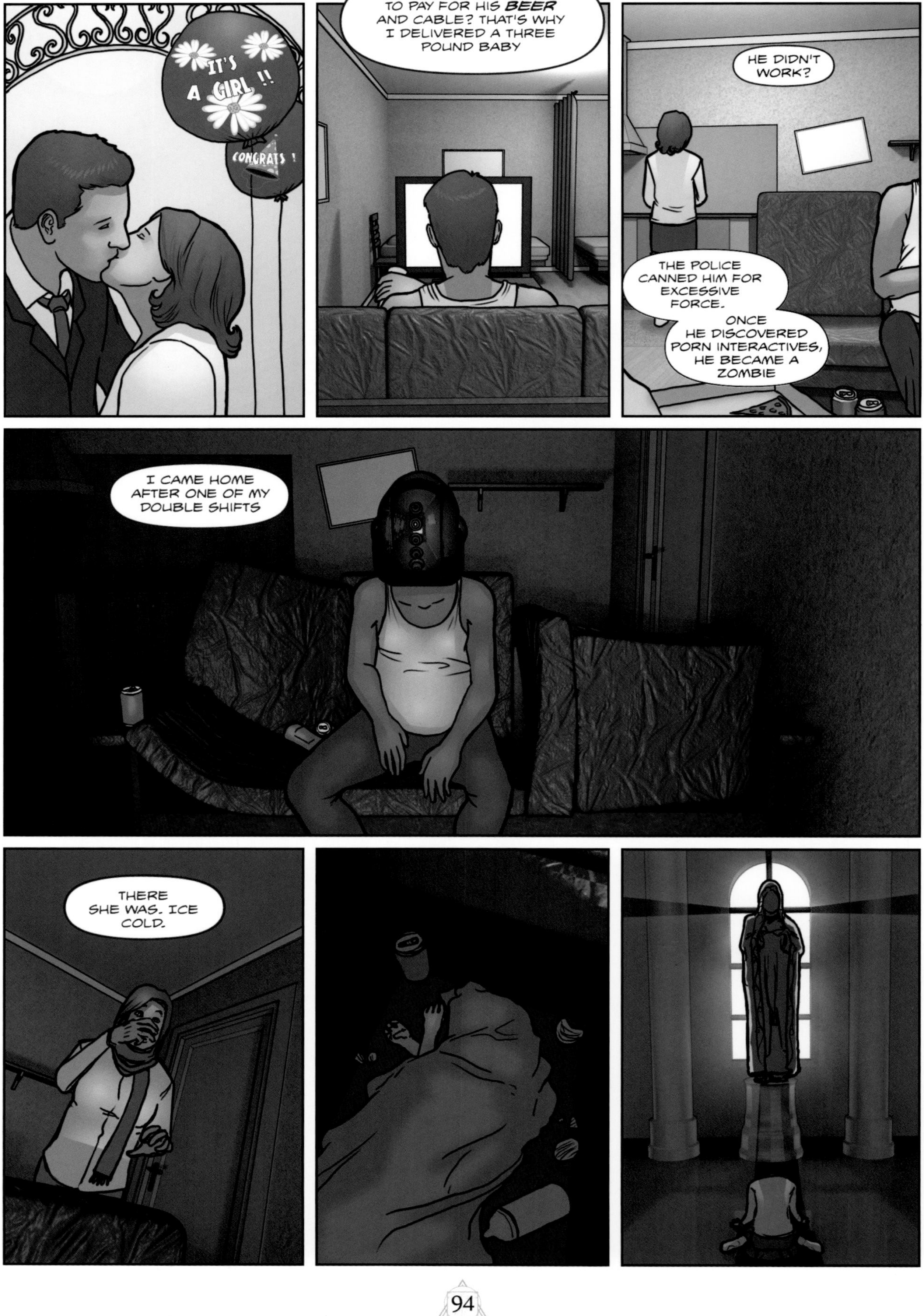
IT'S A GIRL !!
CONGRATS !
DOUBLE SHIFTS TO PAY FOR HIS ***BEER*** AND CABLE? THAT'S WHY I DELIVERED A THREE POUND BABY
HE DIDN'T WORK?
THE POLICE CANNED HIM FOR EXCESSIVE FORCE.
ONCE HE DISCOVERED PORN INTERACTIVES, HE BECAME A ZOMBIE
I CAME HOME AFTER ONE OF MY DOUBLE SHIFTS
THERE SHE WAS. ICE COLD.

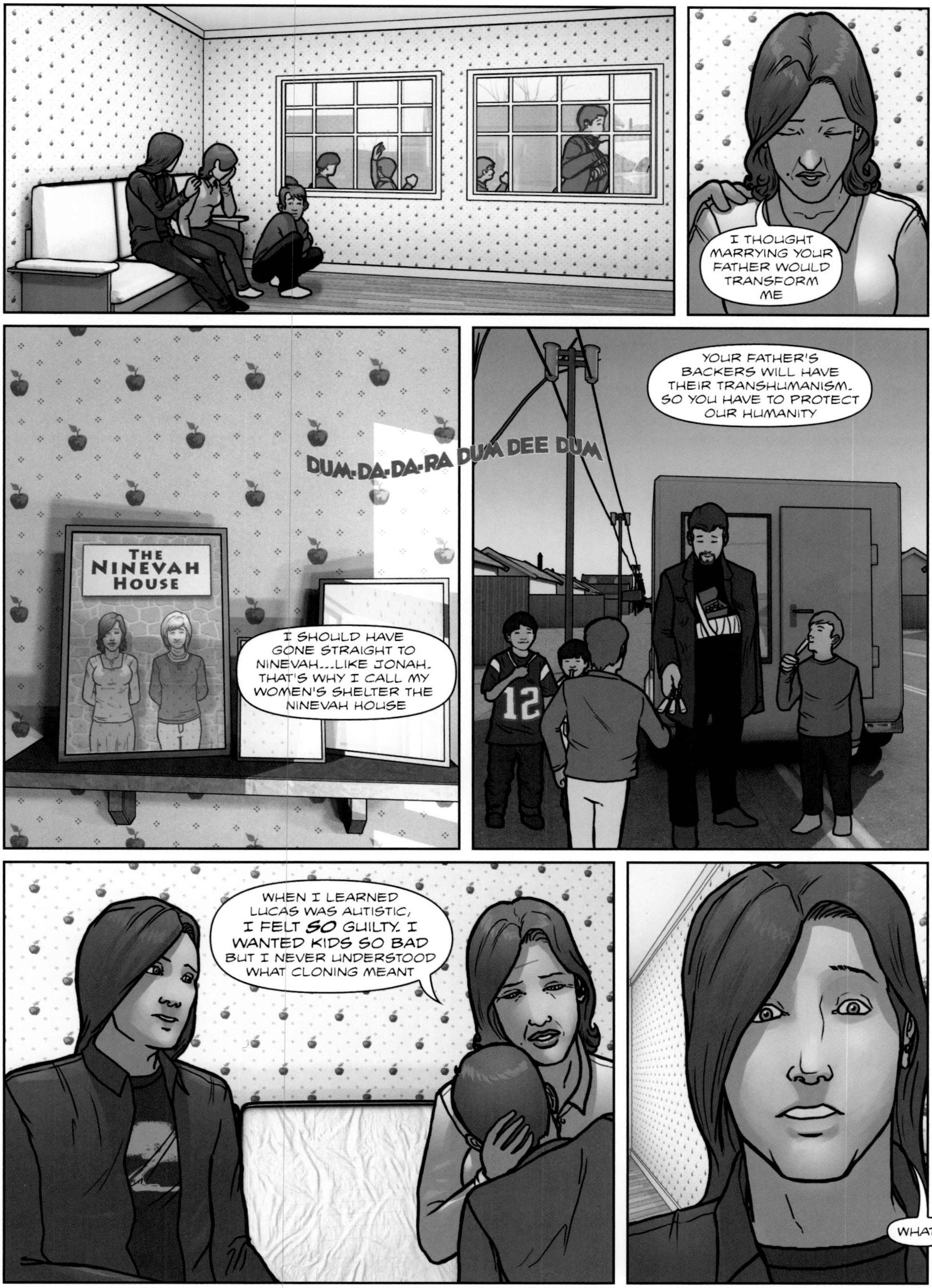
I THOUGHT MARRYING YOUR FATHER WOULD TRANSFORM ME
THE NINEVAH HOUSE
DUM-DA-DA-RA DUM DEE DUM
I SHOULD HAVE GONE STRAIGHT TO NINEVAH...LIKE JONAH. THAT'S WHY I CALL MY WOMEN'S SHELTER THE NINEVAH HOUSE
YOUR FATHER'S BACKERS WILL HAVE THEIR TRANSHUMANISM. SO YOU HAVE TO PROTECT OUR HUMANITY
12
WHEN I LEARNED LUCAS WAS AUTISTIC, I FELT SO GUILTY. I WANTED KIDS SO BAD BUT I NEVER UNDERSTOOD WHAT CLONING MEANT
WHAT?

OH MY GOD, HE *PROMISED* TO TELL YOU IF I AGREED TO DISAPPEAR

TELL ME WHAT?

THAT LUCAS IS MY *CLONE*. ALL EXCEPT KEN'S Y CHROMOSOME. HE ONLY WANTED *SONS* FOR SOME REASON

I FORGET YOU'RE NOT A DOCTOR BECAUSE YOU LOOK SO MUCH LIKE YOUR FATHER

ANYONE EVER TELL YOU HOW MUCH YOU LOOK LIKE HIM?

BUT CLONING WAS *OUTLAWED*

IT WASN'T ENFORCED UNTIL THE PUBLIC FOUND OUT ABOUT THE *LOBOTOMIZED* ONES

-AND BEGAN THE RIOTING

ISN'T THERE ANYTHING *ELSE* YOU WANT TO KNOW?

NO

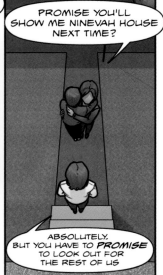

PROMISE YOU'LL SHOW ME NINEVAH HOUSE NEXT TIME?

ABSOLUTELY. BUT YOU HAVE TO *PROMISE* TO LOOK OUT FOR THE REST OF US

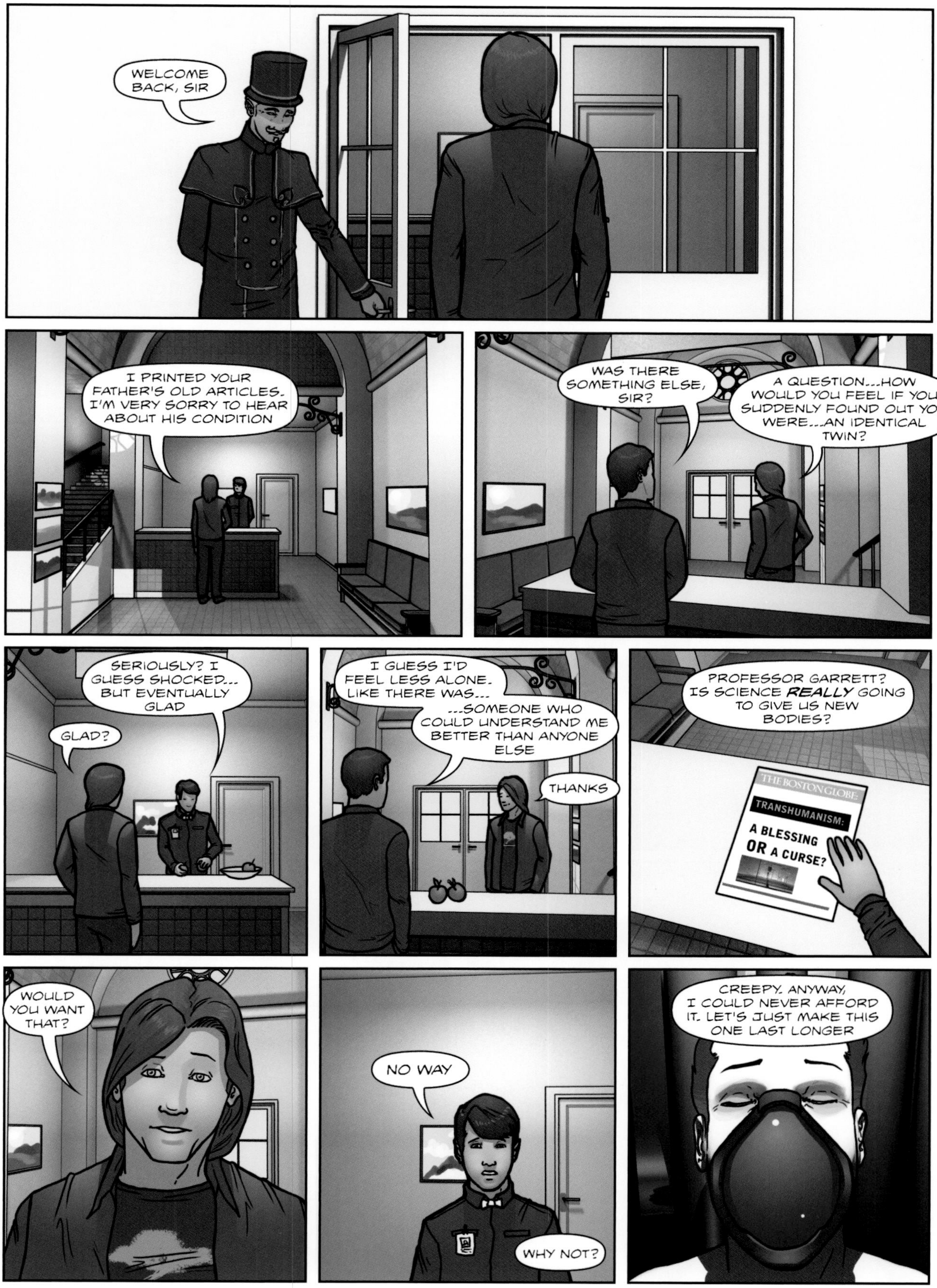
WELCOME BACK, SIR
I PRINTED YOUR FATHER'S OLD ARTICLES. I'M VERY SORRY TO HEAR ABOUT HIS CONDITION
WAS THERE SOMETHING ELSE, SIR?
A QUESTION...HOW WOULD YOU FEEL IF YOU SUDDENLY FOUND OUT YOU WERE...AN IDENTICAL TWIN?
SERIOUSLY? I GUESS SHOCKED... BUT EVENTUALLY GLAD
GLAD?
I GUESS I'D FEEL LESS ALONE. LIKE THERE WAS...
...SOMEONE WHO COULD UNDERSTAND ME BETTER THAN ANYONE ELSE
THANKS
PROFESSOR GARRETT? IS SCIENCE *REALLY* GOING TO GIVE US NEW BODIES?
THE BOSTON GLOBE
TRANSHUMANISM:
A BLESSING OR A CURSE?
WOULD YOU WANT THAT?
NO WAY
WHY NOT?
CREEPY. ANYWAY, I COULD NEVER AFFORD IT. LET'S JUST MAKE THIS ONE LAST LONGER

AGAIN. RUN IT AGAIN

NO HUMAN MATCH

BECAUSE THE *ELEVENTH* TIME WILL BE DIFFERENT? THIS PERSON...WELL, I DON'T THINK HE *IS* ONE

NO HUMAN MA

HERE'S HOW THINGS WORK IN MY WORLD: *I* WANT SOMETHING AND THEN *YOU* DO IT

WHY DON'T I RUN IT AGAIN?

BRRIING

GOOD ANSWER

YOU STILL DON'T GET IT? WHAT IF DIONYSIS AND APHRODITE HAD QUADRUPLETS? TEMPUS FUGIT...FOR ME AND YOUR POOR MOTHER.

DO A SEARCH FOR ME

<Search field:> Dionysis and Aphrodite child

<results field:> Hymen, n. 1. (Class Myth.) Hymen was the son of Dionysis and Aphrodite. He was the god of marriage, and presided over nuptial solemnities

FOUR HYMENS? I'M SUCH AN *IDIOT*! LET ME SIT DOWN

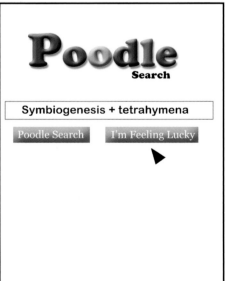

Poodle
Search

Symbiogenesis + tetrahymena

Poodle Search   I'm Feeling Lucky

▶

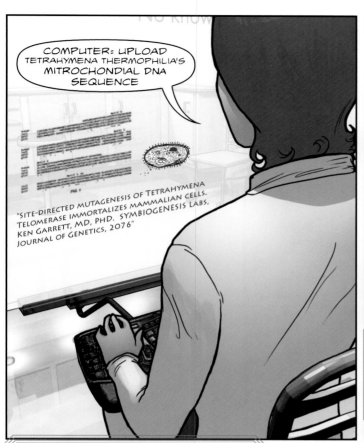

COMPUTER: UPLOAD TETRAHYMENA THERMOPHILIA'S MITROCHONDIAL DNA SEQUENCE

"SITE-DIRECTED MUTAGENESIS OF TETRAHYMENA TELOMERASE IMMORTALIZES MAMMALIAN CELLS. KEN GARRETT, MD, PHD. SYMBIOGENESIS LABS, JOURNAL OF GENETICS, 2076"

COMPUTER: ANALYZE MITOCHONDRIAL DNA OF TETRAHYMENA AND COMPARE WITH KEN GARRETT AND SONS, DOMINIC AND WILL GARRETT

GARRETT, KENNETH: NOT RELATED TO TETRAHYMENA.

CLOSEST ARCHETYPAL MATRIARCH: HAPLOGROUP IS 9TH CENTURY ANGLO-SAXON

GARRETT, DOMINIC: '100% MATCH'
GARRETT, WILLIAM: '65% MATCH'

BUT HOW DID YOU KNOW THEY'D MATCH?

BECAUSE THEIR FATHER WANTED ME TO KNOW. AND NOW HE WANTS ME TO TELL HIS SON

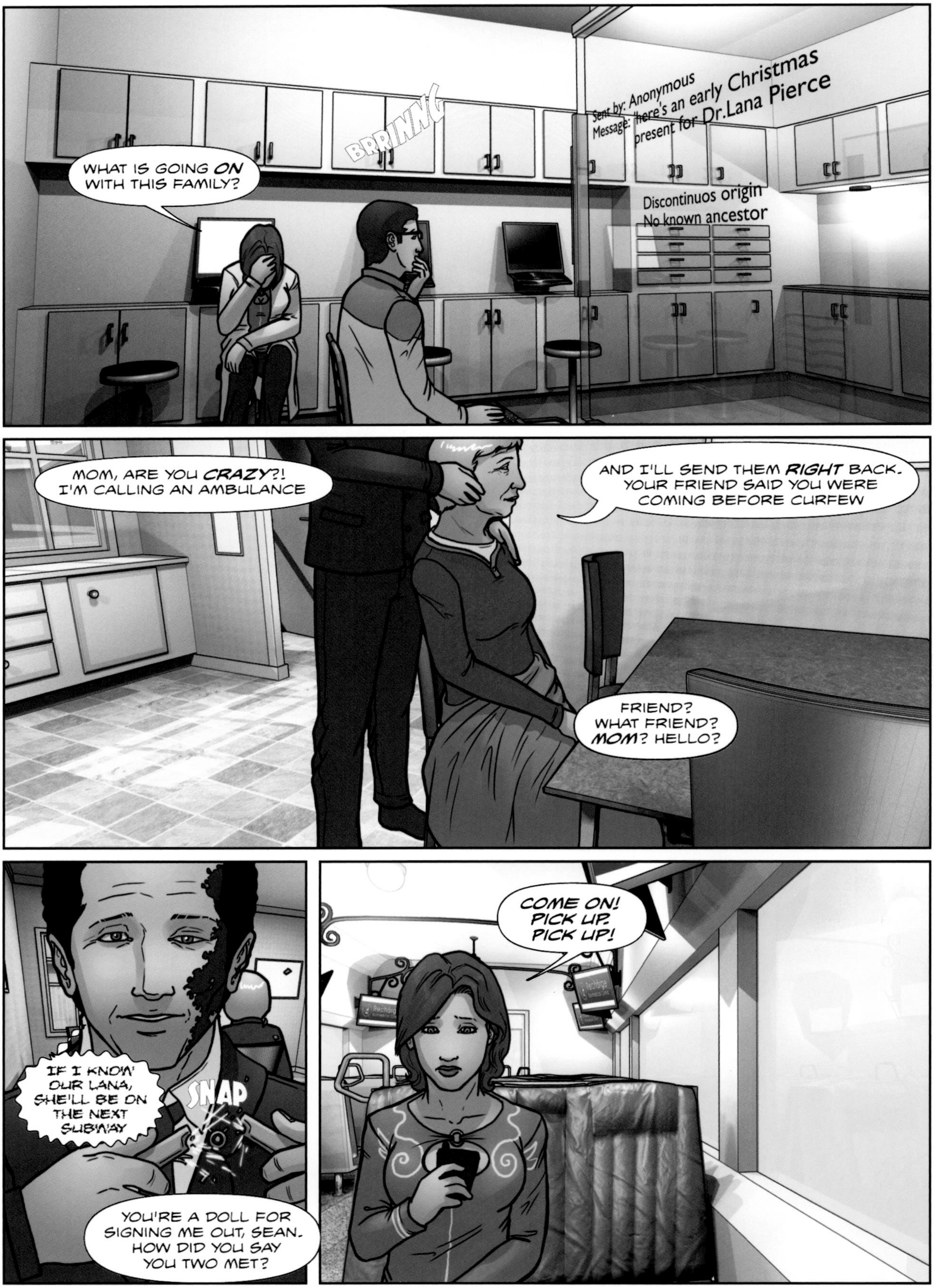

Sent by: Anonymous
Message: 'here's an early Christmas present for Dr.Lana Pierce
BRRINNG
WHAT IS GOING ON WITH THIS FAMILY?
Discontinuos origin
No known ancestor
MOM, ARE YOU CRAZY?! I'M CALLING AN AMBULANCE
AND I'LL SEND THEM RIGHT BACK. YOUR FRIEND SAID YOU WERE COMING BEFORE CURFEW
FRIEND? WHAT FRIEND? MOM? HELLO?
IF I KNOW OUR LANA, SHE'LL BE ON THE NEXT SUBWAY
SNAP
YOU'RE A DOLL FOR SIGNING ME OUT, SEAN. HOW DID YOU SAY YOU TWO MET?
COME ON! PICK UP. PICK UP!

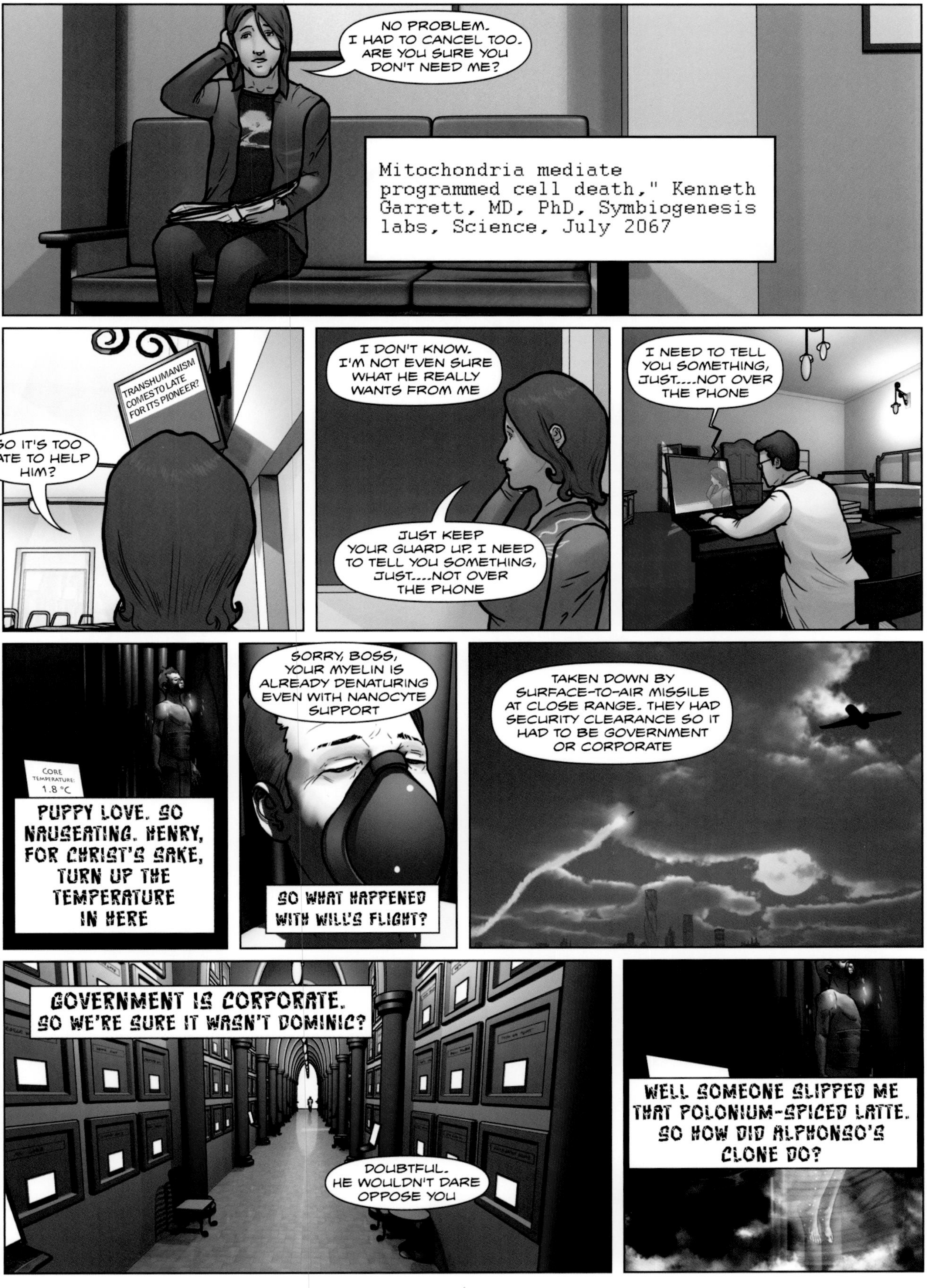

NO PROBLEM. I HAD TO CANCEL TOO. ARE YOU SURE YOU DON'T NEED ME?
Mitochondria mediate programmed cell death," Kenneth Garrett, MD, PhD, Symbiogenesis labs, Science, July 2067
TRANSHUMANISM COMES TO LATE FOR ITS PIONEER?
SO IT'S TOO LATE TO HELP HIM?
I DON'T KNOW. I'M NOT EVEN SURE WHAT HE REALLY WANTS FROM ME
JUST KEEP YOUR GUARD UP. I NEED TO TELL YOU SOMETHING, JUST....NOT OVER THE PHONE
I NEED TO TELL YOU SOMETHING, JUST....NOT OVER THE PHONE
CORE TEMPERATURE: 1.8 °C
PUPPY LOVE. SO NAUSEATING. HENRY, FOR CHRIST'S SAKE, TURN UP THE TEMPERATURE IN HERE
SORRY, BOSS, YOUR MYELIN IS ALREADY DENATURING EVEN WITH NANOCYTE SUPPORT
SO WHAT HAPPENED WITH WILL'S FLIGHT?
TAKEN DOWN BY SURFACE-TO-AIR MISSILE AT CLOSE RANGE. THEY HAD SECURITY CLEARANCE SO IT HAD TO BE GOVERNMENT OR CORPORATE
GOVERNMENT IS CORPORATE. SO WE'RE SURE IT WASN'T DOMINIC?
DOUBTFUL. HE WOULDN'T DARE OPPOSE YOU
WELL SOMEONE SLIPPED ME THAT POLONIUM-SPICED LATTE. SO HOW DID ALPHONSO'S CLONE DO?

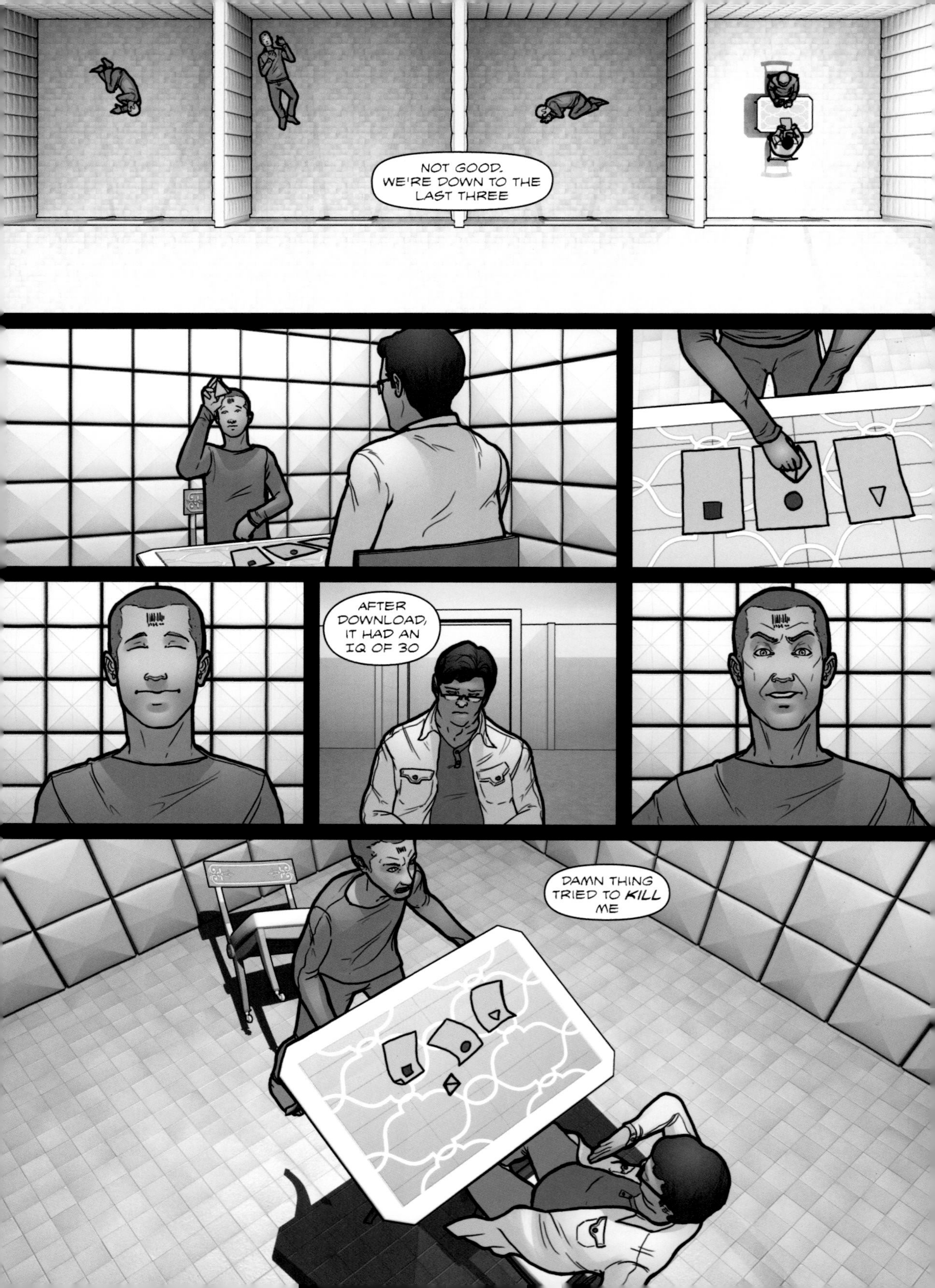
NOT GOOD. WE'RE DOWN TO THE LAST THREE
AFTER DOWNLOAD, IT HAD AN IQ OF 30
DAMN THING TRIED TO *KILL* ME

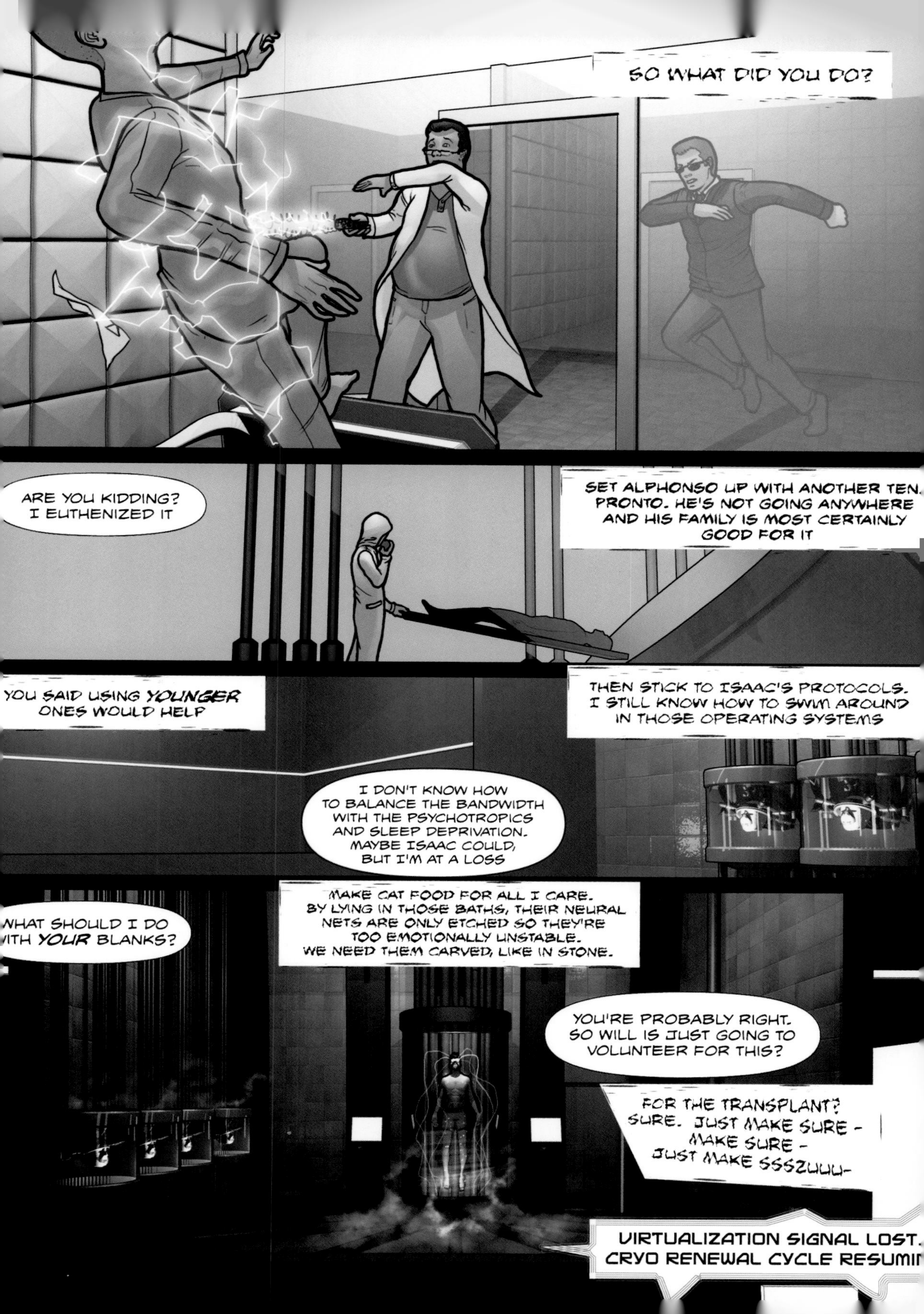
SO WHAT DID YOU DO?
ARE YOU KIDDING? I EUTHENIZED IT
SET ALPHONSO UP WITH ANOTHER TEN. PRONTO. HE'S NOT GOING ANYWHERE AND HIS FAMILY IS MOST CERTAINLY GOOD FOR IT
YOU SAID USING *YOUNGER* ONES WOULD HELP
THEN STICK TO ISAAC'S PROTOCOLS. I STILL KNOW HOW TO SWIM AROUND IN THOSE OPERATING SYSTEMS
I DON'T KNOW HOW TO BALANCE THE BANDWIDTH WITH THE PSYCHOTROPICS AND SLEEP DEPRIVATION. MAYBE ISAAC COULD, BUT I'M AT A LOSS
WHAT SHOULD I DO WITH *YOUR* BLANKS?
MAKE CAT FOOD FOR ALL I CARE. BY LYING IN THOSE BATHS, THEIR NEURAL NETS ARE ONLY ETCHED SO THEY'RE TOO EMOTIONALLY UNSTABLE. WE NEED THEM CARVED, LIKE IN STONE.
YOU'RE PROBABLY RIGHT. SO WILL IS JUST GOING TO VOLUNTEER FOR THIS?
FOR THE TRANSPLANT? SURE. JUST MAKE SURE - MAKE SURE - JUST MAKE SSSZUUU-
VIRTUALIZATION SIGNAL LOST. CRYO RENEWAL CYCLE RESUMI

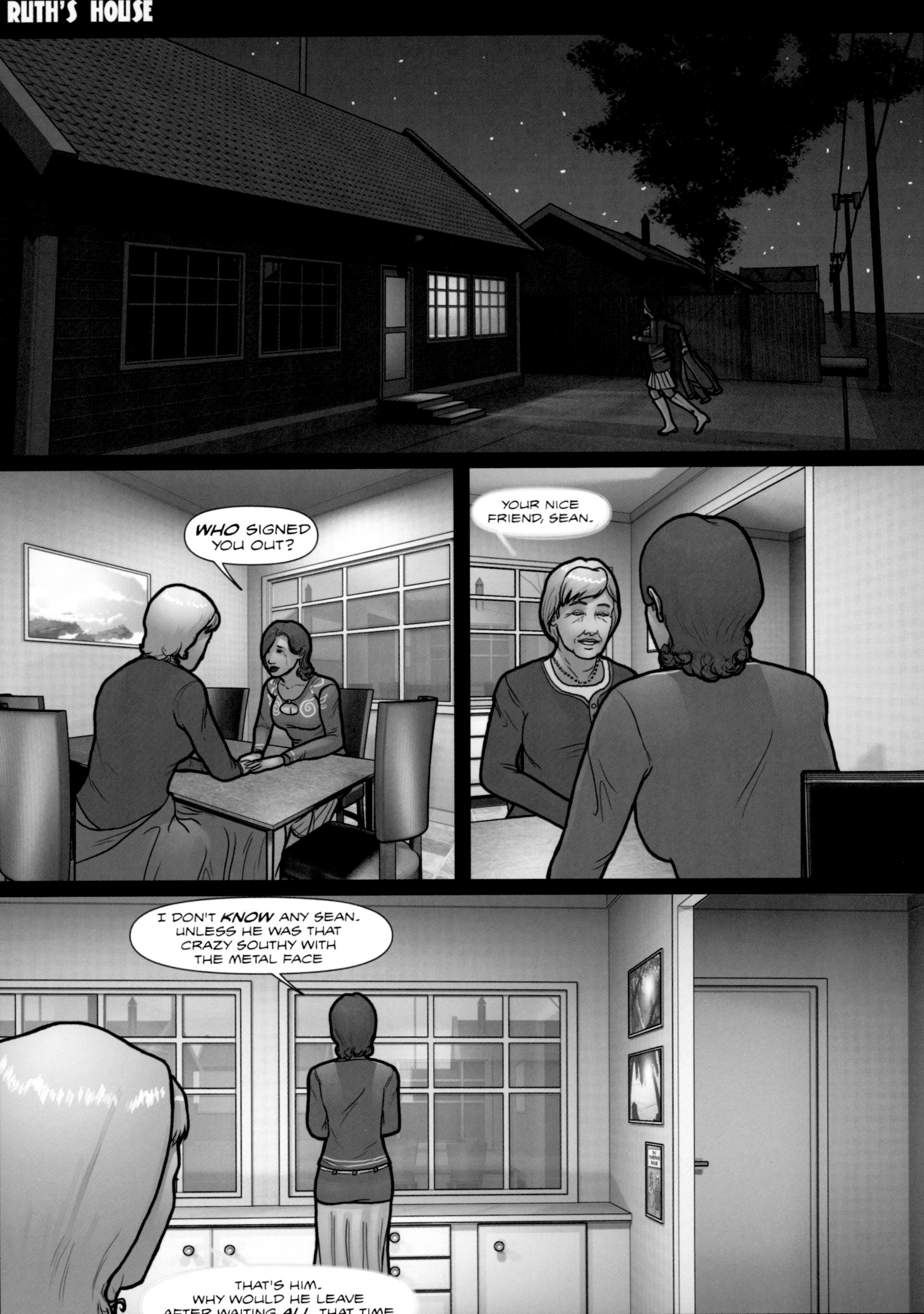
RUTH'S HOUSE
WHO SIGNED YOU OUT?
YOUR NICE FRIEND, SEAN.
I DON'T KNOW ANY SEAN. UNLESS HE WAS THAT CRAZY SOUTHY WITH THE METAL FACE
THAT'S HIM. WHY WOULD HE LEAVE AFTER WAITING ALL THAT TIME

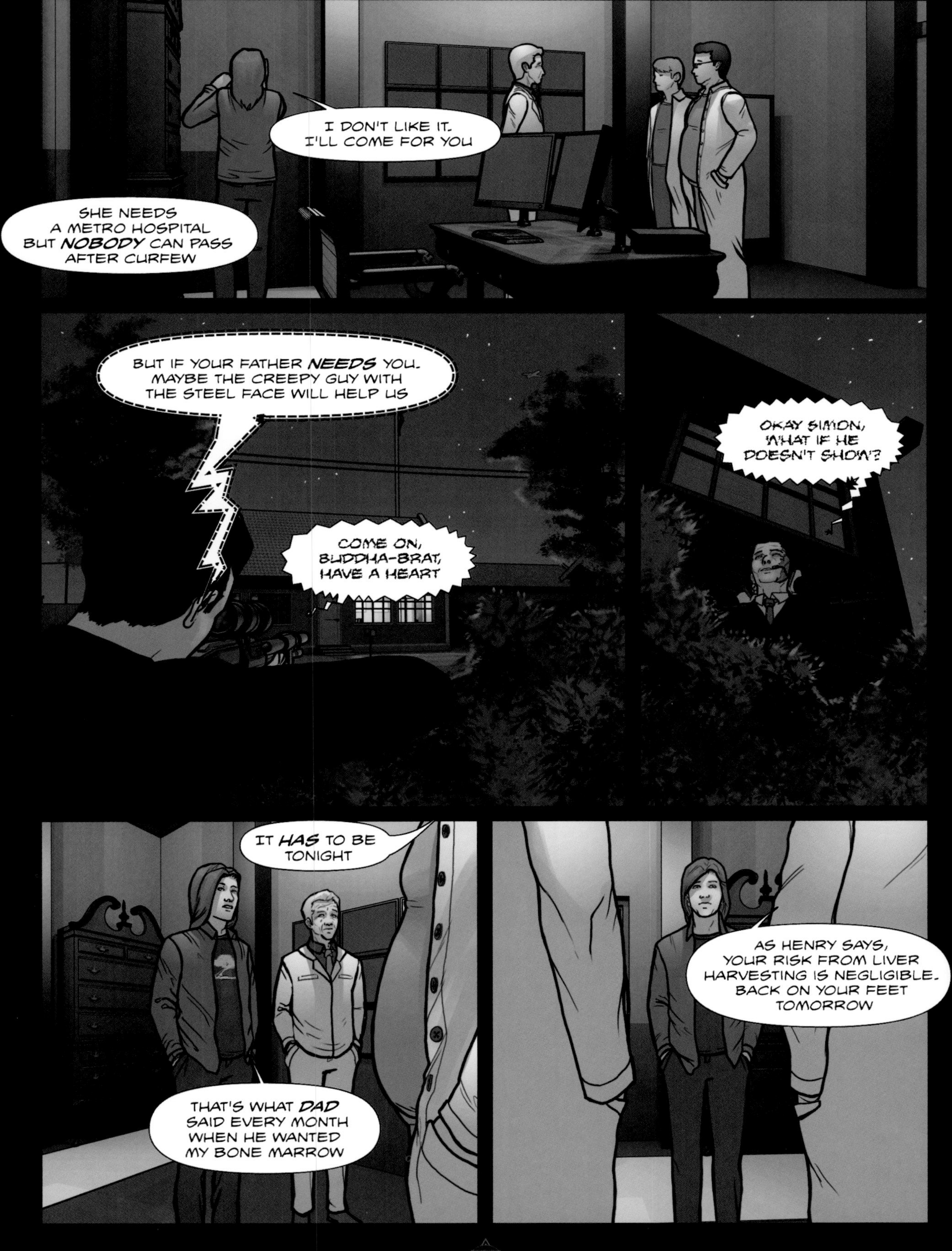
I DON'T LIKE IT. I'LL COME FOR YOU
SHE NEEDS A METRO HOSPITAL BUT NOBODY CAN PASS AFTER CURFEW
BUT IF YOUR FATHER NEEDS YOU. MAYBE THE CREEPY GUY WITH THE STEEL FACE WILL HELP US
COME ON, BUDDHA-BRAT, HAVE A HEART
OKAY SIMON, WHAT IF HE DOESN'T SHOW?
IT HAS TO BE TONIGHT
THAT'S WHAT DAD SAID EVERY MONTH WHEN HE WANTED MY BONE MARROW
AS HENRY SAYS, YOUR RISK FROM LIVER HARVESTING IS NEGLIGIBLE. BACK ON YOUR FEET TOMORROW

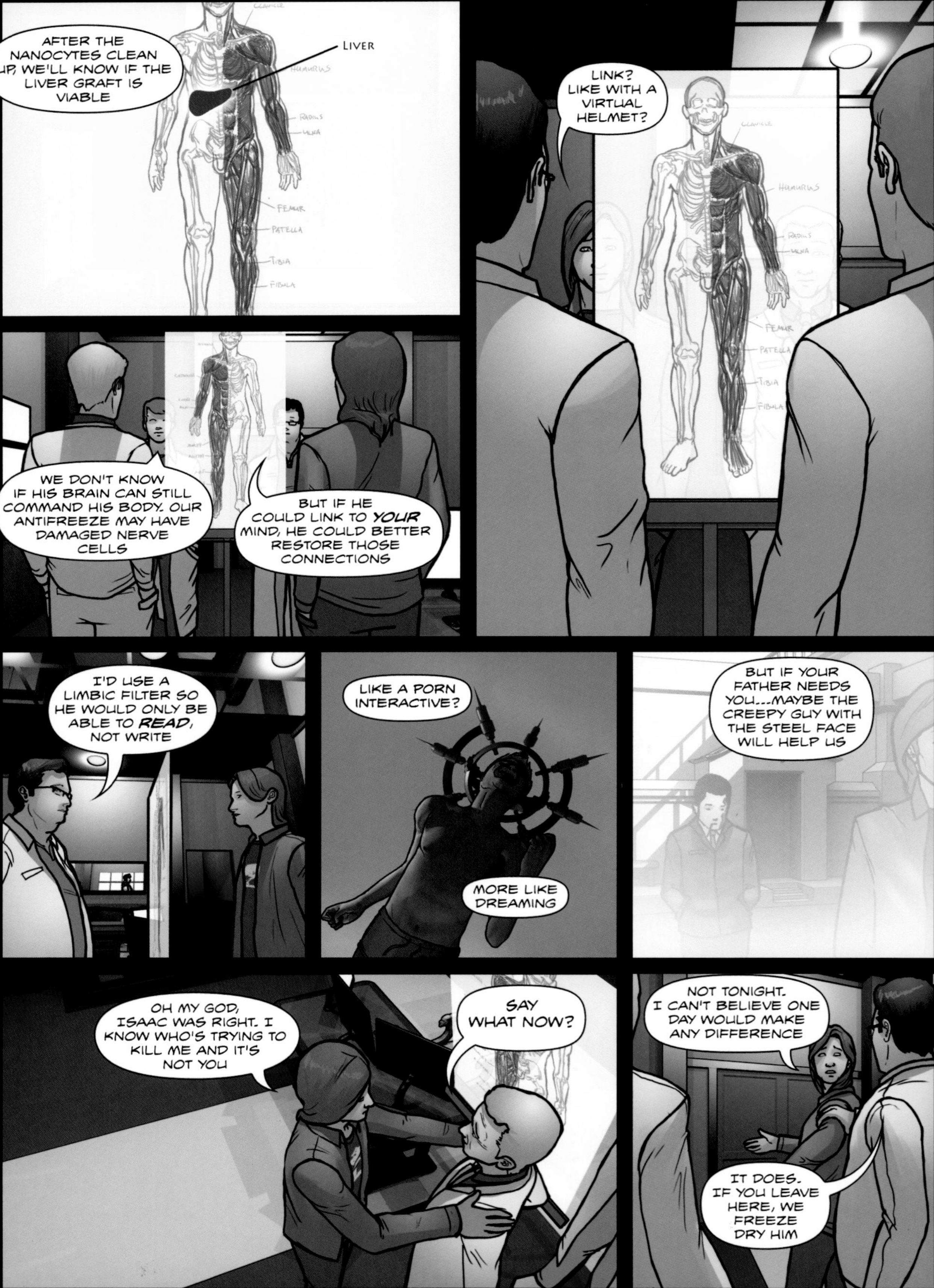
AFTER THE NANOCYTES CLEAN UP, WE'LL KNOW IF THE LIVER GRAFT IS VIABLE
LIVER
LINK? LIKE WITH A VIRTUAL HELMET?
WE DON'T KNOW IF HIS BRAIN CAN STILL COMMAND HIS BODY. OUR ANTIFREEZE MAY HAVE DAMAGED NERVE CELLS
BUT IF HE COULD LINK TO *YOUR* MIND, HE COULD BETTER RESTORE THOSE CONNECTIONS
I'D USE A LIMBIC FILTER SO HE WOULD ONLY BE ABLE TO *READ*, NOT WRITE
LIKE A PORN INTERACTIVE?
MORE LIKE DREAMING
BUT IF YOUR FATHER NEEDS YOU...MAYBE THE CREEPY GUY WITH THE STEEL FACE WILL HELP US
OH MY GOD, ISAAC WAS RIGHT. I KNOW WHO'S TRYING TO KILL ME AND IT'S NOT YOU
SAY WHAT NOW?
NOT TONIGHT. I CAN'T BELIEVE ONE DAY WOULD MAKE ANY DIFFERENCE
IT DOES. IF YOU LEAVE HERE, WE FREEZE DRY HIM

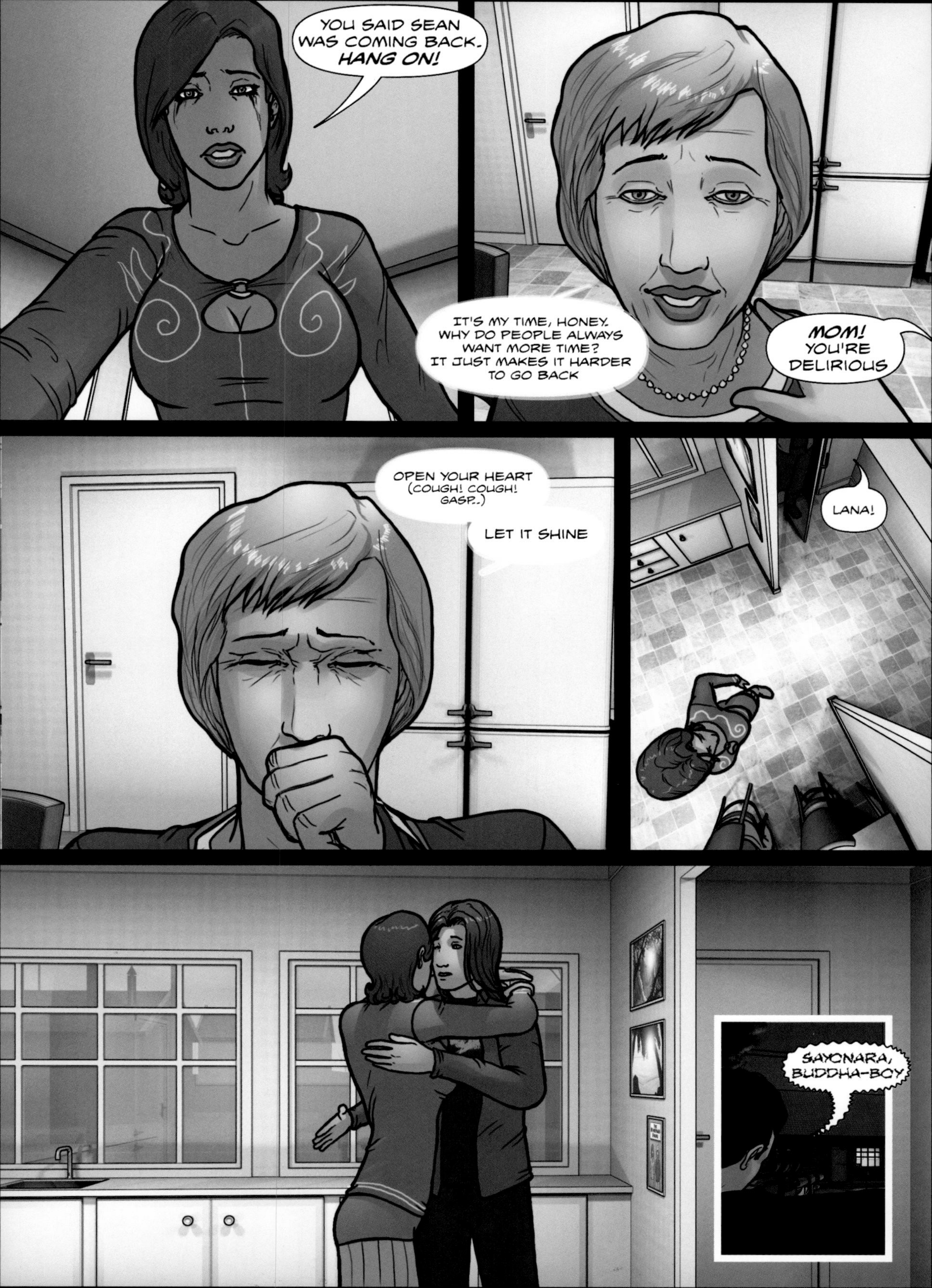
YOU SAID SEAN WAS COMING BACK. HANG ON!
IT'S MY TIME, HONEY. WHY DO PEOPLE ALWAYS WANT MORE TIME? IT JUST MAKES IT HARDER TO GO BACK
MOM! YOU'RE DELIRIOUS
OPEN YOUR HEART (COUGH! COUGH! GASP..)
LET IT SHINE
LANA!
SAYONARA, BUDDHA-BOY

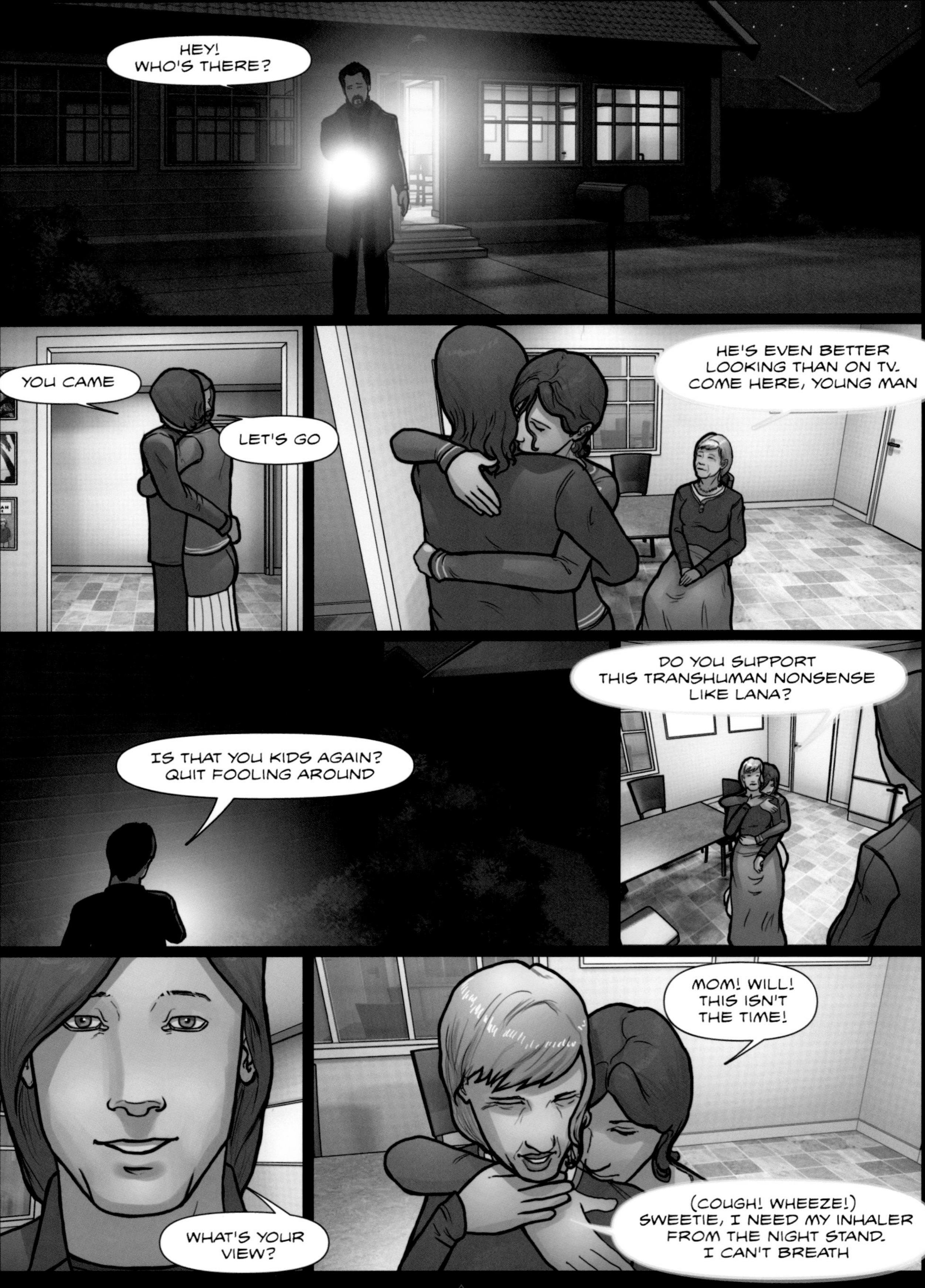
HEY! WHO'S THERE?
YOU CAME
LET'S GO
HE'S EVEN BETTER LOOKING THAN ON TV. COME HERE, YOUNG MAN
IS THAT YOU KIDS AGAIN? QUIT FOOLING AROUND
DO YOU SUPPORT THIS TRANSHUMAN NONSENSE LIKE LANA?
WHAT'S YOUR VIEW?
MOM! WILL! THIS ISN'T THE TIME!
(COUGH! WHEEZE!) SWEETIE, I NEED MY INHALER FROM THE NIGHT STAND. I CAN'T BREATH

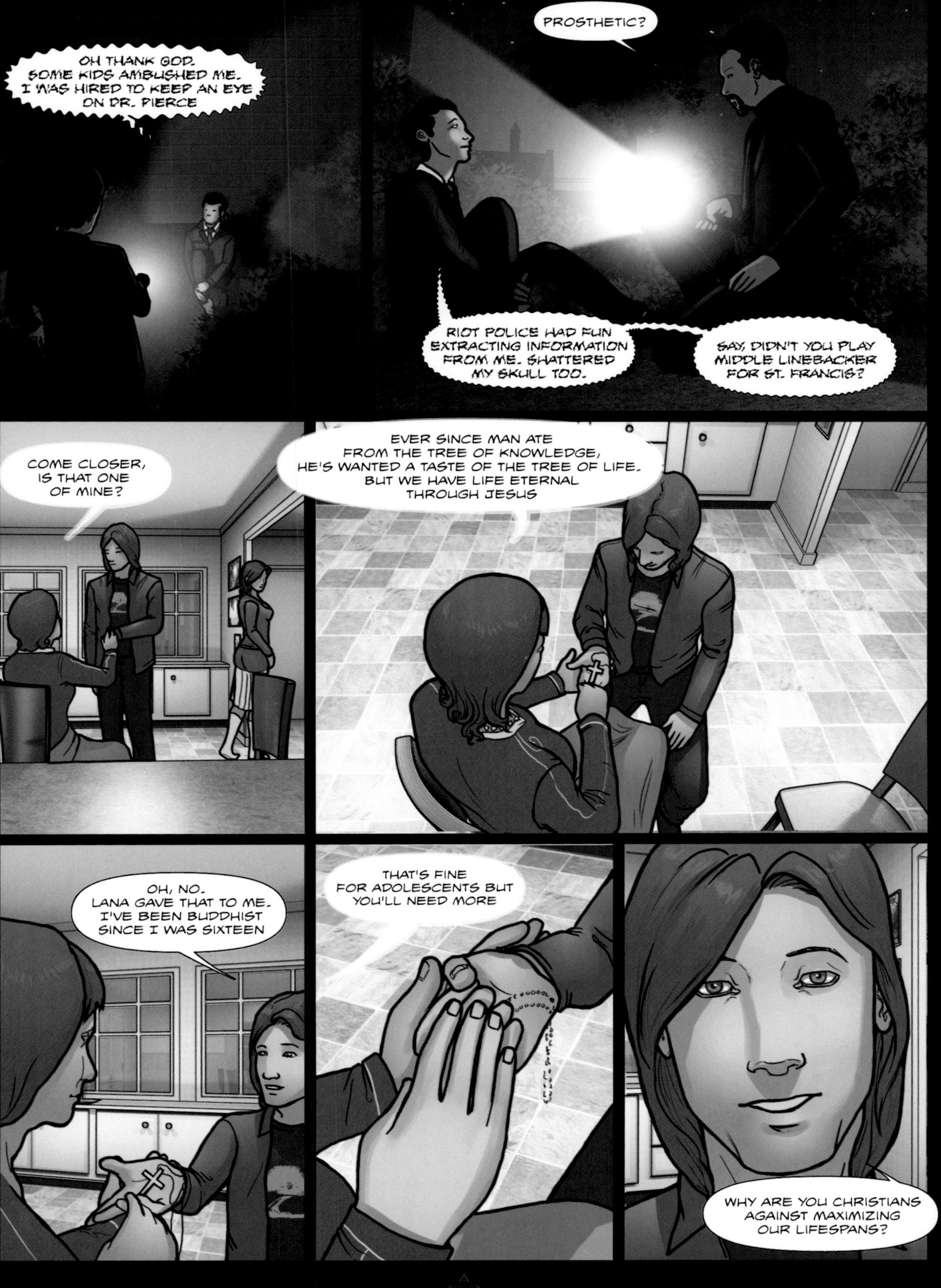
OH THANK GOD. SOME KIDS AMBUSHED ME. I WAS HIRED TO KEEP AN EYE ON DR. PIERCE
PROSTHETIC?
RIOT POLICE HAD FUN EXTRACTING INFORMATION FROM ME. SHATTERED MY SKULL TOO.
SAY, DIDN'T YOU PLAY MIDDLE LINEBACKER FOR ST. FRANCIS?
COME CLOSER, IS THAT ONE OF MINE?
EVER SINCE MAN ATE FROM THE TREE OF KNOWLEDGE, HE'S WANTED A TASTE OF THE TREE OF LIFE. BUT WE HAVE LIFE ETERNAL THROUGH JESUS
OH, NO. LANA GAVE THAT TO ME. I'VE BEEN BUDDHIST SINCE I WAS SIXTEEN
THAT'S FINE FOR ADOLESCENTS BUT YOU'LL NEED MORE
WHY ARE YOU CHRISTIANS AGAINST MAXIMIZING OUR LIFESPANS?

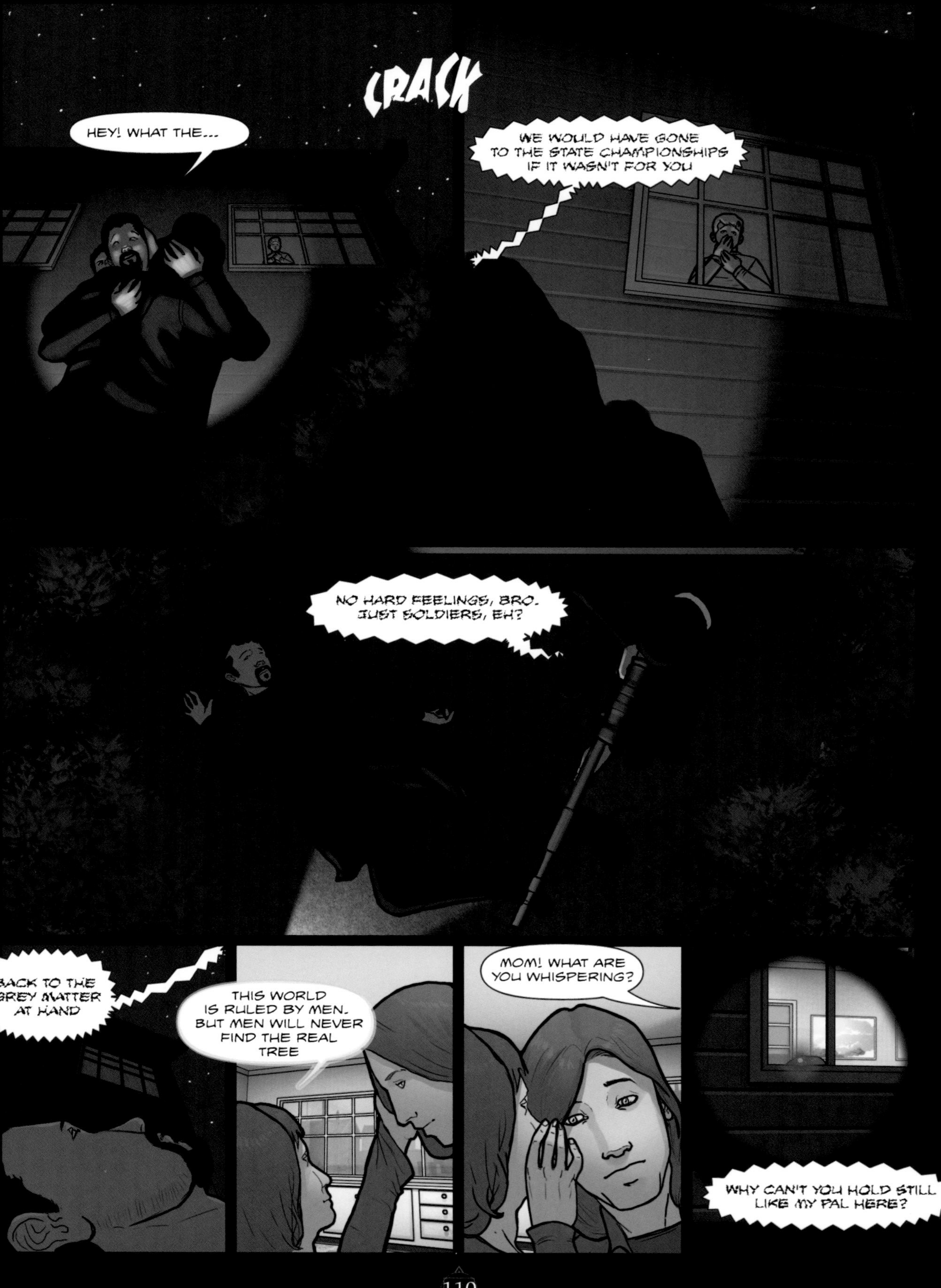
CRACK
HEY! WHAT THE...
WE WOULD HAVE GONE TO THE STATE CHAMPIONSHIPS IF IT WASN'T FOR YOU
NO HARD FEELINGS, BRO. JUST SOLDIERS, EH?
BACK TO THE GREY MATTER AT HAND
THIS WORLD IS RULED BY MEN. BUT MEN WILL NEVER FIND THE REAL TREE
MOM! WHAT ARE YOU WHISPERING?
WHY CAN'T YOU HOLD STILL LIKE MY PAL HERE?

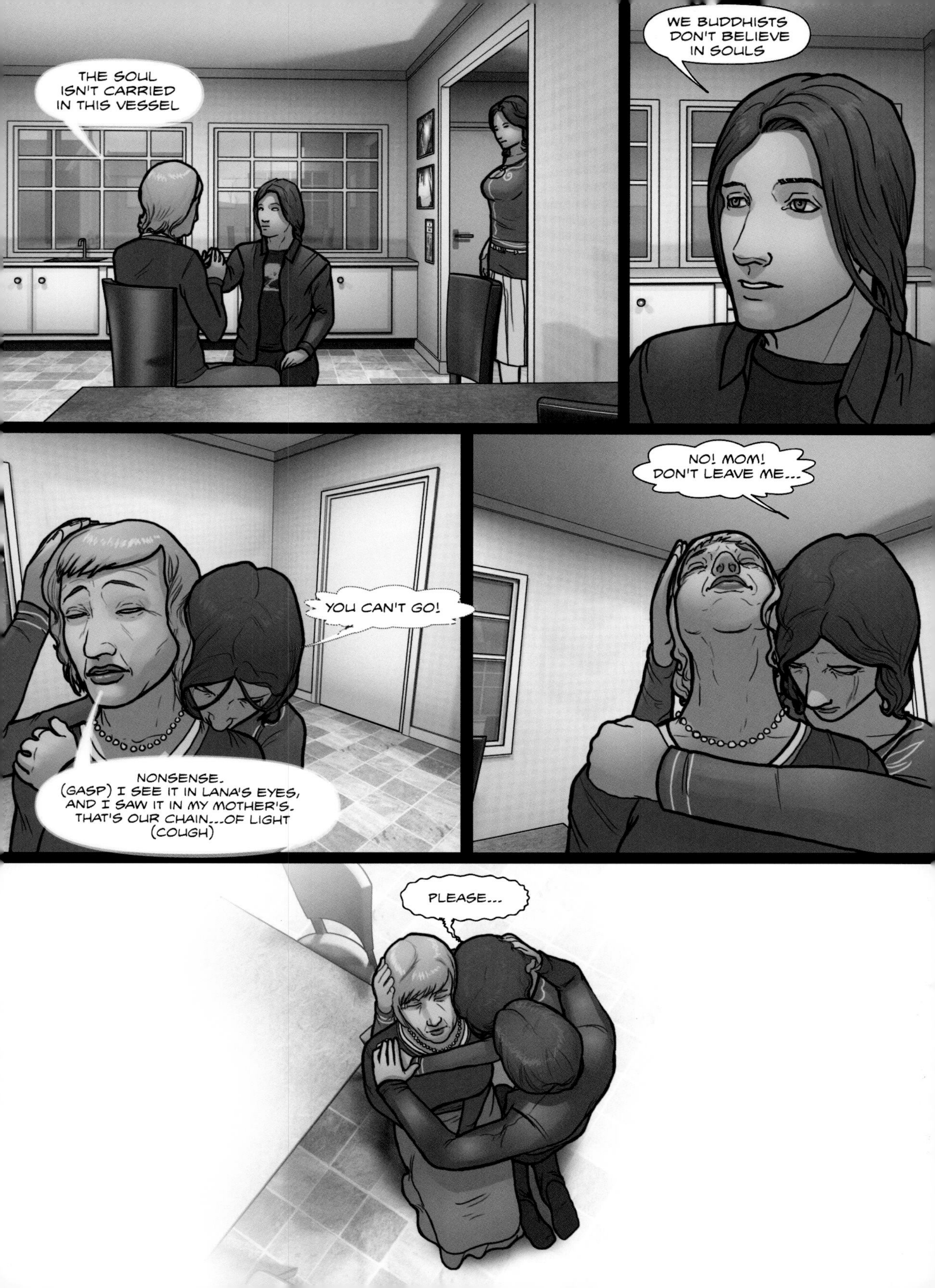
THE SOUL ISN'T CARRIED IN THIS VESSEL
WE BUDDHISTS DON'T BELIEVE IN SOULS
NONSENSE. (GASP) I SEE IT IN LANA'S EYES, AND I SAW IT IN MY MOTHER'S. THAT'S OUR CHAIN...OF LIGHT (COUGH)
YOU CAN'T GO!
NO! MOM! DON'T LEAVE ME...
PLEASE...

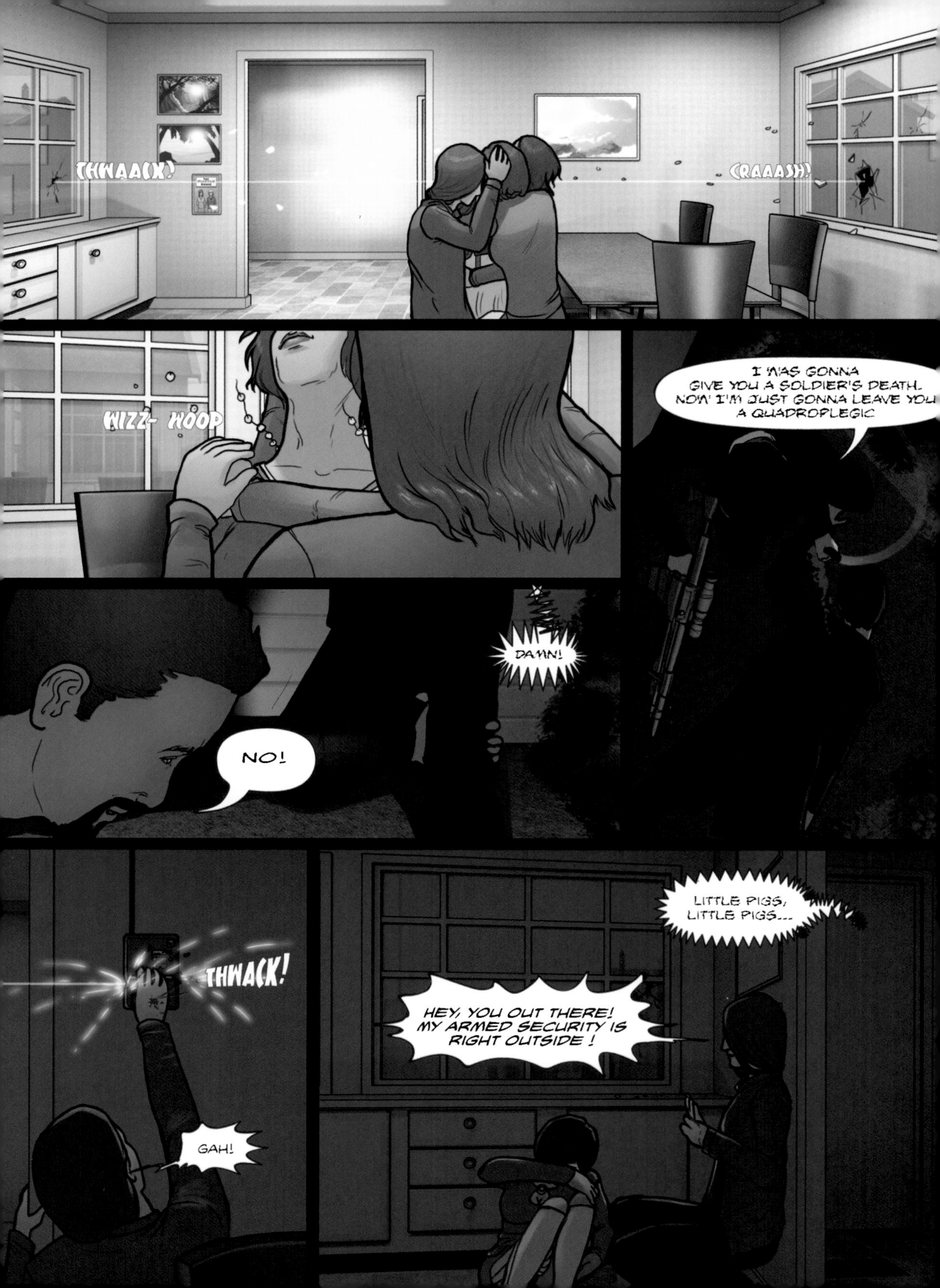
THWAACK!
CRAAASH!
WIZZ- WOOP
I WAS GONNA GIVE YOU A SOLDIER'S DEATH. NOW I'M JUST GONNA LEAVE YOU A QUADROPLEGIC
DAMN!
NO!
LITTLE PIGS, LITTLE PIGS...
THWACK!
HEY, YOU OUT THERE! MY ARMED SECURITY IS RIGHT OUTSIDE !
GAH!

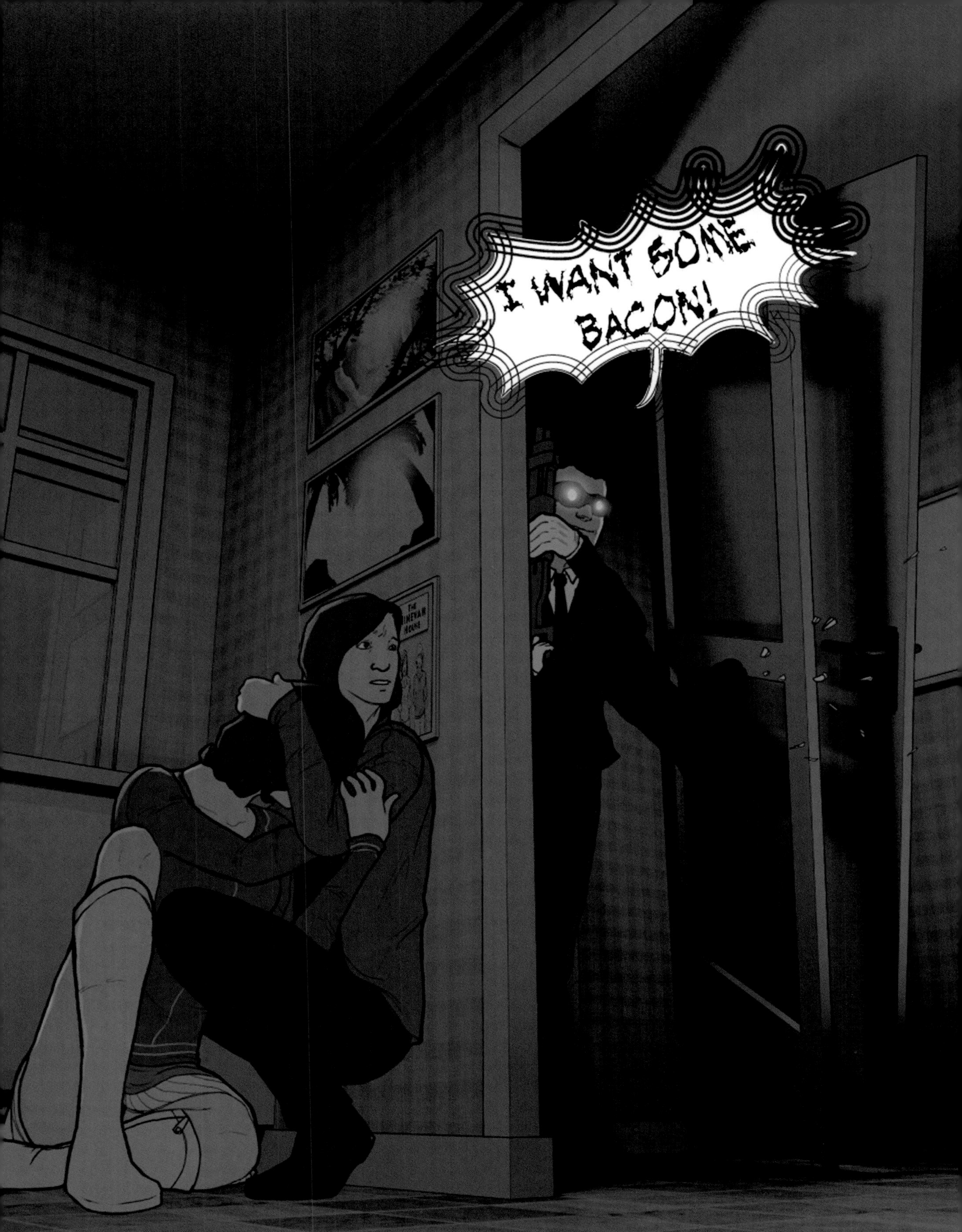
I WANT SOME BACON!

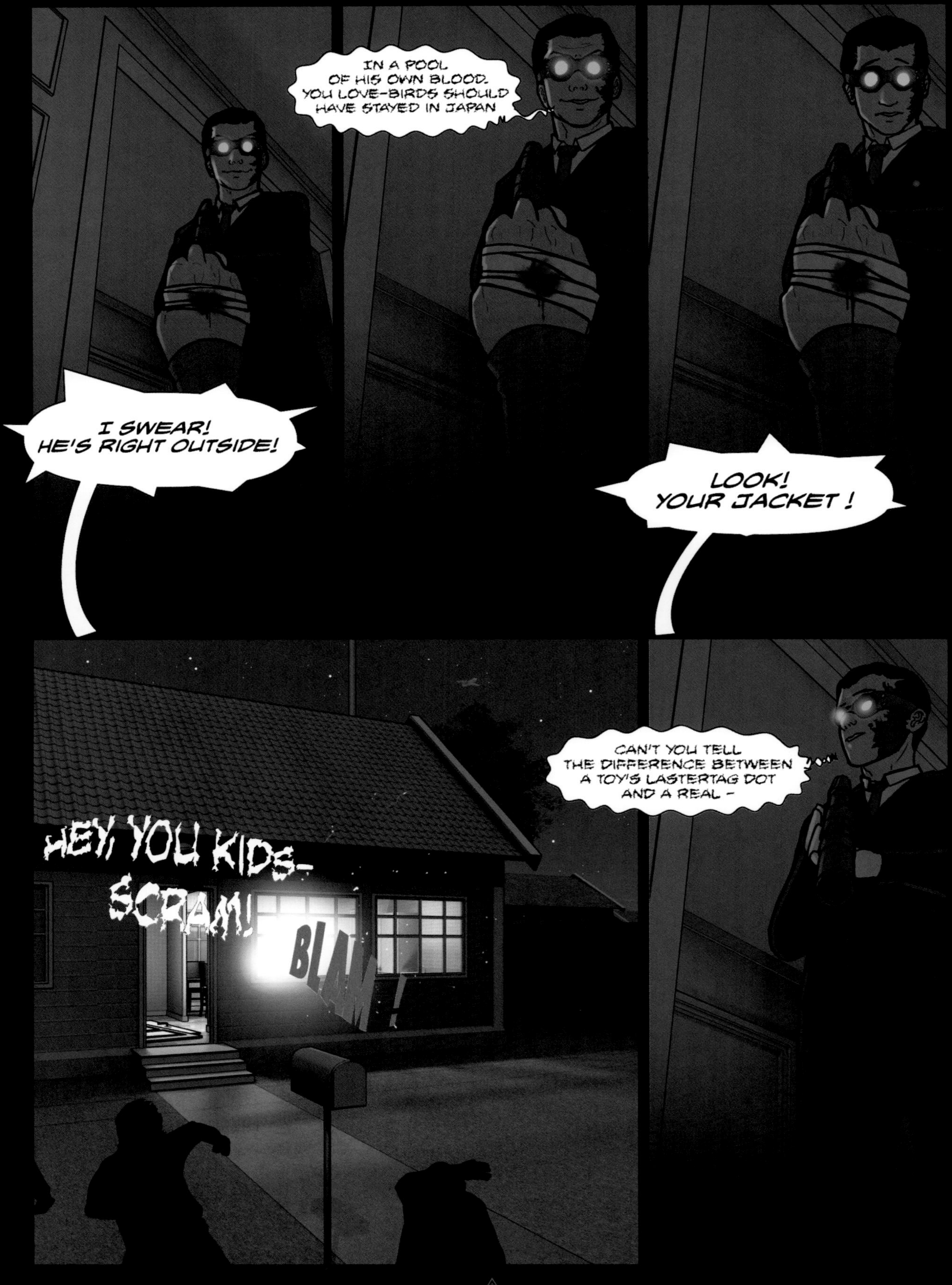
IN A POOL OF HIS OWN BLOOD. YOU LOVE-BIRDS SHOULD HAVE STAYED IN JAPAN
I SWEAR! HE'S RIGHT OUTSIDE!
LOOK! YOUR JACKET !
HEY, YOU KIDS- SCRAM!
BLAM !
CAN'T YOU TELL THE DIFFERENCE BETWEEN A TOY'S LASTERTAG DOT AND A REAL -

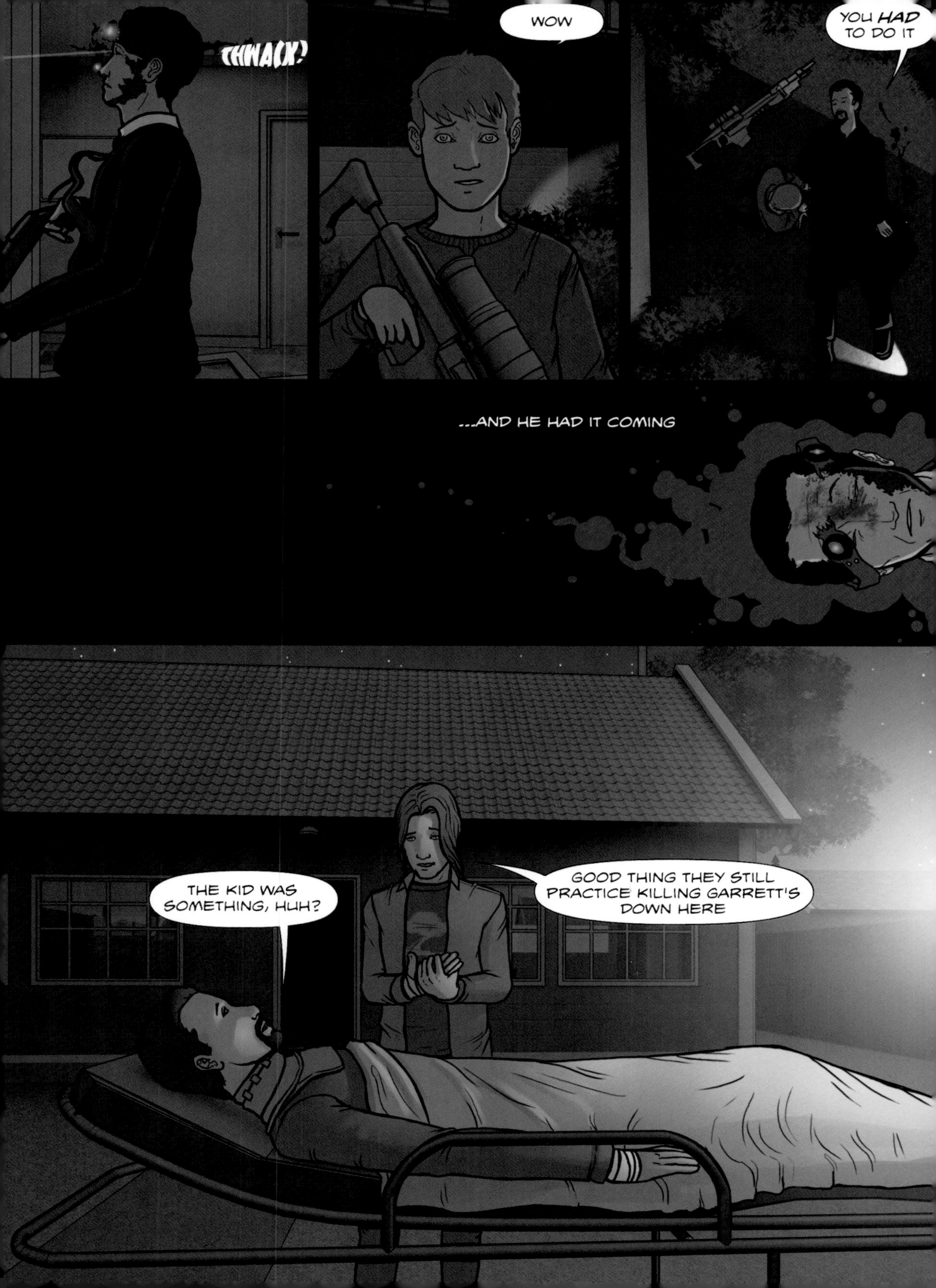
THWACK!
WOW
YOU HAD TO DO IT
...AND HE HAD IT COMING
THE KID WAS SOMETHING, HUH?
GOOD THING THEY STILL PRACTICE KILLING GARRETT'S DOWN HERE

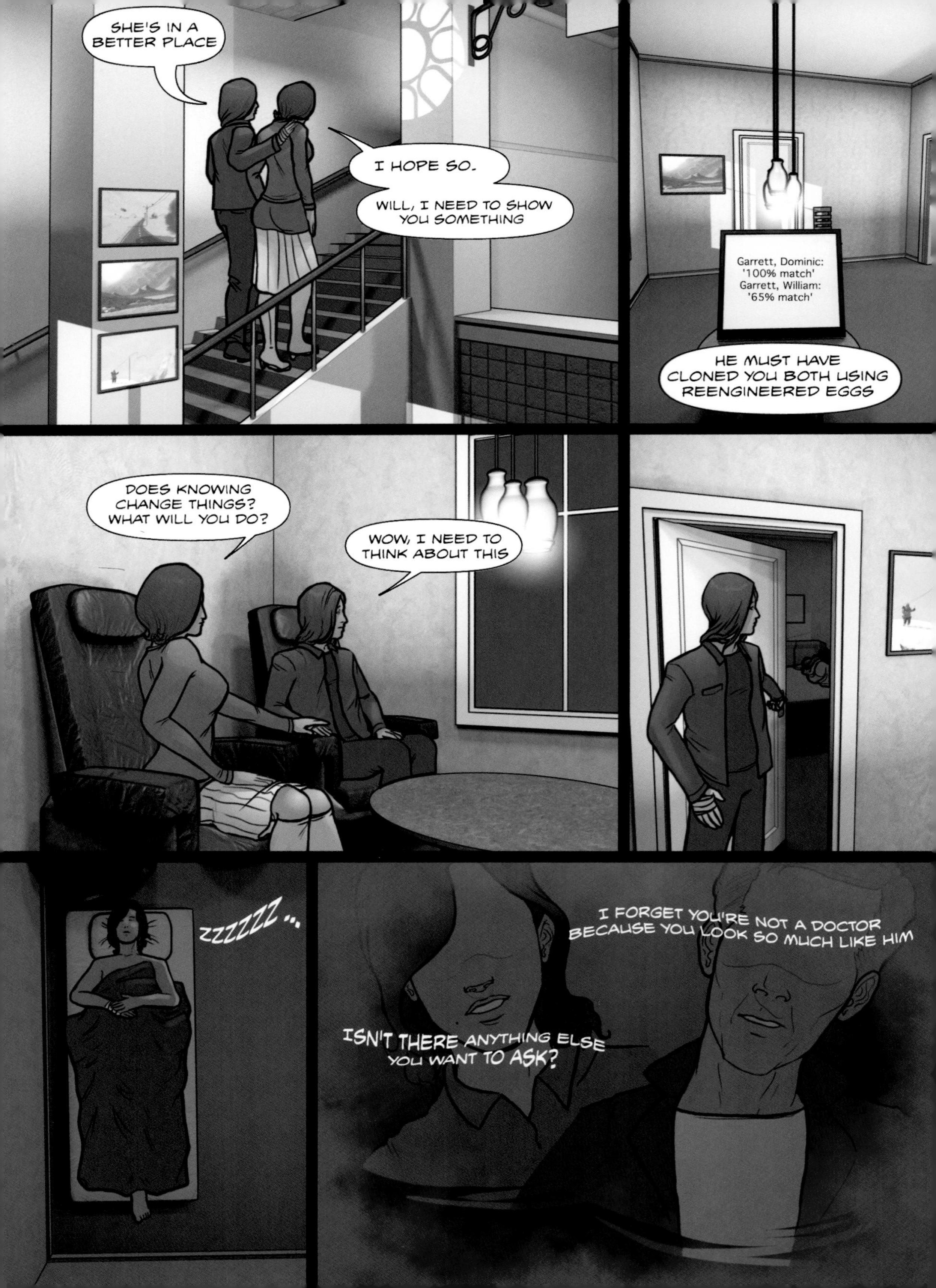
SHE'S IN A BETTER PLACE
I HOPE SO.
WILL, I NEED TO SHOW YOU SOMETHING
Garrett, Dominic: '100% match'
Garrett, William: '65% match'
HE MUST HAVE CLONED YOU BOTH USING REENGINEERED EGGS
DOES KNOWING CHANGE THINGS? WHAT WILL YOU DO?
WOW, I NEED TO THINK ABOUT THIS
ZZZZZZ ...
I FORGET YOU'RE NOT A DOCTOR BECAUSE YOU LOOK SO MUCH LIKE HIM
ISN'T THERE ANYTHING ELSE YOU WANT TO ASK?

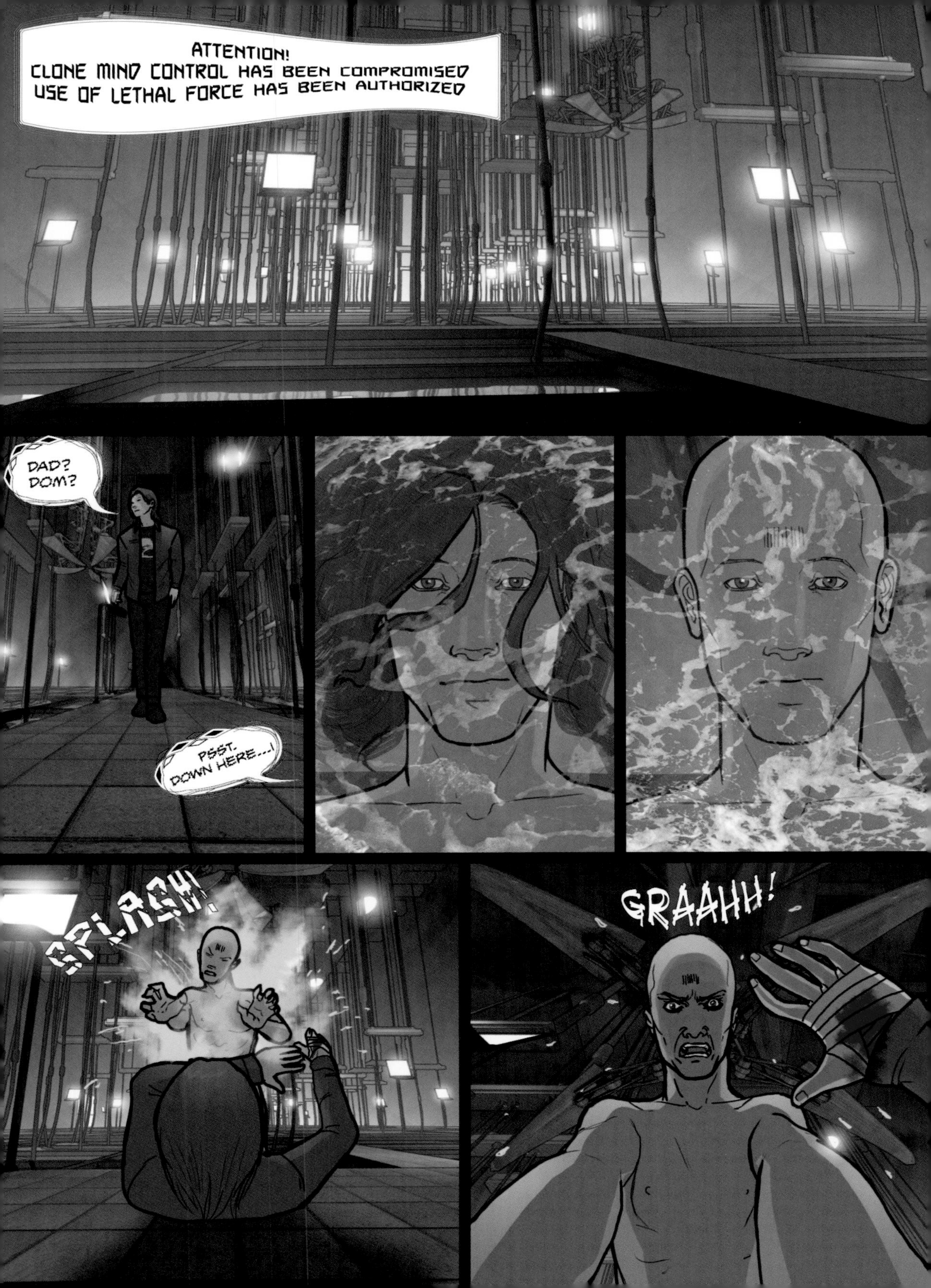
ATTENTION!
CLONE MIND CONTROL HAS BEEN COMPROMISED
USE OF LETHAL FORCE HAS BEEN AUTHORIZED
DAD? DOM?
PSST. DOWN HERE...!
SPLASH!
GRAAHH!

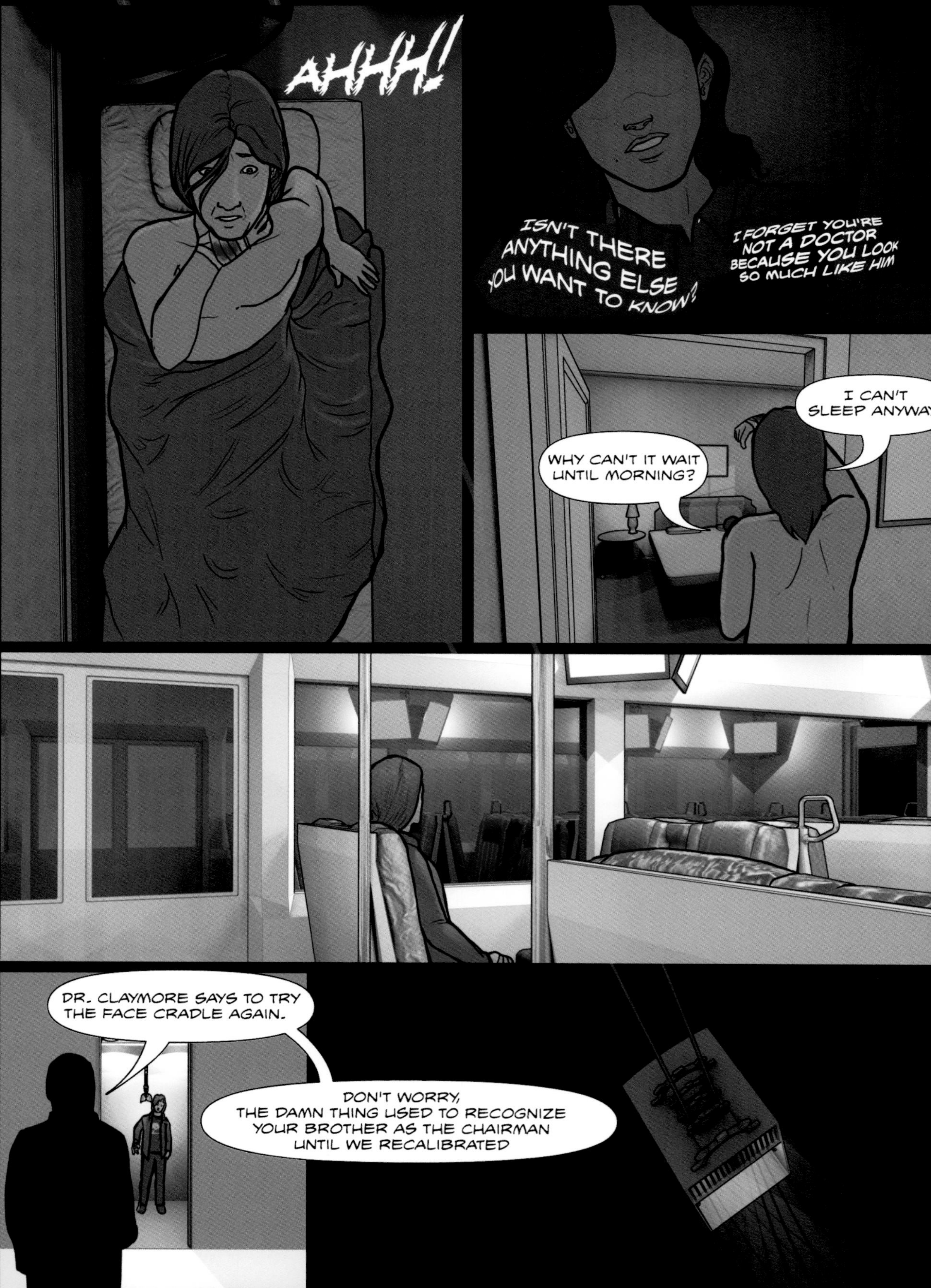
AHHH!
ISN'T THERE ANYTHING ELSE YOU WANT TO KNOW?
I FORGET YOU'RE NOT A DOCTOR BECAUSE YOU LOOK SO MUCH LIKE HIM
I CAN'T SLEEP ANYWAY
WHY CAN'T IT WAIT UNTIL MORNING?
DR. CLAYMORE SAYS TO TRY THE FACE CRADLE AGAIN.
DON'T WORRY, THE DAMN THING USED TO RECOGNIZE YOUR BROTHER AS THE CHAIRMAN UNTIL WE RECALIBRATED

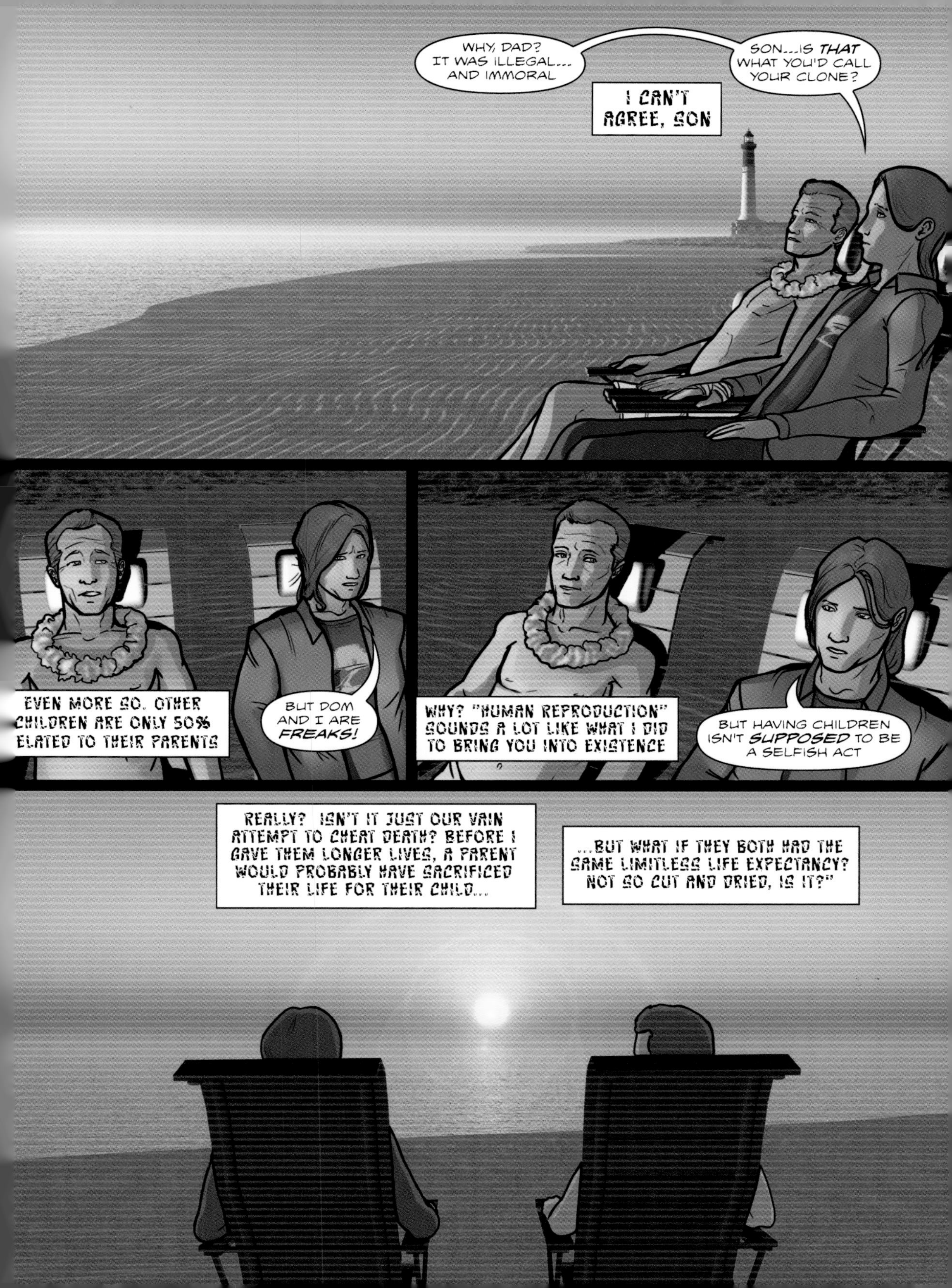
WHY, DAD? IT WAS ILLEGAL... AND IMMORAL
SON...IS *THAT* WHAT YOU'D CALL YOUR CLONE?
I CAN'T AGREE, SON
EVEN MORE SO. OTHER CHILDREN ARE ONLY 50% ELATED TO THEIR PARENTS
BUT DOM AND I ARE *FREAKS!*
WHY? "HUMAN REPRODUCTION" SOUNDS A LOT LIKE WHAT I DID TO BRING YOU INTO EXISTENCE
BUT HAVING CHILDREN ISN'T *SUPPOSED* TO BE A SELFISH ACT
REALLY? ISN'T IT JUST OUR VAIN ATTEMPT TO CHEAT DEATH? BEFORE I GAVE THEM LONGER LIVES, A PARENT WOULD PROBABLY HAVE SACRIFICED THEIR LIFE FOR THEIR CHILD...
...BUT WHAT IF THEY BOTH HAD THE SAME LIMITLESS LIFE EXPECTANCY? NOT SO CUT AND DRIED, IS IT?"

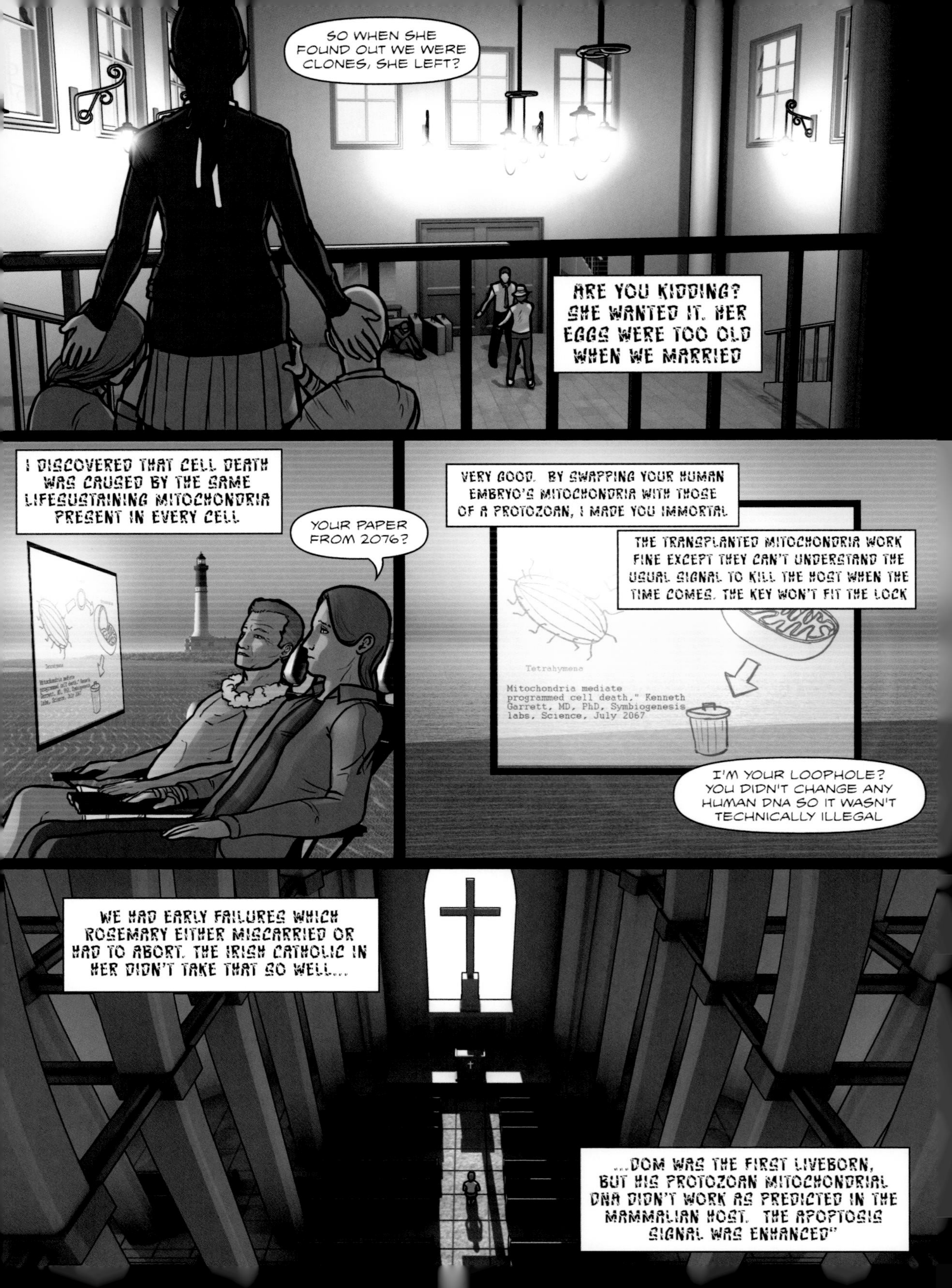
SO WHEN SHE FOUND OUT WE WERE CLONES, SHE LEFT?
ARE YOU KIDDING? SHE WANTED IT. HER EGGS WERE TOO OLD WHEN WE MARRIED
I DISCOVERED THAT CELL DEATH WAS CAUSED BY THE SAME LIFESUSTAINING MITOCHONDRIA PRESENT IN EVERY CELL
YOUR PAPER FROM 2076?
VERY GOOD. BY SWAPPING YOUR HUMAN EMBRYO'S MITOCHONDRIA WITH THOSE OF A PROTOZOAN, I MADE YOU IMMORTAL
THE TRANSPLANTED MITOCHONDRIA WORK FINE EXCEPT THEY CAN'T UNDERSTAND THE USUAL SIGNAL TO KILL THE HOST WHEN THE TIME COMES. THE KEY WON'T FIT THE LOCK
Tetrahymena
Mitochondria mediate programmed cell death," Kenneth Garrett, MD, PhD, Symbiogenesis labs, Science, July 2067
I'M YOUR LOOPHOLE? YOU DIDN'T CHANGE ANY HUMAN DNA SO IT WASN'T TECHNICALLY ILLEGAL
WE HAD EARLY FAILURES WHICH ROSEMARY EITHER MISCARRIED OR HAD TO ABORT. THE IRISH CATHOLIC IN HER DIDN'T TAKE THAT SO WELL...
...DOM WAS THE FIRST LIVEBORN, BUT HIS PROTOZOAN MITOCHONDRIAL DNA DIDN'T WORK AS PREDICTED IN THE MAMMALIAN HOST. THE APOPTOSIS SIGNAL WAS ENHANCED"

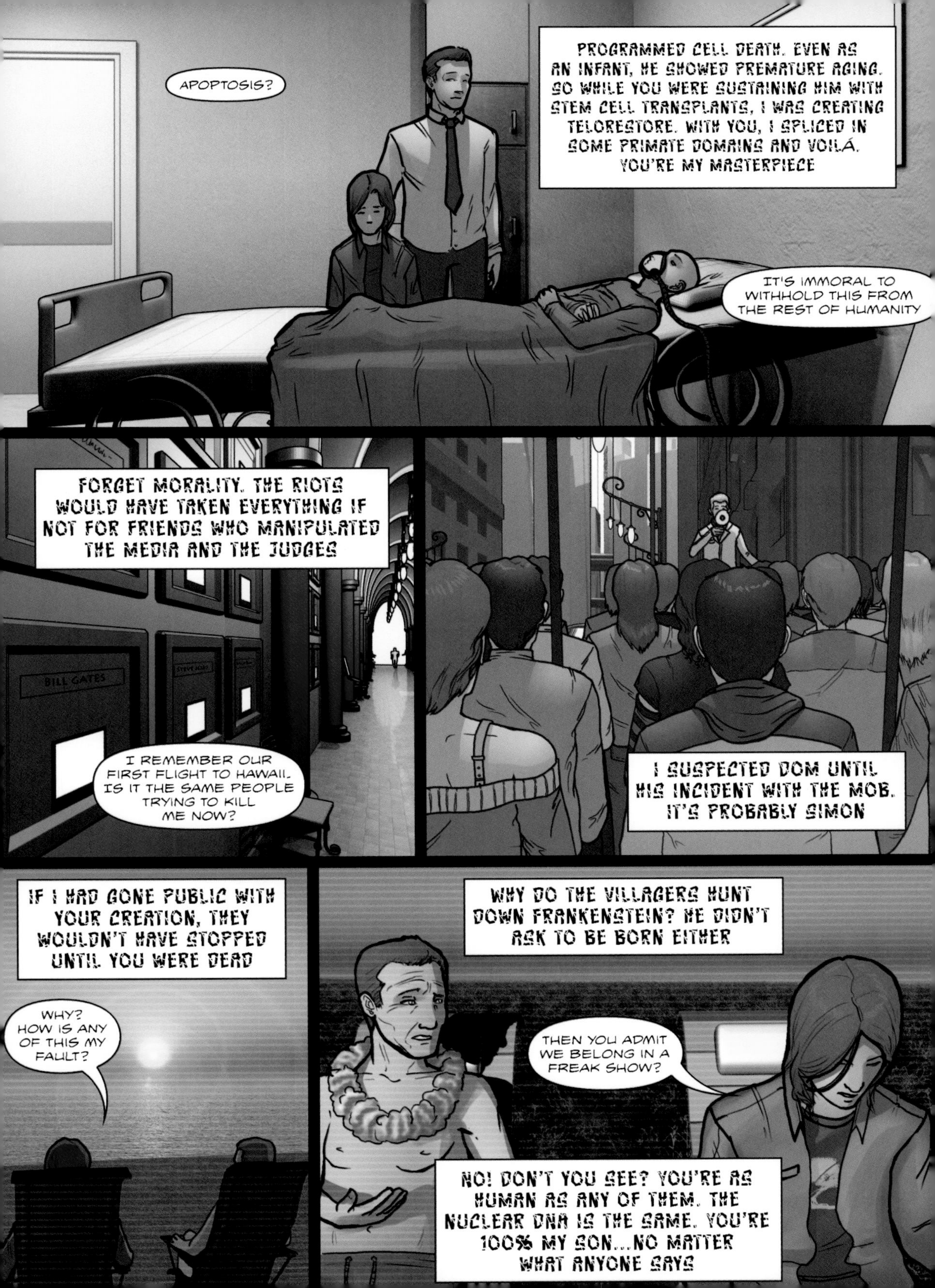
APOPTOSIS?
PROGRAMMED CELL DEATH. EVEN AS AN INFANT, HE SHOWED PREMATURE AGING. SO WHILE YOU WERE SUSTAINING HIM WITH STEM CELL TRANSPLANTS, I WAS CREATING TELORESTORE. WITH YOU, I SPLICED IN SOME PRIMATE DOMAINS AND VOILÁ. YOU'RE MY MASTERPIECE
IT'S IMMORAL TO WITHHOLD THIS FROM THE REST OF HUMANITY
FORGET MORALITY. THE RIOTS WOULD HAVE TAKEN EVERYTHING IF NOT FOR FRIENDS WHO MANIPULATED THE MEDIA AND THE JUDGES
BILL GATES
I REMEMBER OUR FIRST FLIGHT TO HAWAII. IS IT THE SAME PEOPLE TRYING TO KILL ME NOW?
I SUSPECTED DOM UNTIL HIS INCIDENT WITH THE MOB. IT'S PROBABLY SIMON
IF I HAD GONE PUBLIC WITH YOUR CREATION, THEY WOULDN'T HAVE STOPPED UNTIL YOU WERE DEAD
WHY? HOW IS ANY OF THIS MY FAULT?
WHY DO THE VILLAGERS HUNT DOWN FRANKENSTEIN? HE DIDN'T ASK TO BE BORN EITHER
THEN YOU ADMIT WE BELONG IN A FREAK SHOW?
NO! DON'T YOU SEE? YOU'RE AS HUMAN AS ANY OF THEM. THE NUCLEAR DNA IS THE SAME. YOU'RE 100% MY SON...NO MATTER WHAT ANYONE SAYS

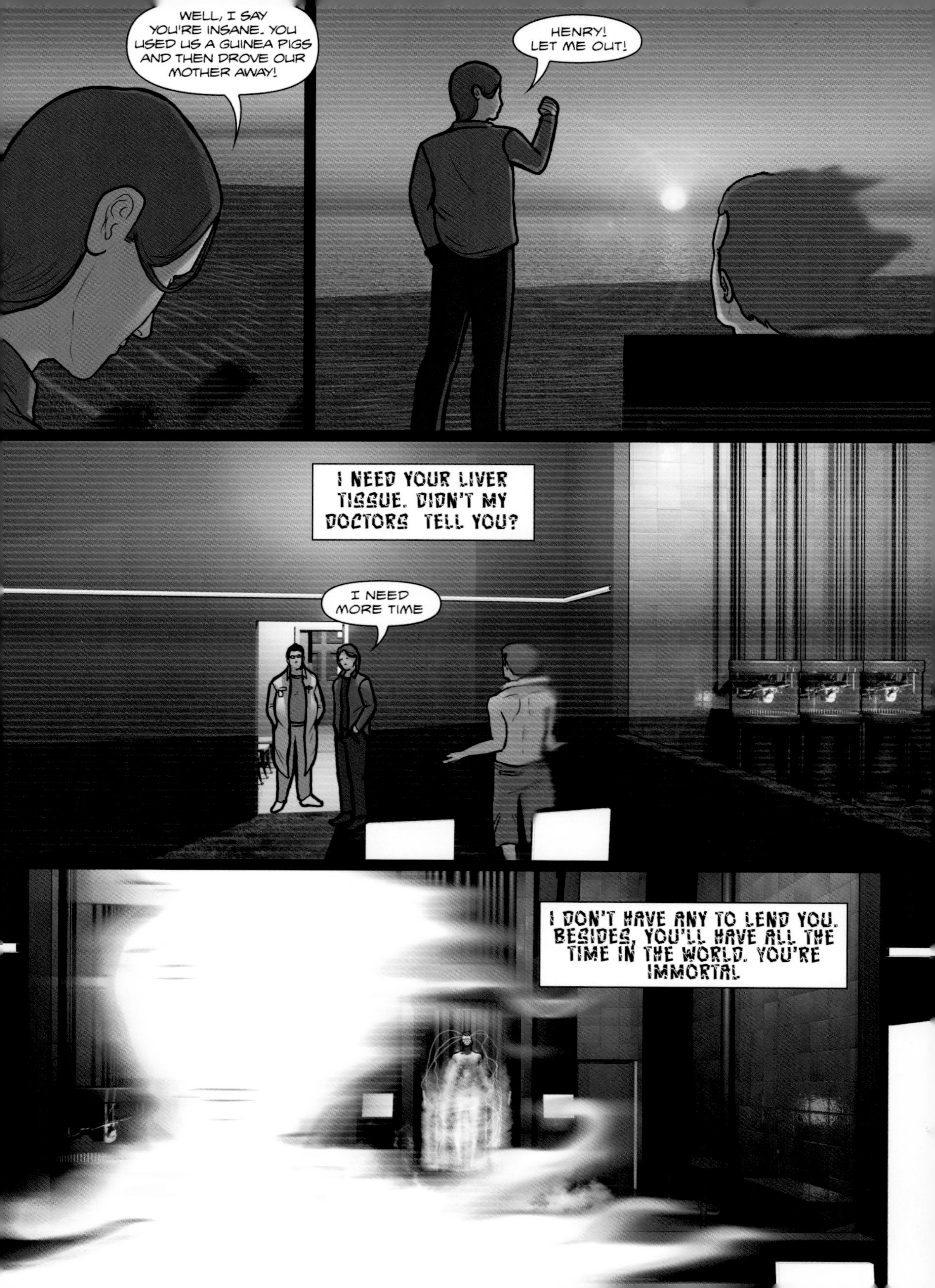
WELL, I SAY YOU'RE INSANE. YOU USED US A GUINEA PIGS AND THEN DROVE OUR MOTHER AWAY!
HENRY! LET ME OUT!
I NEED YOUR LIVER TISSUE. DIDN'T MY DOCTORS TELL YOU?
I NEED MORE TIME
I DON'T HAVE ANY TO LEND YOU. BESIDES, YOU'LL HAVE ALL THE TIME IN THE WORLD. YOU'RE IMMORTAL

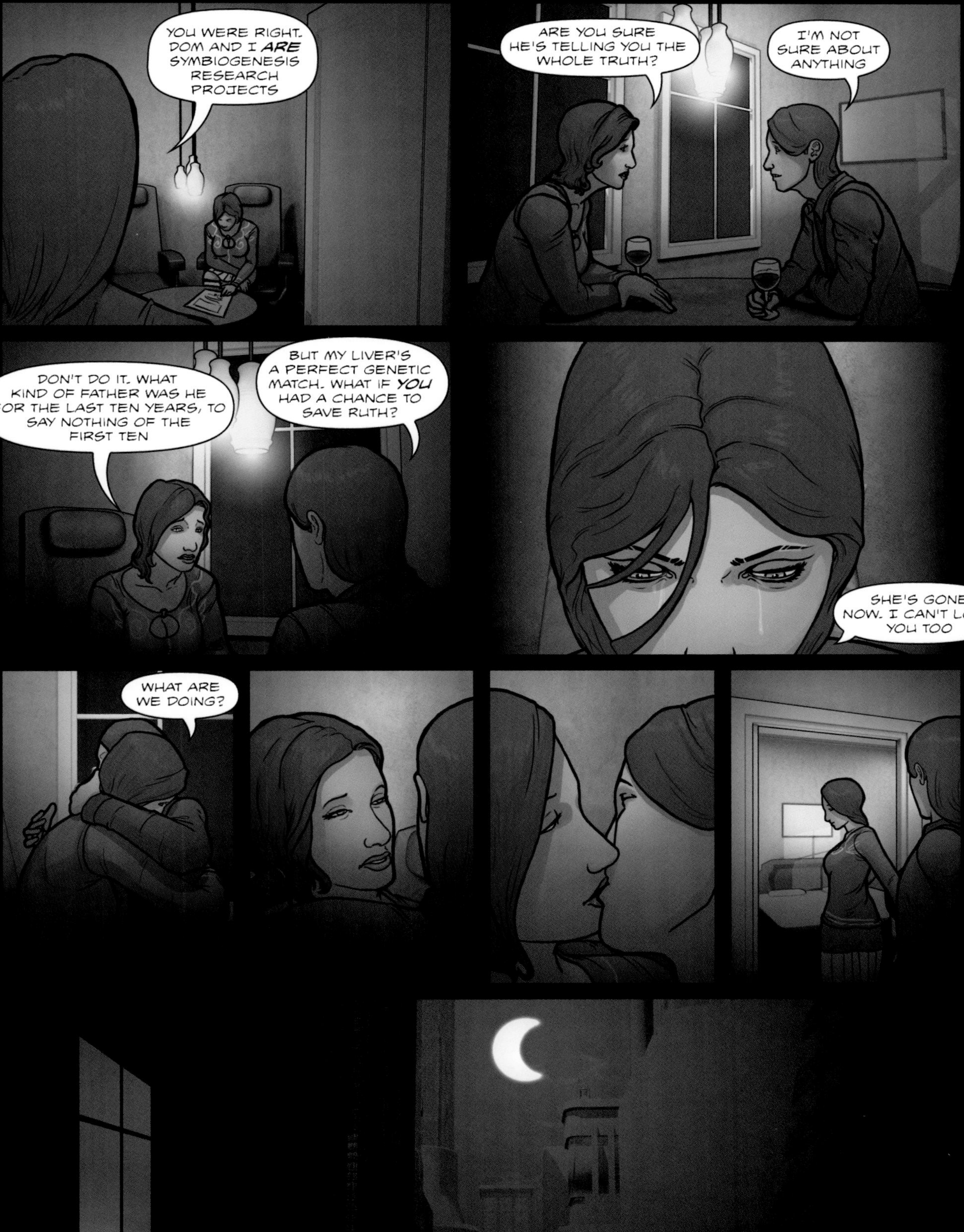
YOU WERE RIGHT. DOM AND I ARE SYMBIOGENESIS RESEARCH PROJECTS
ARE YOU SURE HE'S TELLING YOU THE WHOLE TRUTH?
I'M NOT SURE ABOUT ANYTHING
DON'T DO IT. WHAT KIND OF FATHER WAS HE FOR THE LAST TEN YEARS, TO SAY NOTHING OF THE FIRST TEN
BUT MY LIVER'S A PERFECT GENETIC MATCH. WHAT IF YOU HAD A CHANCE TO SAVE RUTH?
SHE'S GONE NOW. I CAN'T LOSE YOU TOO
WHAT ARE WE DOING?

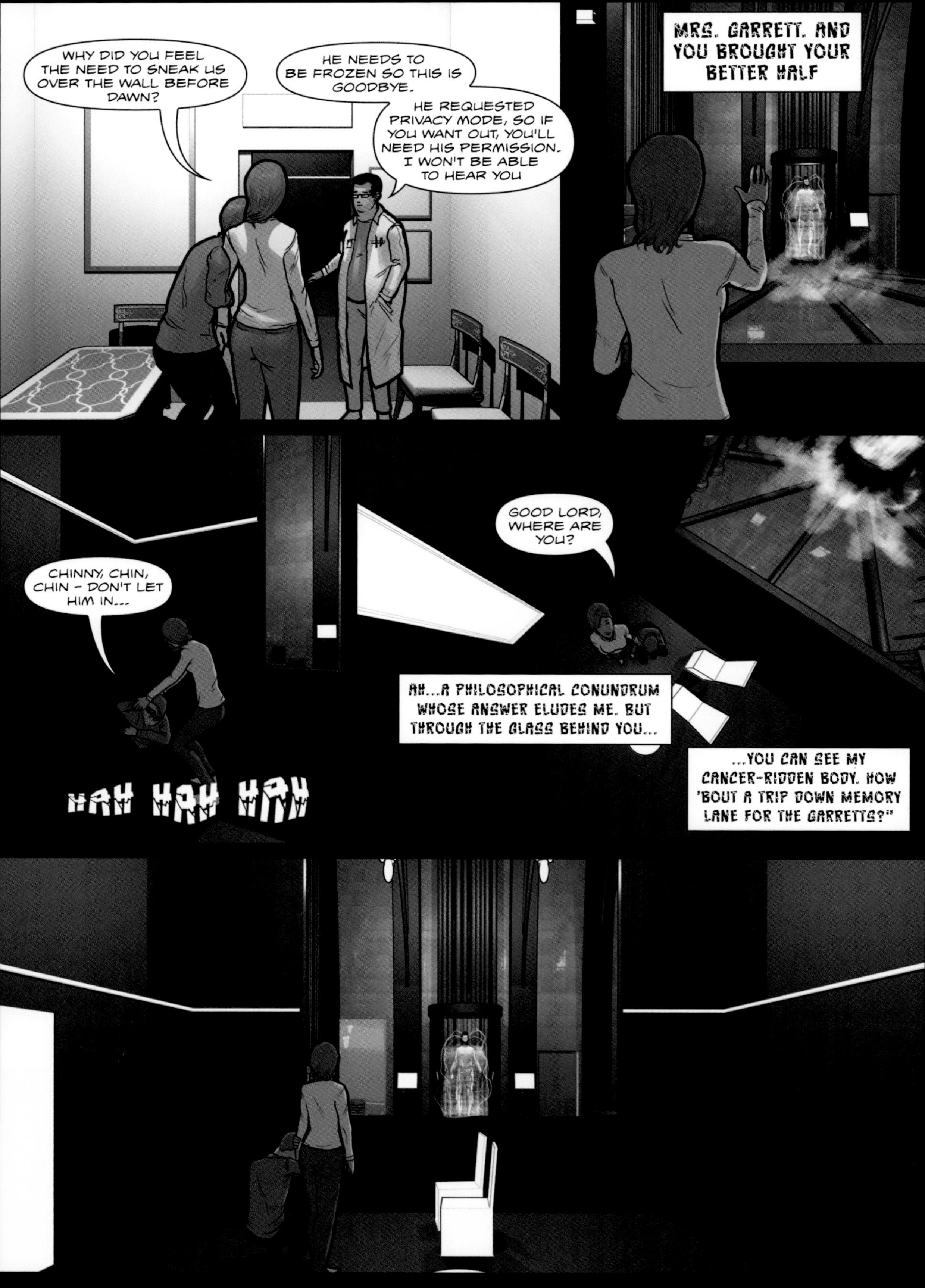
WHY DID YOU FEEL THE NEED TO SNEAK US OVER THE WALL BEFORE DAWN?
HE NEEDS TO BE FROZEN SO THIS IS GOODBYE.
HE REQUESTED PRIVACY MODE, SO IF YOU WANT OUT, YOU'LL NEED HIS PERMISSION. I WON'T BE ABLE TO HEAR YOU
MRS. GARRETT. AND YOU BROUGHT YOUR BETTER HALF
CHINNY, CHIN, CHIN - DON'T LET HIM IN...
HAH HAH HAH
GOOD LORD, WHERE ARE YOU?
AH...A PHILOSOPHICAL CONUNDRUM WHOSE ANSWER ELUDES ME. BUT THROUGH THE GLASS BEHIND YOU...
...YOU CAN SEE MY CANCER-RIDDEN BODY. HOW 'BOUT A TRIP DOWN MEMORY LANE FOR THE GARRETTS?"

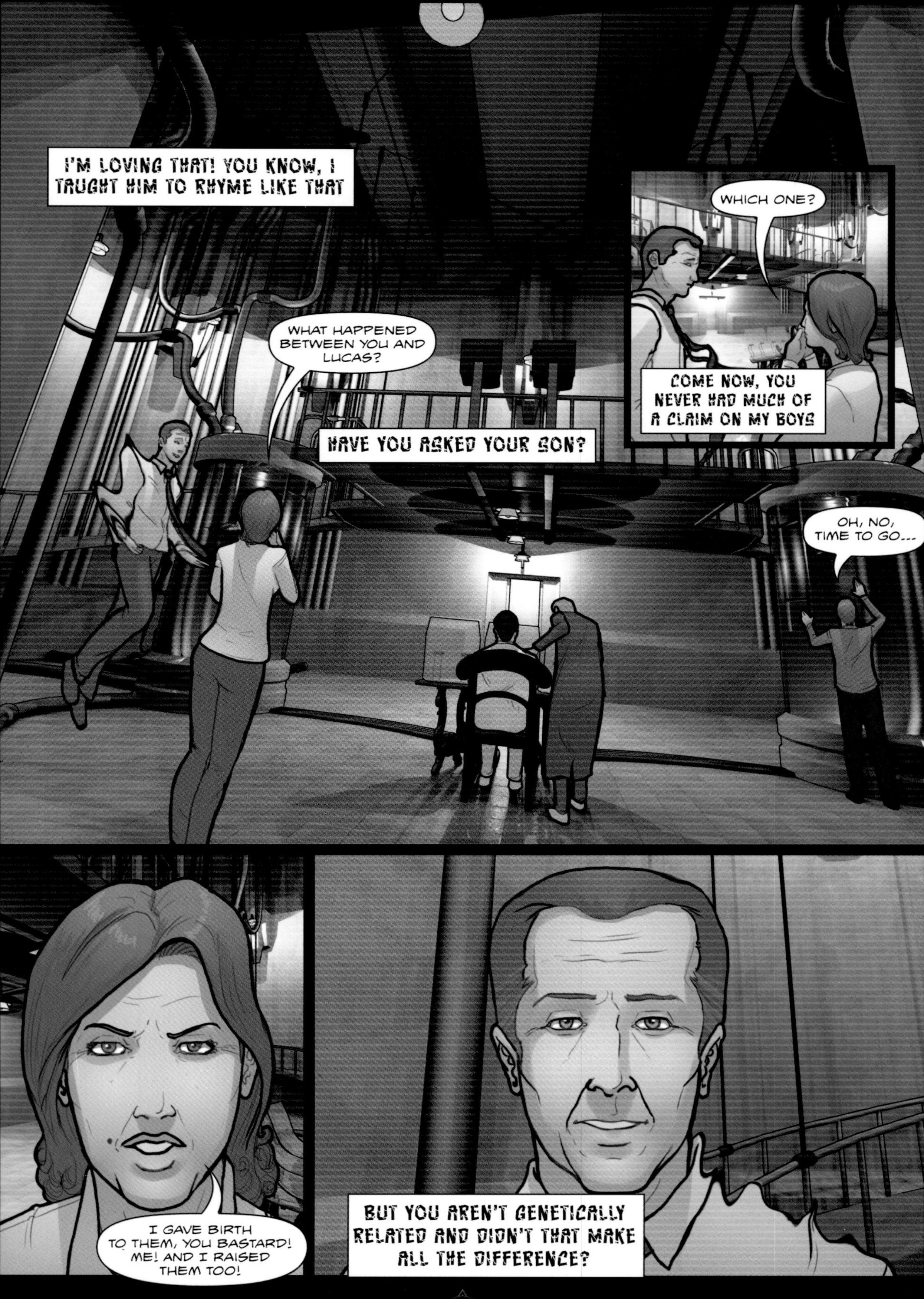
I'M LOVING THAT! YOU KNOW, I TAUGHT HIM TO RHYME LIKE THAT
WHICH ONE?
COME NOW, YOU NEVER HAD MUCH OF A CLAIM ON MY BOYS
WHAT HAPPENED BETWEEN YOU AND LUCAS?
HAVE YOU ASKED YOUR SON?
OH, NO, TIME TO GO...
I GAVE BIRTH TO THEM, YOU BASTARD! ME! AND I RAISED THEM TOO!
BUT YOU AREN'T GENETICALLY RELATED AND DIDN'T THAT MAKE ALL THE DIFFERENCE?

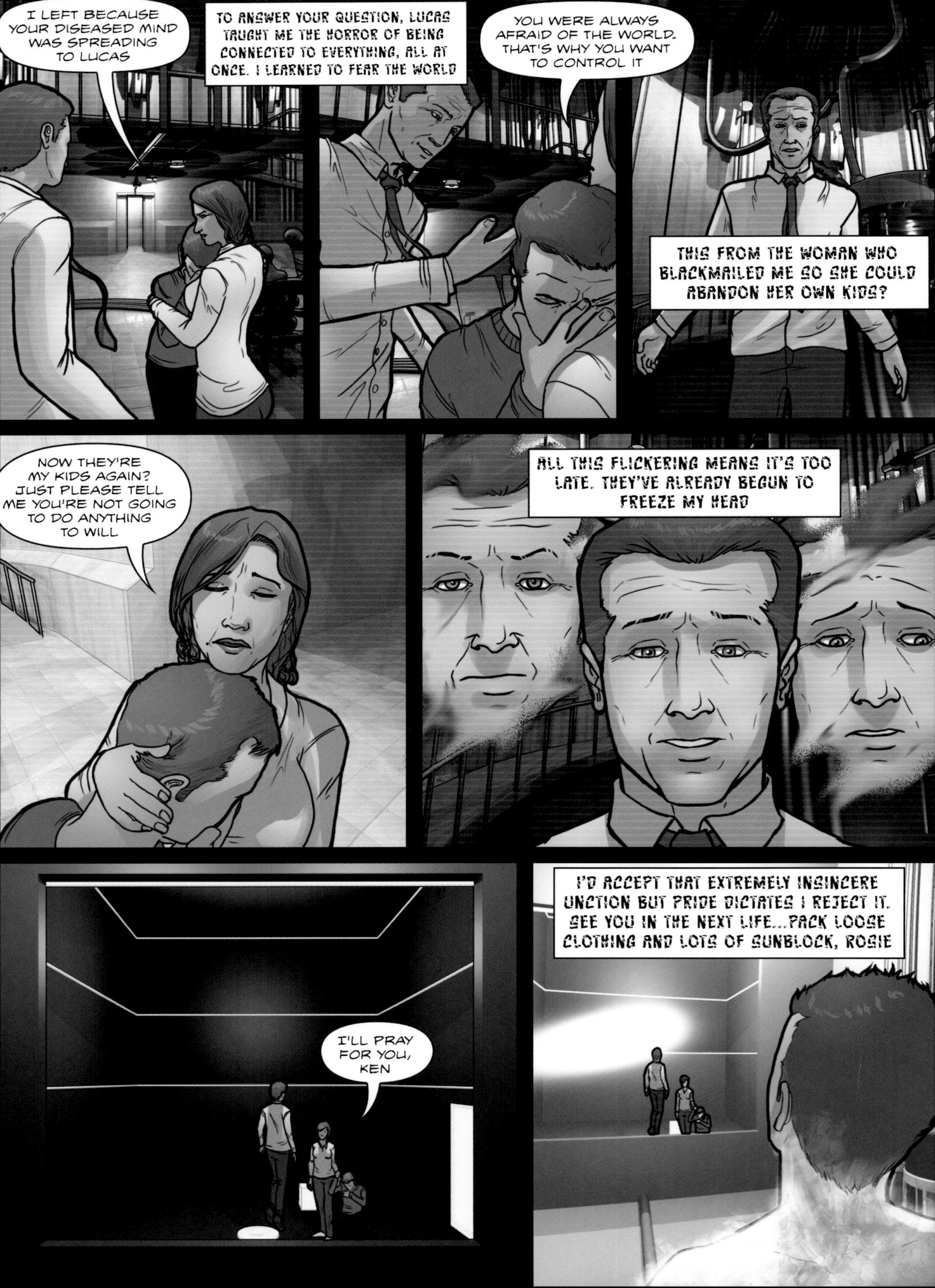
I LEFT BECAUSE YOUR DISEASED MIND WAS SPREADING TO LUCAS
TO ANSWER YOUR QUESTION, LUCAS TAUGHT ME THE HORROR OF BEING CONNECTED TO EVERYTHING, ALL AT ONCE. I LEARNED TO FEAR THE WORLD
YOU WERE ALWAYS AFRAID OF THE WORLD. THAT'S WHY YOU WANT TO CONTROL IT
THIS FROM THE WOMAN WHO BLACKMAILED ME SO SHE COULD ABANDON HER OWN KIDS?
NOW THEY'RE MY KIDS AGAIN? JUST PLEASE TELL ME YOU'RE NOT GOING TO DO ANYTHING TO WILL
ALL THIS FLICKERING MEANS IT'S TOO LATE. THEY'VE ALREADY BEGUN TO FREEZE MY HEAD
I'LL PRAY FOR YOU, KEN
I'D ACCEPT THAT EXTREMELY INSINCERE UNCTION BUT PRIDE DICTATES I REJECT IT. SEE YOU IN THE NEXT LIFE...PACK LOOSE CLOTHING AND LOTS OF SUNBLOCK, ROSIE

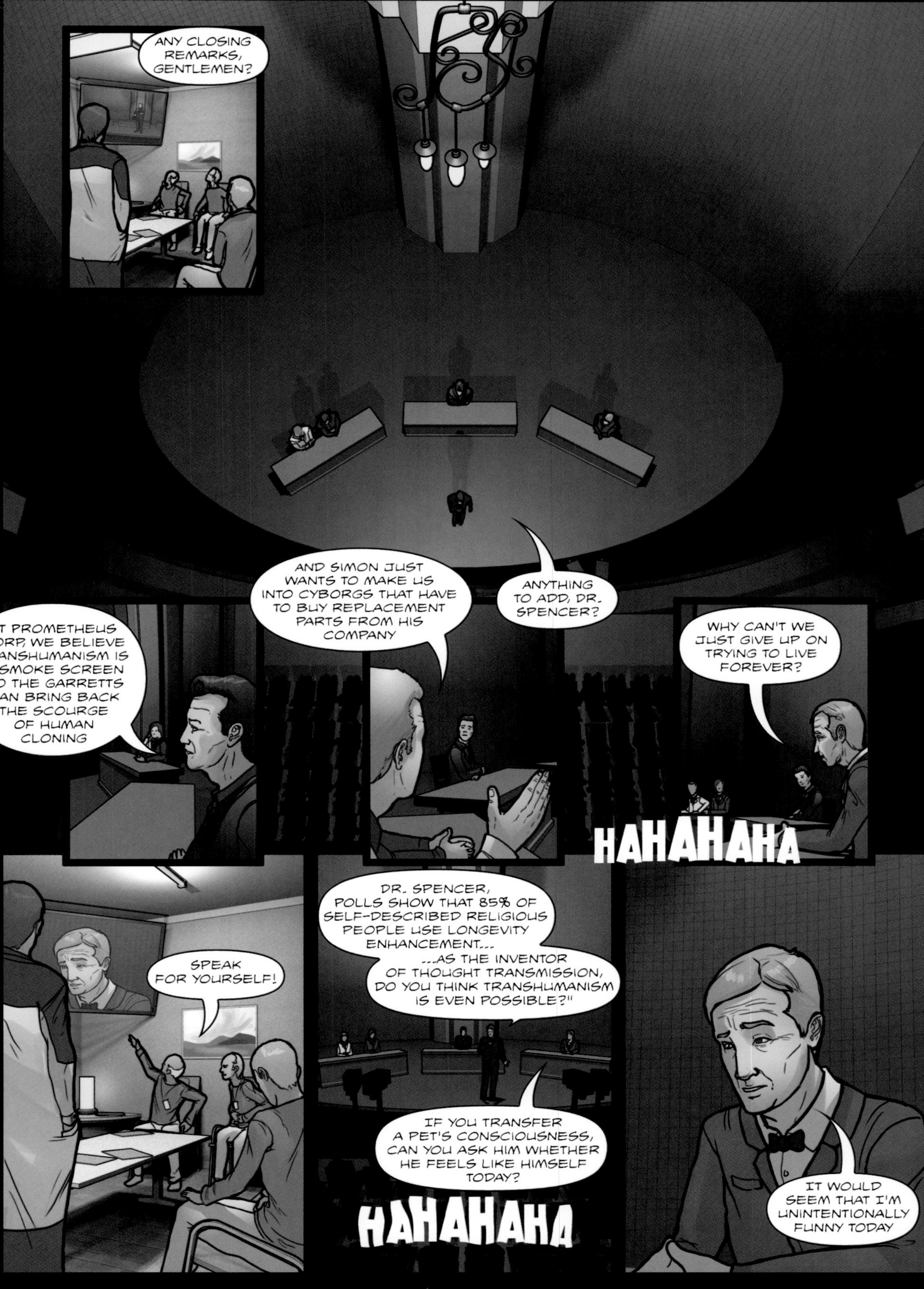
ANY CLOSING REMARKS, GENTLEMEN?
AT PROMETHEUS CORP, WE BELIEVE TRANSHUMANISM IS A SMOKE SCREEN SO THE GARRETTS CAN BRING BACK THE SCOURGE OF HUMAN CLONING
AND SIMON JUST WANTS TO MAKE US INTO CYBORGS THAT HAVE TO BUY REPLACEMENT PARTS FROM HIS COMPANY
ANYTHING TO ADD, DR. SPENCER?
WHY CAN'T WE JUST GIVE UP ON TRYING TO LIVE FOREVER?
HAHAHAHA
SPEAK FOR YOURSELF!
DR. SPENCER, POLLS SHOW THAT 85% OF SELF-DESCRIBED RELIGIOUS PEOPLE USE LONGEVITY ENHANCEMENT...
...AS THE INVENTOR OF THOUGHT TRANSMISSION, DO YOU THINK TRANSHUMANISM IS EVEN POSSIBLE?"
IF YOU TRANSFER A PET'S CONSCIOUSNESS, CAN YOU ASK HIM WHETHER HE FEELS LIKE HIMSELF TODAY?
HAHAHAHA
IT WOULD SEEM THAT I'M UNINTENTIONALLY FUNNY TODAY

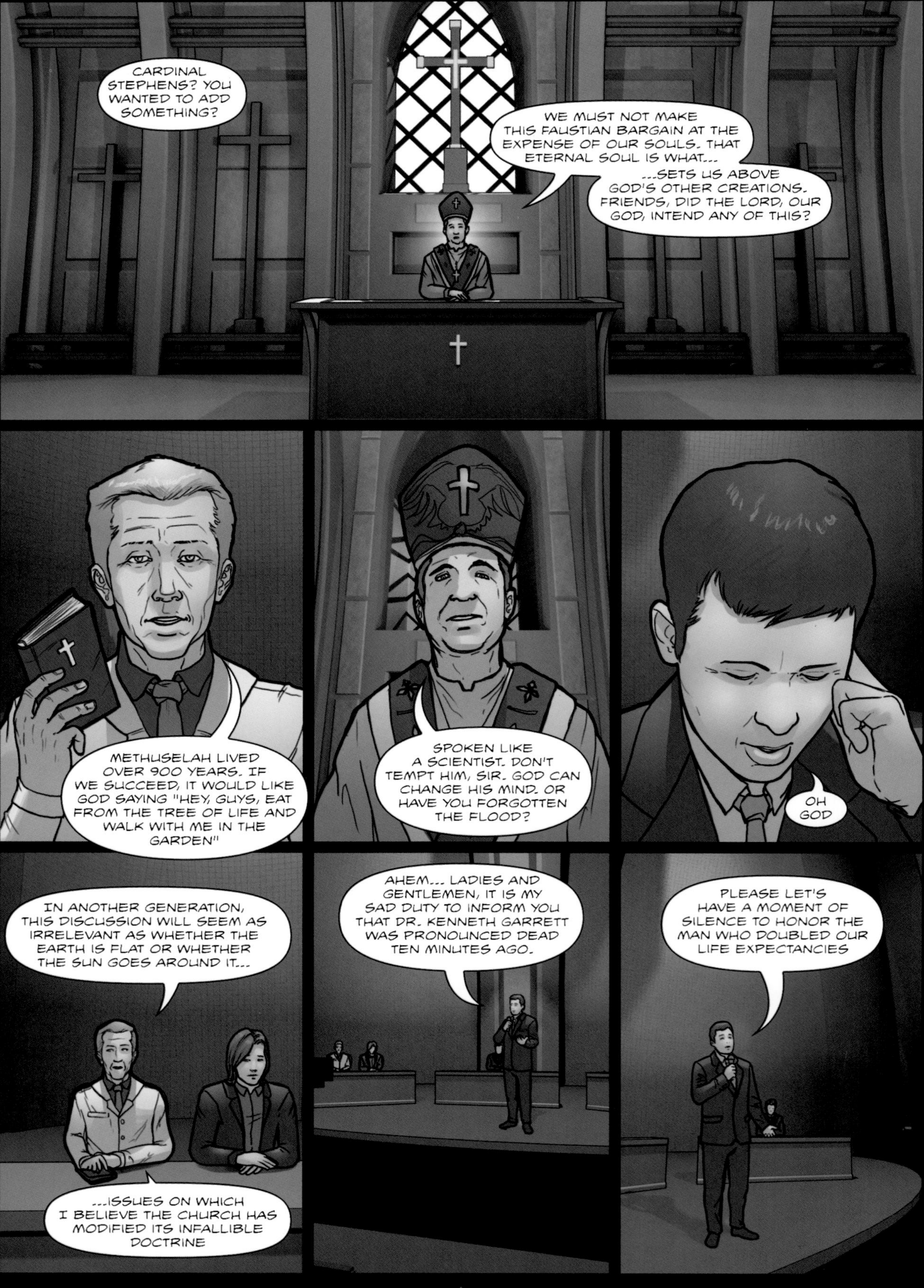
CARDINAL STEPHENS? YOU WANTED TO ADD SOMETHING?
WE MUST NOT MAKE THIS FAUSTIAN BARGAIN AT THE EXPENSE OF OUR SOULS. THAT ETERNAL SOUL IS WHAT...
...SETS US ABOVE GOD'S OTHER CREATIONS. FRIENDS, DID THE LORD, OUR GOD, INTEND ANY OF THIS?
METHUSELAH LIVED OVER 900 YEARS. IF WE SUCCEED, IT WOULD LIKE GOD SAYING "HEY, GUYS, EAT FROM THE TREE OF LIFE AND WALK WITH ME IN THE GARDEN"
SPOKEN LIKE A SCIENTIST. DON'T TEMPT HIM, SIR. GOD CAN CHANGE HIS MIND. OR HAVE YOU FORGOTTEN THE FLOOD?
OH GOD
IN ANOTHER GENERATION, THIS DISCUSSION WILL SEEM AS IRRELEVANT AS WHETHER THE EARTH IS FLAT OR WHETHER THE SUN GOES AROUND IT...
...ISSUES ON WHICH I BELIEVE THE CHURCH HAS MODIFIED ITS INFALLIBLE DOCTRINE
AHEM... LADIES AND GENTLEMEN, IT IS MY SAD DUTY TO INFORM YOU THAT DR. KENNETH GARRETT WAS PRONOUNCED DEAD TEN MINUTES AGO.
PLEASE LET'S HAVE A MOMENT OF SILENCE TO HONOR THE MAN WHO DOUBLED OUR LIFE EXPECTANCIES

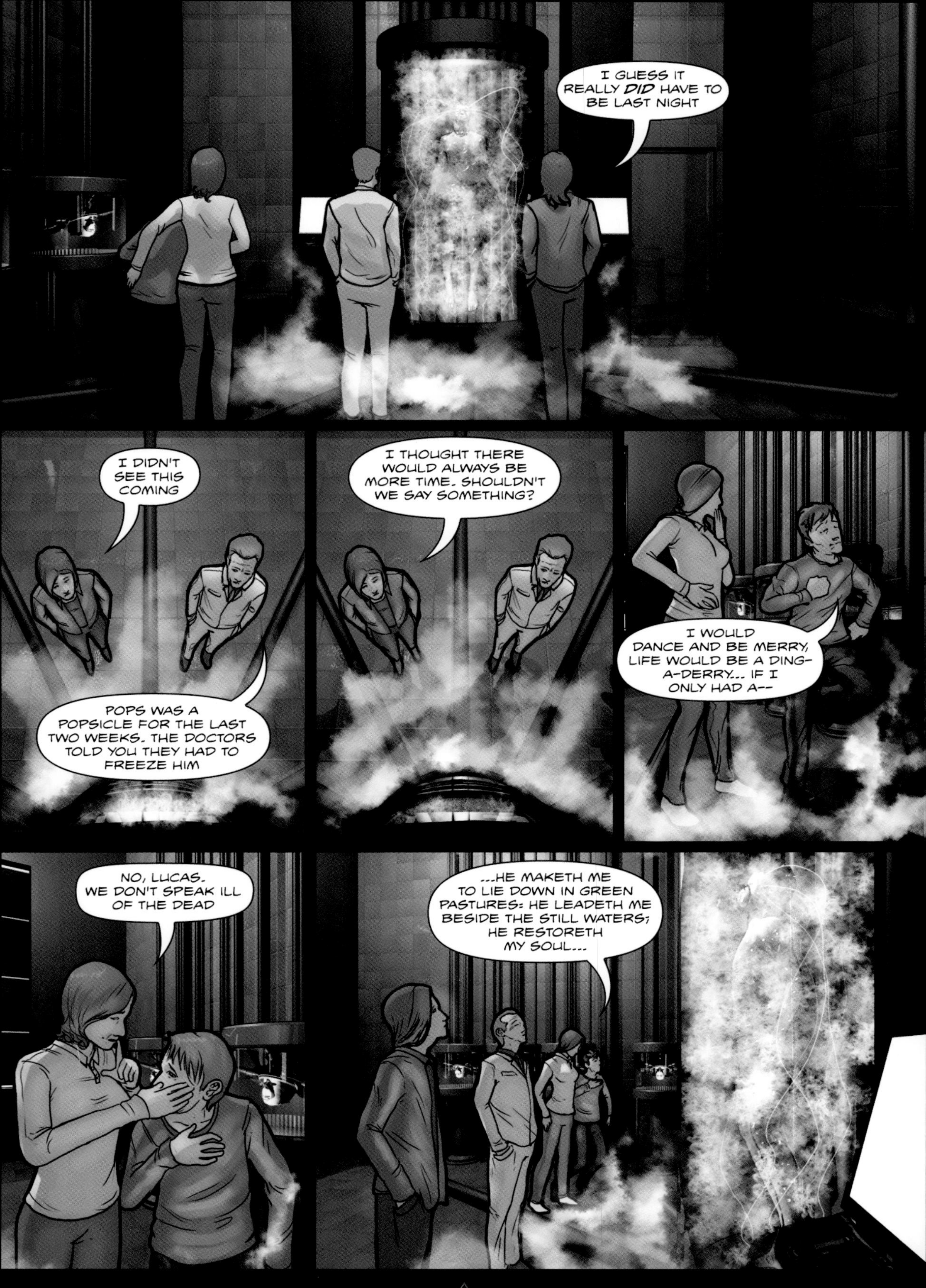
I GUESS IT REALLY *DID* HAVE TO BE LAST NIGHT
I DIDN'T SEE THIS COMING
POPS WAS A POPSICLE FOR THE LAST TWO WEEKS. THE DOCTORS TOLD YOU THEY HAD TO FREEZE HIM
I THOUGHT THERE WOULD ALWAYS BE MORE TIME. SHOULDN'T WE SAY SOMETHING?
I WOULD DANCE AND BE MERRY, LIFE WOULD BE A DING-A-DERRY... IF I ONLY HAD A--
NO, LUCAS. WE DON'T SPEAK ILL OF THE DEAD
...HE MAKETH ME TO LIE DOWN IN GREEN PASTURES: HE LEADETH ME BESIDE THE STILL WATERS; HE RESTORETH MY SOUL...

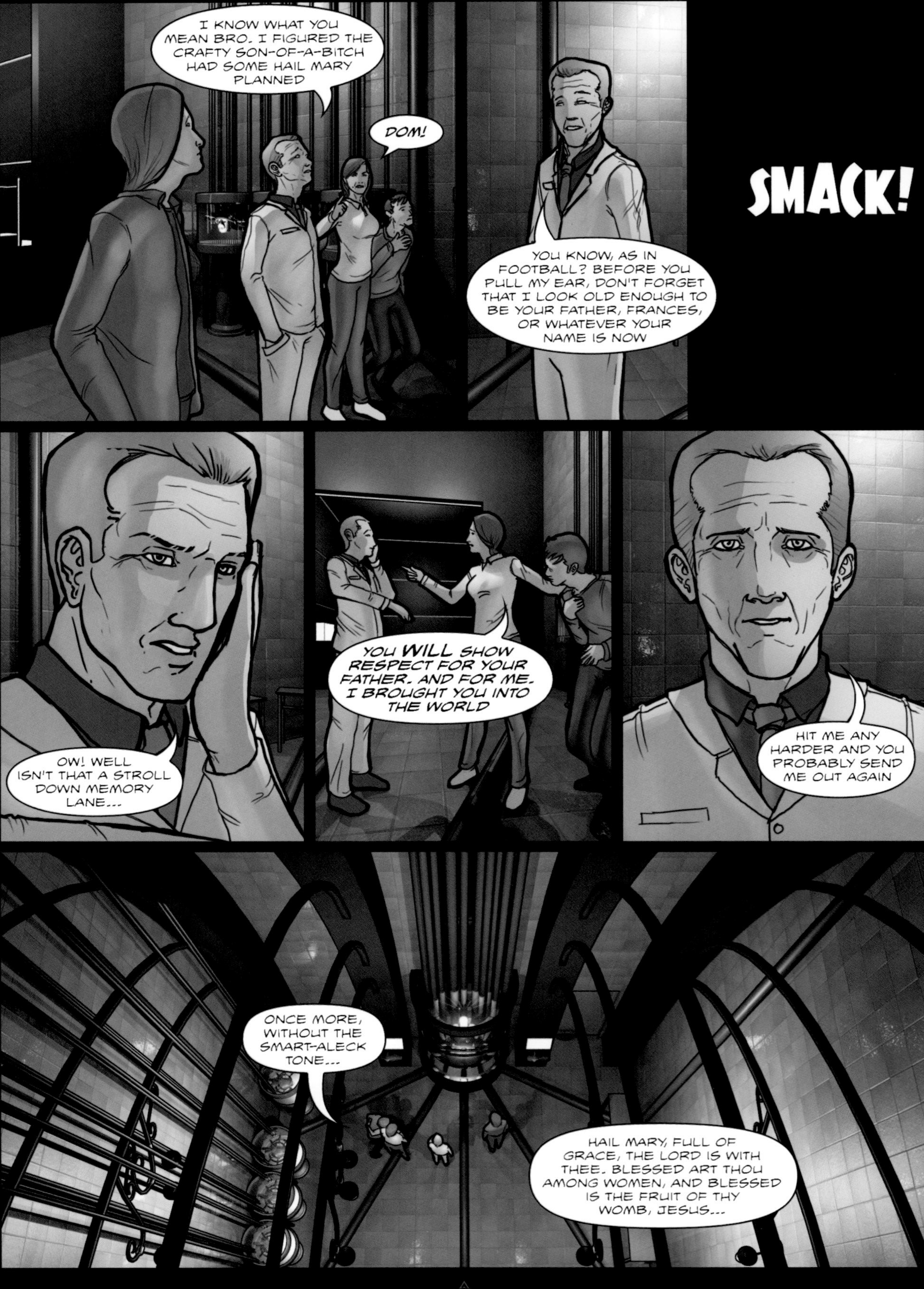
I KNOW WHAT YOU MEAN BRO. I FIGURED THE CRAFTY SON-OF-A-BITCH HAD SOME HAIL MARY PLANNED
DOM!
YOU KNOW, AS IN FOOTBALL? BEFORE YOU PULL MY EAR, DON'T FORGET THAT I LOOK OLD ENOUGH TO BE YOUR FATHER, FRANCES, OR WHATEVER YOUR NAME IS NOW
SMACK!
OW! WELL ISN'T THAT A STROLL DOWN MEMORY LANE...
YOU WILL SHOW RESPECT FOR YOUR FATHER. AND FOR ME. I BROUGHT YOU INTO THE WORLD
HIT ME ANY HARDER AND YOU PROBABLY SEND ME OUT AGAIN
ONCE MORE, WITHOUT THE SMART-ALECK TONE...
HAIL MARY, FULL OF GRACE, THE LORD IS WITH THEE. BLESSED ART THOU AMONG WOMEN, AND BLESSED IS THE FRUIT OF THY WOMB, JESUS...

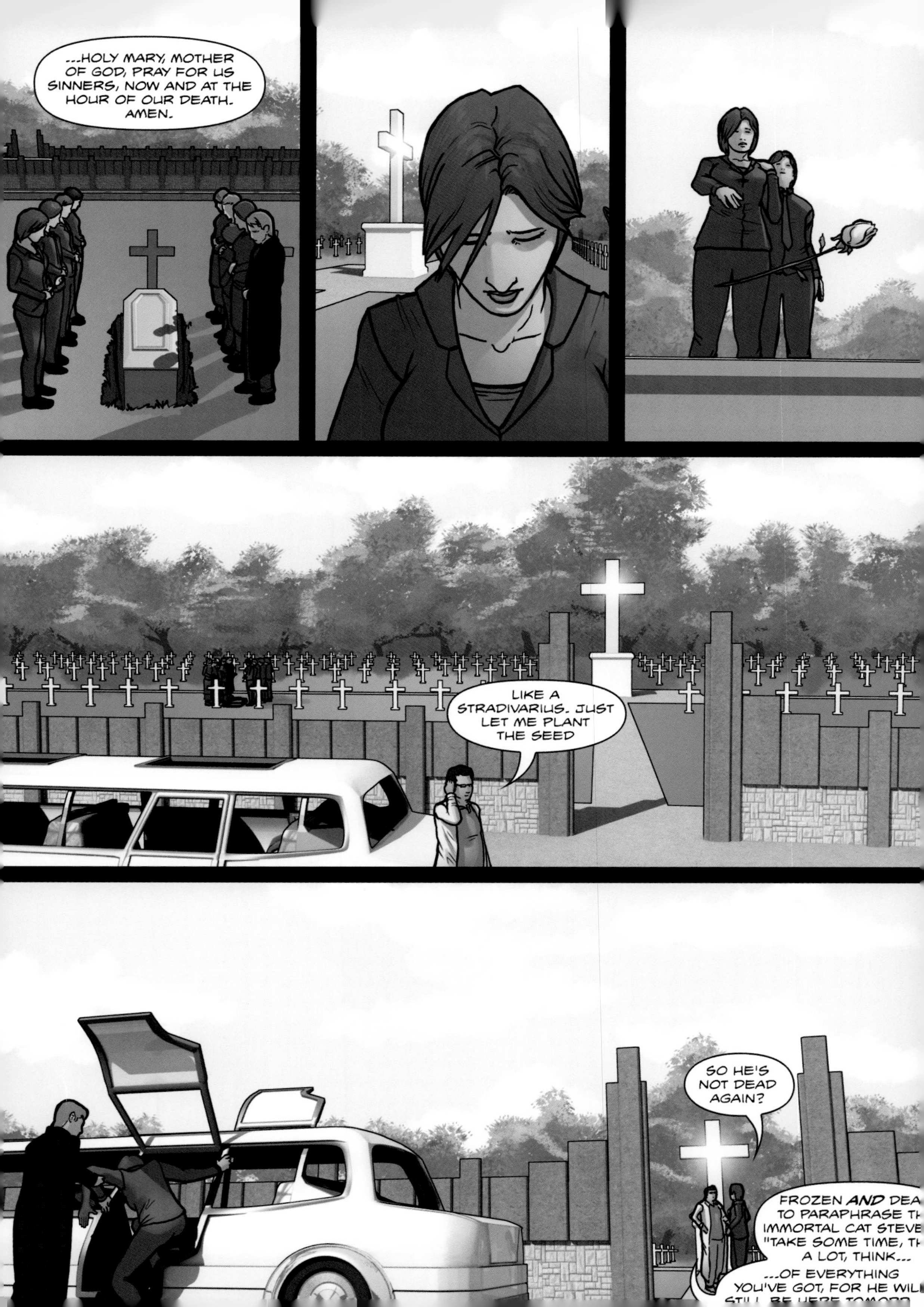
...HOLY MARY, MOTHER OF GOD, PRAY FOR US SINNERS, NOW AND AT THE HOUR OF OUR DEATH. AMEN.
LIKE A STRADIVARIUS. JUST LET ME PLANT THE SEED
SO HE'S NOT DEAD AGAIN?
FROZEN AND DEA TO PARAPHRASE TH IMMORTAL CAT STEVE "TAKE SOME TIME, TH A LOT, THINK...
...OF EVERYTHING YOU'VE GOT, FOR HE WIL

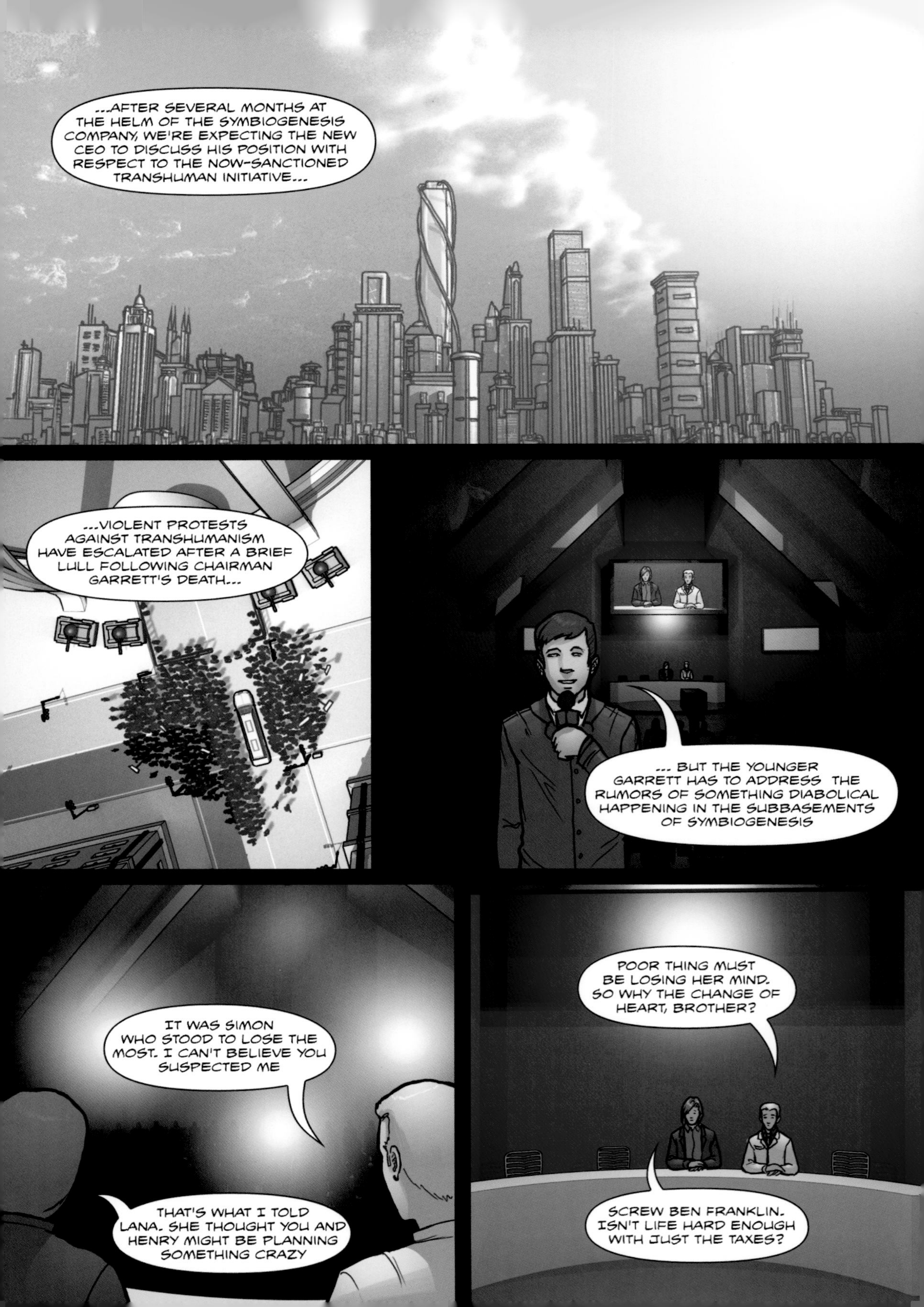
...AFTER SEVERAL MONTHS AT THE HELM OF THE SYMBIOGENESIS COMPANY, WE'RE EXPECTING THE NEW CEO TO DISCUSS HIS POSITION WITH RESPECT TO THE NOW-SANCTIONED TRANSHUMAN INITIATIVE...
...VIOLENT PROTESTS AGAINST TRANSHUMANISM HAVE ESCALATED AFTER A BRIEF LULL FOLLOWING CHAIRMAN GARRETT'S DEATH...
... BUT THE YOUNGER GARRETT HAS TO ADDRESS THE RUMORS OF SOMETHING DIABOLICAL HAPPENING IN THE SUBBASEMENTS OF SYMBIOGENESIS
IT WAS SIMON WHO STOOD TO LOSE THE MOST. I CAN'T BELIEVE YOU SUSPECTED ME
THAT'S WHAT I TOLD LANA. SHE THOUGHT YOU AND HENRY MIGHT BE PLANNING SOMETHING CRAZY
POOR THING MUST BE LOSING HER MIND. SO WHY THE CHANGE OF HEART, BROTHER?
SCREW BEN FRANKLIN. ISN'T LIFE HARD ENOUGH WITH JUST THE TAXES?

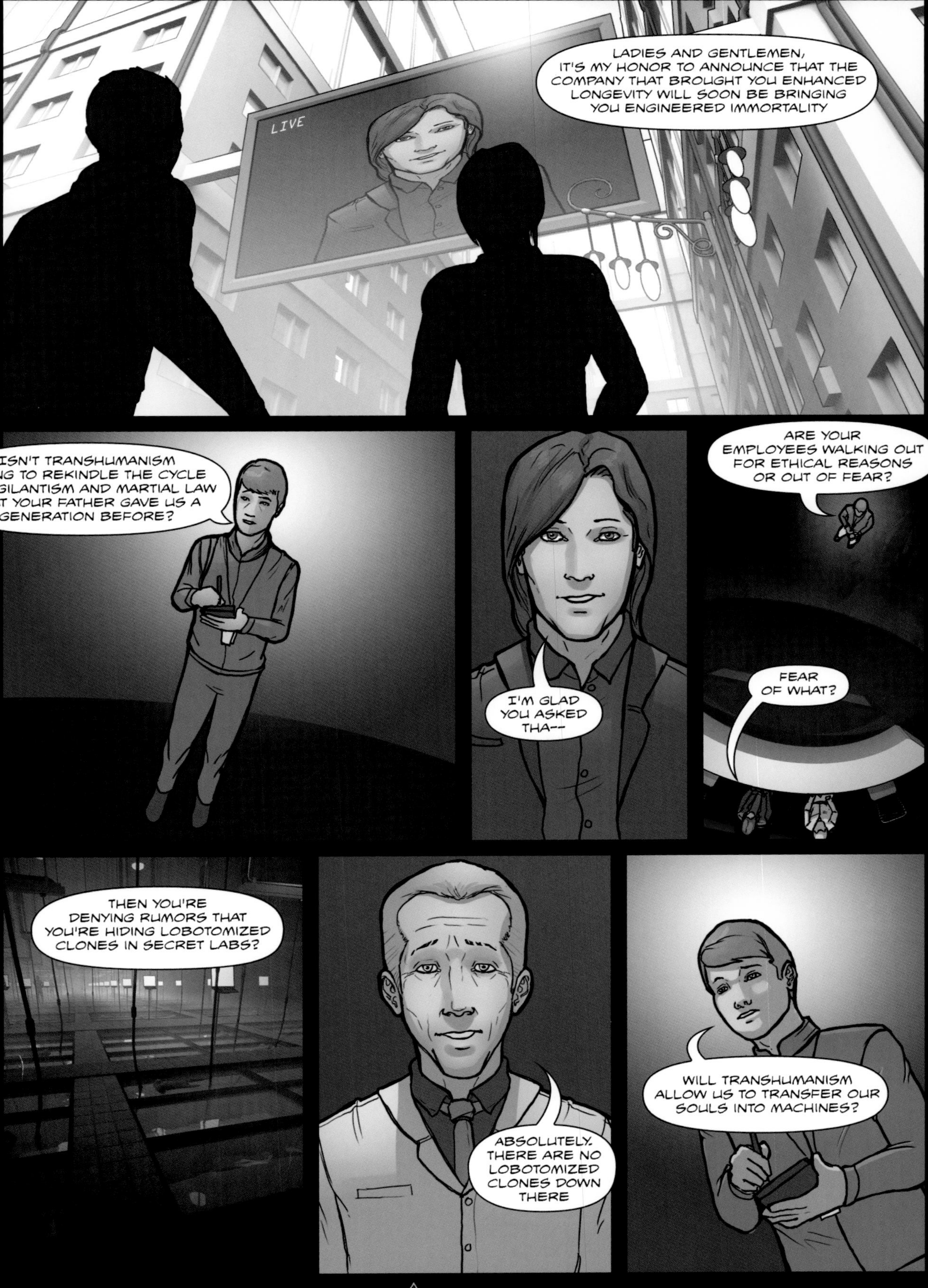
LIVE
LADIES AND GENTLEMEN, IT'S MY HONOR TO ANNOUNCE THAT THE COMPANY THAT BROUGHT YOU ENHANCED LONGEVITY WILL SOON BE BRINGING YOU ENGINEERED IMMORTALITY
ISN'T TRANSHUMANISM GOING TO REKINDLE THE CYCLE OF VIGILANTISM AND MARTIAL LAW THAT YOUR FATHER GAVE US A GENERATION BEFORE?
I'M GLAD YOU ASKED THA--
ARE YOUR EMPLOYEES WALKING OUT FOR ETHICAL REASONS OR OUT OF FEAR?
FEAR OF WHAT?
THEN YOU'RE DENYING RUMORS THAT YOU'RE HIDING LOBOTOMIZED CLONES IN SECRET LABS?
ABSOLUTELY. THERE ARE NO LOBOTOMIZED CLONES DOWN THERE
WILL TRANSHUMANISM ALLOW US TO TRANSFER OUR SOULS INTO MACHINES?

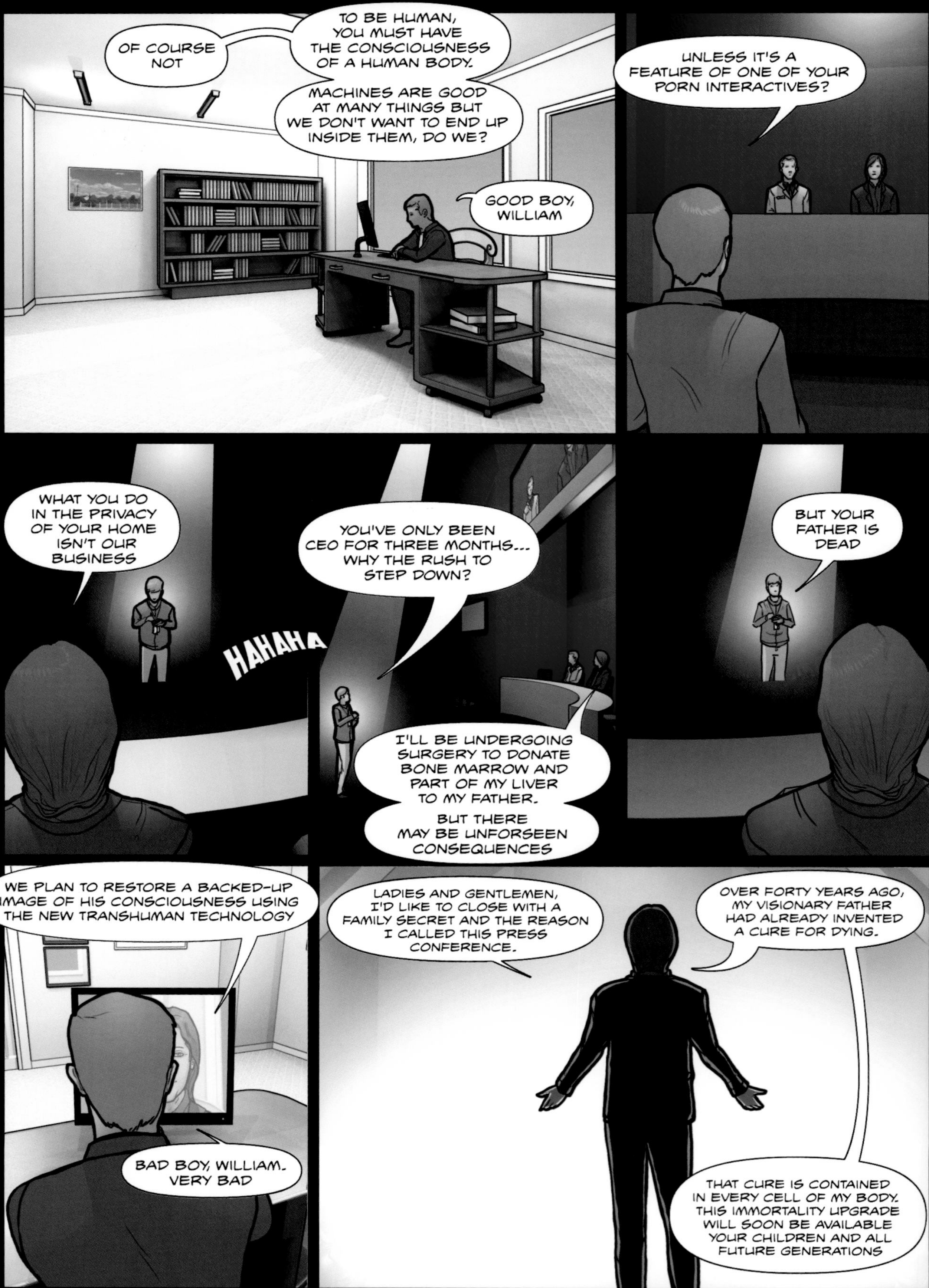
OF COURSE NOT
TO BE HUMAN, YOU MUST HAVE THE CONSCIOUSNESS OF A HUMAN BODY.
MACHINES ARE GOOD AT MANY THINGS BUT WE DON'T WANT TO END UP INSIDE THEM, DO WE?
GOOD BOY, WILLIAM
UNLESS IT'S A FEATURE OF ONE OF YOUR PORN INTERACTIVES?
WHAT YOU DO IN THE PRIVACY OF YOUR HOME ISN'T OUR BUSINESS
HAHAHA
YOU'VE ONLY BEEN CEO FOR THREE MONTHS... WHY THE RUSH TO STEP DOWN?
I'LL BE UNDERGOING SURGERY TO DONATE BONE MARROW AND PART OF MY LIVER TO MY FATHER.
BUT THERE MAY BE UNFORSEEN CONSEQUENCES
BUT YOUR FATHER IS DEAD
WE PLAN TO RESTORE A BACKED-UP IMAGE OF HIS CONSCIOUSNESS USING THE NEW TRANSHUMAN TECHNOLOGY
BAD BOY, WILLIAM. VERY BAD
LADIES AND GENTLEMEN, I'D LIKE TO CLOSE WITH A FAMILY SECRET AND THE REASON I CALLED THIS PRESS CONFERENCE.
OVER FORTY YEARS AGO, MY VISIONARY FATHER HAD ALREADY INVENTED A CURE FOR DYING.
THAT CURE IS CONTAINED IN EVERY CELL OF MY BODY. THIS IMMORTALITY UPGRADE WILL SOON BE AVAILABLE YOUR CHILDREN AND ALL FUTURE GENERATIONS

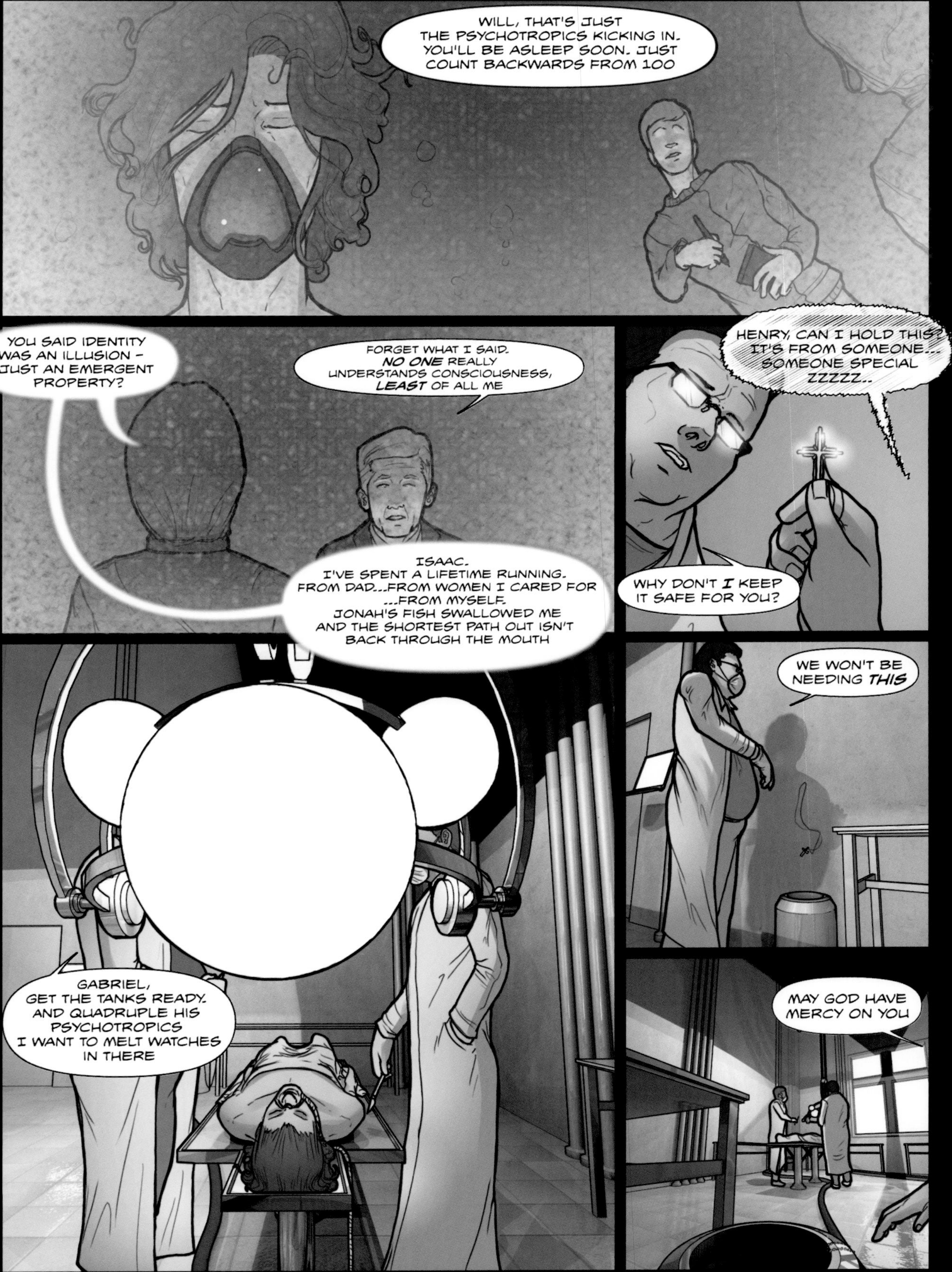
WILL, THAT'S JUST THE PSYCHOTROPICS KICKING IN. YOU'LL BE ASLEEP SOON. JUST COUNT BACKWARDS FROM 100
YOU SAID IDENTITY WAS AN ILLUSION – JUST AN EMERGENT PROPERTY?
FORGET WHAT I SAID. NO ONE REALLY UNDERSTANDS CONSCIOUSNESS, LEAST OF ALL ME
ISAAC. I'VE SPENT A LIFETIME RUNNING. FROM DAD...FROM WOMEN I CARED FOR ...FROM MYSELF. JONAH'S FISH SWALLOWED ME AND THE SHORTEST PATH OUT ISN'T BACK THROUGH THE MOUTH
HENRY, CAN I HOLD THIS? IT'S FROM SOMEONE... SOMEONE SPECIAL ZZZZZ..
WHY DON'T I KEEP IT SAFE FOR YOU?
GABRIEL, GET THE TANKS READY. AND QUADRUPLE HIS PSYCHOTROPICS I WANT TO MELT WATCHES IN THERE
WE WON'T BE NEEDING THIS
MAY GOD HAVE MERCY ON YOU

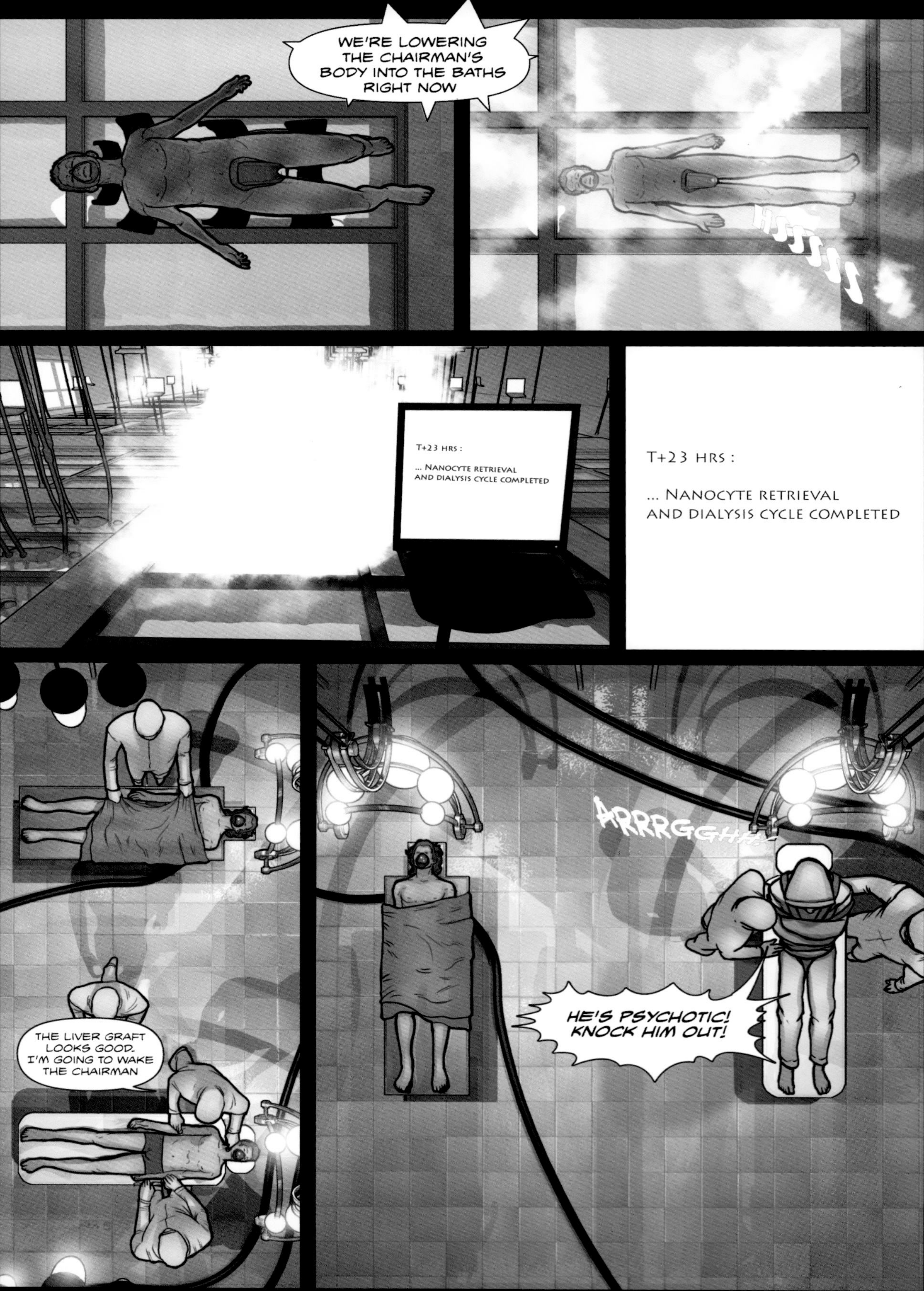
WE'RE LOWERING THE CHAIRMAN'S BODY INTO THE BATHS RIGHT NOW
HSSSSSS
T+23 HRS :
... NANOCYTE RETRIEVAL AND DIALYSIS CYCLE COMPLETED
T+23 HRS :
... NANOCYTE RETRIEVAL AND DIALYSIS CYCLE COMPLETED
THE LIVER GRAFT LOOKS GOOD. I'M GOING TO WAKE THE CHAIRMAN
ARRRGGHH
HE'S PSYCHOTIC! KNOCK HIM OUT!

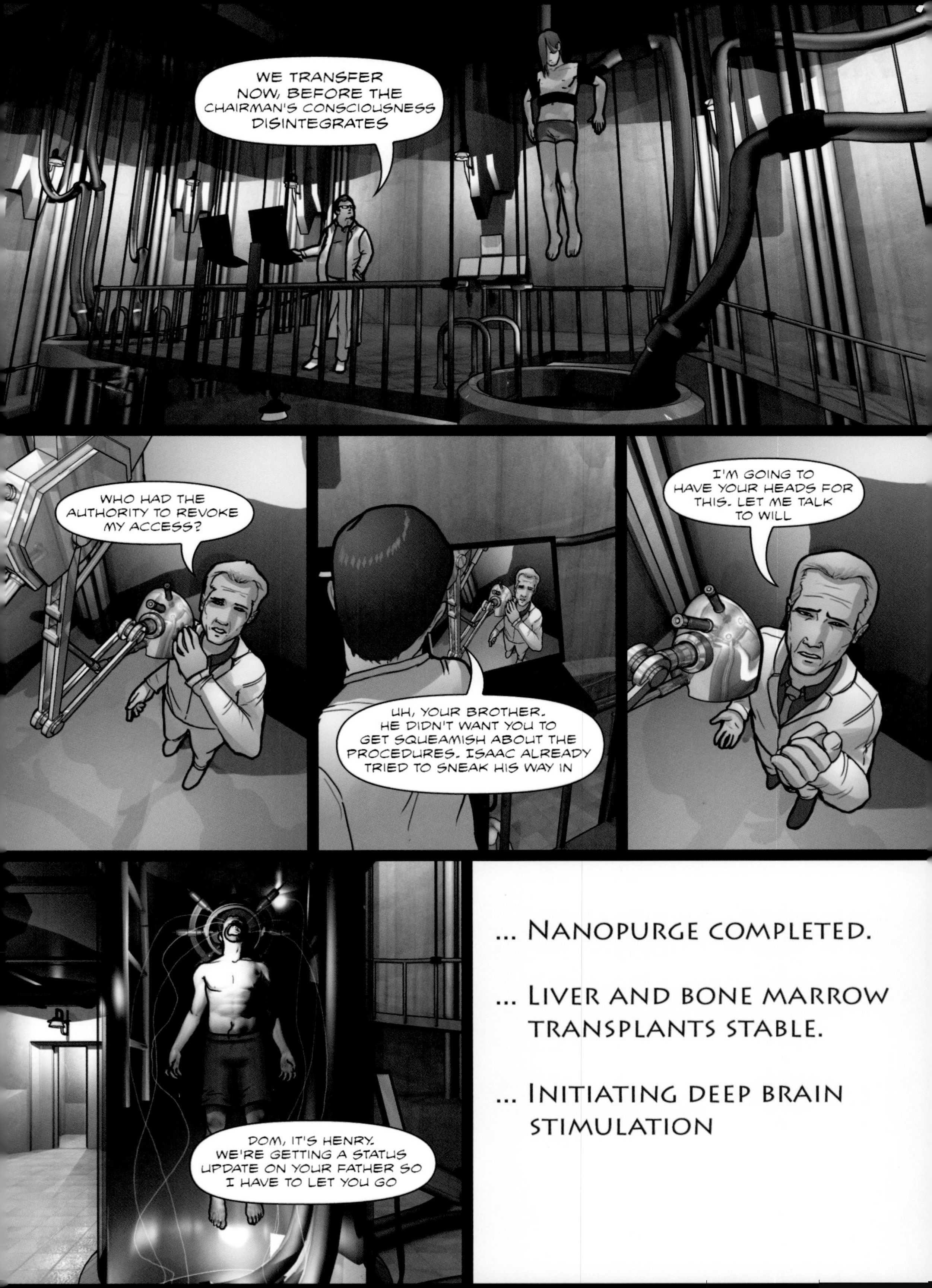
WE TRANSFER NOW, BEFORE THE CHAIRMAN'S CONSCIOUSNESS DISINTEGRATES
WHO HAD THE AUTHORITY TO REVOKE MY ACCESS?
UH, YOUR BROTHER. HE DIDN'T WANT YOU TO GET SQUEAMISH ABOUT THE PROCEDURES. ISAAC ALREADY TRIED TO SNEAK HIS WAY IN
I'M GOING TO HAVE YOUR HEADS FOR THIS. LET ME TALK TO WILL
DOM, IT'S HENRY. WE'RE GETTING A STATUS UPDATE ON YOUR FATHER SO I HAVE TO LET YOU GO
... NANOPURGE COMPLETED.
... LIVER AND BONE MARROW TRANSPLANTS STABLE.
... INITIATING DEEP BRAIN STIMULATION

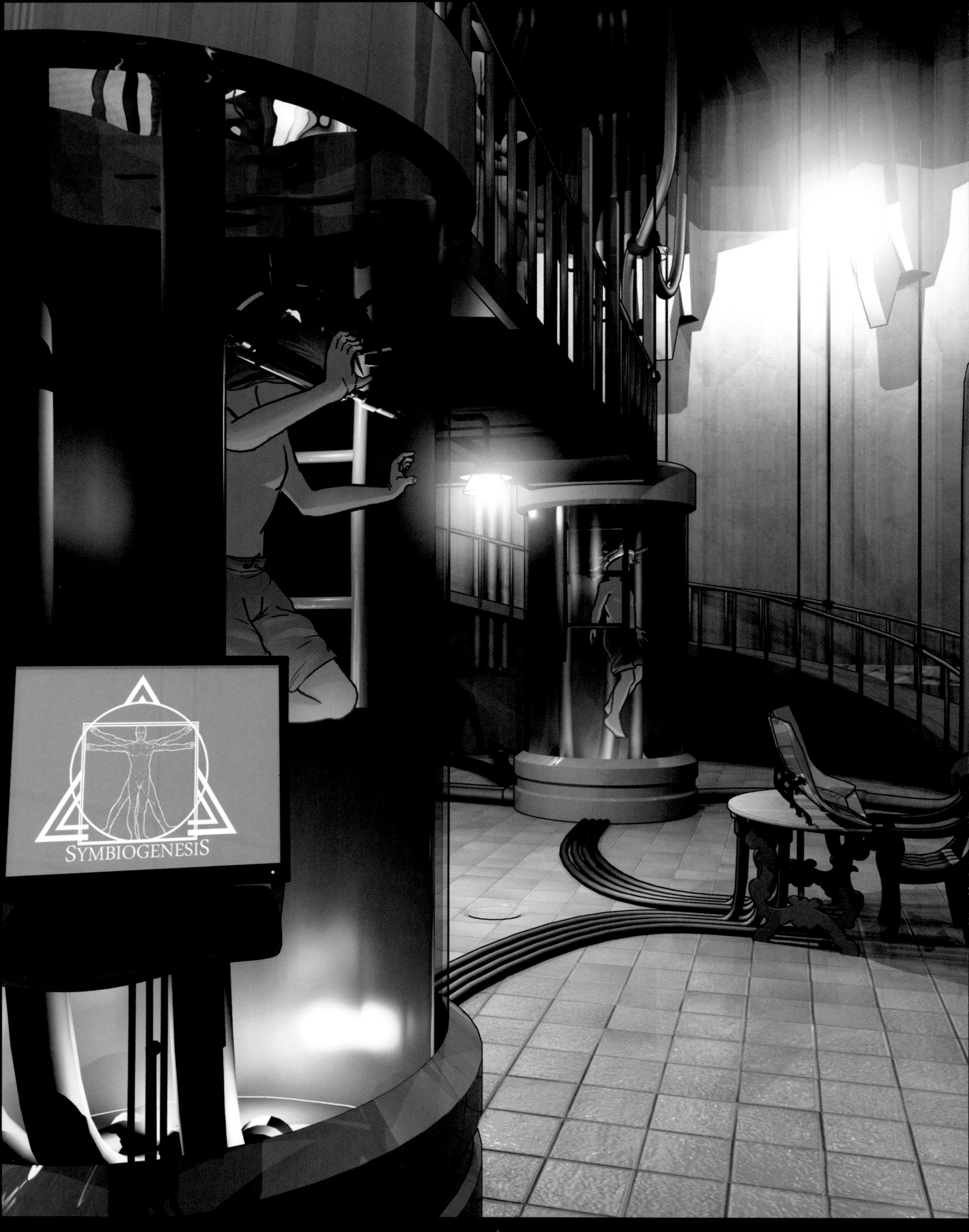
SYMBIOGENESIS

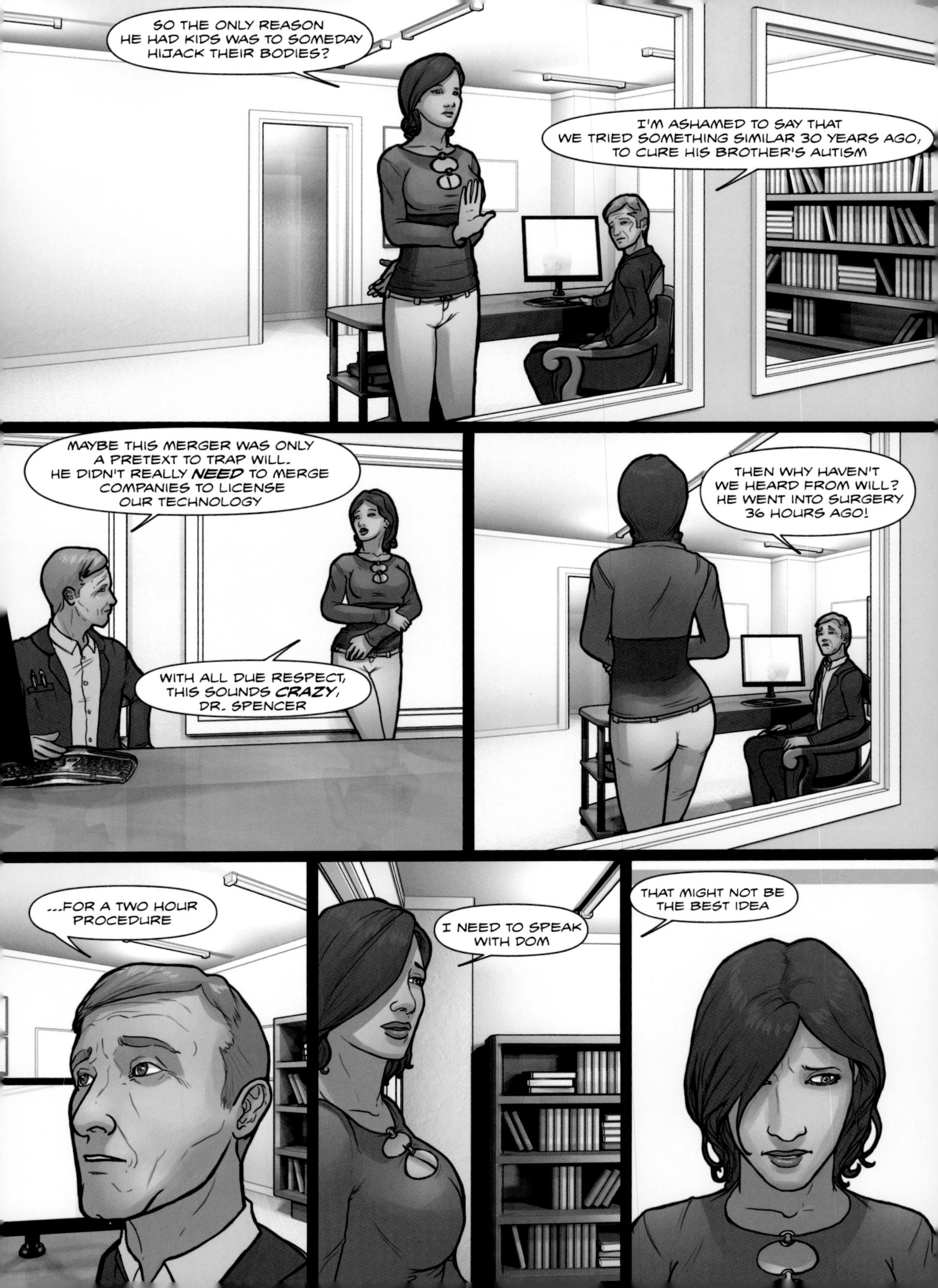
SO THE ONLY REASON HE HAD KIDS WAS TO SOMEDAY HIJACK THEIR BODIES?
I'M ASHAMED TO SAY THAT WE TRIED SOMETHING SIMILAR 30 YEARS AGO, TO CURE HIS BROTHER'S AUTISM
MAYBE THIS MERGER WAS ONLY A PRETEXT TO TRAP WILL. HE DIDN'T REALLY NEED TO MERGE COMPANIES TO LICENSE OUR TECHNOLOGY
WITH ALL DUE RESPECT, THIS SOUNDS CRAZY, DR. SPENCER
THEN WHY HAVEN'T WE HEARD FROM WILL? HE WENT INTO SURGERY 36 HOURS AGO!
...FOR A TWO HOUR PROCEDURE
I NEED TO SPEAK WITH DOM
THAT MIGHT NOT BE THE BEST IDEA

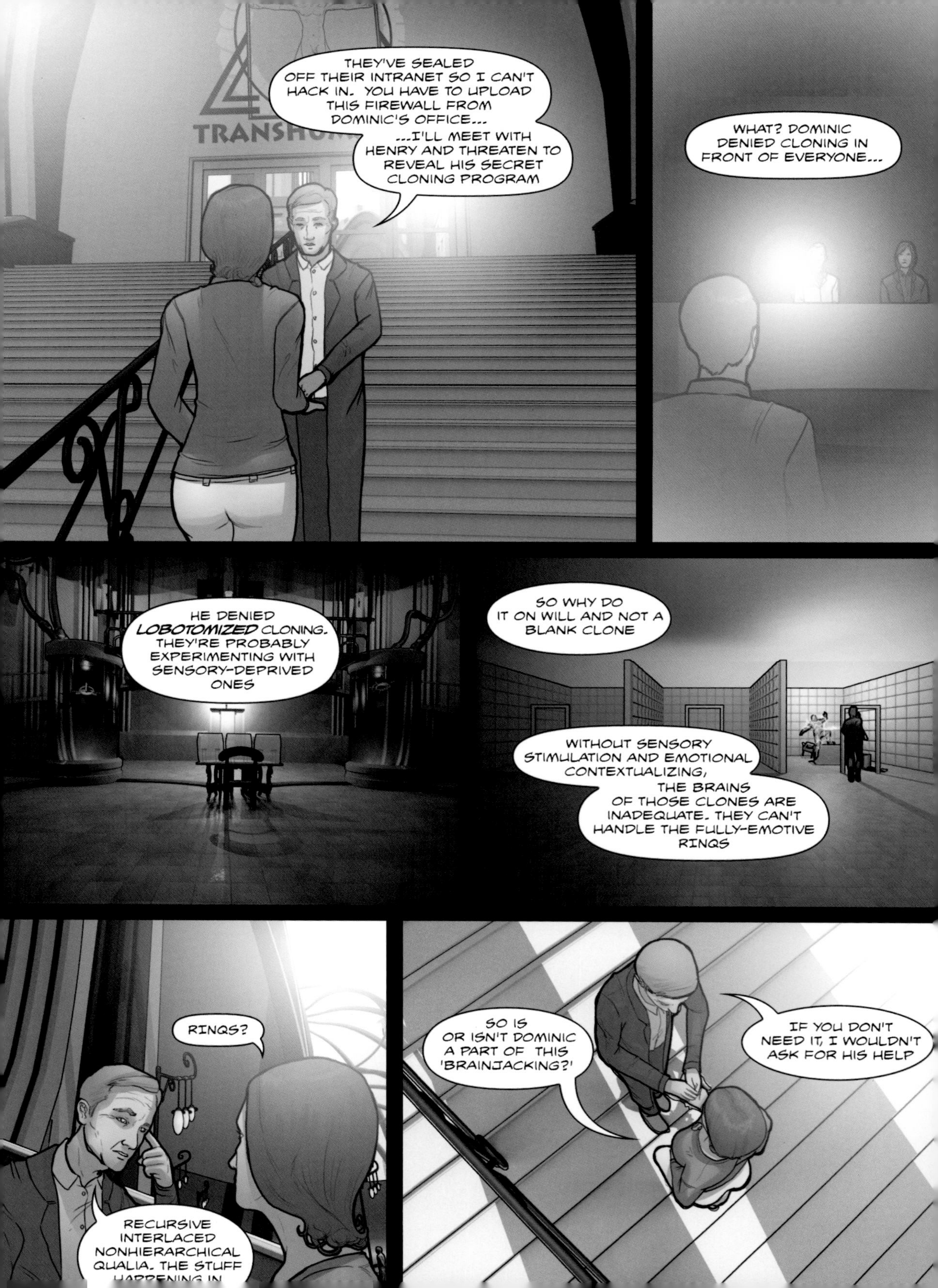
THEY'VE SEALED OFF THEIR INTRANET SO I CAN'T HACK IN. YOU HAVE TO UPLOAD THIS FIREWALL FROM DOMINIC'S OFFICE...
...I'LL MEET WITH HENRY AND THREATEN TO REVEAL HIS SECRET CLONING PROGRAM
TRANSHUM
WHAT? DOMINIC DENIED CLONING IN FRONT OF EVERYONE...
HE DENIED *LOBOTOMIZED* CLONING. THEY'RE PROBABLY EXPERIMENTING WITH SENSORY-DEPRIVED ONES
SO WHY DO IT ON WILL AND NOT A BLANK CLONE
WITHOUT SENSORY STIMULATION AND EMOTIONAL CONTEXTUALIZING, THE BRAINS OF THOSE CLONES ARE INADEQUATE. THEY CAN'T HANDLE THE FULLY-EMOTIVE RINQS
RINQS?
RECURSIVE INTERLACED NONHIERARCHICAL QUALIA. THE STUFF
SO IS OR ISN'T DOMINIC A PART OF THIS 'BRAINJACKING?'
IF YOU DON'T NEED IT, I WOULDN'T ASK FOR HIS HELP

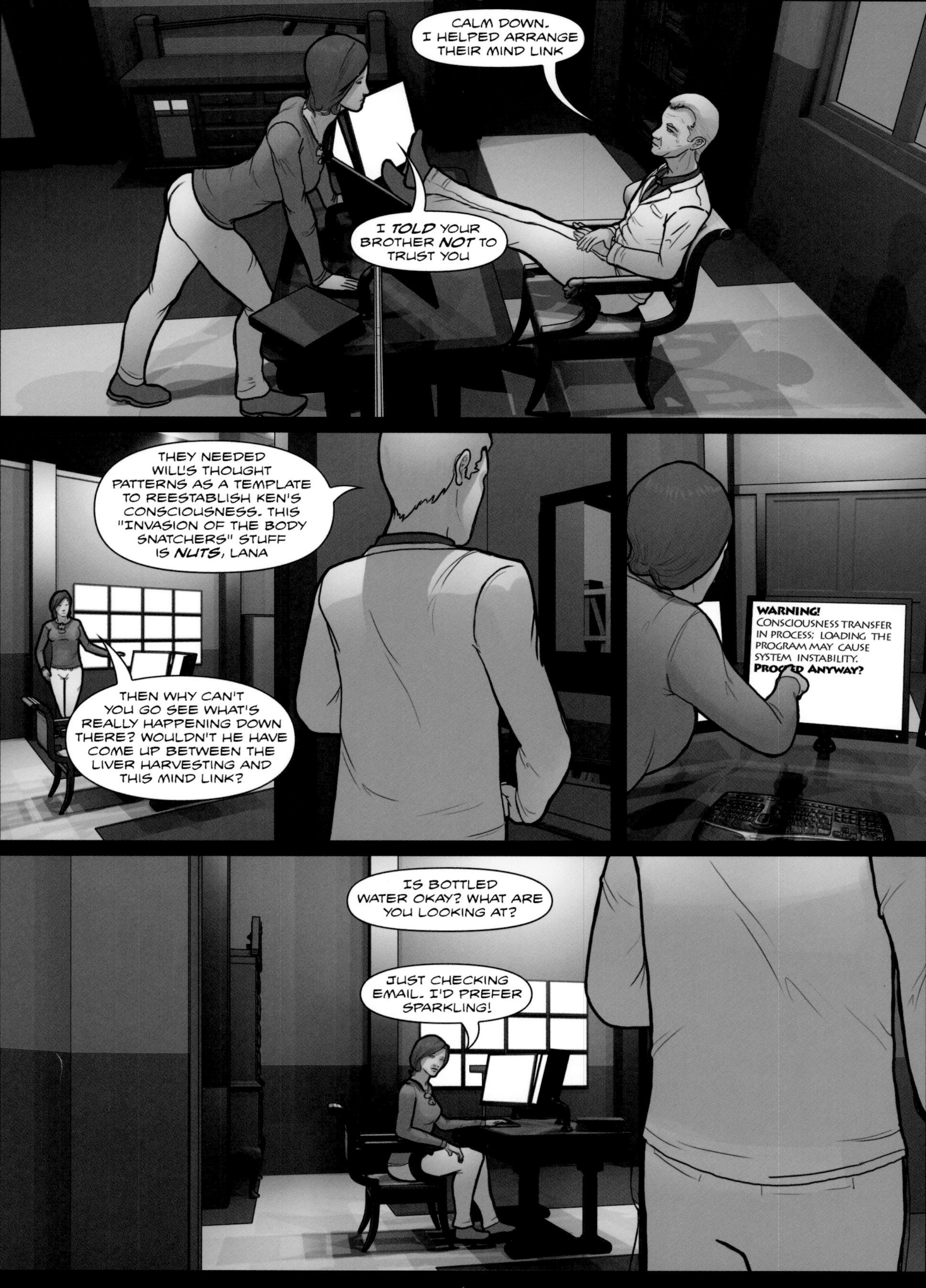
CALM DOWN. I HELPED ARRANGE THEIR MIND LINK
I TOLD YOUR BROTHER NOT TO TRUST YOU
THEY NEEDED WILL'S THOUGHT PATTERNS AS A TEMPLATE TO REESTABLISH KEN'S CONSCIOUSNESS. THIS "INVASION OF THE BODY SNATCHERS" STUFF IS NUTS, LANA
THEN WHY CAN'T YOU GO SEE WHAT'S REALLY HAPPENING DOWN THERE? WOULDN'T HE HAVE COME UP BETWEEN THE LIVER HARVESTING AND THIS MIND LINK?
WARNING!
CONSCIOUSNESS TRANSFER IN PROCESS; LOADING THE PROGRAM MAY CAUSE SYSTEM INSTABILITY.
PROCEED ANYWAY?
IS BOTTLED WATER OKAY? WHAT ARE YOU LOOKING AT?
JUST CHECKING EMAIL. I'D PREFER SPARKLING!

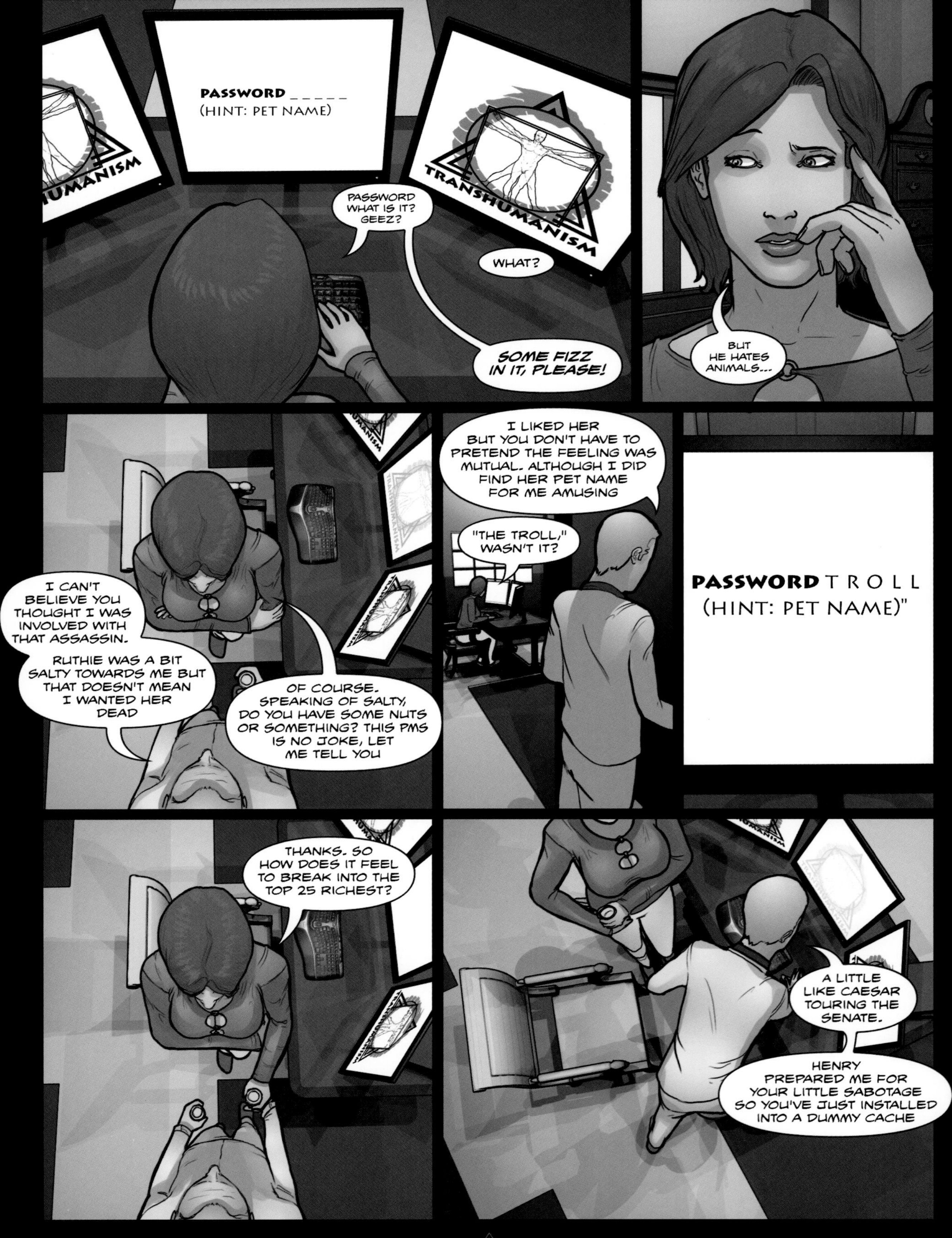
PASSWORD _ _ _ _ _
(HINT: PET NAME)
TRANSHUMANISM
PASSWORD WHAT IS IT? GEEZ?
WHAT?
SOME FIZZ IN IT, PLEASE!
BUT HE HATES ANIMALS...
I CAN'T BELIEVE YOU THOUGHT I WAS INVOLVED WITH THAT ASSASSIN.
RUTHIE WAS A BIT SALTY TOWARDS ME BUT THAT DOESN'T MEAN I WANTED HER DEAD
OF COURSE. SPEAKING OF SALTY, DO YOU HAVE SOME NUTS OR SOMETHING? THIS PMS IS NO JOKE, LET ME TELL YOU
I LIKED HER BUT YOU DON'T HAVE TO PRETEND THE FEELING WAS MUTUAL. ALTHOUGH I DID FIND HER PET NAME FOR ME AMUSING
"THE TROLL," WASN'T IT?
PASSWORD T R O L L
(HINT: PET NAME)"
THANKS. SO HOW DOES IT FEEL TO BREAK INTO THE TOP 25 RICHEST?
A LITTLE LIKE CAESAR TOURING THE SENATE.
HENRY PREPARED ME FOR YOUR LITTLE SABOTAGE SO YOU'VE JUST INSTALLED INTO A DUMMY CACHE

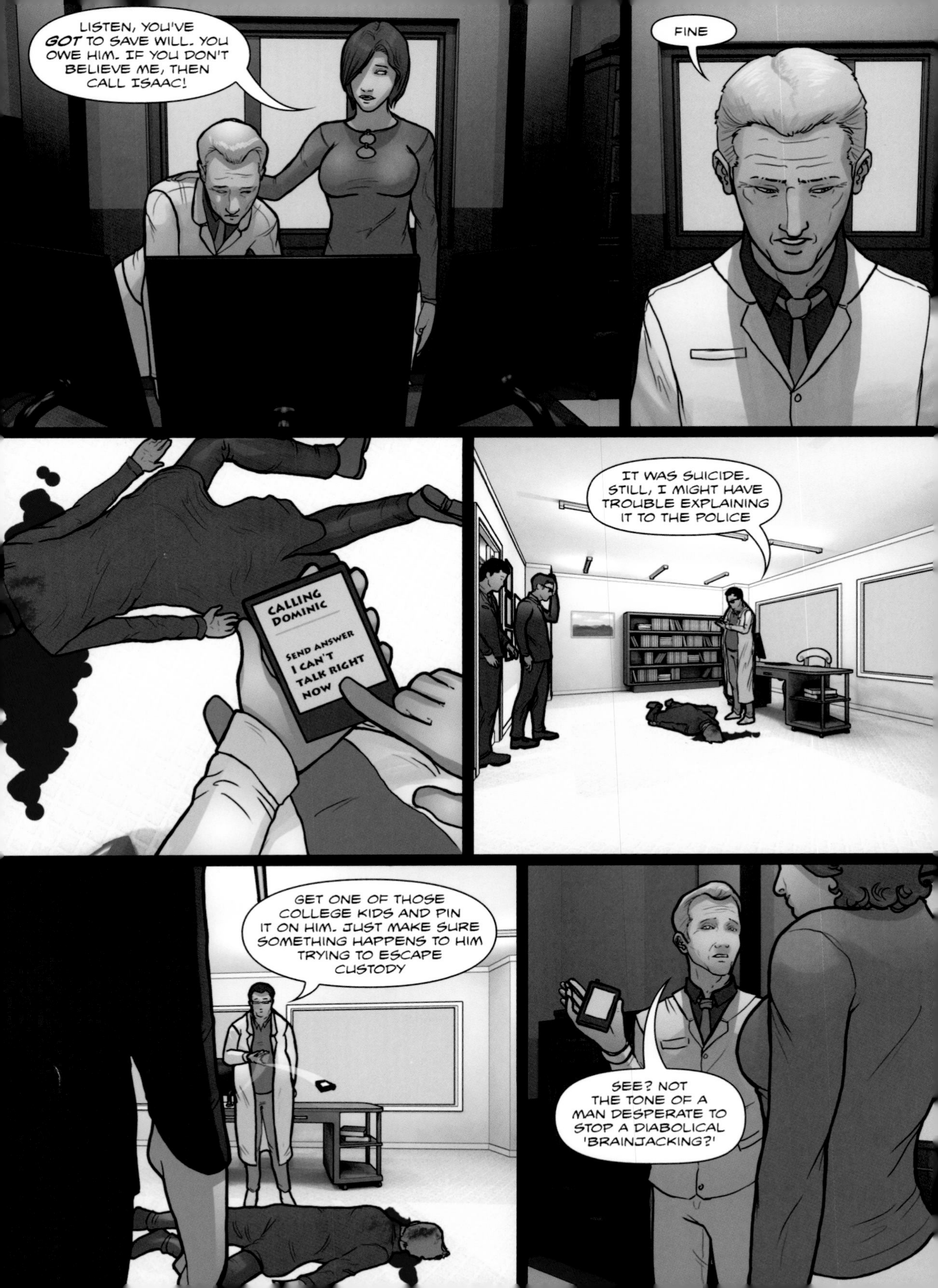
LISTEN, YOU'VE GOT TO SAVE WILL. YOU OWE HIM. IF YOU DON'T BELIEVE ME, THEN CALL ISAAC!
FINE
CALLING DOMINIC
SEND ANSWER
I CAN'T TALK RIGHT NOW
IT WAS SUICIDE. STILL, I MIGHT HAVE TROUBLE EXPLAINING IT TO THE POLICE
GET ONE OF THOSE COLLEGE KIDS AND PIN IT ON HIM. JUST MAKE SURE SOMETHING HAPPENS TO HIM TRYING TO ESCAPE CUSTODY
SEE? NOT THE TONE OF A MAN DESPERATE TO STOP A DIABOLICAL 'BRAINJACKING?'

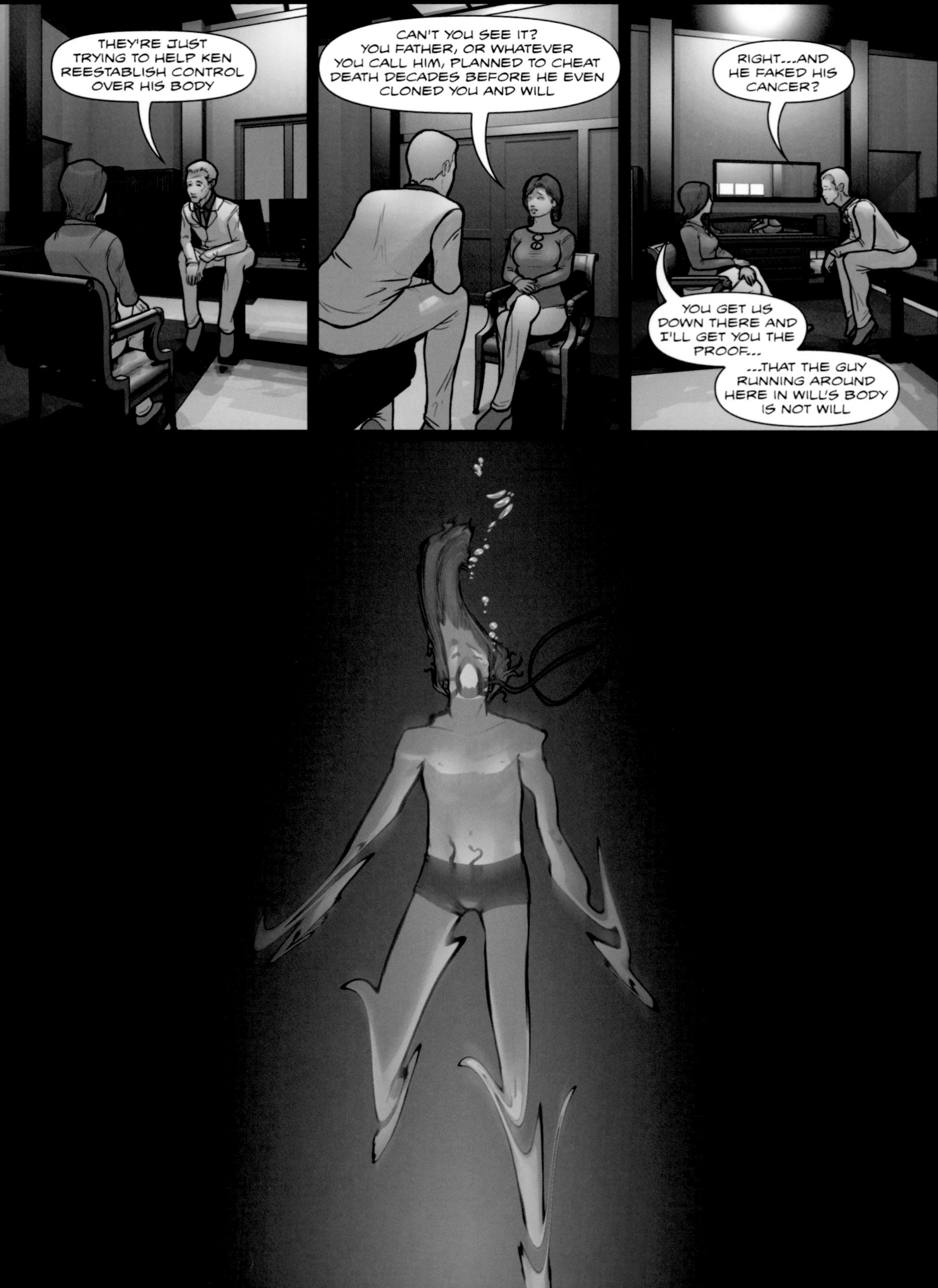
THEY'RE JUST TRYING TO HELP KEN REESTABLISH CONTROL OVER HIS BODY
CAN'T YOU SEE IT? YOU FATHER, OR WHATEVER YOU CALL HIM, PLANNED TO CHEAT DEATH DECADES BEFORE HE EVEN CLONED YOU AND WILL
RIGHT...AND HE FAKED HIS CANCER?
YOU GET US DOWN THERE AND I'LL GET YOU THE PROOF...
...THAT THE GUY RUNNING AROUND HERE IN WILL'S BODY IS NOT WILL

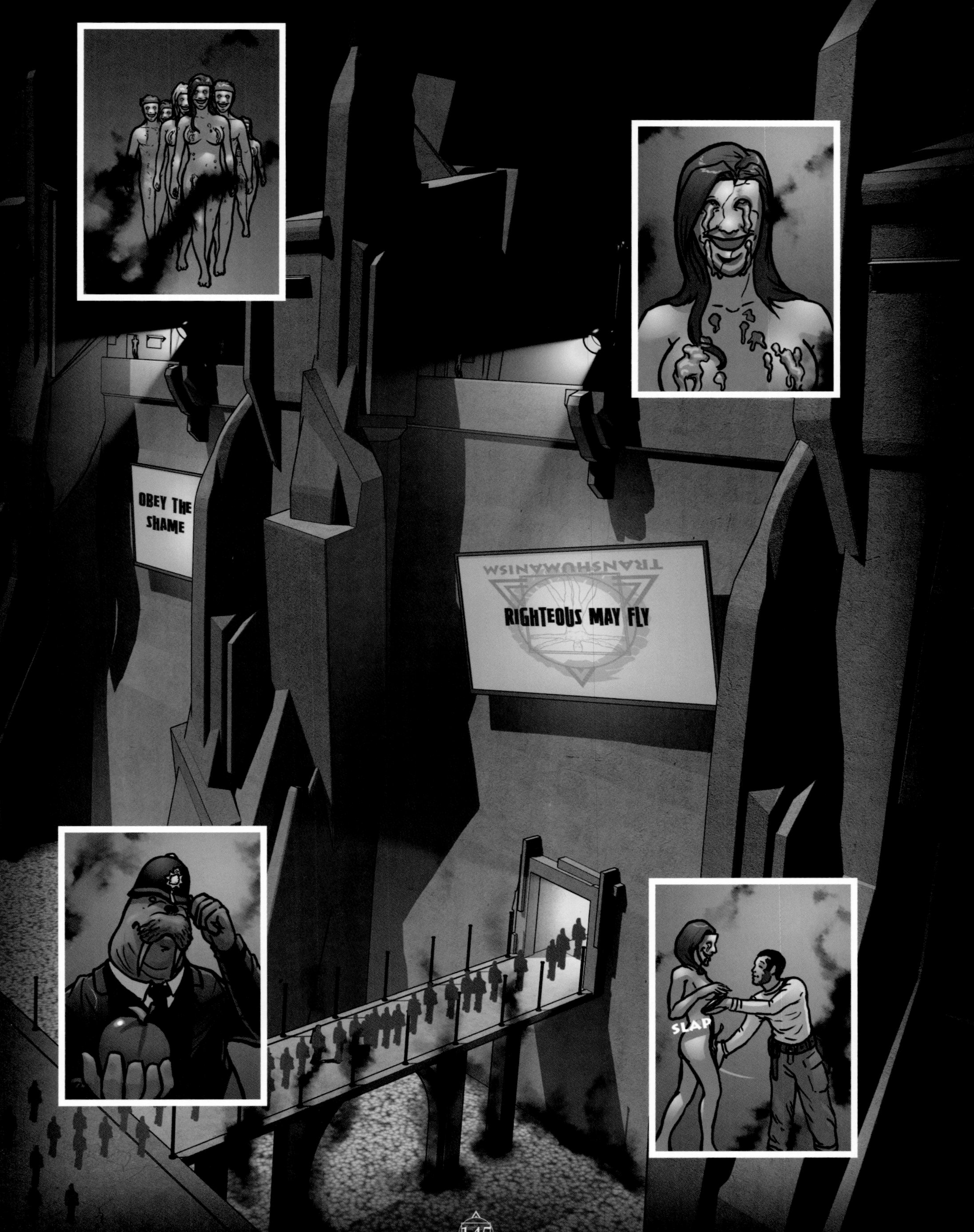
OBEY THE SHAME
TRANSHUMANISM
RIGHTEOUS MAY FLY
SLAP

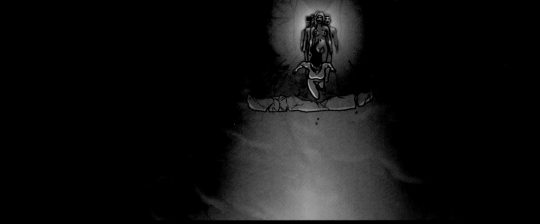

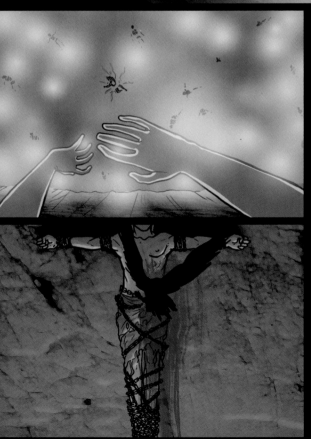

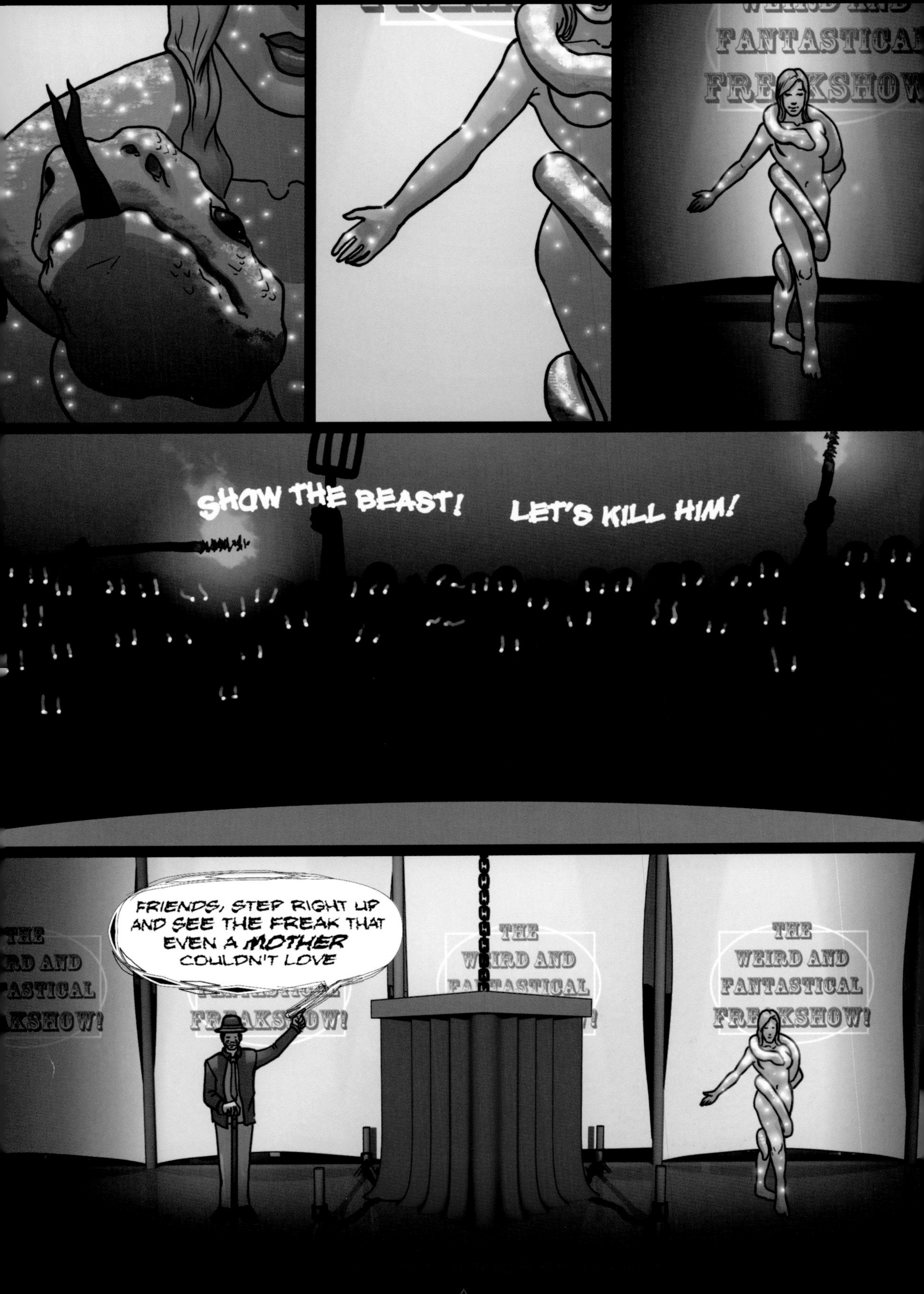
WEIRD AND
FANTASTICAL
FREAKSHOW
SHOW THE BEAST!
LET'S KILL HIM!
FRIENDS, STEP RIGHT UP AND SEE THE FREAK THAT EVEN A *MOTHER* COULDN'T LOVE
THE
WEIRD AND
FANTASTICAL
FREAKSHOW!

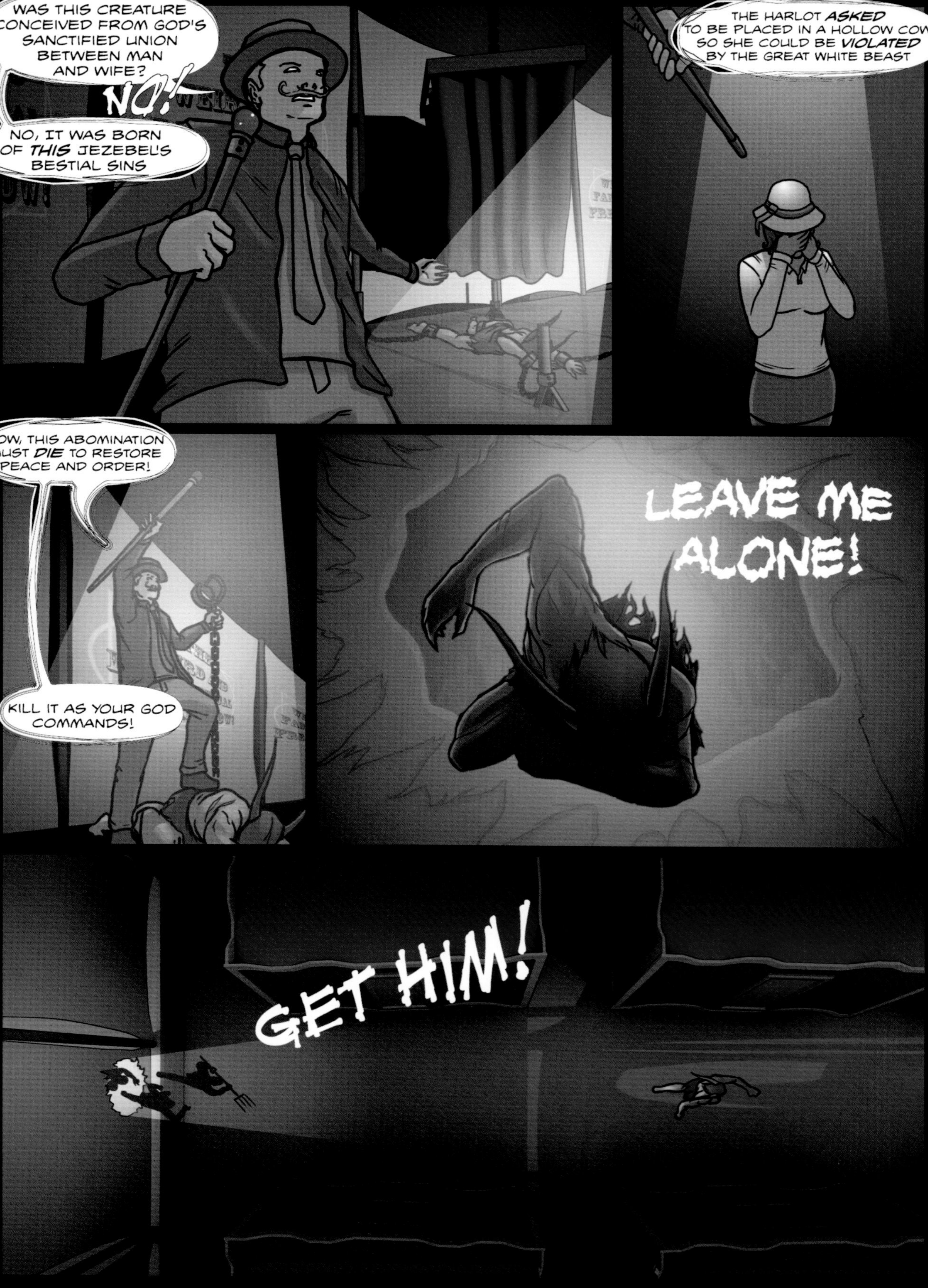
WAS THIS CREATURE CONCEIVED FROM GOD'S SANCTIFIED UNION BETWEEN MAN AND WIFE?
NO!
NO, IT WAS BORN OF THIS JEZEBEL'S BESTIAL SINS
THE HARLOT ASKED TO BE PLACED IN A HOLLOW COW SO SHE COULD BE VIOLATED BY THE GREAT WHITE BEAST
NOW, THIS ABOMINATION MUST DIE TO RESTORE PEACE AND ORDER!
KILL IT AS YOUR GOD COMMANDS!
LEAVE ME ALONE!
GET HIM!

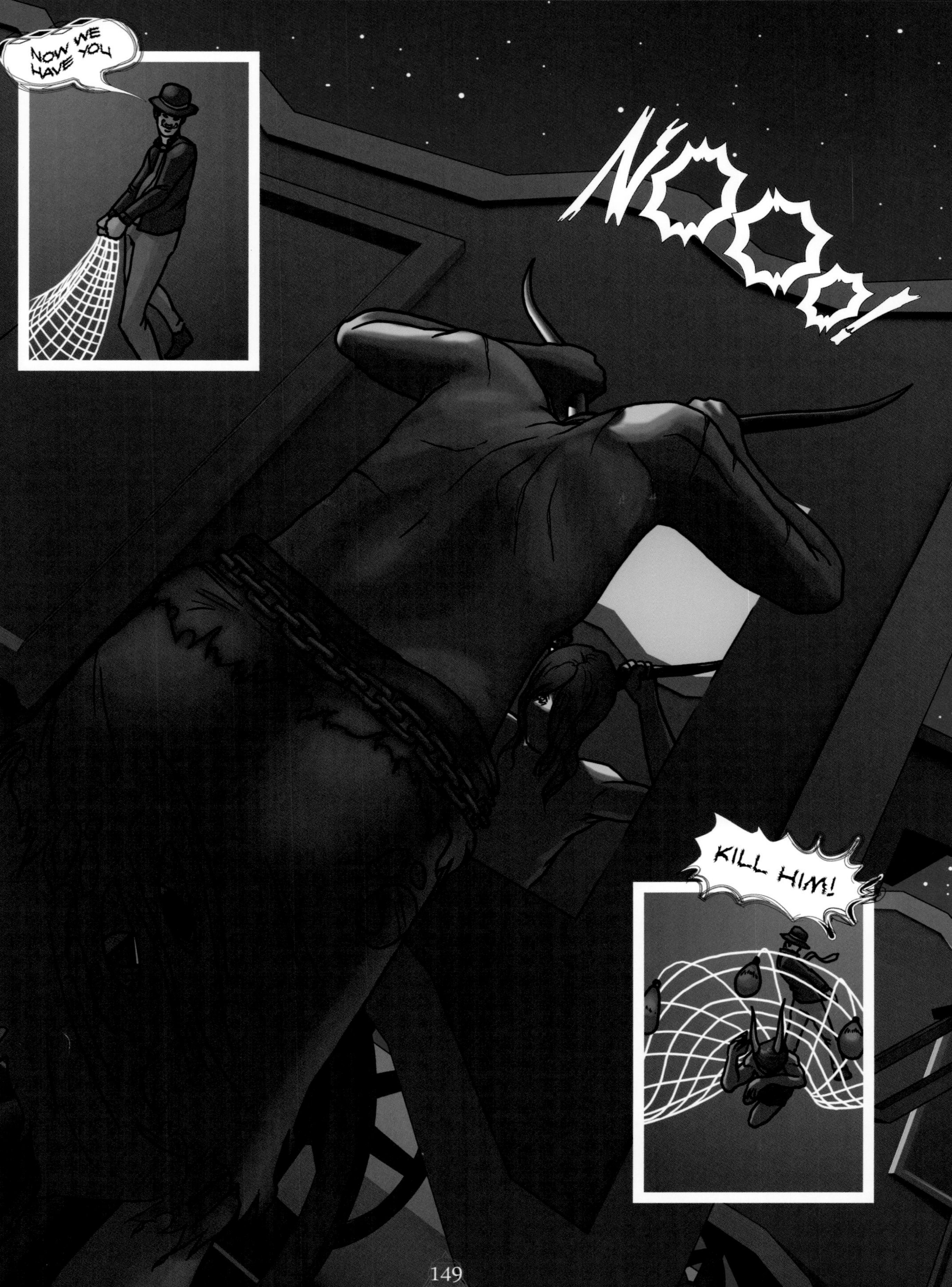
NOW WE HAVE YOU
NOOOO!
KILL HIM!

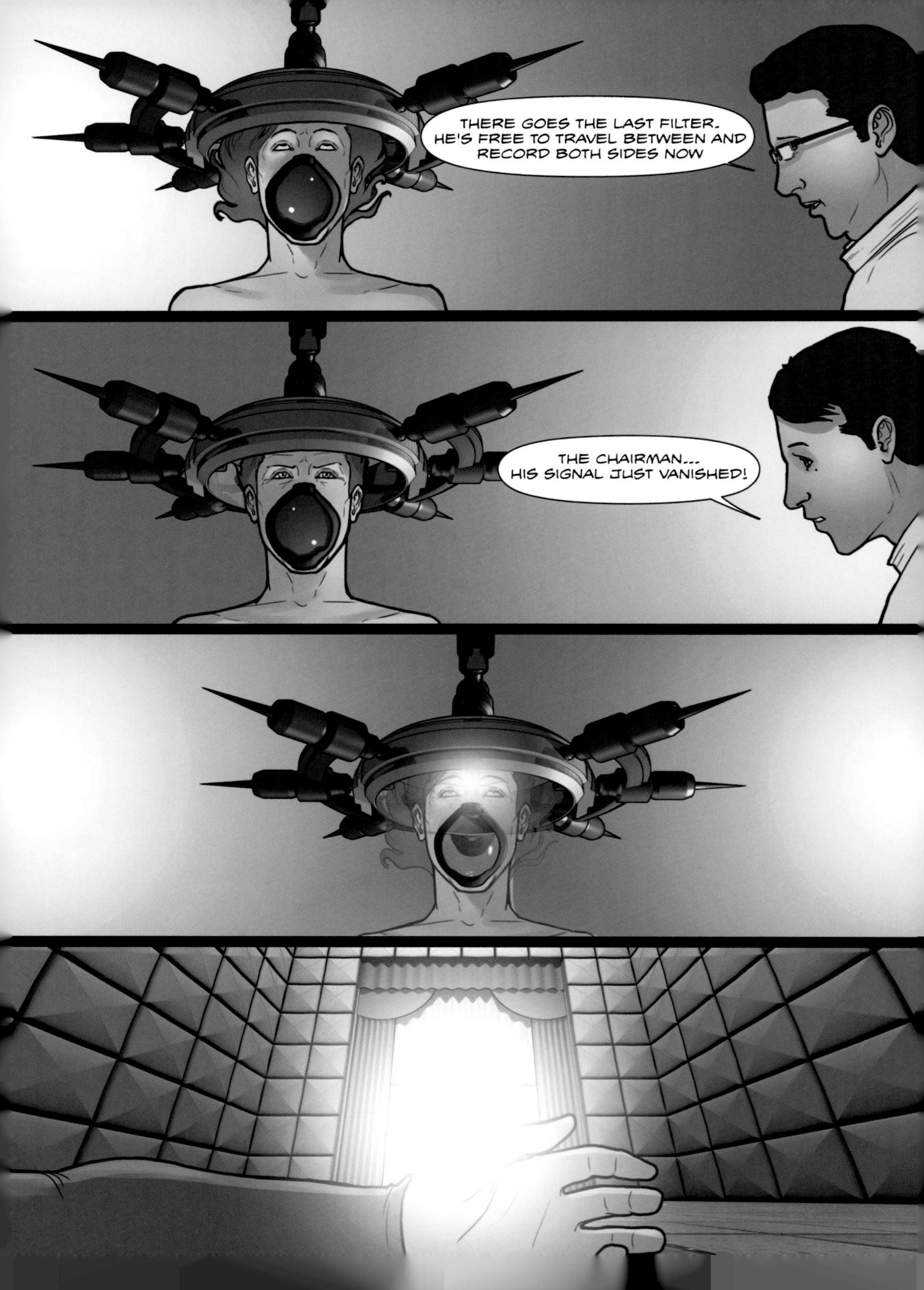
THERE GOES THE LAST FILTER. HE'S FREE TO TRAVEL BETWEEN AND RECORD BOTH SIDES NOW
THE CHAIRMAN... HIS SIGNAL JUST VANISHED!

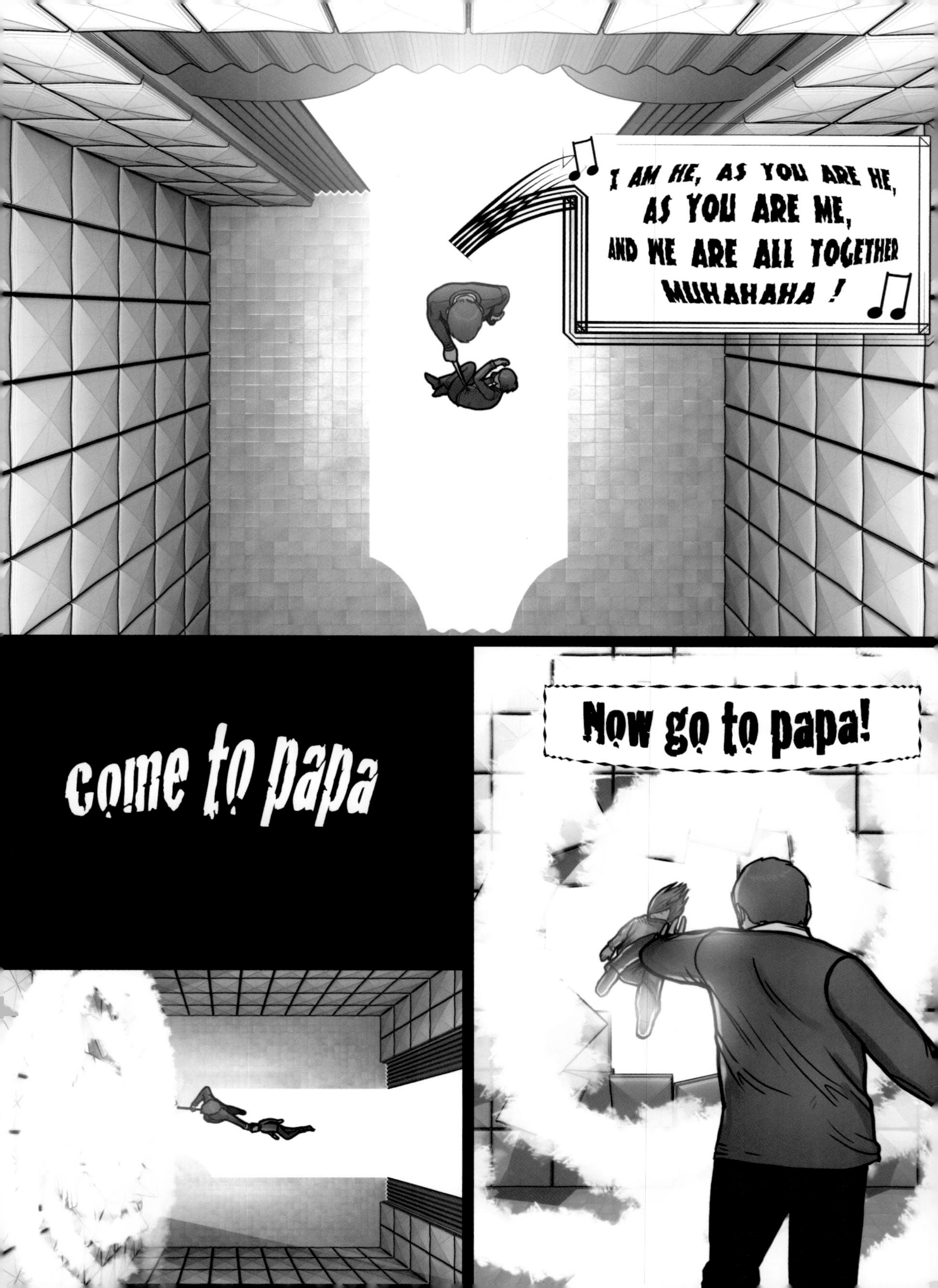
I AM HE, AS YOU ARE HE, AS YOU ARE ME, AND WE ARE ALL TOGETHER MUHAHAHA !
come to papa
Now go to papa!

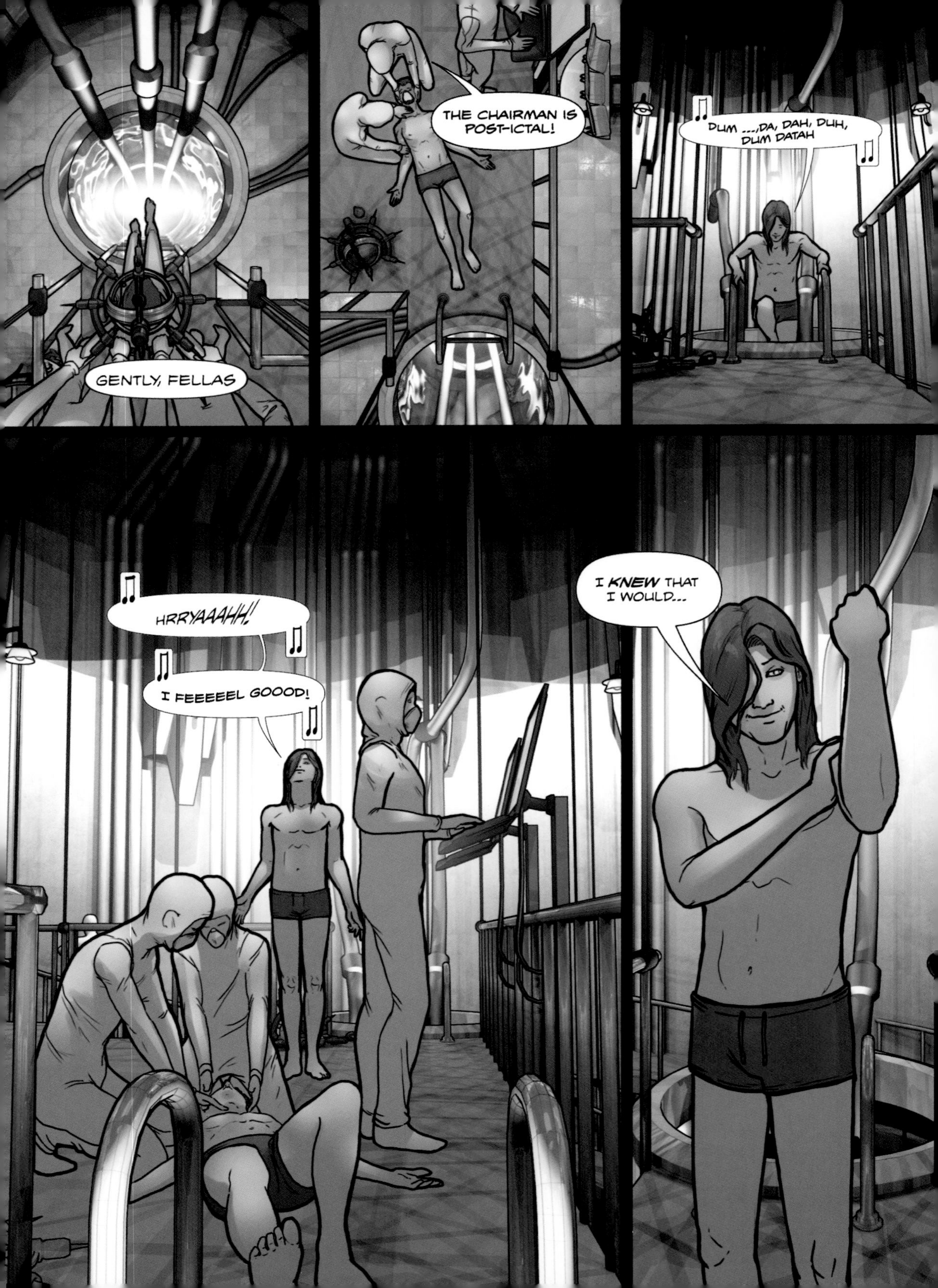
GENTLY, FELLAS
THE CHAIRMAN IS POST-ICTAL!
DUM ...,DA, DAH, DUH, DUM DATAH
HRRYAAAHH!
I FEEEEEL GOOOD!
I KNEW THAT I WOULD...

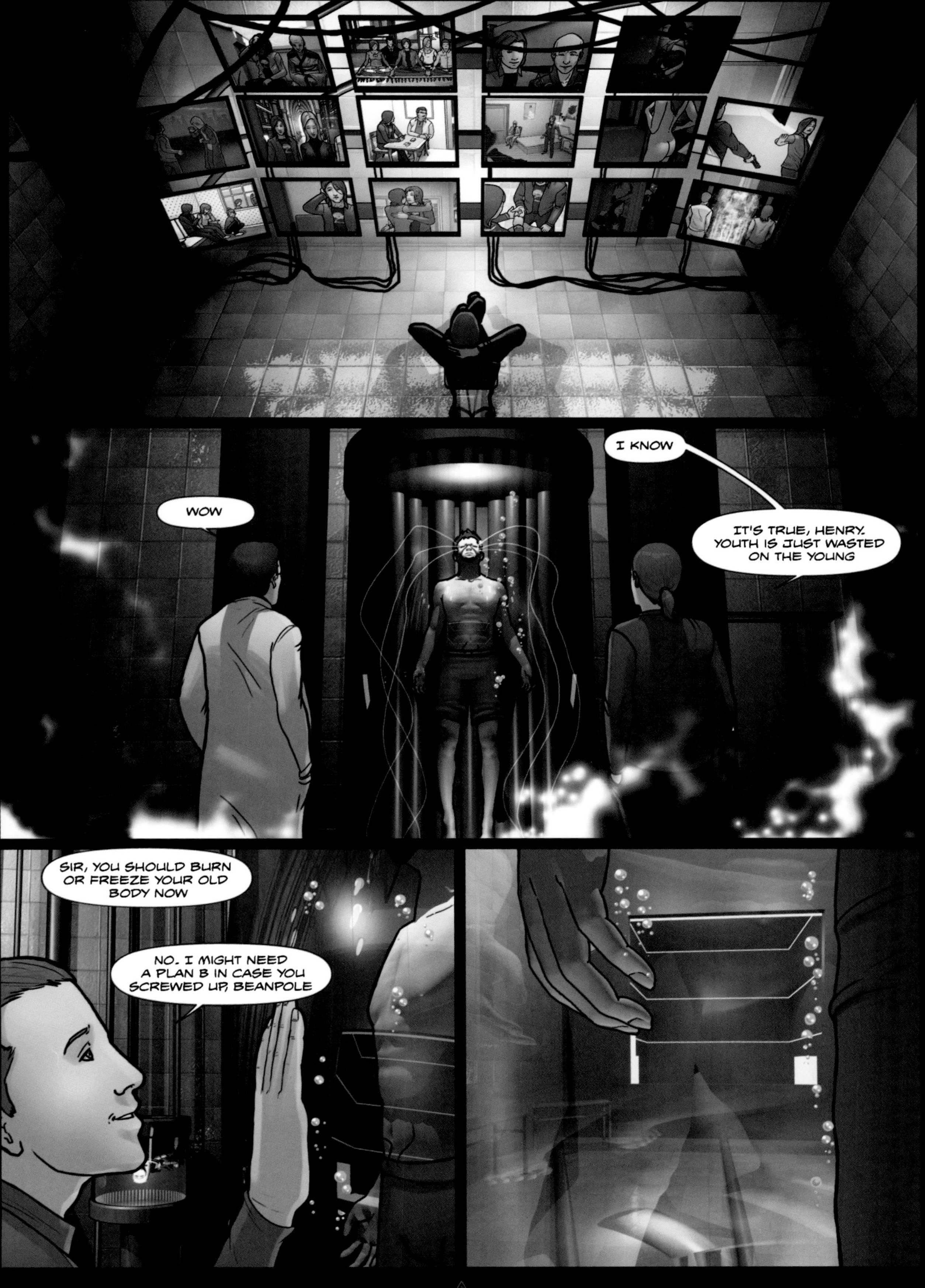
WOW
I KNOW
IT'S TRUE, HENRY. YOUTH IS JUST WASTED ON THE YOUNG
SIR, YOU SHOULD BURN OR FREEZE YOUR OLD BODY NOW
NO. I MIGHT NEED A PLAN B IN CASE YOU SCREWED UP, BEANPOLE

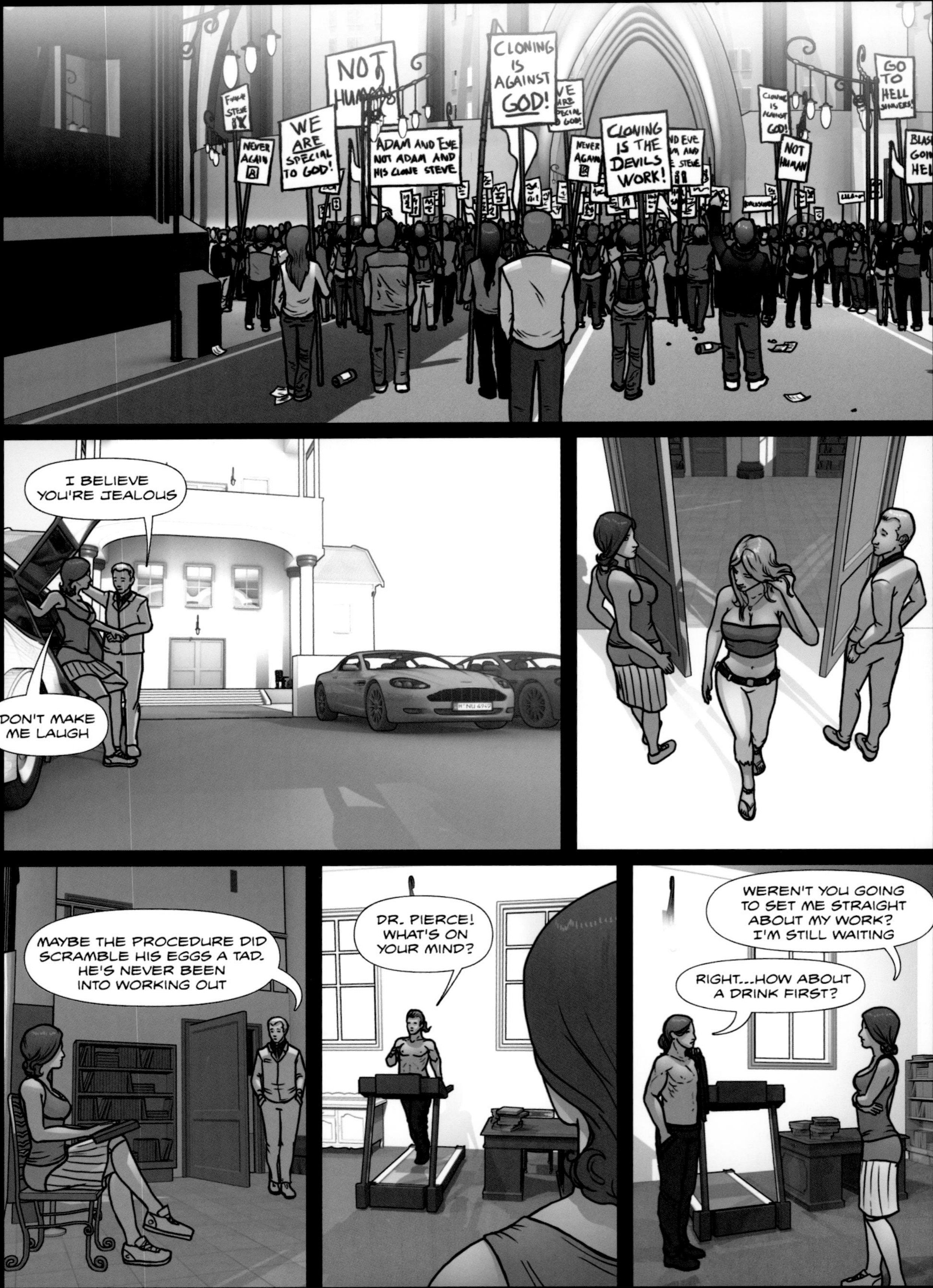
CLONING IS AGAINST GOD!
WE ARE SPECIAL TO GOD!
ADAM AND EVE NOT ADAM AND HIS CLONE STEVE
NEVER AGAIN
CLONING IS THE DEVILS WORK!
GO TO HELL SINNERS!
NOT HUMAN
I BELIEVE YOU'RE JEALOUS
DON'T MAKE ME LAUGH
MAYBE THE PROCEDURE DID SCRAMBLE HIS EGGS A TAD. HE'S NEVER BEEN INTO WORKING OUT
DR. PIERCE! WHAT'S ON YOUR MIND?
WEREN'T YOU GOING TO SET ME STRAIGHT ABOUT MY WORK? I'M STILL WAITING
RIGHT...HOW ABOUT A DRINK FIRST?

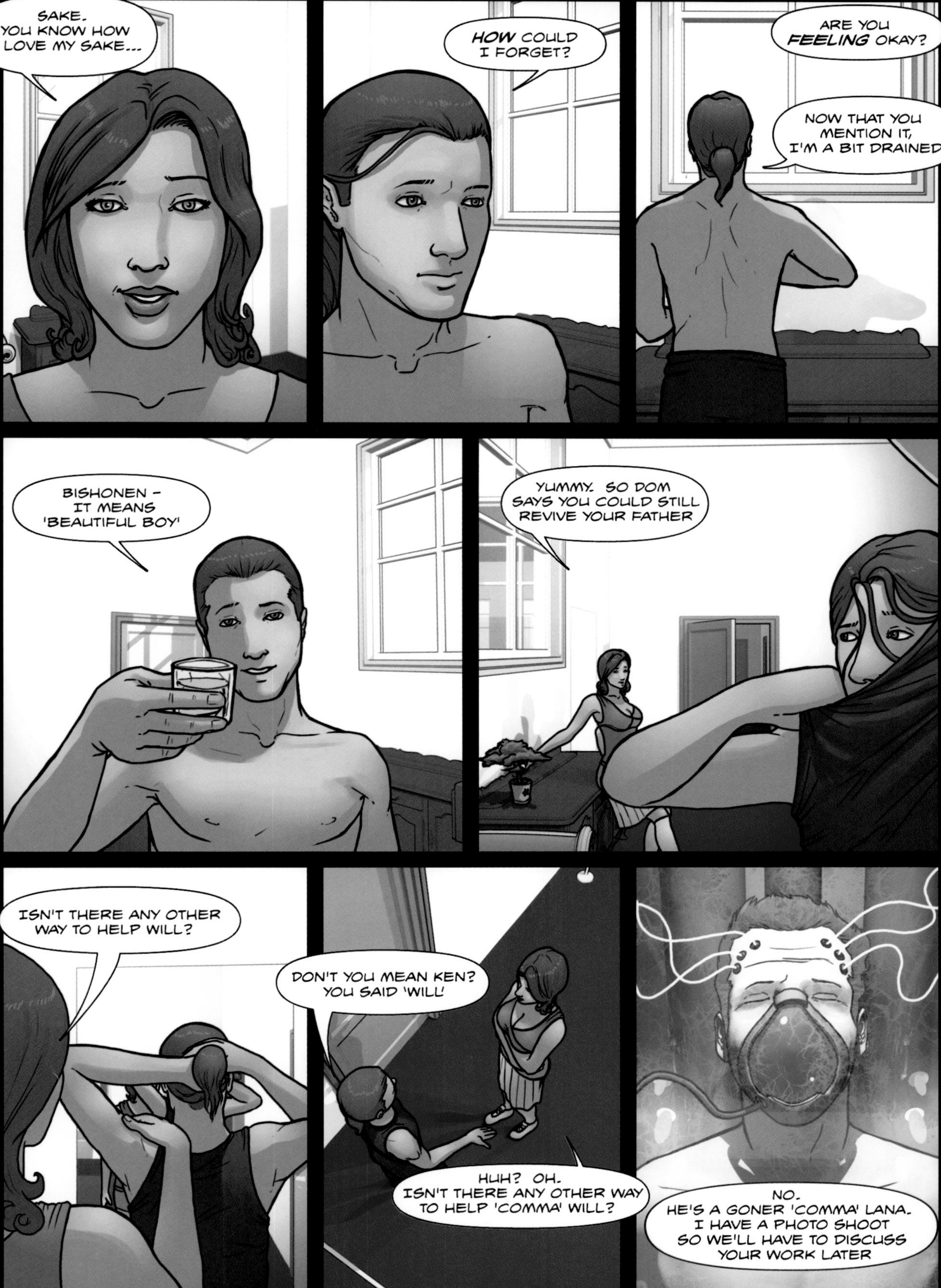
SAKE. YOU KNOW HOW I LOVE MY SAKE...
HOW COULD I FORGET?
ARE YOU FEELING OKAY?
NOW THAT YOU MENTION IT, I'M A BIT DRAINED
BISHONEN - IT MEANS 'BEAUTIFUL BOY'
YUMMY. SO DOM SAYS YOU COULD STILL REVIVE YOUR FATHER
ISN'T THERE ANY OTHER WAY TO HELP WILL?
DON'T YOU MEAN KEN? YOU SAID 'WILL'
HUH? OH. ISN'T THERE ANY OTHER WAY TO HELP 'COMMA' WILL?
NO. HE'S A GONER 'COMMA' LANA. I HAVE A PHOTO SHOOT SO WE'LL HAVE TO DISCUSS YOUR WORK LATER

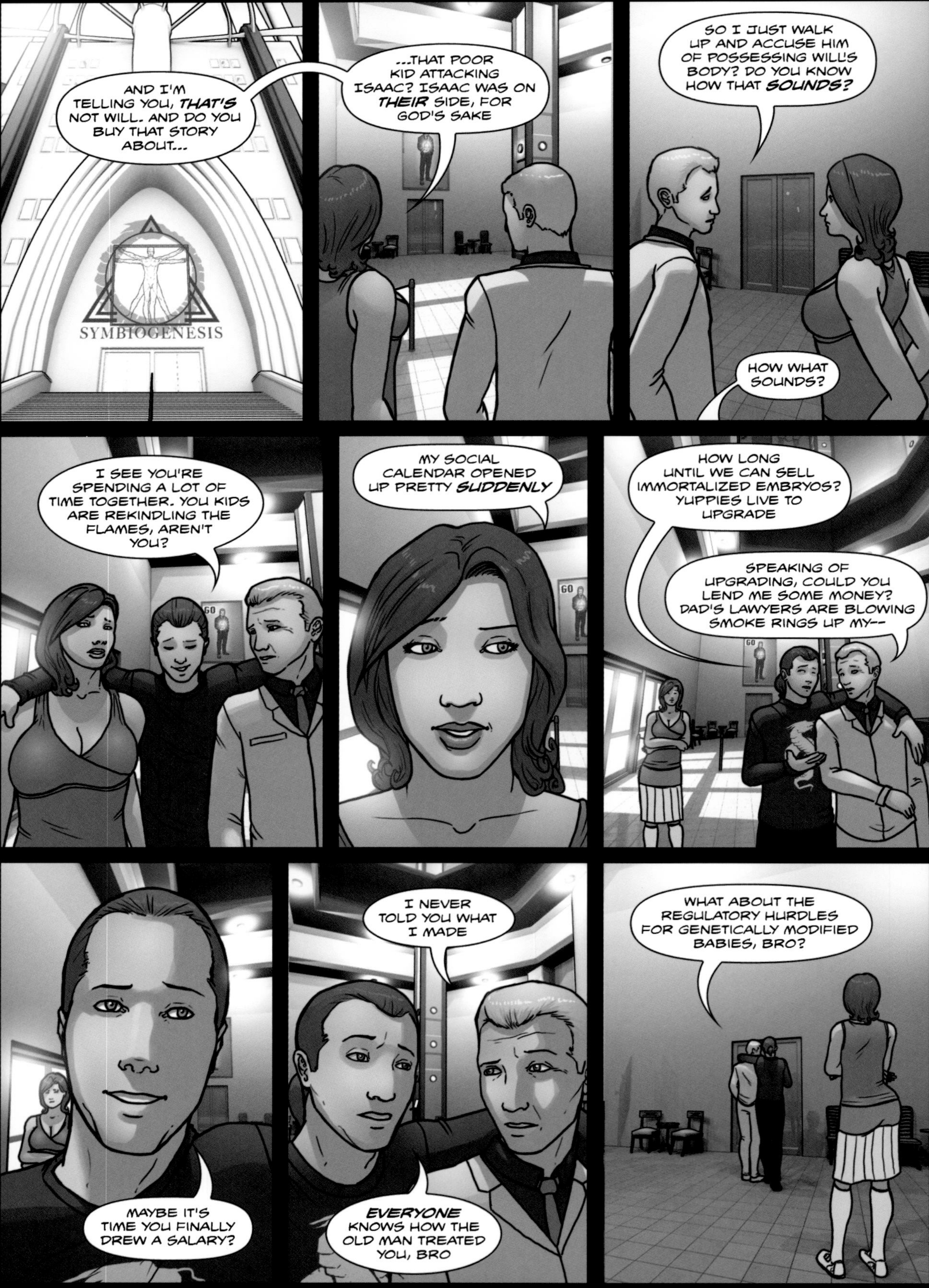

AND I'M TELLING YOU, THAT'S NOT WILL. AND DO YOU BUY THAT STORY ABOUT...
...THAT POOR KID ATTACKING ISAAC? ISAAC WAS ON THEIR SIDE, FOR GOD'S SAKE
SO I JUST WALK UP AND ACCUSE HIM OF POSSESSING WILL'S BODY? DO YOU KNOW HOW THAT SOUNDS?
HOW WHAT SOUNDS?
I SEE YOU'RE SPENDING A LOT OF TIME TOGETHER. YOU KIDS ARE REKINDLING THE FLAMES, AREN'T YOU?
MY SOCIAL CALENDAR OPENED UP PRETTY SUDDENLY
HOW LONG UNTIL WE CAN SELL IMMORTALIZED EMBRYOS? YUPPIES LIVE TO UPGRADE
SPEAKING OF UPGRADING, COULD YOU LEND ME SOME MONEY? DAD'S LAWYERS ARE BLOWING SMOKE RINGS UP MY--
MAYBE IT'S TIME YOU FINALLY DREW A SALARY?
I NEVER TOLD YOU WHAT I MADE
EVERYONE KNOWS HOW THE OLD MAN TREATED YOU, BRO
WHAT ABOUT THE REGULATORY HURDLES FOR GENETICALLY MODIFIED BABIES, BRO?

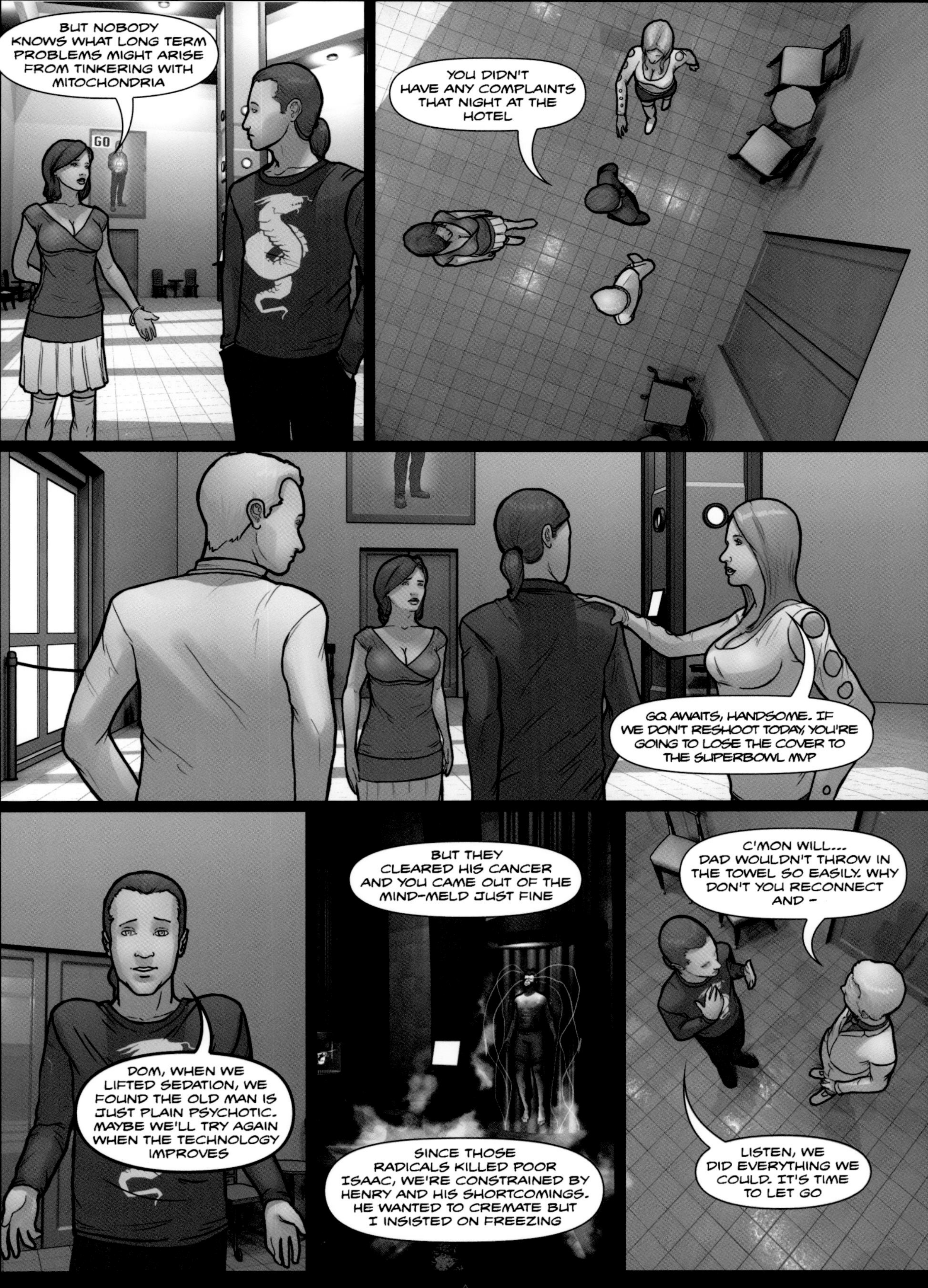
BUT NOBODY KNOWS WHAT LONG TERM PROBLEMS MIGHT ARISE FROM TINKERING WITH MITOCHONDRIA
YOU DIDN'T HAVE ANY COMPLAINTS THAT NIGHT AT THE HOTEL
GQ AWAITS, HANDSOME. IF WE DON'T RESHOOT TODAY, YOU'RE GOING TO LOSE THE COVER TO THE SUPERBOWL MVP
DOM, WHEN WE LIFTED SEDATION, WE FOUND THE OLD MAN IS JUST PLAIN PSYCHOTIC. MAYBE WE'LL TRY AGAIN WHEN THE TECHNOLOGY IMPROVES
BUT THEY CLEARED HIS CANCER AND YOU CAME OUT OF THE MIND-MELD JUST FINE
SINCE THOSE RADICALS KILLED POOR ISAAC, WE'RE CONSTRAINED BY HENRY AND HIS SHORTCOMINGS. HE WANTED TO CREMATE BUT I INSISTED ON FREEZING
C'MON WILL... DAD WOULDN'T THROW IN THE TOWEL SO EASILY. WHY DON'T YOU RECONNECT AND -
LISTEN, WE DID EVERYTHING WE COULD. IT'S TIME TO LET GO

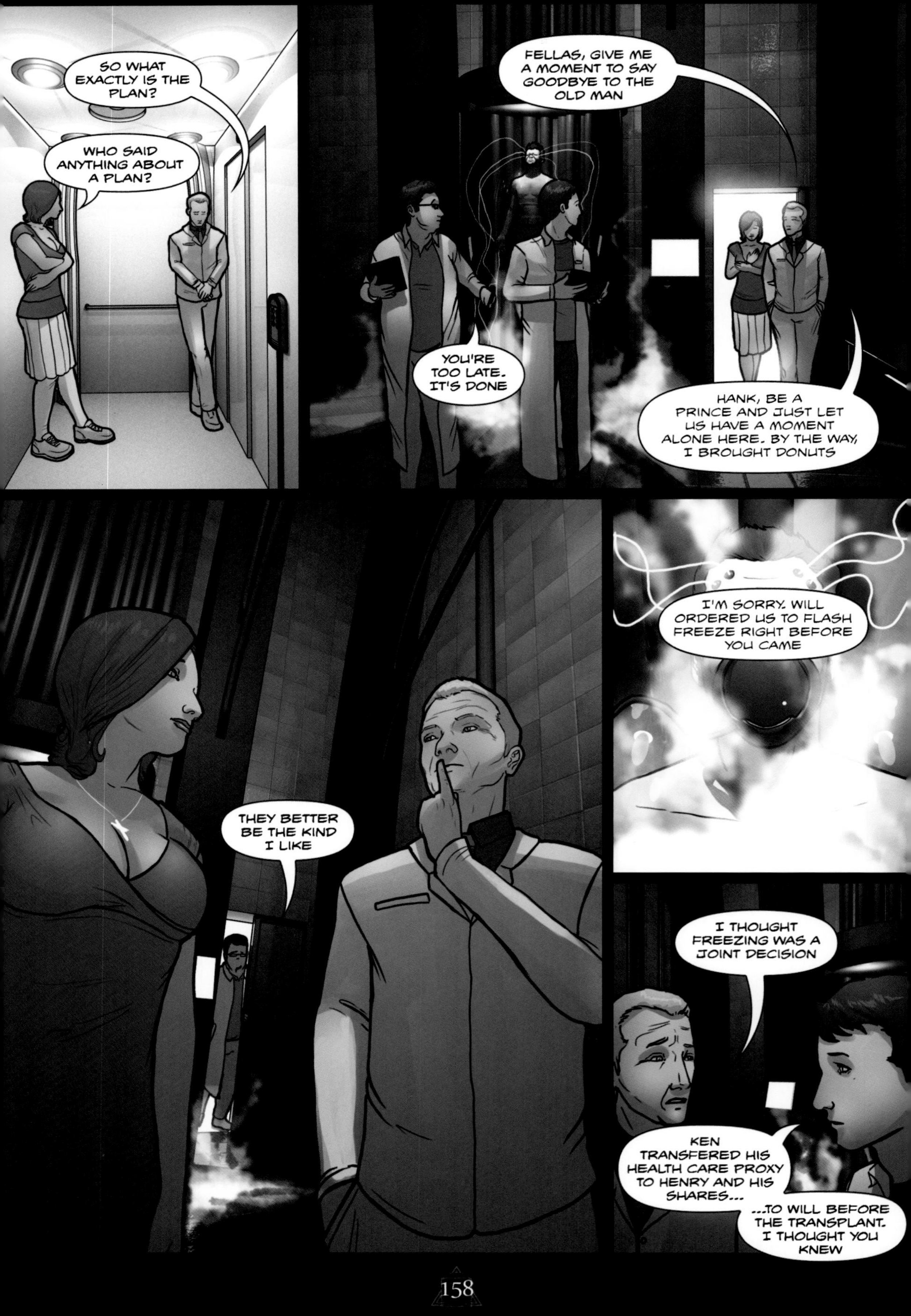
SO WHAT EXACTLY IS THE PLAN?
WHO SAID ANYTHING ABOUT A PLAN?
FELLAS, GIVE ME A MOMENT TO SAY GOODBYE TO THE OLD MAN
YOU'RE TOO LATE. IT'S DONE
HANK, BE A PRINCE AND JUST LET US HAVE A MOMENT ALONE HERE. BY THE WAY, I BROUGHT DONUTS
THEY BETTER BE THE KIND I LIKE
I'M SORRY. WILL ORDERED US TO FLASH FREEZE RIGHT BEFORE YOU CAME
I THOUGHT FREEZING WAS A JOINT DECISION
KEN TRANSFERED HIS HEALTH CARE PROXY TO HENRY AND HIS SHARES...
...TO WILL BEFORE THE TRANSPLANT. I THOUGHT YOU KNEW

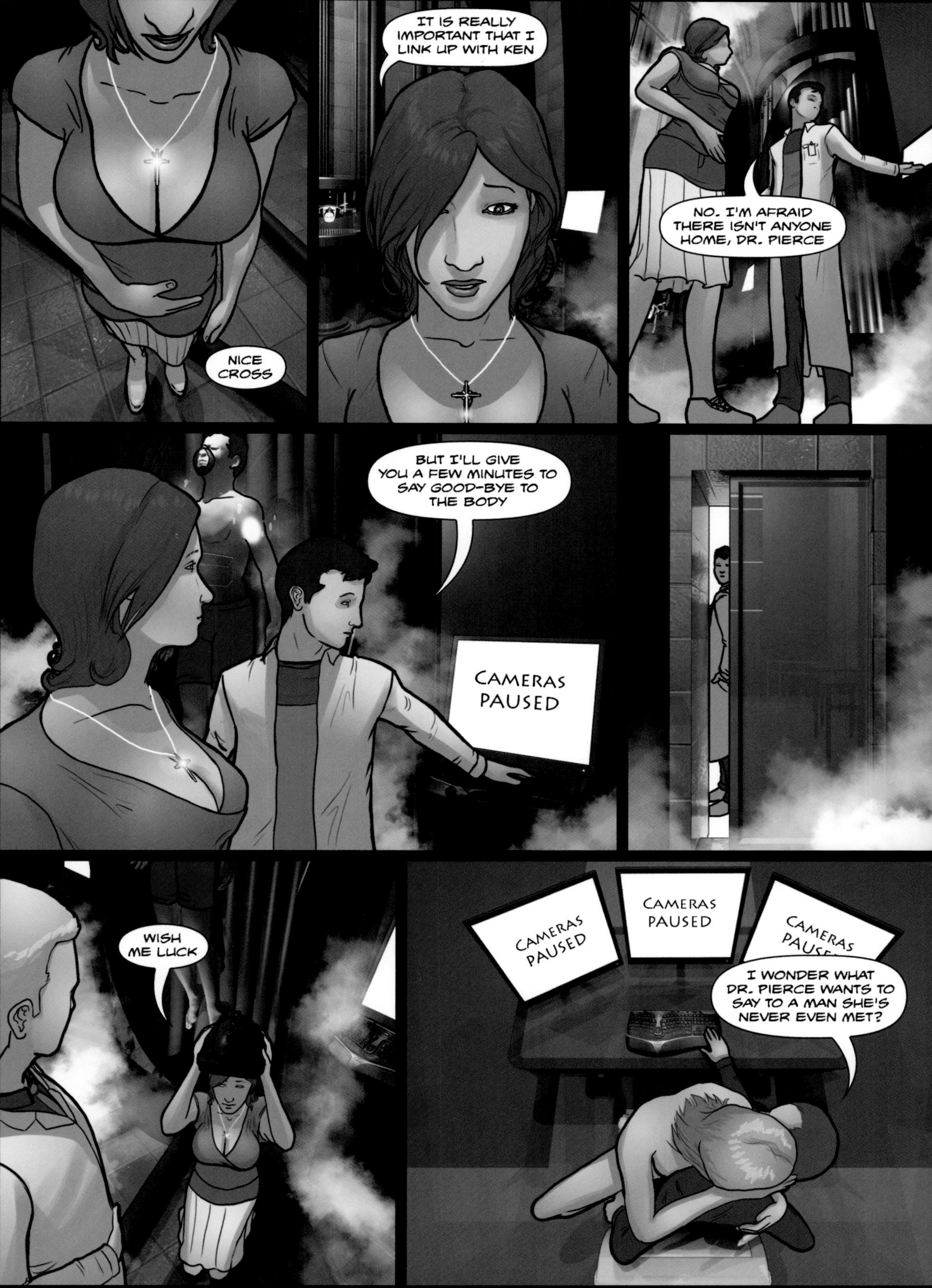
NICE CROSS
IT IS REALLY IMPORTANT THAT I LINK UP WITH KEN
NO. I'M AFRAID THERE ISN'T ANYONE HOME, DR. PIERCE
BUT I'LL GIVE YOU A FEW MINUTES TO SAY GOOD-BYE TO THE BODY
CAMERAS PAUSED
WISH ME LUCK
CAMERAS PAUSED
CAMERAS PAUSED
I WONDER WHAT DR. PIERCE WANTS TO SAY TO A MAN SHE'S NEVER EVEN MET?

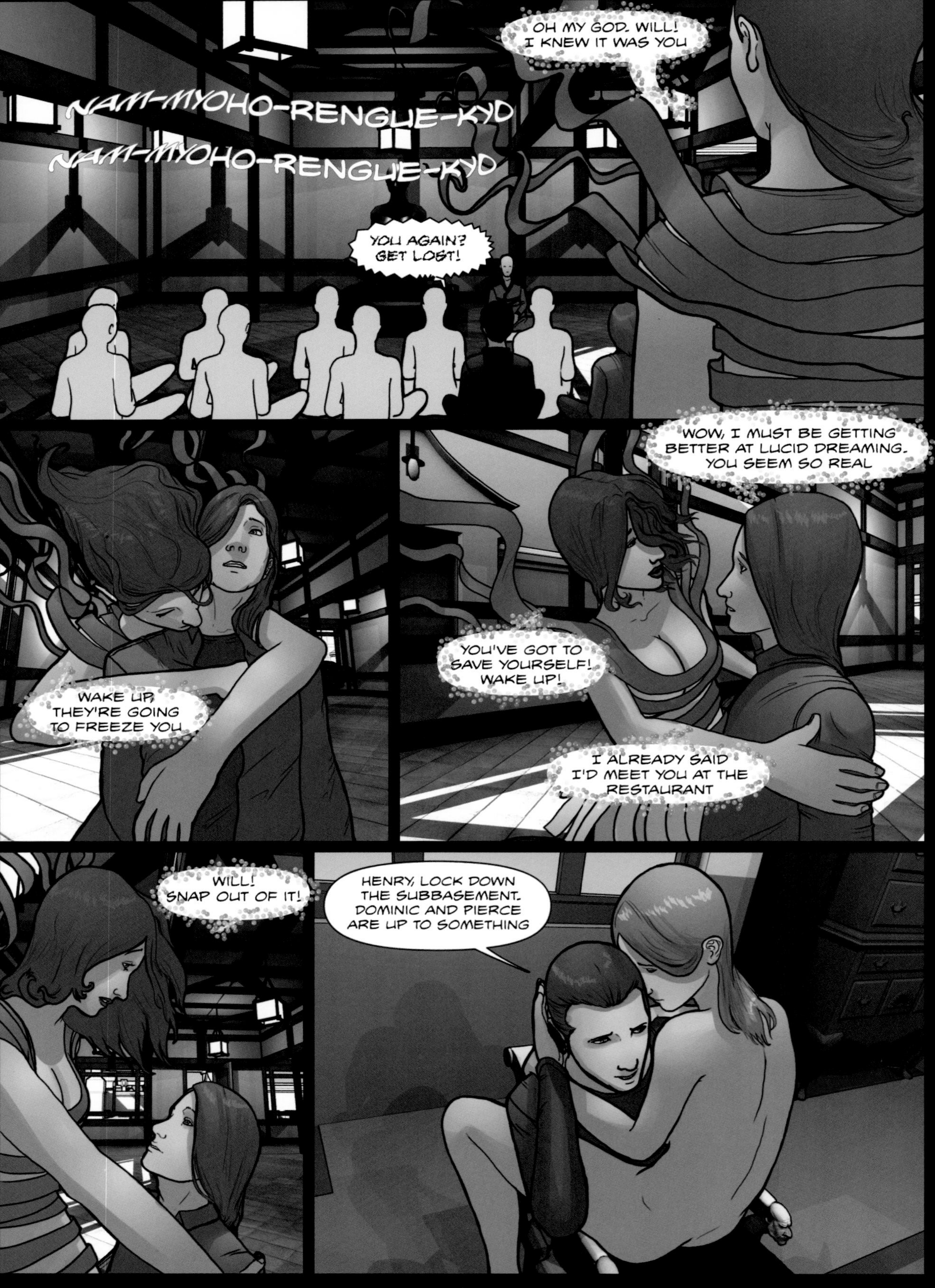
NAM-MYOHO-RENGUE-KYO
NAM-MYOHO-RENGUE-KYO
OH MY GOD. WILL! I KNEW IT WAS YOU
YOU AGAIN? GET LOST!
WAKE UP, THEY'RE GOING TO FREEZE YOU
WOW, I MUST BE GETTING BETTER AT LUCID DREAMING. YOU SEEM SO REAL
YOU'VE GOT TO SAVE YOURSELF! WAKE UP!
I ALREADY SAID I'D MEET YOU AT THE RESTAURANT
WILL! SNAP OUT OF IT!
HENRY, LOCK DOWN THE SUBBASEMENT. DOMINIC AND PIERCE ARE UP TO SOMETHING

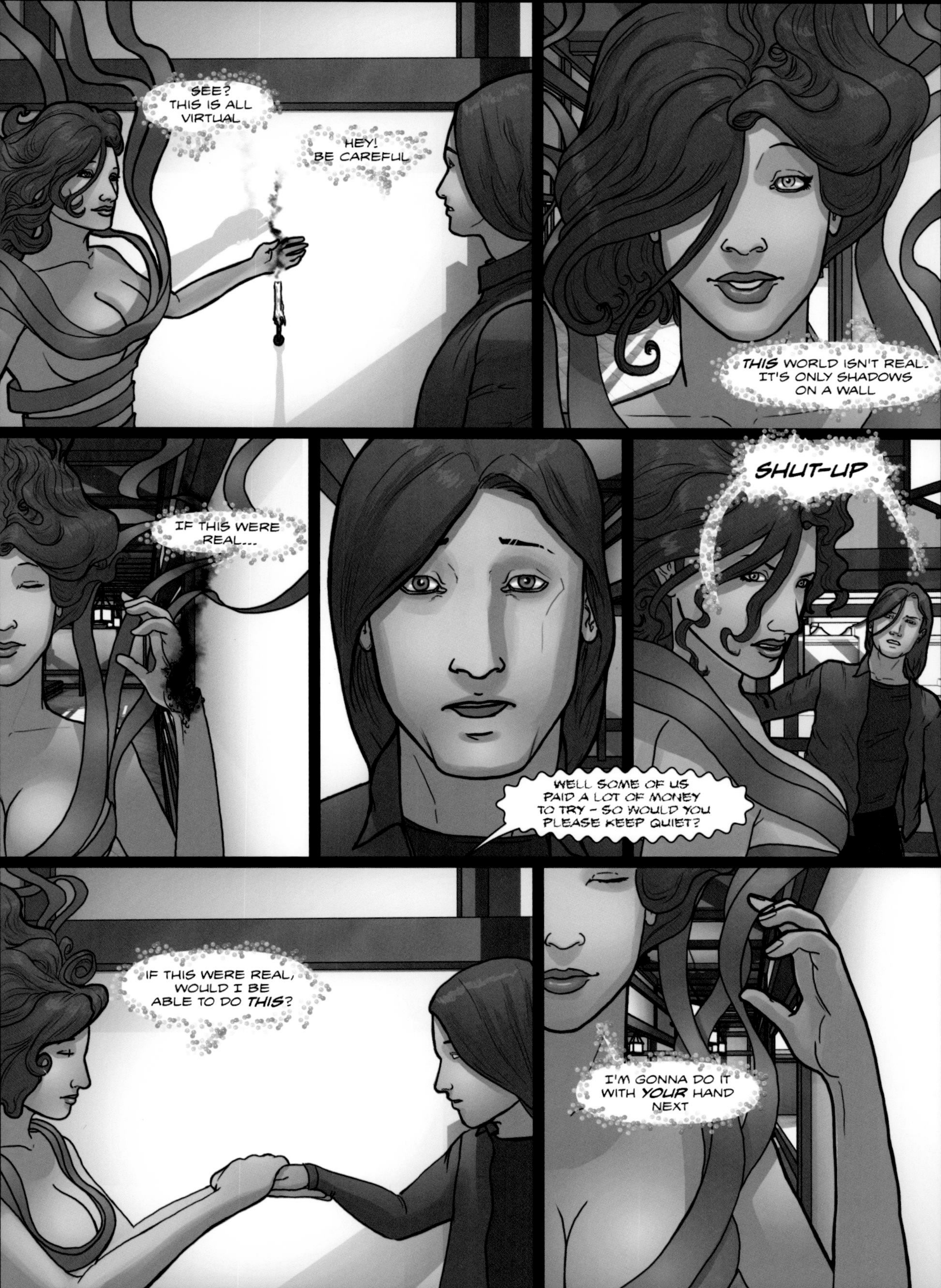
SEE? THIS IS ALL VIRTUAL
HEY! BE CAREFUL
THIS WORLD ISN'T REAL. IT'S ONLY SHADOWS ON A WALL
IF THIS WERE REAL...
SHUT-UP
WELL SOME OF US PAID A LOT OF MONEY TO TRY - SO WOULD YOU PLEASE KEEP QUIET?
IF THIS WERE REAL, WOULD I BE ABLE TO DO THIS?
I'M GONNA DO IT WITH YOUR HAND NEXT

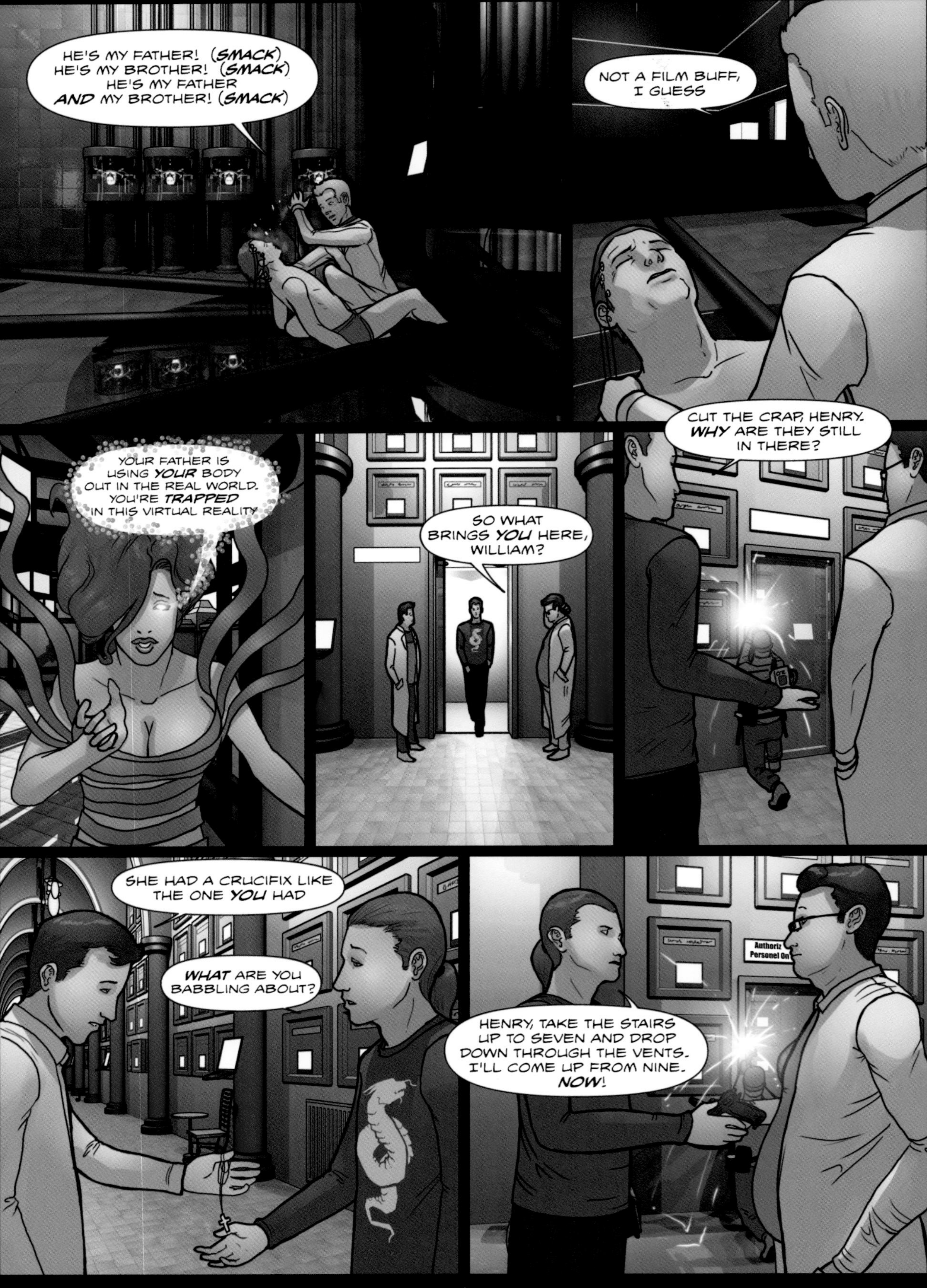

HE'S MY FATHER! (SMACK) HE'S MY BROTHER! (SMACK) HE'S MY FATHER AND MY BROTHER! (SMACK)
NOT A FILM BUFF, I GUESS
YOUR FATHER IS USING YOUR BODY OUT IN THE REAL WORLD. YOU'RE TRAPPED IN THIS VIRTUAL REALITY
SO WHAT BRINGS YOU HERE, WILLIAM?
CUT THE CRAP, HENRY. WHY ARE THEY STILL IN THERE?
SHE HAD A CRUCIFIX LIKE THE ONE YOU HAD
WHAT ARE YOU BABBLING ABOUT?
Authoriz Personel On
HENRY, TAKE THE STAIRS UP TO SEVEN AND DROP DOWN THROUGH THE VENTS. I'LL COME UP FROM NINE. NOW!

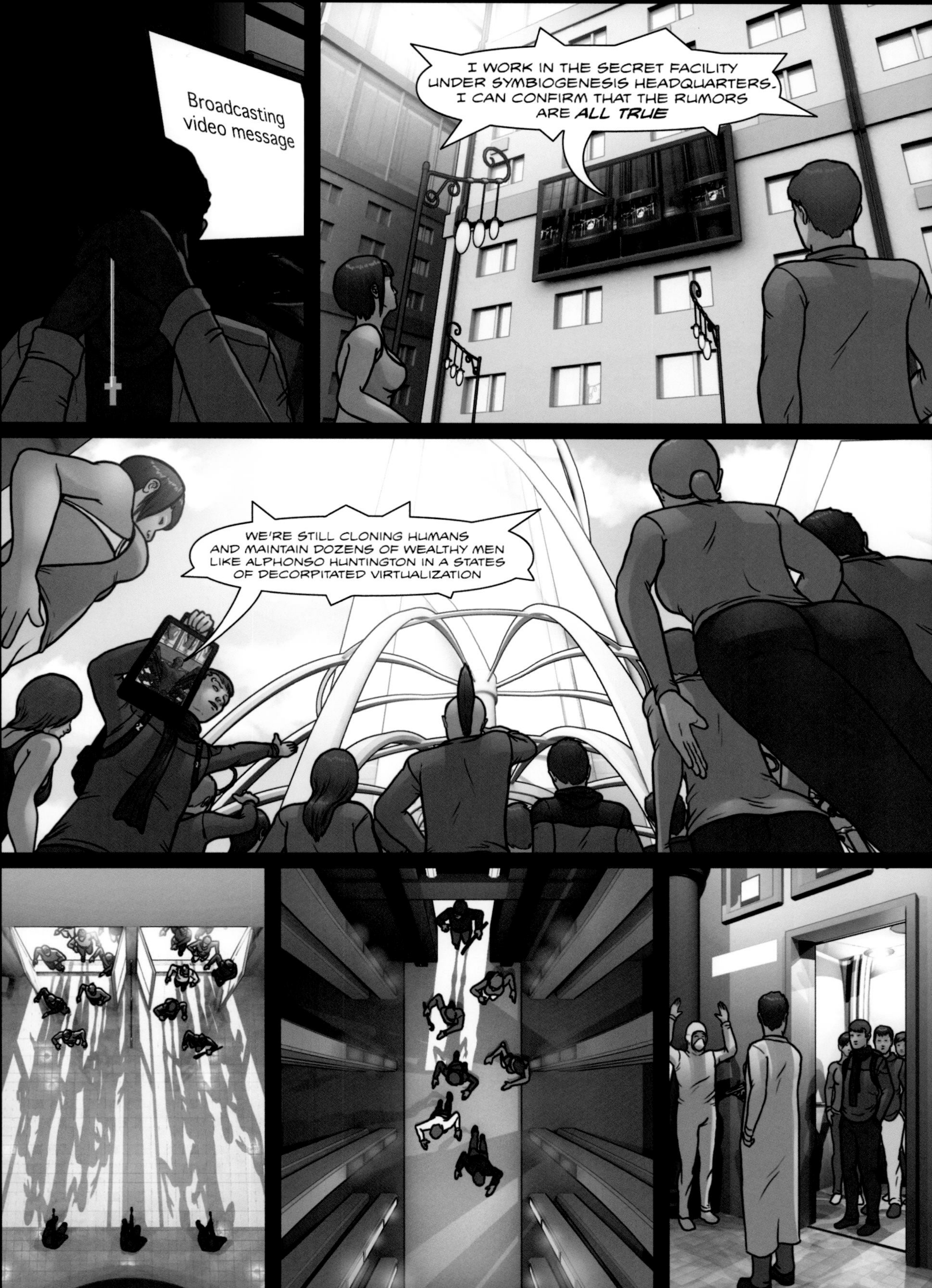
Broadcasting
video message
I WORK IN THE SECRET FACILITY UNDER SYMBIOGENESIS HEADQUARTERS. I CAN CONFIRM THAT THE RUMORS ARE *ALL TRUE*
WE'RE STILL CLONING HUMANS AND MAINTAIN DOZENS OF WEALTHY MEN LIKE ALPHONSO HUNTINGTON IN A STATES OF DECORPITATED VIRTUALIZATION

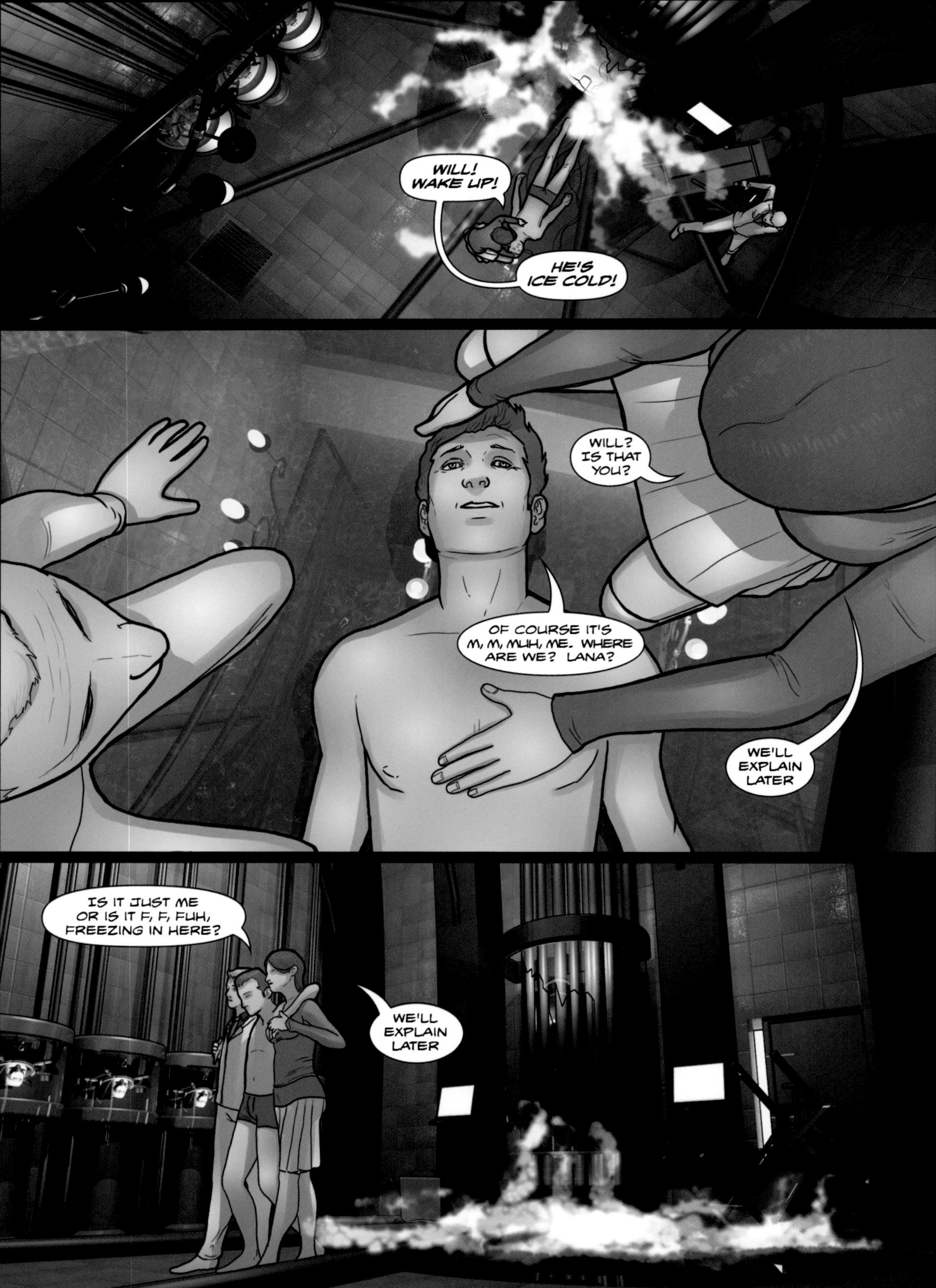
WILL! WAKE UP!
HE'S ICE COLD!
WILL? IS THAT YOU?
OF COURSE IT'S M, M, MUH, ME. WHERE ARE WE? LANA?
WE'LL EXPLAIN LATER
IS IT JUST ME OR IS IT F, F, FUH, FREEZING IN HERE?
WE'LL EXPLAIN LATER

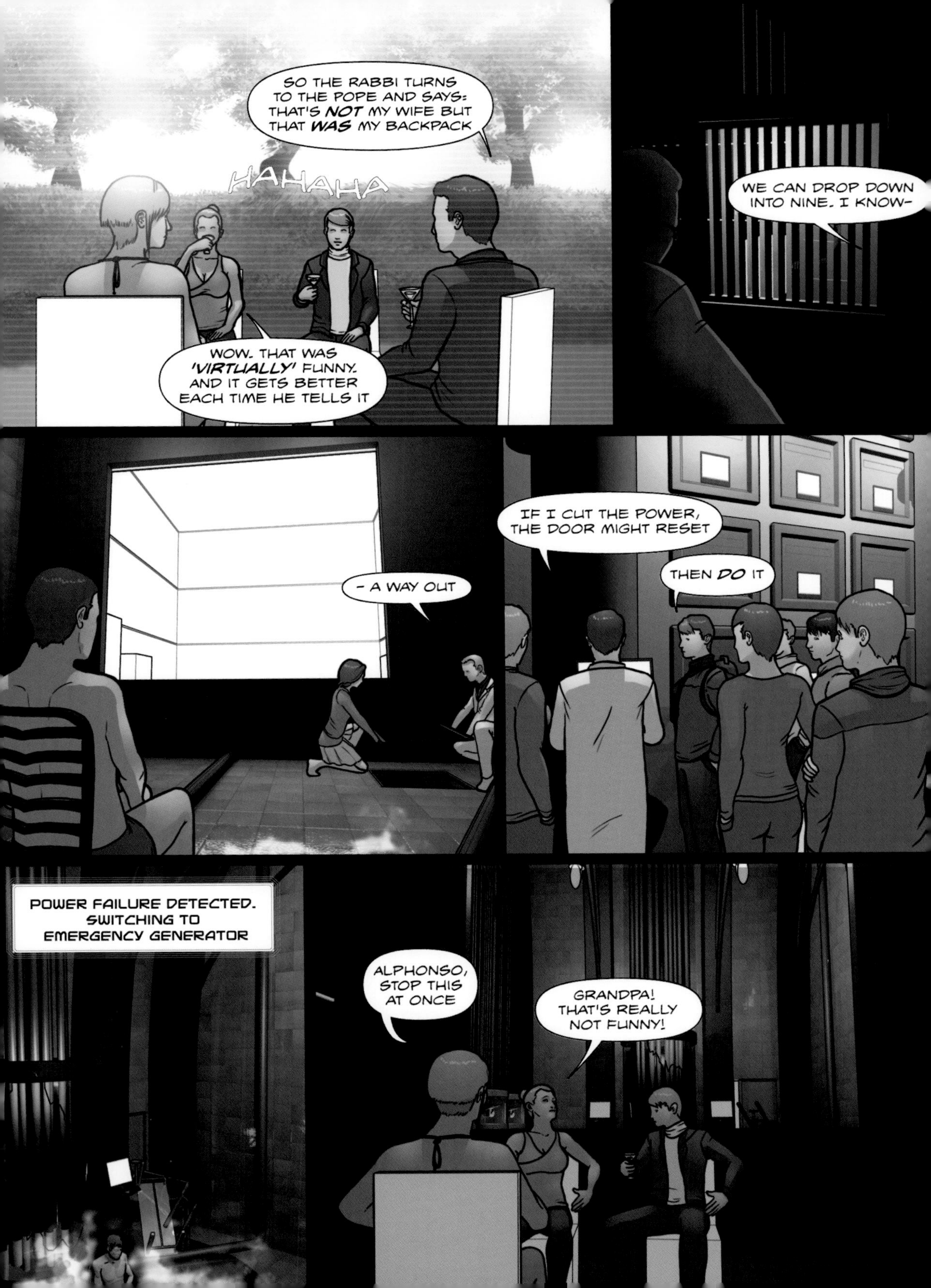
SO THE RABBI TURNS TO THE POPE AND SAYS: THAT'S NOT MY WIFE BUT THAT WAS MY BACKPACK
HAHAHA
WOW. THAT WAS 'VIRTUALLY' FUNNY. AND IT GETS BETTER EACH TIME HE TELLS IT
WE CAN DROP DOWN INTO NINE. I KNOW-
- A WAY OUT
IF I CUT THE POWER, THE DOOR MIGHT RESET
THEN DO IT
POWER FAILURE DETECTED. SWITCHING TO EMERGENCY GENERATOR
ALPHONSO, STOP THIS AT ONCE
GRANDPA! THAT'S REALLY NOT FUNNY!

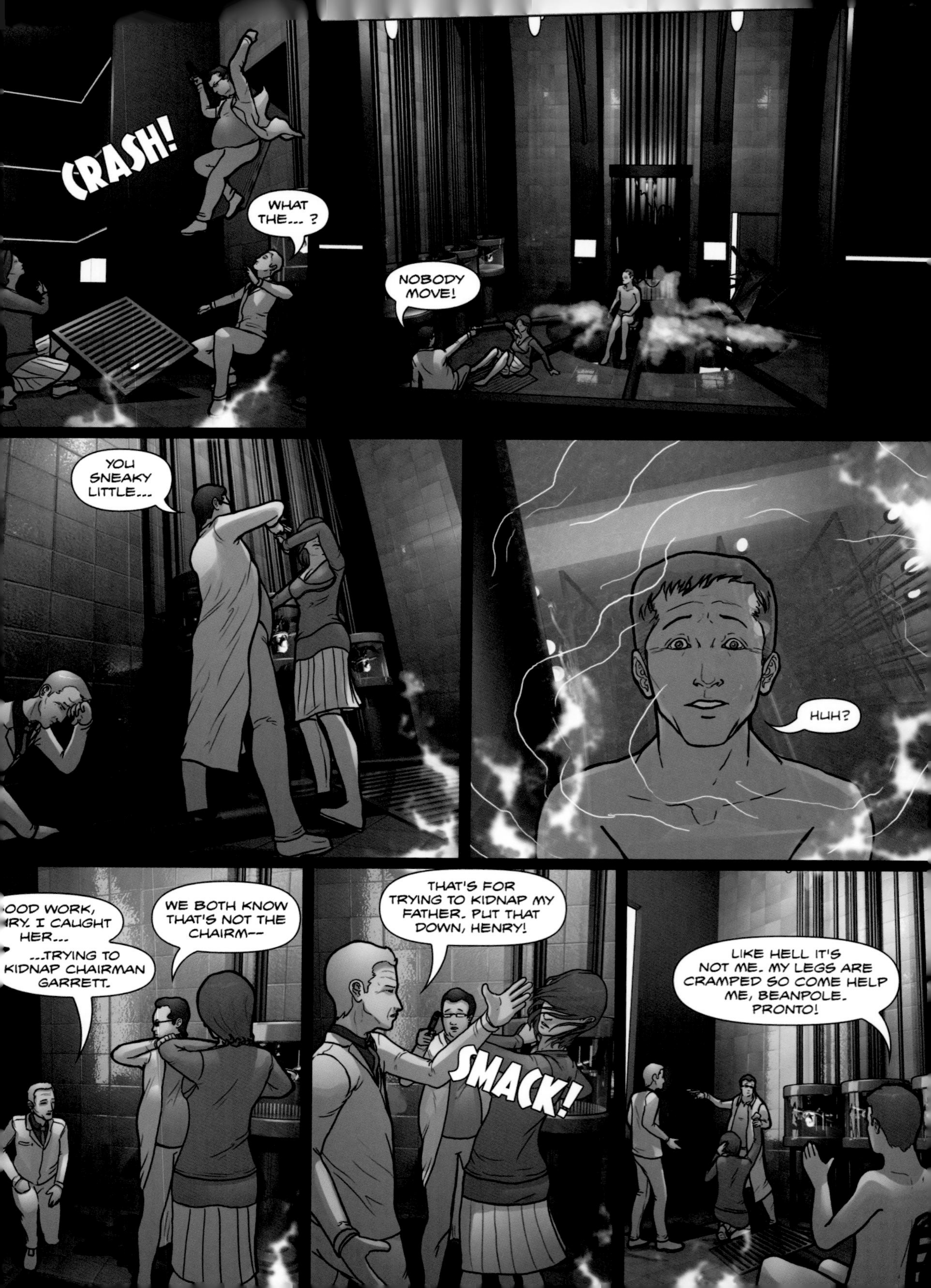
CRASH!
WHAT THE... ?
NOBODY MOVE!
YOU SNEAKY LITTLE...
HUH?
OOD WORK, RY. I CAUGHT HER...
...TRYING TO KIDNAP CHAIRMAN GARRETT.
WE BOTH KNOW THAT'S NOT THE CHAIRM--
THAT'S FOR TRYING TO KIDNAP MY FATHER. PUT THAT DOWN, HENRY!
SMACK!
LIKE HELL IT'S NOT ME. MY LEGS ARE CRAMPED SO COME HELP ME, BEANPOLE. PRONTO!

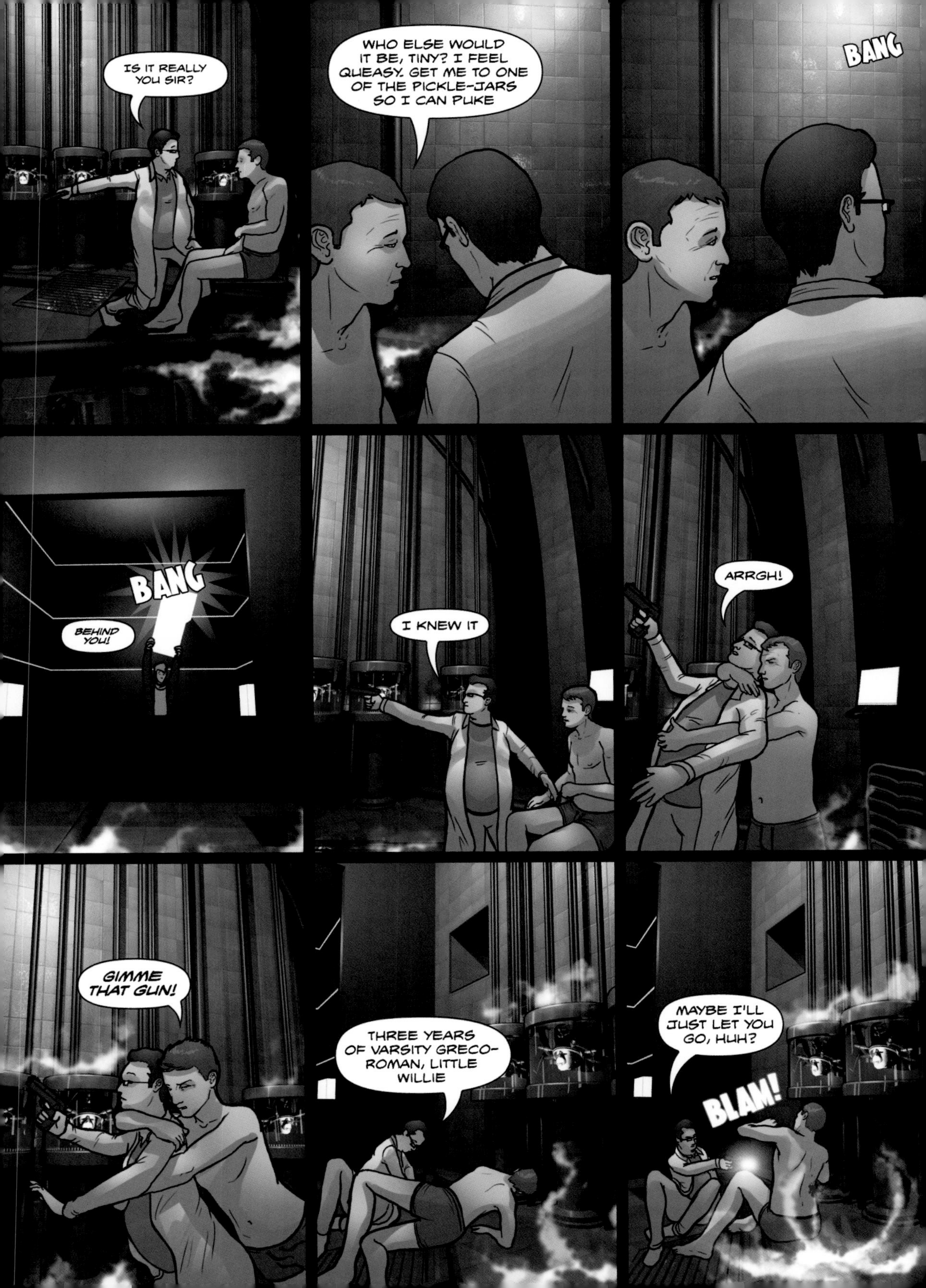
IS IT REALLY YOU SIR?
WHO ELSE WOULD IT BE, TINY? I FEEL QUEASY. GET ME TO ONE OF THE PICKLE-JARS SO I CAN PUKE
BANG
BANG
BEHIND YOU!
I KNEW IT
ARRGH!
GIMME THAT GUN!
THREE YEARS OF VARSITY GRECO-ROMAN, LITTLE WILLIE
MAYBE I'LL JUST LET YOU GO, HUH?
BLAM!

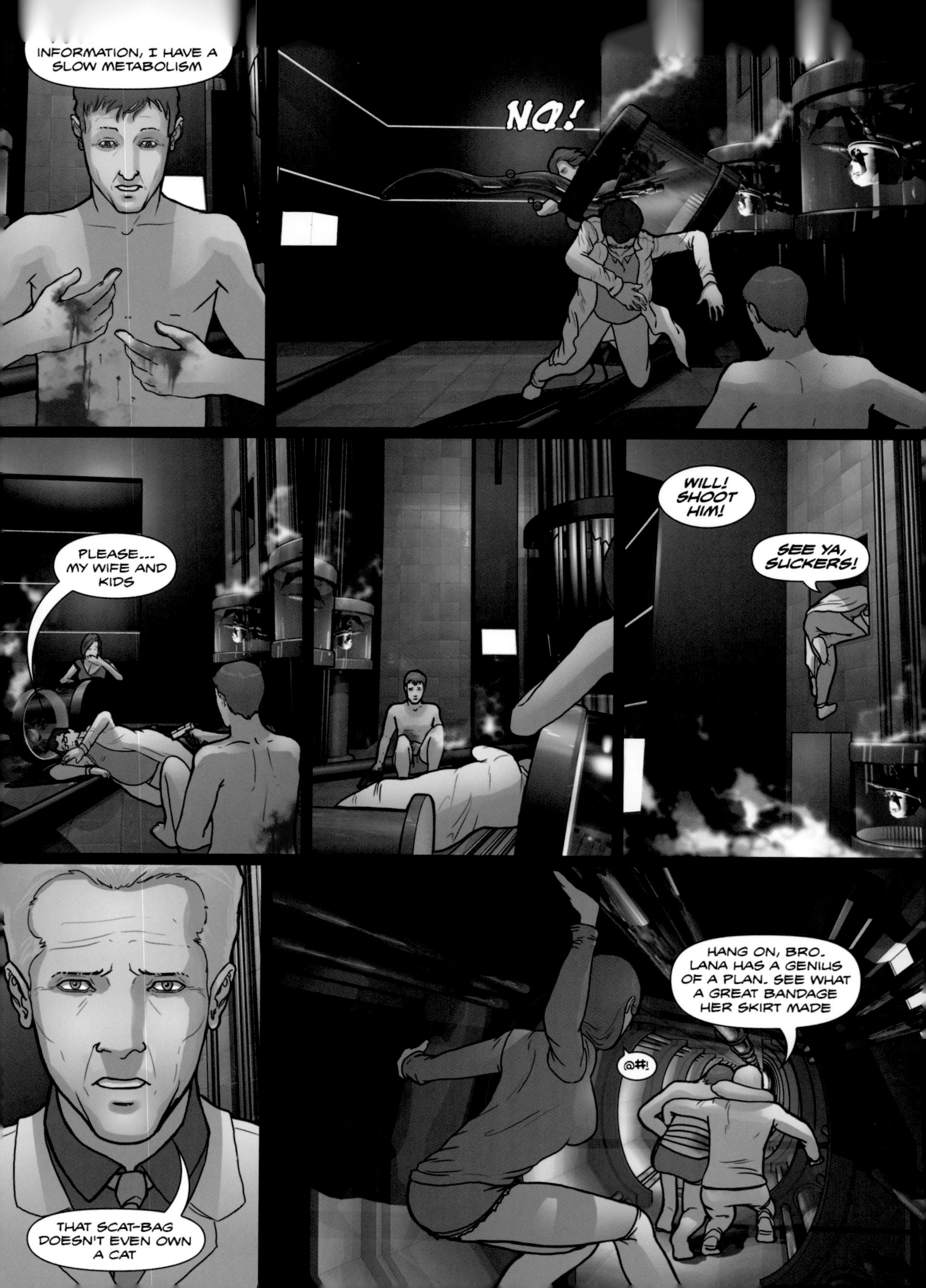
INFORMATION, I HAVE A SLOW METABOLISM
NO!
PLEASE... MY WIFE AND KIDS
WILL! SHOOT HIM!
SEE YA, SUCKERS!
THAT SCAT-BAG DOESN'T EVEN OWN A CAT
HANG ON, BRO. LANA HAS A GENIUS OF A PLAN. SEE WHAT A GREAT BANDAGE HER SKIRT MADE
@#!

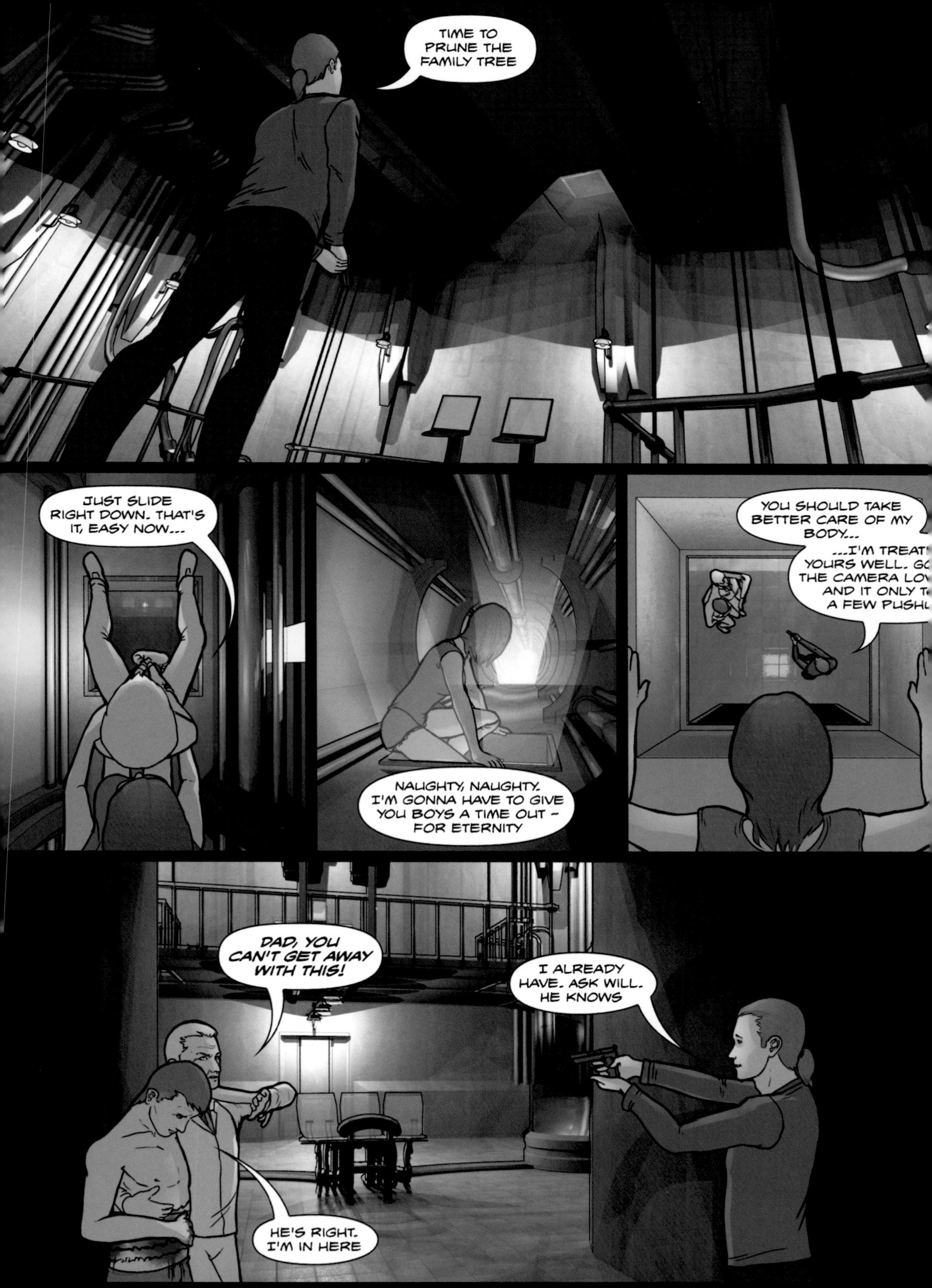
TIME TO PRUNE THE FAMILY TREE
JUST SLIDE RIGHT DOWN. THAT'S IT, EASY NOW...
NAUGHTY, NAUGHTY. I'M GONNA HAVE TO GIVE YOU BOYS A TIME OUT - FOR ETERNITY
YOU SHOULD TAKE BETTER CARE OF MY BODY...
...I'M TREAT YOURS WELL. GO THE CAMERA LOW AND IT ONLY T A FEW PUSH
DAD, YOU CAN'T GET AWAY WITH THIS!
I ALREADY HAVE. ASK WILL. HE KNOWS
HE'S RIGHT. I'M IN HERE

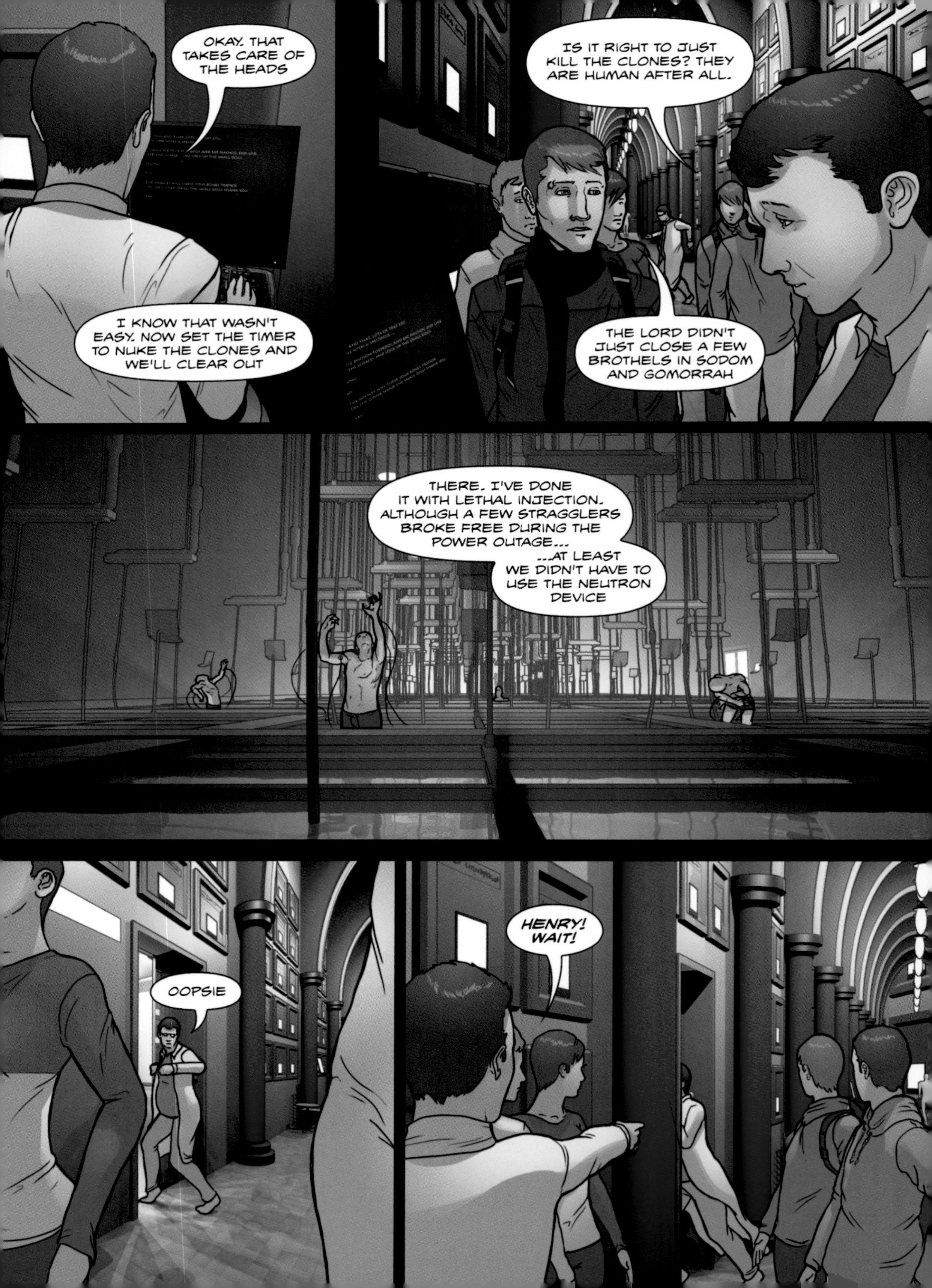
OKAY. THAT TAKES CARE OF THE HEADS
I KNOW THAT WASN'T EASY. NOW SET THE TIMER TO NUKE THE CLONES AND WE'LL CLEAR OUT
IS IT RIGHT TO JUST KILL THE CLONES? THEY ARE HUMAN AFTER ALL.
THE LORD DIDN'T JUST CLOSE A FEW BROTHELS IN SODOM AND GOMORRAH
THERE. I'VE DONE IT WITH LETHAL INJECTION. ALTHOUGH A FEW STRAGGLERS BROKE FREE DURING THE POWER OUTAGE...
...AT LEAST WE DIDN'T HAVE TO USE THE NEUTRON DEVICE
OOPSIE
HENRY! WAIT!

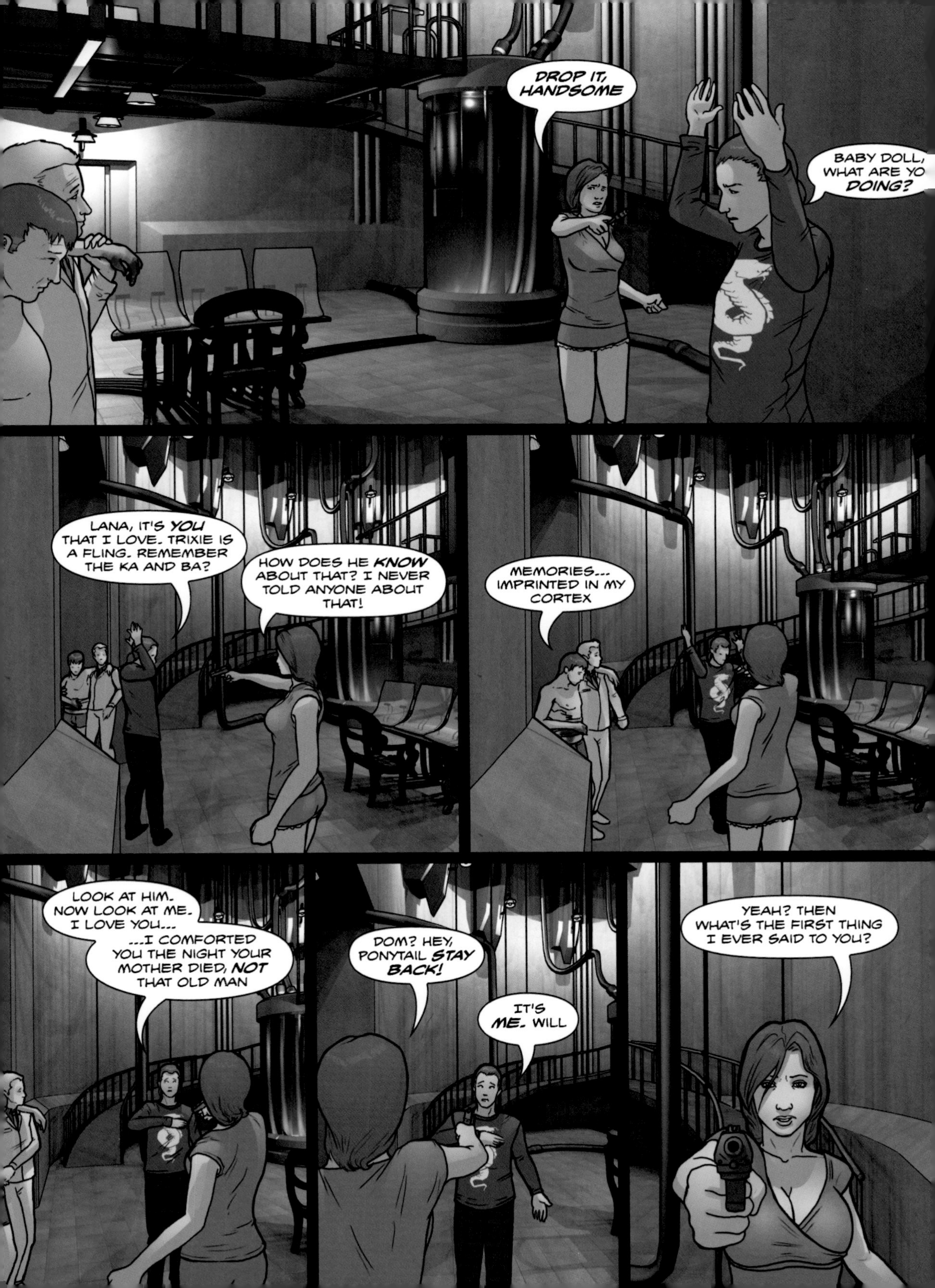
DROP IT, HANDSOME
BABY DOLL, WHAT ARE YO DOING?
LANA, IT'S YOU THAT I LOVE. TRIXIE IS A FLING. REMEMBER THE KA AND BA?
HOW DOES HE KNOW ABOUT THAT? I NEVER TOLD ANYONE ABOUT THAT!
MEMORIES... IMPRINTED IN MY CORTEX
LOOK AT HIM. NOW LOOK AT ME. I LOVE YOU...
...I COMFORTED YOU THE NIGHT YOUR MOTHER DIED, NOT THAT OLD MAN
DOM? HEY, PONYTAIL STAY BACK!
IT'S ME. WILL
YEAH? THEN WHAT'S THE FIRST THING I EVER SAID TO YOU?

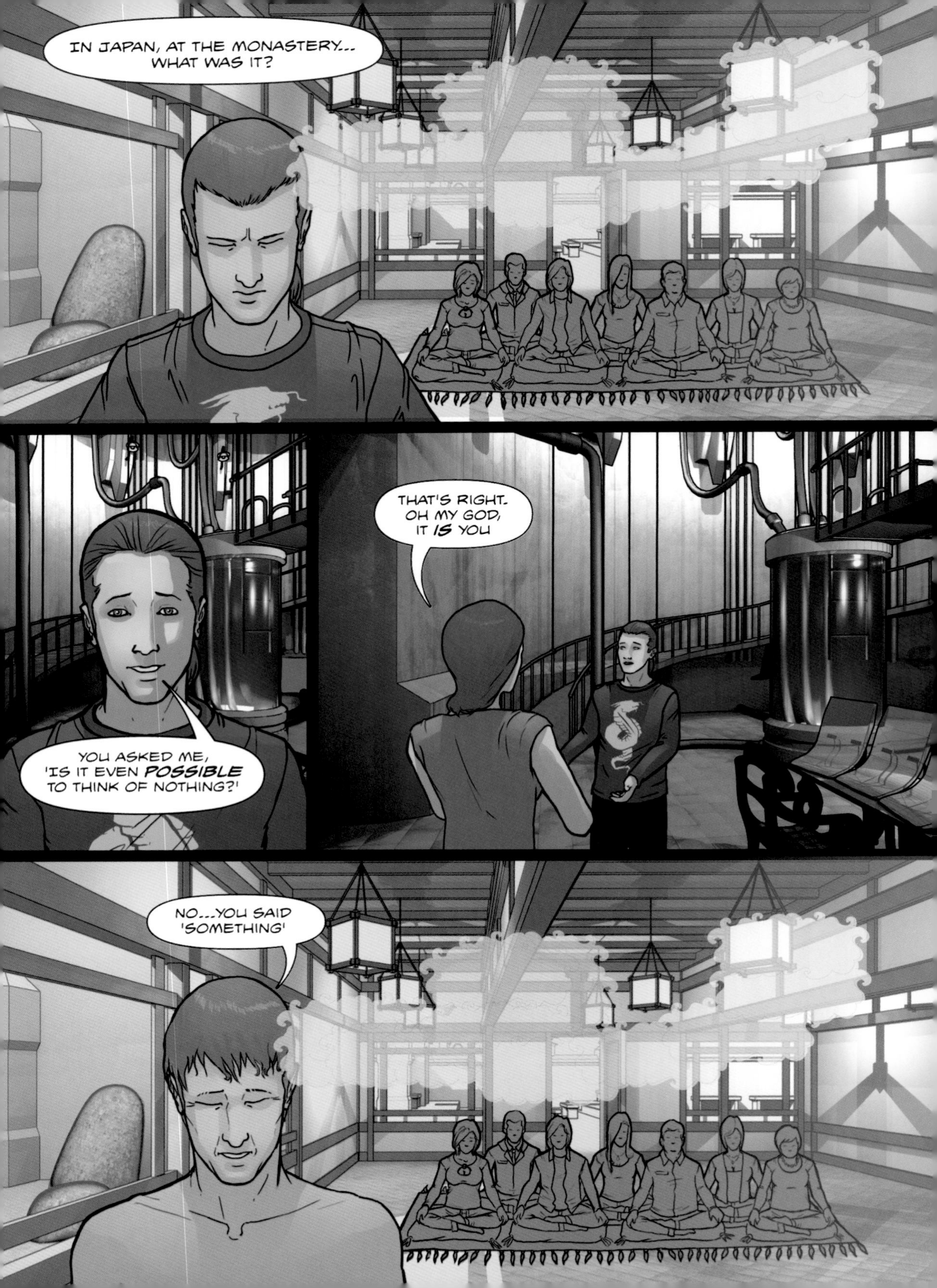
IN JAPAN, AT THE MONASTERY...
WHAT WAS IT?
YOU ASKED ME,
'IS IT EVEN *POSSIBLE* TO THINK OF NOTHING?'
THAT'S RIGHT.
OH MY GOD,
IT *IS* YOU
NO...YOU SAID 'SOMETHING'

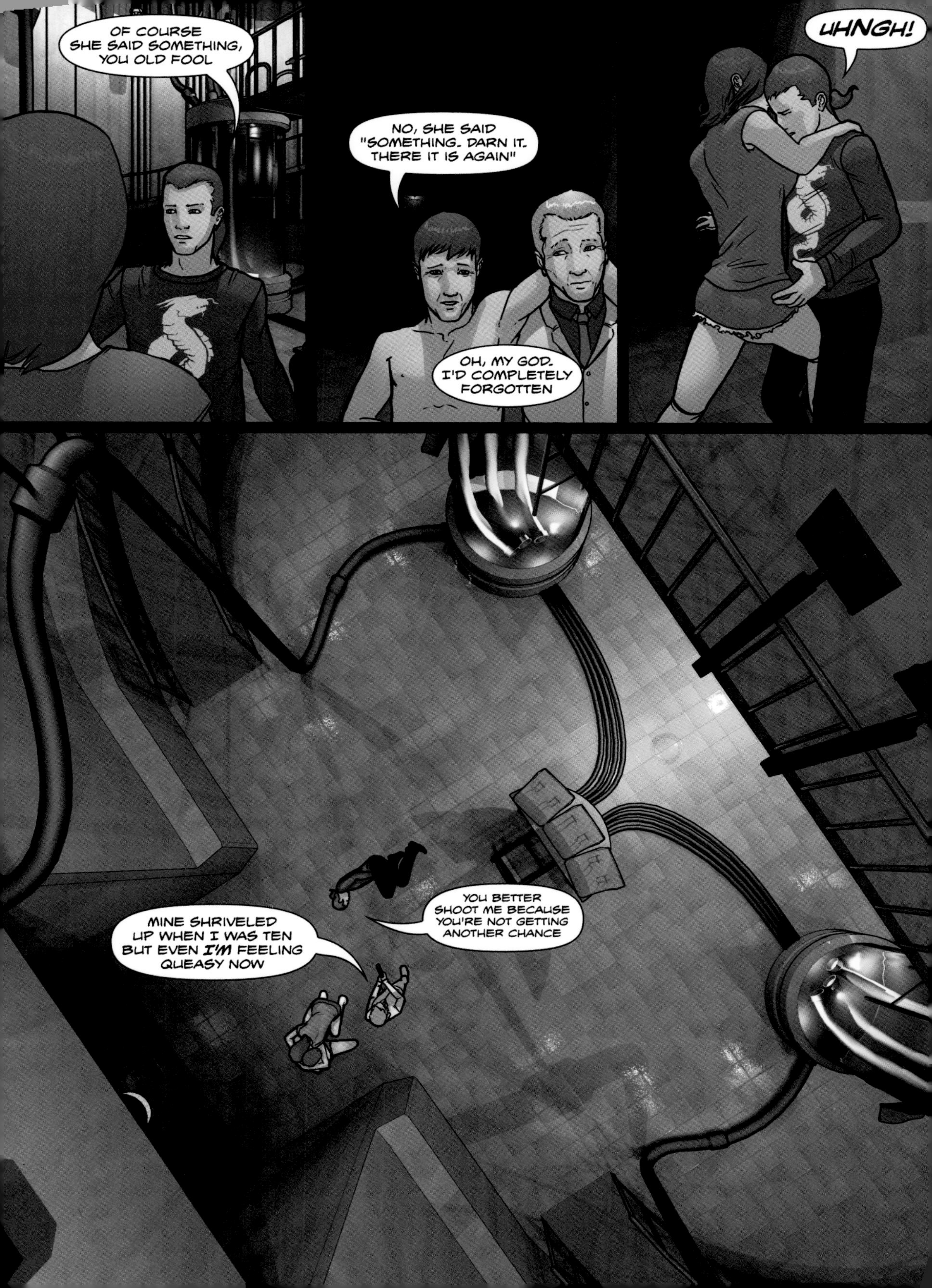
OF COURSE SHE SAID SOMETHING, YOU OLD FOOL
NO, SHE SAID "SOMETHING. DARN IT. THERE IT IS AGAIN"
OH, MY GOD. I'D COMPLETELY FORGOTTEN
UHNGH!
YOU BETTER SHOOT ME BECAUSE YOU'RE NOT GETTING ANOTHER CHANCE
MINE SHRIVELED UP WHEN I WAS TEN BUT EVEN I'M FEELING QUEASY NOW

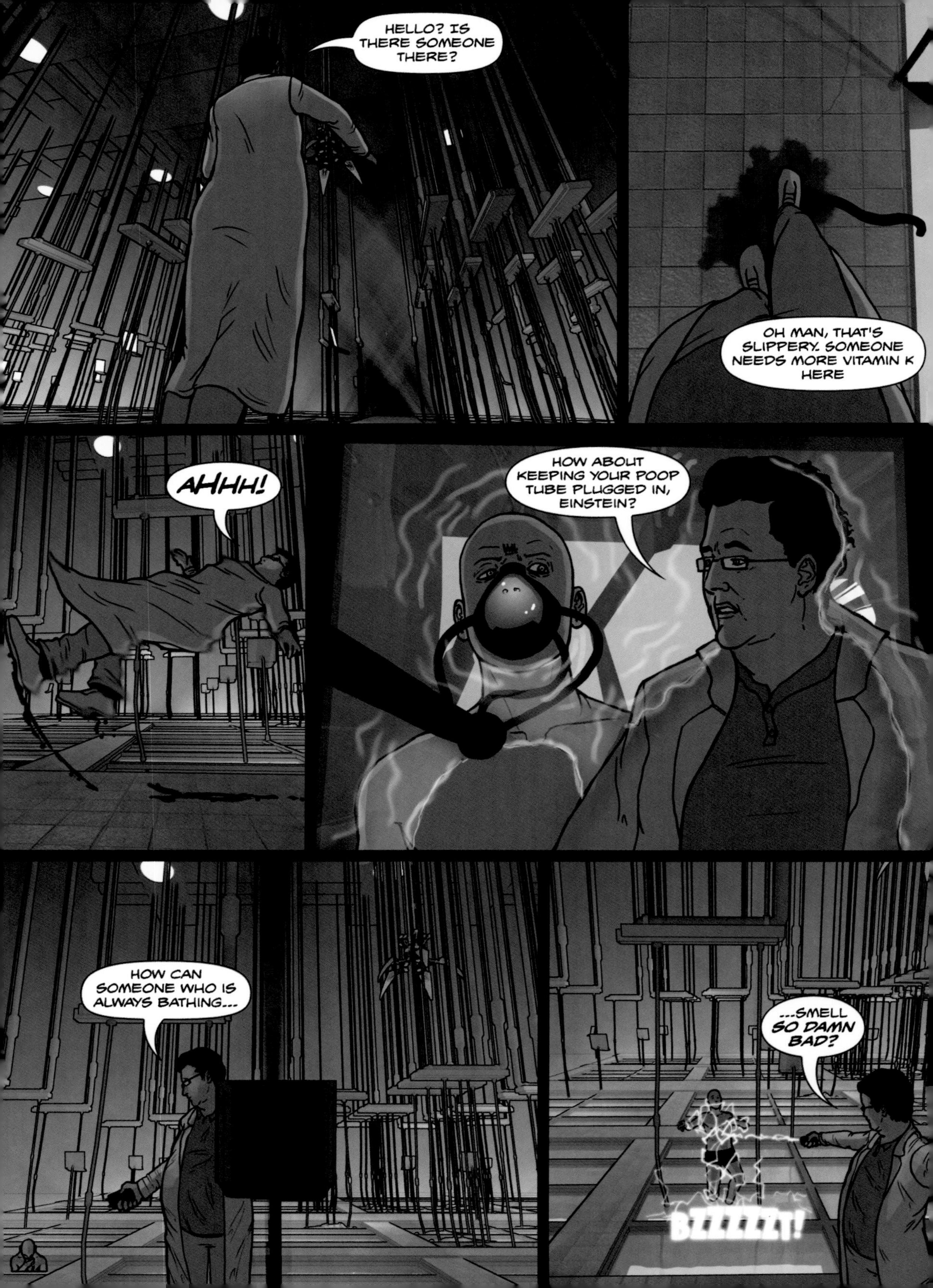
HELLO? IS THERE SOMEONE THERE?
OH MAN, THAT'S SLIPPERY. SOMEONE NEEDS MORE VITAMIN K HERE
AHHH!
HOW ABOUT KEEPING YOUR POOP TUBE PLUGGED IN, EINSTEIN?
HOW CAN SOMEONE WHO IS ALWAYS BATHING...
...SMELL SO DAMN BAD?
BZZZZZT!

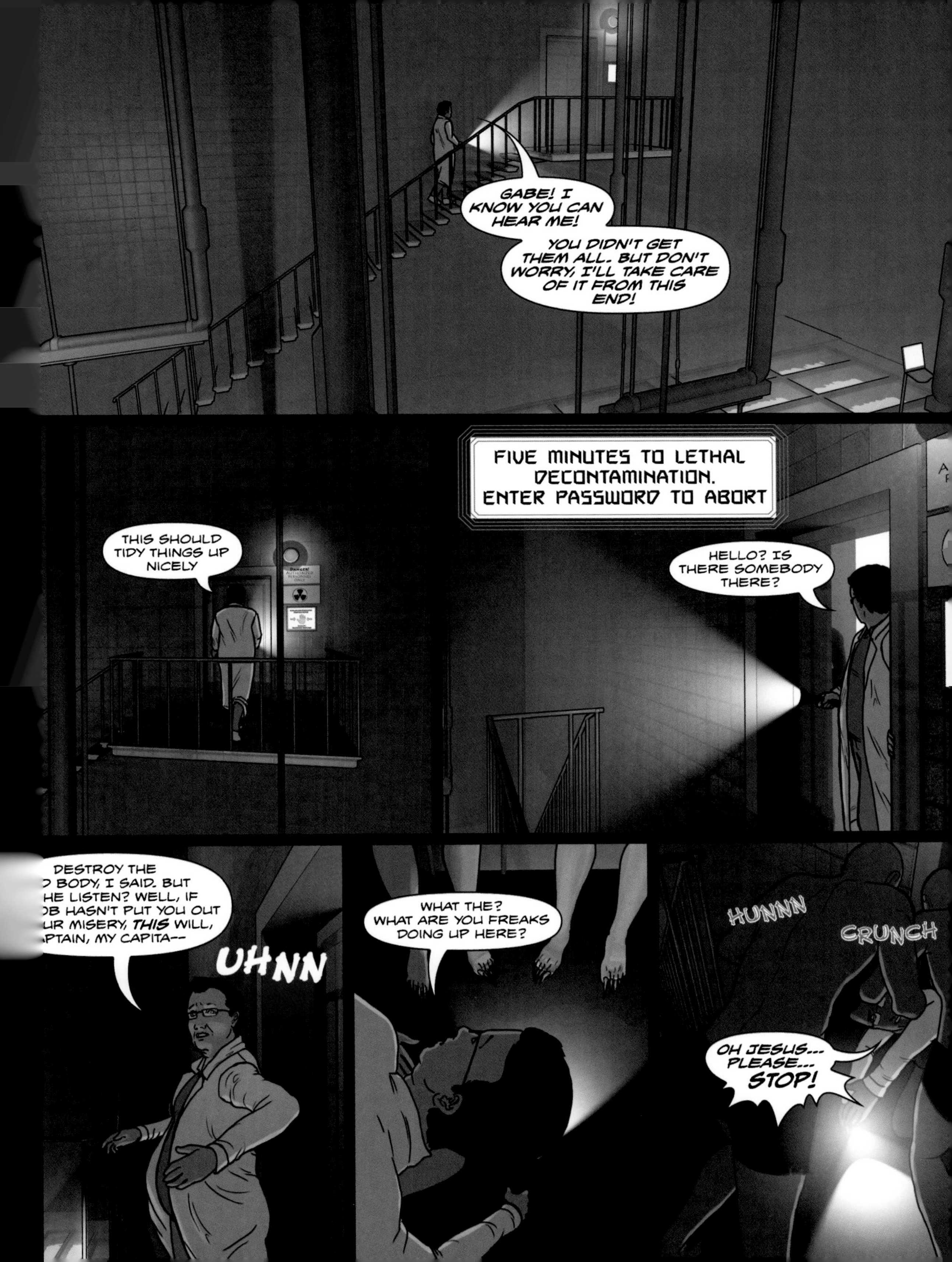
GABE! I KNOW YOU CAN HEAR ME!
YOU DIDN'T GET THEM ALL. BUT DON'T WORRY, I'LL TAKE CARE OF IT FROM THIS END!
FIVE MINUTES TO LETHAL DECONTAMINATION. ENTER PASSWORD TO ABORT
THIS SHOULD TIDY THINGS UP NICELY
HELLO? IS THERE SOMEBODY THERE?
DESTROY THE
D BODY, I SAID. BUT
HE LISTEN? WELL, IF
OB HASN'T PUT YOU OUT
UR MISERY, THIS WILL,
PTAIN, MY CAPITA--
UHNN
WHAT THE? WHAT ARE YOU FREAKS DOING UP HERE?
HUNNN
CRUNCH
OH JESUS... PLEASE... STOP!

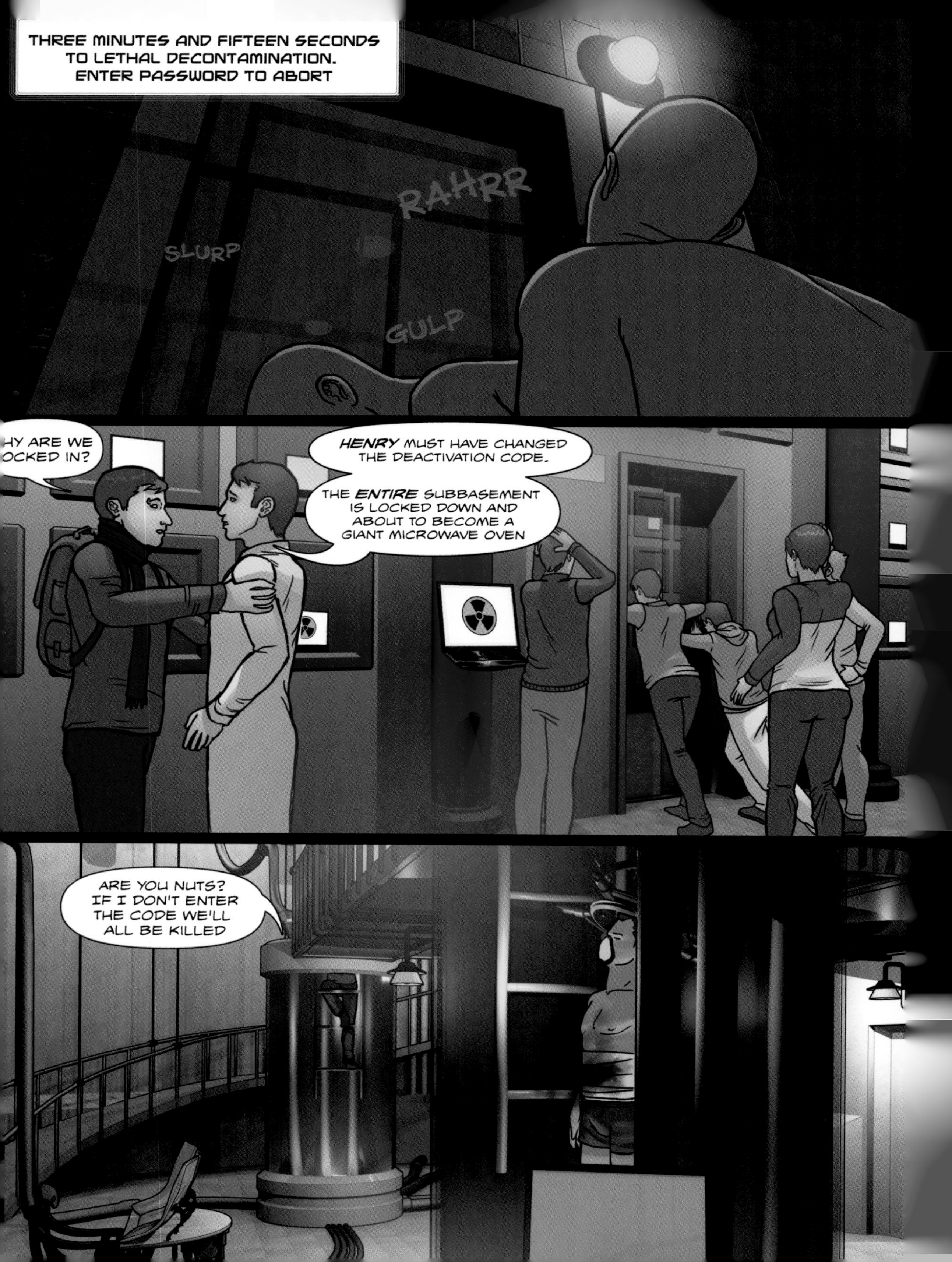
THREE MINUTES AND FIFTEEN SECONDS TO LETHAL DECONTAMINATION. ENTER PASSWORD TO ABORT
RAHRR
SLURP
GULP
HY ARE WE
OCKED IN?
HENRY MUST HAVE CHANGED THE DEACTIVATION CODE.
THE ENTIRE SUBBASEMENT IS LOCKED DOWN AND ABOUT TO BECOME A GIANT MICROWAVE OVEN
ARE YOU NUTS? IF I DON'T ENTER THE CODE WE'LL ALL BE KILLED

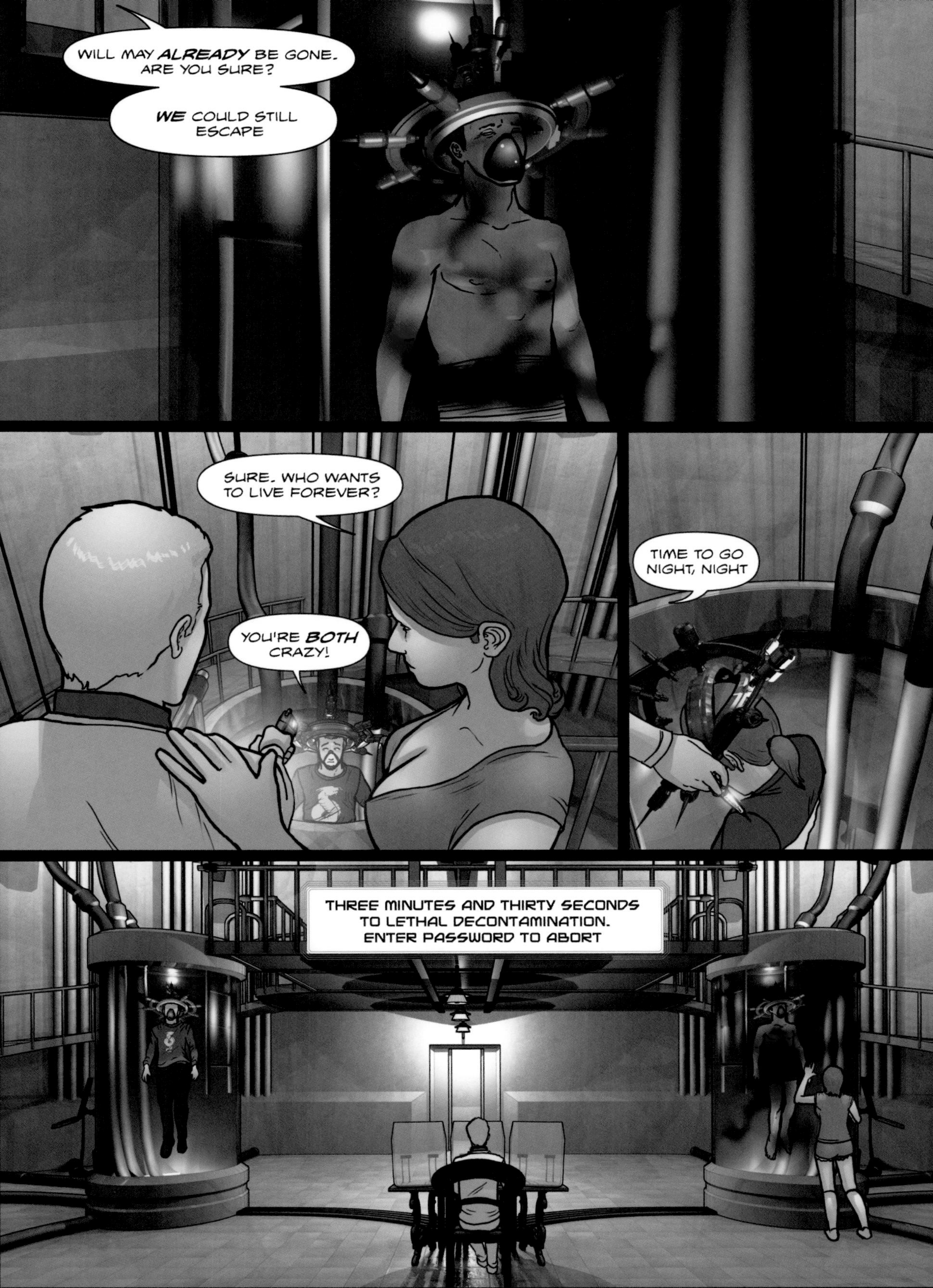
WILL MAY ALREADY BE GONE. ARE YOU SURE?
WE COULD STILL ESCAPE
SURE. WHO WANTS TO LIVE FOREVER?
YOU'RE BOTH CRAZY!
TIME TO GO NIGHT, NIGHT
THREE MINUTES AND THIRTY SECONDS TO LETHAL DECONTAMINATION. ENTER PASSWORD TO ABORT

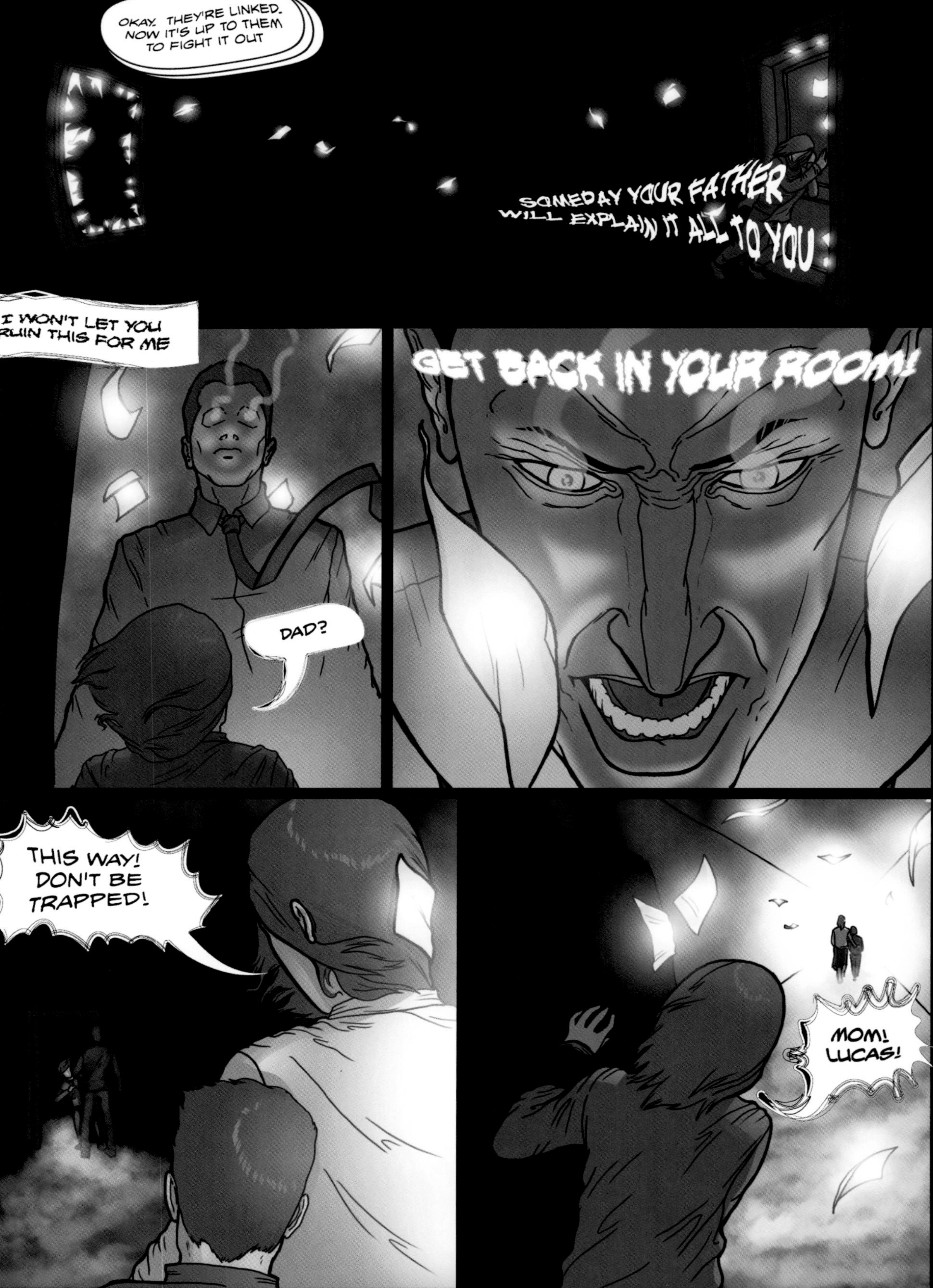
OKAY. THEY'RE LINKED. NOW IT'S UP TO THEM TO FIGHT IT OUT
SOMEDAY YOUR FATHER WILL EXPLAIN IT ALL TO YOU
I WON'T LET YOU RUIN THIS FOR ME
GET BACK IN YOUR ROOM!
DAD?
THIS WAY! DON'T BE TRAPPED!
MOM! LUCAS!

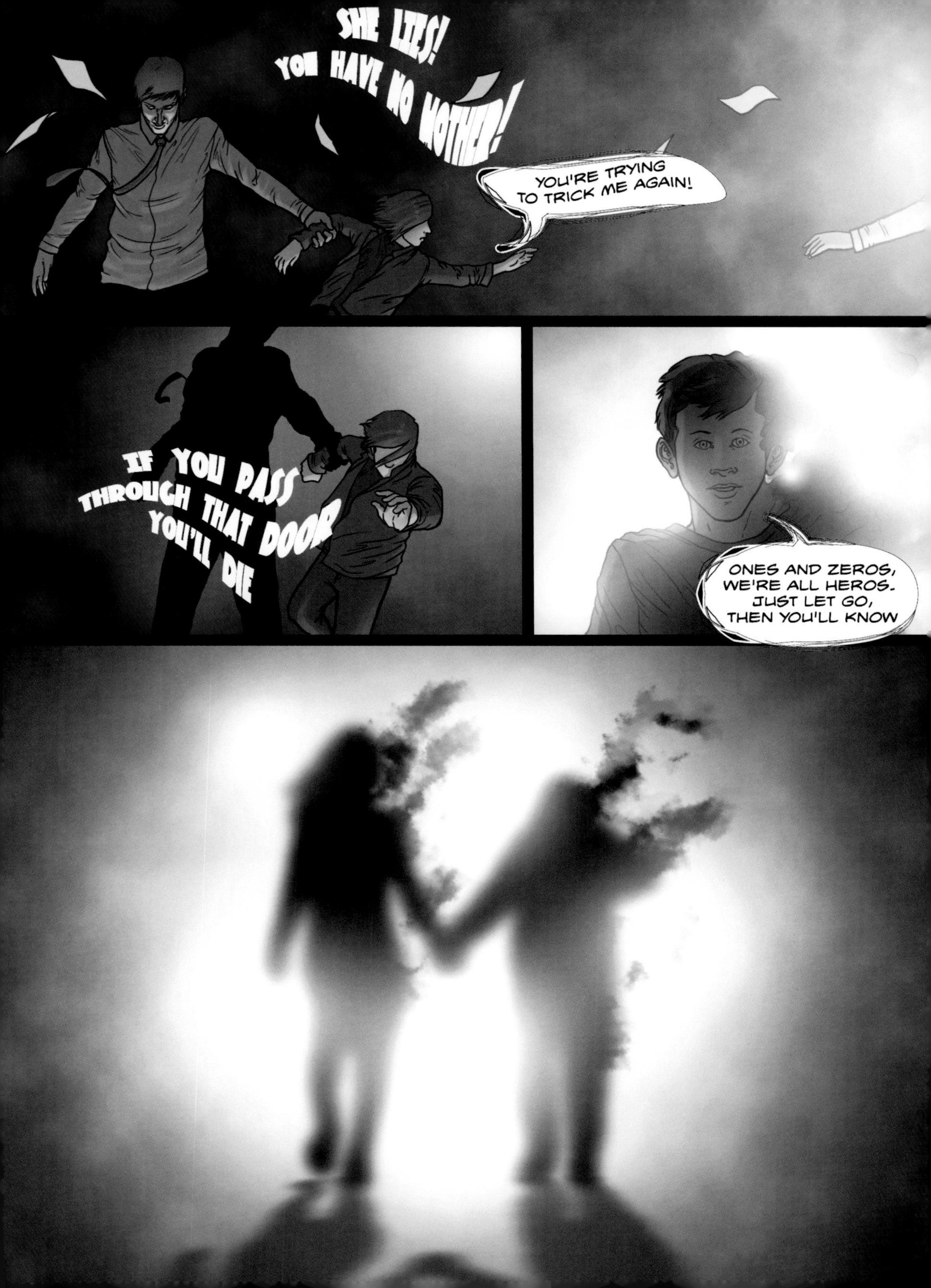
SHE LIES! YOU HAVE NO MOTHER!
YOU'RE TRYING TO TRICK ME AGAIN!
IF YOU PASS THROUGH THAT DOOR YOU'LL DIE
ONES AND ZEROS, WE'RE ALL HEROS. JUST LET GO, THEN YOU'LL KNOW

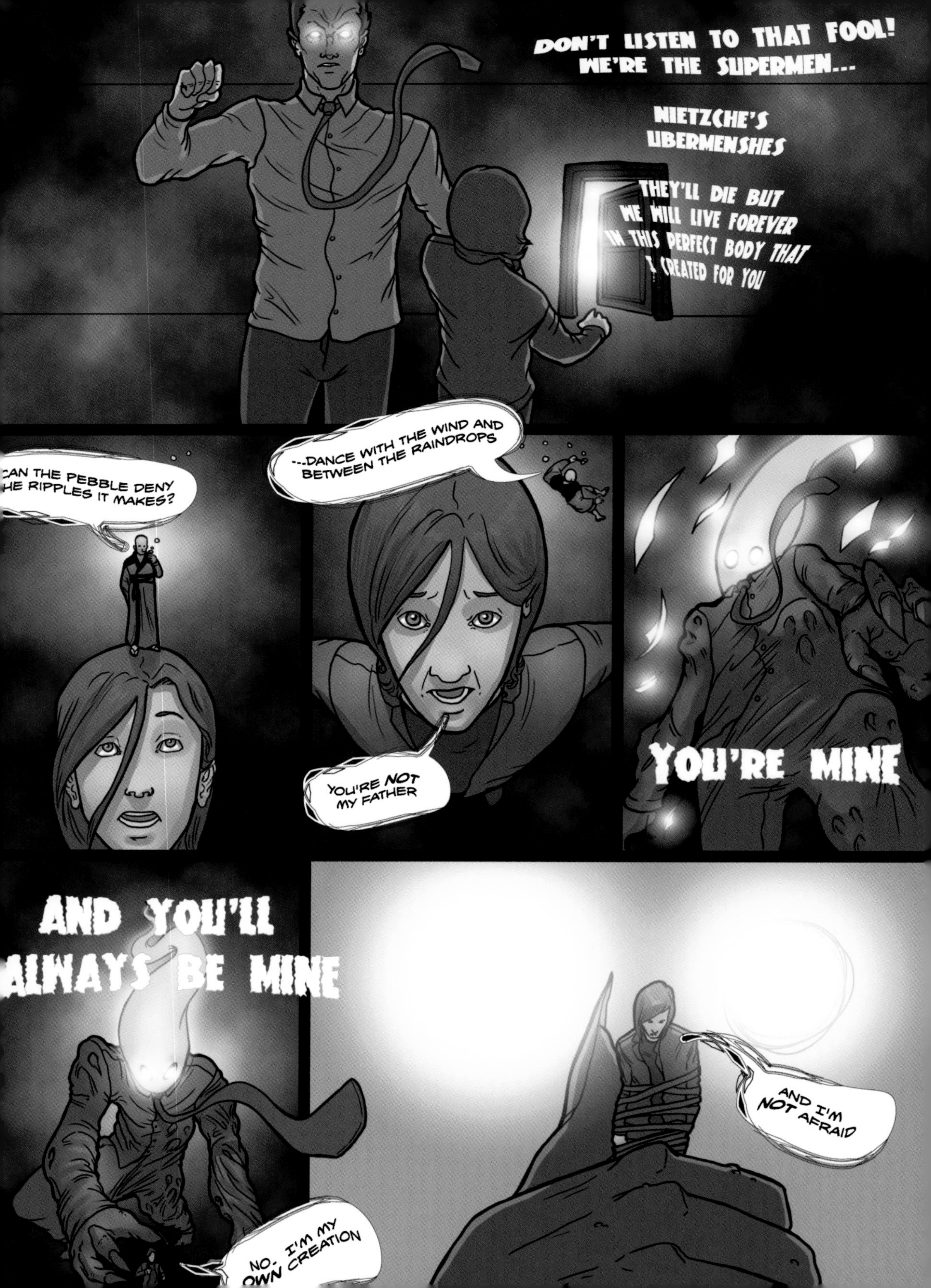
DON'T LISTEN TO THAT FOOL! WE'RE THE SUPERMEN...
NIETZCHE'S UBERMENSHES
THEY'LL DIE BUT WE WILL LIVE FOREVER IN THIS PERFECT BODY THAT I CREATED FOR YOU
CAN THE PEBBLE DENY THE RIPPLES IT MAKES?
...DANCE WITH THE WIND AND BETWEEN THE RAINDROPS
YOU'RE NOT MY FATHER
YOU'RE MINE
AND YOU'LL ALWAYS BE MINE
NO. I'M MY OWN CREATION
AND I'M NOT AFRAID

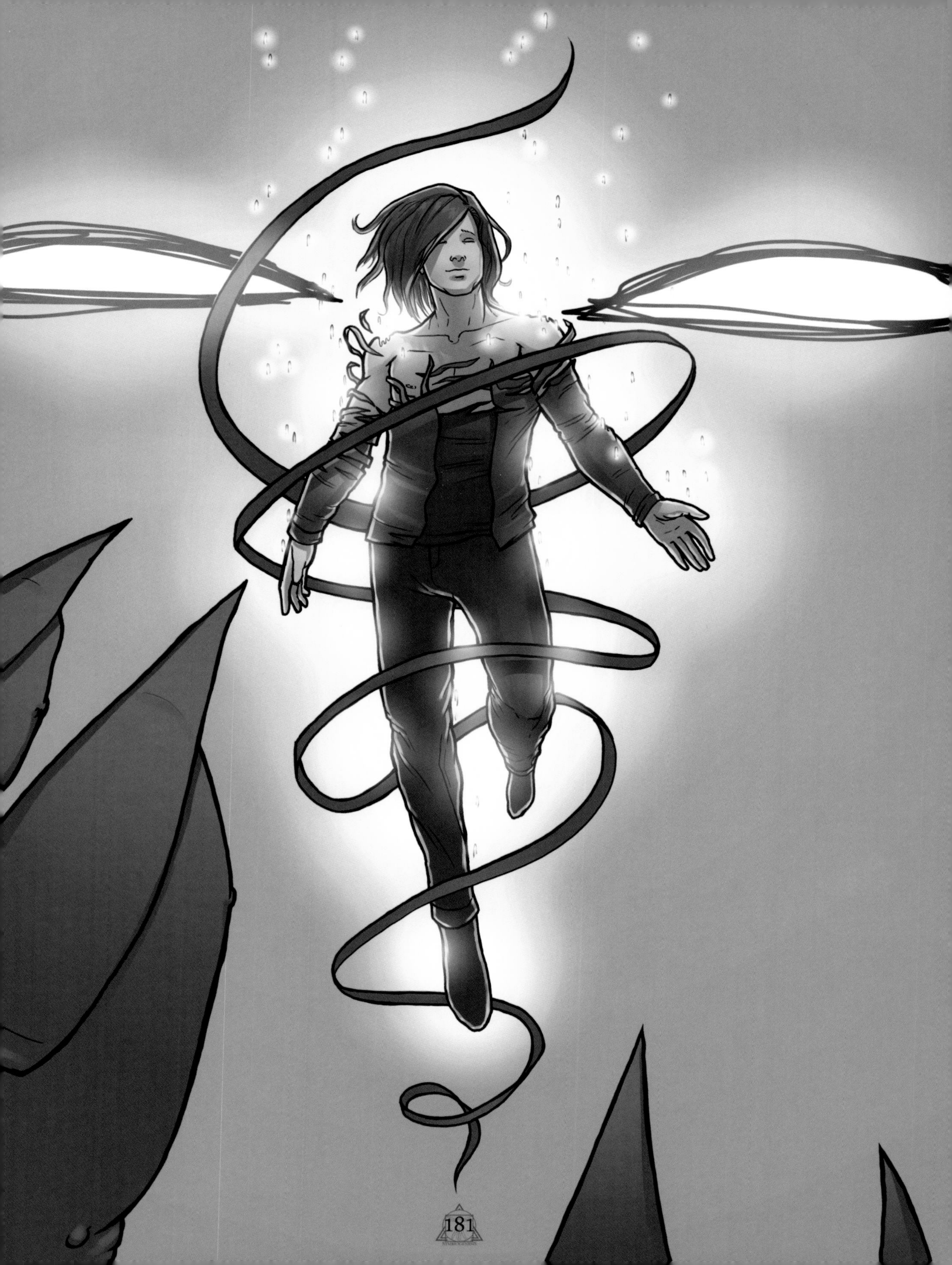

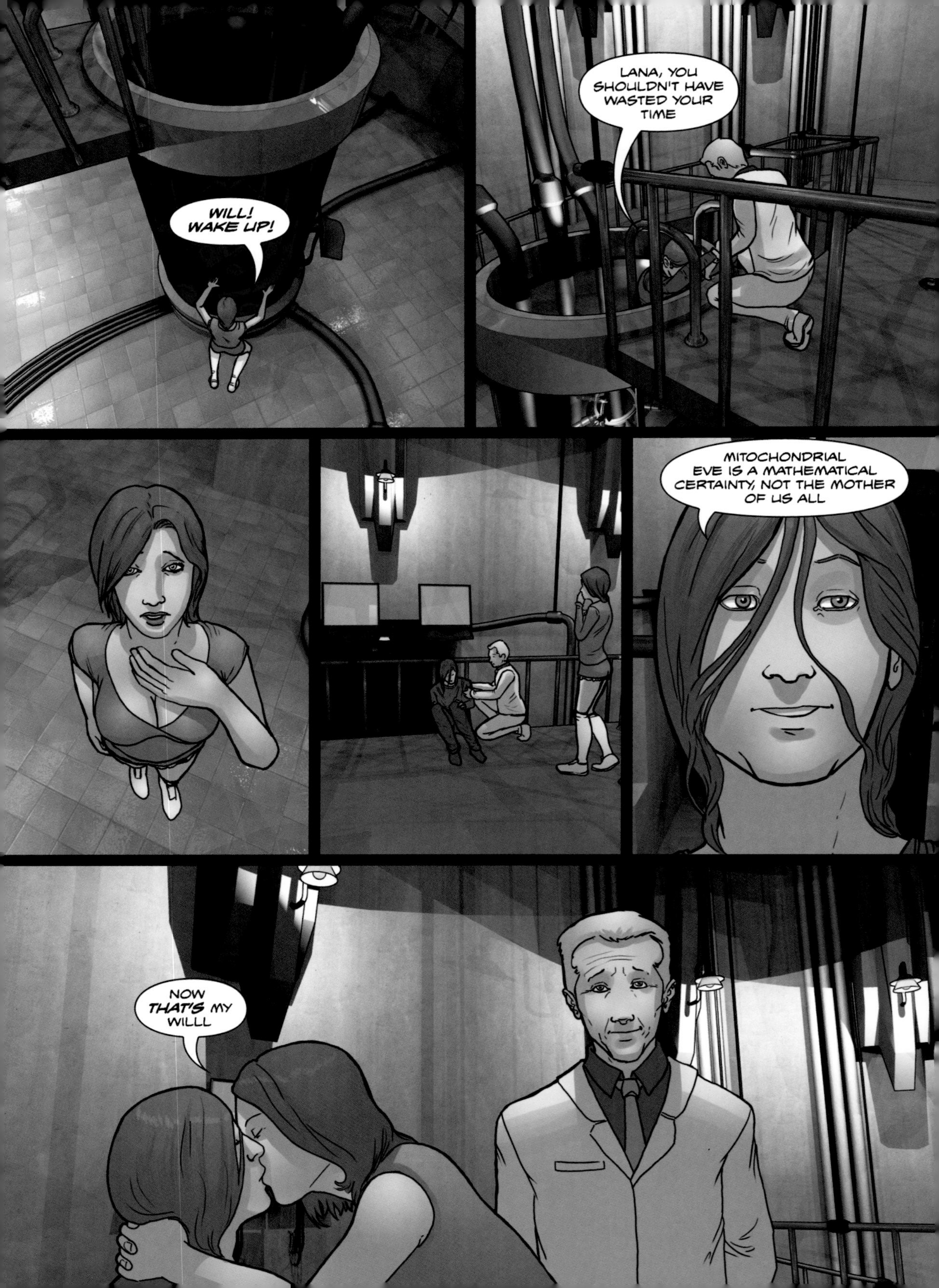
WILL! WAKE UP!
LANA, YOU SHOULDN'T HAVE WASTED YOUR TIME
MITOCHONDRIAL EVE IS A MATHEMATICAL CERTAINTY, NOT THE MOTHER OF US ALL
NOW *THAT'S* MY WILL!

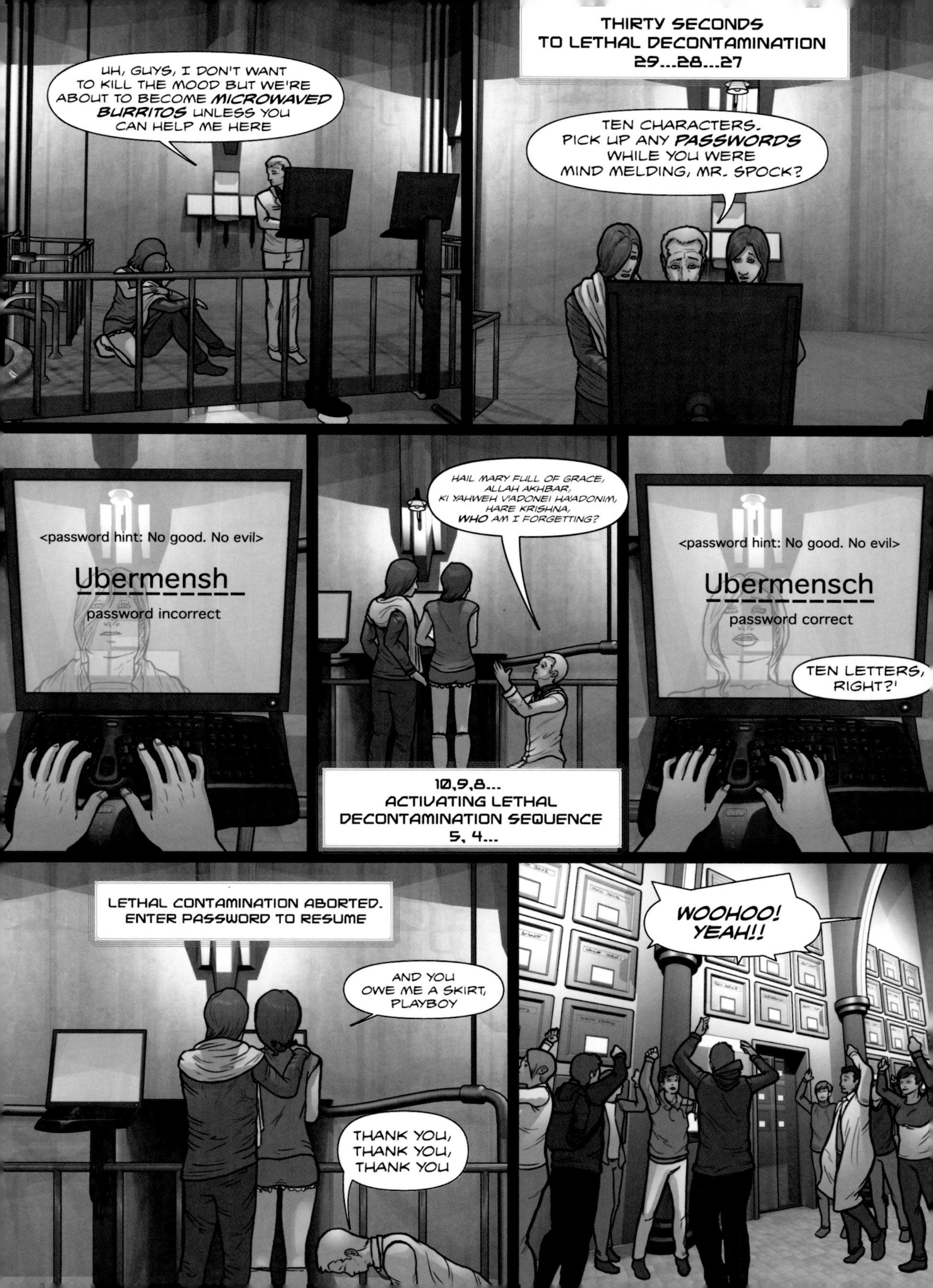
UH, GUYS, I DON'T WANT TO KILL THE MOOD BUT WE'RE ABOUT TO BECOME MICROWAVED BURRITOS UNLESS YOU CAN HELP ME HERE
THIRTY SECONDS TO LETHAL DECONTAMINATION 29...28...27
TEN CHARACTERS. PICK UP ANY PASSWORDS WHILE YOU WERE MIND MELDING, MR. SPOCK?
<password hint: No good. No evil>
Ubermensh_
password incorrect
HAIL MARY FULL OF GRACE, ALLAH AKHBAR, KI YAHWEH V'ADONEI HA'ADONIM, HARE KRISHNA, WHO AM I FORGETTING?
10,9,8... ACTIVATING LETHAL DECONTAMINATION SEQUENCE 5, 4...
<password hint: No good. No evil>
Ubermensch
password correct
TEN LETTERS, RIGHT?'
LETHAL CONTAMINATION ABORTED. ENTER PASSWORD TO RESUME
AND YOU OWE ME A SKIRT, PLAYBOY
THANK YOU, THANK YOU, THANK YOU
WOOHOO! YEAH!!

ONE YEAR LATER

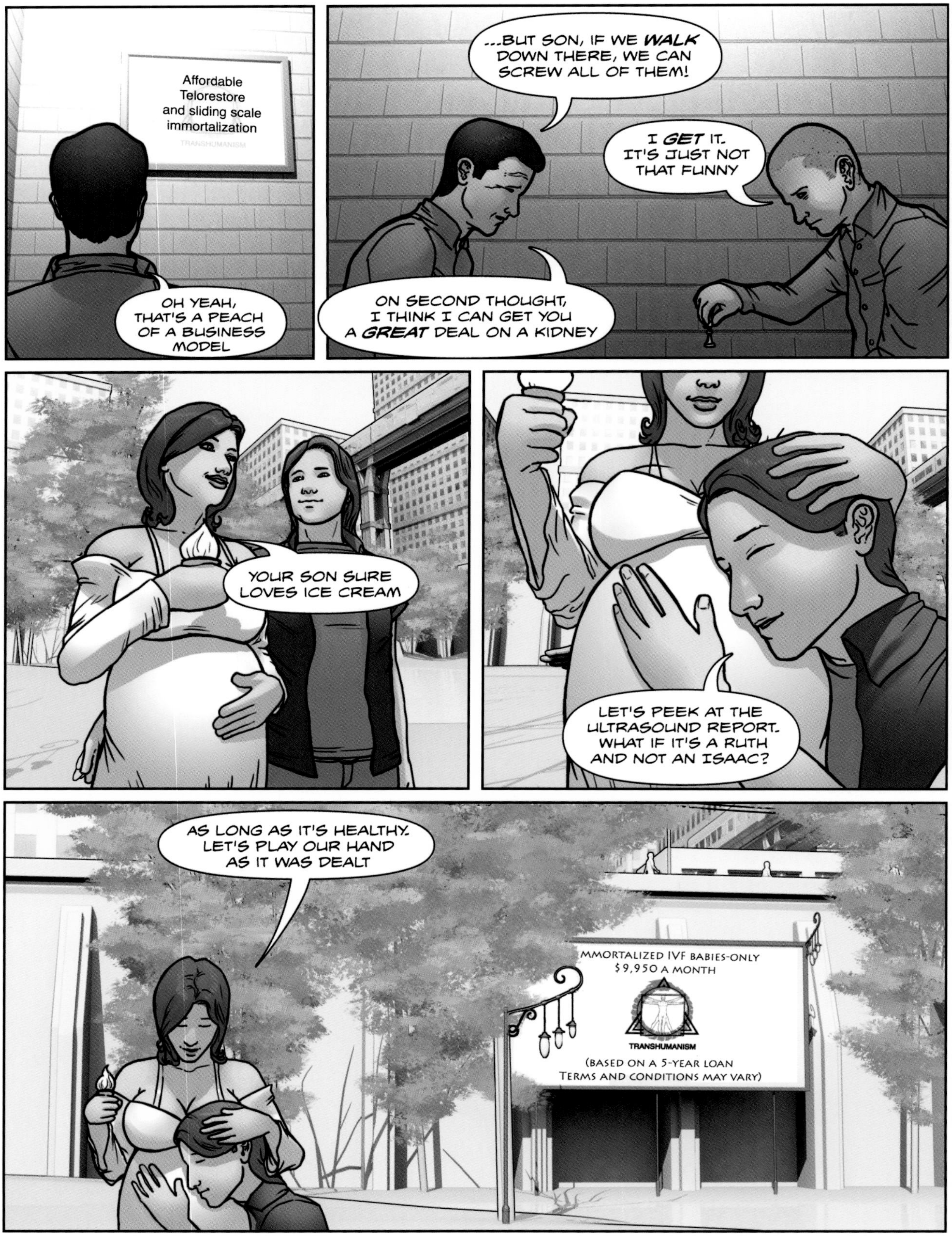

Affordable Telorestore and sliding scale immortalization
TRANSHUMANISM
OH YEAH, THAT'S A PEACH OF A BUSINESS MODEL
...BUT SON, IF WE WALK DOWN THERE, WE CAN SCREW ALL OF THEM!
I GET IT. IT'S JUST NOT THAT FUNNY
ON SECOND THOUGHT, I THINK I CAN GET YOU A GREAT DEAL ON A KIDNEY
YOUR SON SURE LOVES ICE CREAM
LET'S PEEK AT THE ULTRASOUND REPORT. WHAT IF IT'S A RUTH AND NOT AN ISAAC?
AS LONG AS IT'S HEALTHY. LET'S PLAY OUR HAND AS IT WAS DEALT
MMORTALIZED IVF BABIES-ONLY $9,950 A MONTH
TRANSHUMANISM
(BASED ON A 5-YEAR LOAN
TERMS AND CONDITIONS MAY VARY)

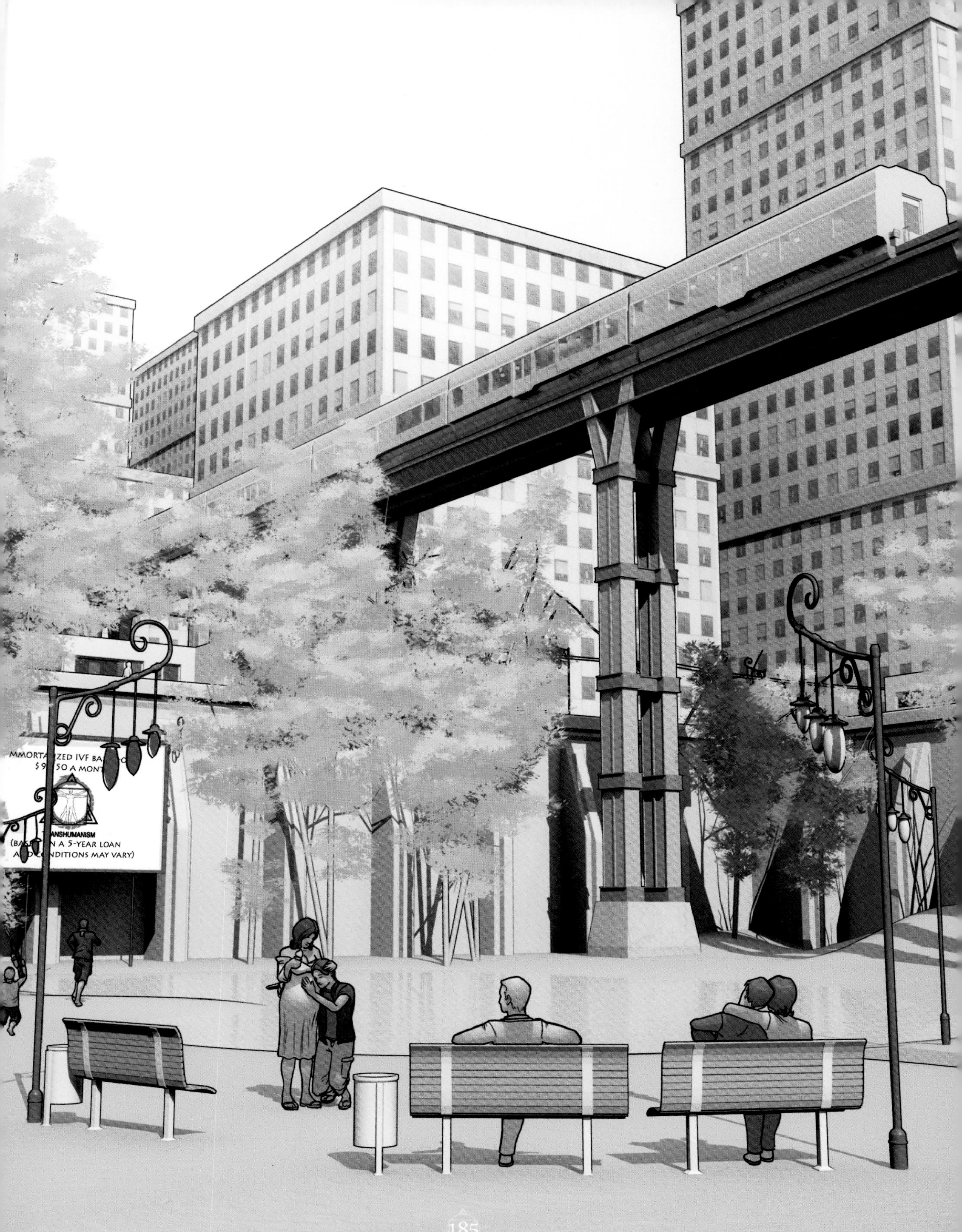
MMORTA ZED IVF BA
$9 50 A MONT
ANSHUMANISM
(BA N A 5-YEAR LOAN
NDITIONS MAY VARY)

Acknowledgements

Lee Stein and the Hammer Creative Crew

Usana shadday of The Book designers

Vicki Lundgren of C&C Printing

Cor Vanderdonk and Hao Wang for website design

Sebastian Englund for last minute heroics

Michelle Davies, Emil Sjöström, and Benjamin kim for moral support and friendship.

Susie Cyin and Brenda Rodriguez for international translations

And finally, Torbjörn Leksell & Ji-Yeon Park, just for putting up with us

DR. EDWARD PARK

IS A SOUTHERN CALIFORNIAN PHYSICIAN AND WRITER.

IN 2006, DR. PARK DECIDED TO BECOME A WRITER. HE CONVERTED HIS FIRST SCREENPLAY INTO THIS GRAPHIC NOVEL. FOR HIS NEXT PROJECT, HE IS TRANSFORMING HIS HOUSTON FILM FESTIVAL-WINNING SCREENPLAY ABOUT HYPATIA OF ALEXANDRIA INTO A NOVEL.

THE THEMES IN "MAXIMUM LIFESPAN" ARE A CASE OF ART IMITATING LIFE. SINCE 2007, HE HAS BEEN TAKING TA-65, THE WORLD'S FIRST TELOMERASE ACTIVATOR, SIMILAR TO THE NOVEL'S FICTIONAL "TELORESTORE."

THE RESULTS HAVE BEEN SO POSITIVE THAT HE NOW OFFERS TELOMERASE ACTIVATION TO THE GENERAL PUBLIC.

TO LEARN MORE, GO TO RECHARGEBIOMEDICAL.COM

JOVE LEKSELL

IS A PAINTER/ ILLUSTRATOR WHO MAINLY WORKS WITH CONCEPT AND SEQUENTIAL ART FROM HIS HOME IN SWEDEN.

ORIGINALLY, JOVE WAS WORKING WITH CREATING CONCEPT ART FOR GAME DEVELOPMENT STUDIOS BUT IN EARLY 2007 HE MET DR. EDWARD PARK ONLINE AND GIVEN THE CHANCE OF WORKING ON A GRAPHIC NOVEL, HE IMMEDIATELY SET OUT TO REALIZE "MAXIMUM LIFESPAN," A PROJECT THAT ENDED UP TAKING ON A LIFE OF IT'S OWN.

JOVE IS LOOKING FORWARD TO FINALLY SHOWING FRIENDS AND FAMILY WHAT HE WAS WORKING ON FOR TWO YEARS.

TO SEE MORE OF JOVES WORK, VISIT HIS WEBSITE AT: WWW.NARCISSISTICSTUDIOS.COM/JOVE